Exchange-Rate Policies for Emerging Market Economics

The Political Economy of Global Interdependence
Thomas D. Willett, Series Editor

Exchange-Rate Policies for Emerging Market Economies

EDITED BY

Richard J. Sweeney, Clas G. Wihlborg, and Thomas D. Willett

Westview Press
A Member of the Perseus Books Group

Political Economy of Global Interdependence

Copyright © 1999 by Westview Press, A Member of the Perseus Books Group

Published in 1999 in the United States of America by Westview Press, 5500 Central Avenue, Boulder, Colorado 80301-2877, and in the United Kingdom by Westview Press, 12 Hid's Copse Road, Cumnor Hill, Oxford OX2 9JJ

A CIP catalog record for this book is available from the Library of Congress.
ISBN 0-8133-3019-X

The paper used in this publication meets the requirements of the American National Standard for Permanence of Paper for Printed Library Materials Z39.48-1984.

10   9   8   7   6   5   4   3   2   1

Contents

Acknowledgments

This is the third and final volume resulting from a collaborative project on international and monetary aspects of economic reform in the former communist countries undertaken by the Claremont Colleges, Georgetown University and the School of Economics and Commercial Law at Göteborg University. The two previous volumes are *Establishing Monetary Stability in Emerging Market Economies* (1995) and *Capital Controls in Emerging Market Economies* (1997), also published by Westview Press. The Claremont portion of the project was administered through the Claremont Institute for Economic Policy Studies at the Claremont Graduate University and the Lowe Institute of Political Economy at Claremont McKenna College and was funded primarily through a generous grant from the Lincoln Foundation.

The Georgetown School of Business at Georgetown University provided further support through faculty summer grants, and workshop funding was provided from Georgetown's Finance/Accounting seminar series. Professor Sweeney also wishes to thank the Georgetown University Center for International Business Education and Research for travel and workshop funds, and the Georgetown University Center for Business-Government Relations for supplying summer research assistance.

Activities of the Swedish research group and conferences in Göteborg, Sweden, and Tallinn, Estonia, were funded by the Royal Academy of Sciences, the Research Council for Humanities and Social Research, and the School of Economics and Commercial Law at Göteborg University, Sweden. Additional funding for conferences in Tallinn was provided by the Bank of Keila and the Open Estonian Foundation in Estonia.

A major purpose of the project was to establish economic policy dialogues between Western economists and economists and policy officials from the former communist countries. The emphasis was not on having Western economists tell Eastern economists what to do, but rather to enter into discussions which would culminate in shared agreement about the nature of the key issues—even if there was not always agreement about policy recommendations. To this end we organized a substantial number of conferences and workshops which brought economists and officials from the former commu-

nist countries to Claremont, Georgetown, and Göteborg and brought groups of Western economists to locations in Central Europe and the former Soviet Union. We especially appreciate the cooperation of local host institutions: the Czech National Bank in Prague, the Czech Republic; Tallinn Technical University in Tallinn, Estonia; the Institute for World Economics in Budapest, Hungary; and the Institute for Advanced Studies and the Austrian National Bank in Vienna, Austria.

Special thanks go to Pamela Martin of the Claremont Institute of Economic Policy Studies and Karin Hane of Göteborg University for their excellent work in preparing the manuscript for publication.

Richard J. Sweeney
Clas Wihlborg
Thomas D. Willett

Exchange-Rate Policies for Emerging Market Economics

Introduction

Richard J. Sweeney, Clas Wihlborg and Thomas D. Willett

Exchange Rate Regime Choice: The Debate

The merits and limitations of fixed versus flexible exchange rate regimes are the focus of one of the most long-standing debates in economics. There are important costs to both fixed and flexible rates, the relative costs of each depending on a country's characteristics and circumstances. As a consequence, policymakers in many countries have attempted to avoid choosing between these extremes and have opted for compromise regimes of adjustable or crawling pegs. This was the basic philosophy of the Bretton Woods international monetary system set up at the end of World War II. However, both economic and political considerations make such compromise systems difficult to manage effectively. This is especially true in a world of high international capital mobility.

The adjustably pegged exchange rate regime of the Bretton Woods system broke down in the early 1970s, but the lessons of this experience were not always remembered. In the 1980s and 1990s, various forms of pegged rate regimes again became popular across the globe, being adopted in Western and Eastern Europe, Asia and Latin America. In the 1990s, the difficulties of managing adjustably pegged exchange rates have once again been dramatically illustrated. The latest example of this point is the Asian currency crises of 1997–98, but many others abound, including the crises surrounding the Bulgarian lev, the Mexican peso, and the Russian ruble in 1994, the European monetary crises in 1992 and 1993 and the failure of the Bretton Woods system itself in the early 1970s. As the workability of compromise exchange rate regimes has become questionable, the choices facing policymakers have become more difficult. To a large extent the current controversy over exchange rate policies in the emerging market economies has simply transferred an ongoing debate to a new battleground. There are, however, arguments about the applicability of fixed or flexible exchange rate regimes based on the special circumstances of the emerging market economies.

The break-up of the Soviet Union and its loss of control over Central and Eastern Europe, along with the moves toward economic liberalization in many developing countries, has led to a huge increase in the number of convertible currencies worldwide in the last decade. Trade and financial relations are affected by, but also constrain management of, these currencies. Many developing and transitional countries are trying to establish their external and internal economic relationships on liberal economic principles. These principles, however, give no clear guidance about what type of exchange rate arrangements a country should adopt. A market-oriented economy may function effectively under either fixed or flexible exchange rates, as long as heavy use of exchange or capital controls is avoided. Thus, a country's choice of exchange rate regime will depend on how different exchange rate regimes perform in terms of macroeconomic independence and stability, and in terms of inflation control.

The contributions to this volume focus on issues that determine the answers to these questions. Economists from Central Europe and the former Soviet Union, as well as the United States and Western Europe, analyze the experiences of the formerly communist and developing countries and draw lessons for future exchange rate policies there and elsewhere.

The debate about exchange rate regimes is confused, and sometime confusing, for several reasons. One is that most countries' exchange rate arrangements are not easily classified as fixed or flexible. Another is that the objectives underlying the choice of exchange rate regime often are not clearly stated. These objectives may be as much political as economic, as documented in many of the contributions in this volume. Most of the debate over the superiority of fixed or flexible rates concerns the use of exchange rate changes as an adjustment mechanism, and is only implicitly about the higher order objectives which the exchange rate regime will help achieve.

The principal argument for allowing exchange rate changes to adjust balance of payments disequilibria is that under some circumstances it provides a lower cost method of adjustment than do changes in domestic macroeconomic policies. The chief arguments against it are that fluctuating exchange rates may increase transactions and uncertainty costs for firms and households, and that expected or actual exchange rate changes could be destabilizing to the domestic economy in one way or another. A considered review of the available theory and evidence does not indicate a general advantage to either regime. Advocates of flexible exchange rates can point to cases where they have worked well and critics can point to cases where they have not. The same can be said for fixed exchange rates. The debate continues.

As discussed in Part I of this volume, the development of the optimum currency area (OCA) approach to exchange rate analysis has provided us with a conceptual framework for analyzing these issues. A major insight of this approach is that there are costs and benefits to any exchange rate regime for any country, but the ratio of costs to benefits associated with each regime varies systematically depending upon a country's characteristics and the external economic environment it faces.

The early literature on optimum currency areas focused on criteria for the choice between a credibly fixed exchange rate[1] and a flexible or adjustable rate responding either to market forces or to policy-induced shocks. The optimum currency area was determined by a tradeoff between the microeconomic benefits of fixing the relative price among monies, thereby expanding the domain of a single currency, and the macroeconomic costs of giving up independent exchange-rate and monetary policies. Giving up these policy options reduces a country's ability to achieve balance of payments equilibrium (external balance) at noninflationary full employment (internal balance). The analytical contributions of the OCA approach have focused on the macroeconomic aspects while the microeconomic benefits of establishing a currency area have been asserted or taken for granted.[2]

In the real world, most countries face a choice between pegging with more or less adjustment and floating with more or less intervention. A highly credible pegged rate requires a nearly irrevocably fixed rate. Once we depart from such a regime, there is no well-defined scale of increasing flexibility. Intermediate regimes between a pure float and a highly credible fixed rate have characteristics of both fixed and flexible rates as defined in OCA theory.

Although OCA theory has relevance for the analysis of benefits and costs of different intermediate regimes, the criteria of this theory may be insufficient to evaluate the relative superiority of different intermediate regimes. For example, the tendency for a particular regime to cause the real exchange rate to deviate from an equilibrium rate (by some definition) would depend on the efficiency of the market mechanism to the extent the exchange rate floats, and on the government's exchange rate policy objectives to the extent the government intervenes in the foreign exchange market. Evaluation of different regimes is, therefore, going to depend on the general objectives underlying the choice of exchange rate regime.

In this introductory chapter, we offer a brief perspective on some of the key issues of dispute concerning exchange rate policy, paying particular attention to the special circumstances facing emerging market economies. In the next section we discuss alternative objectives that determine, more or less explicitly, a government's choice of exchange rate regime. Specific characteristics of transition economies that could influence the objectives for exchange rate regime choice and the conflicts among such objectives are discussed. In the third section we review the issues addressed in this volume, referring to specific chapters.

Exchange Rate Regime Objectives and
Characteristics of Transition Economies

General Objectives of Regime Choice

The traditional OCA approach takes the view that a country's exchange rate regime should enable its economy to restore balance in international payments after various shocks with the smallest possible costs in terms of output, employment and inflation. A second objective is a stable price level. This objective gained importance after inflation theory incorporated inter-temporal considerations which imply that a simple Phillips-curve tradeoff is valid, if at all, only in the short run, before expectations about future inflation adjust.

A third objective underlying exchange rate regime choice, mentioned but not analyzed in detail in the OCA literature, is microeconomic efficiency.[3] This objective has been addressed by monetary theorists such as Hayek (1977), and it has gained some attention in the debate about the European Monetary Union (EMU). In this debate, factors influencing microeconomic efficiency include transactions costs, uncertainty about prices and returns on investments, and the information value of prices.[4]

Microeconomic efficiency is clearly of great economic relevance, but it is a multifaceted objective. It includes conventional static efficiency and is linked to factors that enhance growth opportunities. Exchange rate policy may enhance static efficiency by reducing transactions costs and uncertainty that is endogenous to exchange rate regimes as opposed to uncertainty caused by exogenous factors, such as preferences, technology, oil price shocks, etc. Static efficiency is also influenced by the exchange rate's deviation from an equilibrium based on real and monetary factors.

These factors influencing static efficiency are also important for growth opportunities (see, e.g., Baldwin 1989). This aspect of efficiency can also be expected to be influenced by the information value of prices. Uncertainly about the relevance of an observed price, for investment decisions in particular, would affect growth as well as the static efficiency of, for example, consumption choice and international trade patterns. Although a high information value of prices is not conceptually identical to low uncertainty about future prices, we regard reduced uncertainty as a good approximation for increased information value. Thus, to the extent an exchange rate regime reduces uncertainty, it should also increase the information value of prices.

As noted, microeconomic efficiency has played an important role in the debate about the EMU. However, observers such as Eichengreen (1992), Krugman (1995), and Goodhart (1995) have argued that in the case of the EMU such potential gains are likely to be small, although there is some dispute about the importance of reduced exchange rate uncertainty.[5] Microeconomic efficiency aspects may nevertheless be important for developing and transition economies, where macroeconomic conditions are more unstable and unpredictable. Furthermore, the efficiency losses associated with disequilibrium exchange rates are likely to be relatively more serious in such poor economies than in Western Europe.

A fourth objective of exchange rate regime choice could be export promotion and trade-sector expansion with the government consciously manipulating the nominal exchange rate to attain a real exchange rate objective. Economists rarely consider this purpose in normative models, but it is more or less explicitly used by many governments' policymakers, as is noted in several country studies in this volume.[6] Trade expansion and real exchange rate objectives appear in the development literature, however, where it is assumed that foreign exchange markets are characterized by rationing and that the objective of government policies is to fill a "foreign exchange gap" and a "savings gap."

Traded sector expansion is often linked to economic growth in popular debate. If trade barriers or specific market failures have hindered the expansion of the traded goods sector, then their removal will clearly enhance economic efficiency. Going beyond this to give direct or indirect subsides to exports enjoys little academic credibility, however. Using exchange rate policy to make the traded goods sector highly competitive may stimulate the movement of factors into this sector, but at the expense of activities in the non-traded goods sector, with a net welfare loss for the country. There is a popular view that export-oriented production somehow is more valuable, but it is hard to pinpoint the external effects of such production that would justify a subsidization of exports across the board. To the extent that such positive externalities exist, they are likely to be associated only with particular industries. In such cases the theory of economic policy suggests that it is less costly to target those industries directly rather than attempt to use exchange rate policy as a second-best strategy. Lack of foreign exchange is often referred to as an argument for favoring export production. However, the "foreign exchange gap" is usually caused by exchange rate and other policies that discourage exports rather than market failure in the exporting sector in particular.

A country's exchange rate regime and other aspects of monetary policy are generally determined with one or more of these policy objectives explicitly or implicitly in the minds of policymakers. These policy objectives are not generally the primary objectives of economic policy, however. Economic growth, an equitable income distribution and a reduction of risk of loss of income are examples of primary objectives for different aspects of economic policy. It can be expected that exchange rate regime choice is part of an economic strategy to achieve these more general primary objectives.

Regime Objectives in Transition Economies

Are the primary objectives for transition economies different from those of industrialized market economies and, if so, what are the implications for the choice of exchange rate regime? One working hypothesis is that long-run economic growth has relatively greater weight for transition economies. At the same time, their recent history is characterized by strong egalitarianism and little individual risk-taking. Remnants of these objectives are still institutionalized in, for example, financial, labor and housing markets as noted by Goldberg in Part I and by Banaian and Zhukov in Part V of this volume. This legacy of the central planning period has two implications of relevance here. First, the institutional remnants causing rigidities in factor markets increase the short-term costs of growth-oriented policies that require rapid structural change. Second, policy measures to dismantle remaining institutional structures are positive from a growth point of view.

Among the four objectives mentioned above, microeconomic efficiency has the most obvious bearing on long-run growth. Thus, it could be argued that this objective should be of primary importance in the choice of exchange rate regime in transition economies. However, price and output stability also have a strong bearing on microeconomic efficiency. Price-level stability enhances the information content of prices, while output stability provides a more stable environment for economic activities.

Granted the importance of price-level stability, there is a question whether high inflation should be viewed as exogenous relative to the exchange rate regime or whether the regime should be chosen in order to reduce inflation. Different transition economies have chosen different paths with respect to the role of price-level stabilization in the transition process.

Here political economy considerations are paramount. An increasing number of economists and organizations such as the International Monetary Fund have advocated the use of fixed exchange rates to discipline domestic macroeconomic policymakers and thus fight inflation. Ultimately, however, domestic political stability appears to be the most important condition for controlling inflation (see Willett, Burdekin, Sweeney and Wihlborg 1995). Where domestic political conditions are highly unstable, efforts to promote discipline through an exchange rate constraint are likely to succeed only in producing balance of payments crises and economic disruptions. On the other hand, with domestic political stability and a sound institutional framework there is no need for an external constraint. In a middle range of domestic political and institutional situations, however, the use of the exchange rate as an anchor for domestic monetary policy may be helpful. The Czech Republic, Estonia and Lithuania are possible examples. It is crucial, however, that the potential contributions of genuinely fixed exchange rates not be falsely conferred on adjustably pegged exchange rate regimes.[7]

If high inflation is so embedded in an economy that exchange rate and monetary policy will not reduce it without high costs in terms of unemployment and growth, then it is necessary to accommodate inflation with a high degree of exchange rate flexibility. For transition economies, this view is backed by the argument that inflation can be reduced at much less cost after state enterprises have been privatized and the banking sector has new incentives to impose budget constraints on large state enterprises. In the absence of such reforms restrictive monetary policy will particularly hinder the expansion of emerging private enterprises. Price-level stabilization could lead to unemployment in exactly the "wrong" sector from an economic growth perspective.[8]

There are important arguments against delaying stabilization, however. Most Western economists favor stabilization of the price level at an early stage in the transition process, arguing that macroeconomic stabilization is a precondition for long-run growth. Some economists also argue that price-level stability should be given priority at an early stage in the transition because governments will likely enjoy an initial "honeymoon" with the public during which the initial economic costs of stabilization may impose lower political costs on the government initiating such policies. Furthermore, high unemployment will induce policymakers to speed up market-oriented reforms such as privatization and other measures increasing the responsiveness of output to economic incentives. On the other hand, high unemployment in emerging sectors could increase the reluctance of policymakers to expose state enterprises to market forces, slowing down reforms. These conflicting considerations are evident in the country studies in this volume. Experiences in a few transition countries, with Estonia as the primary example, indicate that it is possible both to conduct a restrictive monetary policy and promote privatization and reform of the financial sector (see the contribution by Ross in Chapter 13.) The political conditions in each country will determine the timing of anti-inflation efforts that will best enhance growth objectives. It is important to remember, however, that there is substantial empirical evidence that, contrary to the short-term tradeoffs that may be involved, over the medium term high inflation hurts growth.[9] Thus, an anti-inflation policy is an important element in promoting microeconomic efficiency and growth.

We have argued that the objective of output and employment stabilization is consistent with microeconomic efficiency in important respects. It does not necessarily follow, however, that such stabilization should be a factor in choosing the exchange rate regime. The OCA approach emphasizes that exchange rate adjustment may substitute for labor mobility and wage flexibility as an adjustment mechanism after temporary aggregate shocks. By the same token, knowledge in labor markets that exchange rates or macroeconomic policy will be adjusted to reduce unemployment could reduce labor mobility and the incentives to reform institutions, thereby contributing to factor immobility. This risk seems particularly high under pegged but adjustable exchange rates where exchange rate adjustment is a political decision. The risk could be less under flexible rates. Sweeney discusses in Chapter 12 under what circumstances a currency board may or may not contribute to improved adjustment in an economy.

We conclude that factors influencing output, employment and price-level stabilization should be important considerations in the choice of exchange rate regime, but on grounds of microeconomic efficiency the choice should take into account both that the chosen regime could influence factor mobility and wage adjustment and that inflation in some countries can be seen as exogenous to some extent at early stages in the transition process. The country studies in this volume certainly indicate that policymakers in, for example, Poland and Russia took the latter position in the initial stages of the transition. In these countries trade sector expansion has been a policy objective and therefore contributed to disequilibrium real exchange rates. (See the chapters by Kowalski and Stawarska and by Banaian and Zhukov in Part V of this volume.[10]) This objective certainly stands in conflict with microeconomic efficiency.

Microeconomic and Macroeconomic Objectives: Is There a Trade-off?

Is there a tradeoff between microeconomic efficiency and the other objectives of exchange rate regime choice? Clearly, there is a tradeoff between export promotion and efficiency unless the case for export promotion rests on broad market failures in traded-goods industries. We argued above that such failures are not the common reason for trying to peg the real exchange rate at a disequilibrium level.

The objectives of microeconomic efficiency and a stable price level are more likely to coincide than collide. A stable price level or a stable inflation rate reduces transactions costs and uncertainty, and it enhances the information value of prices. Note also that stable inflation rates are usually associated with low inflation rates. Yet another reason why the two objectives coincide is that attempts to peg a real exchange rate at an export-promoting level are likely to cause imported inflation or direct controls on trade and prices.

The question whether there is a tradeoff between the objectives of microeconomic efficiency and the costs in terms of output and employment to restore external balance in response to shocks is more complex. Output uncertainty caused by uncertainty about the level of aggregate demand is clearly as much a concern from a firm's point of view as is exchange rate uncertainty. Thus, to the extent a flexible and uncertain exchange rate is expected to stabilize demand and output, overall uncertainty may be reduced by exchange rate flexibility. In this sense, the objective of overall microeconomic efficiency and the macroeconomic objective most commonly assumed in the OCA literature may be reinforcing rather than conflicting.

In some circumstances short-run output stabilization and macroeconomic policies oriented towards external balance are associated with microeconomic costs, however. For example, adjustment to productivity declines, like those induced by the oil price shocks during the 1970s, may require a temporary fall in output and employment as well as a current account deficit to induce the required decline in real wages and the sectoral reallocation of resources. Similarly, demand shifts among sectors will require relative price and wage adjustments, but to the extent such shifts affect output, employment, and inflation, they may induce macroeconomic policy responses that may slow adjustment in relative prices and wages.

In both the above examples there is a conflict between microeconomic efficiency and output stabilization. Macroeconomic output-stabilization policies are likely to contribute to inflationary pressure in the economy. Thus, in these cases inflation can be seen as an indicator of macroeconomic disequilibrium. It follows that the conflict between microeconomic efficiency and economic stabilization coincides in these cases with the conflict between inflation and output stabilization. Therefore, it can be argued that the microeconomic efficiency objective is often subsumed in the analysis of conflicts between output stability and inflation in macroeconomic analyses.

Although the microeconomic efficiency objective is often implicitly taken into account in macroeconomic analyses of exchange rate regime choice based on OCA theory, there are reasons to think of microeconomic efficiency separately and explicitly as an independent and sometime conflicting objective. For example, using the objectives in OCA theory, the analyst may find that limited convertibility of a currency increases the ability of firms and households to obtain financial asset and liability portfolios that optimize their risk-return tradeoffs.

A second important reason to treat microeconomic efficiency as a separate objective is that many governments equate external balance with short-term balance in the current account, or even with a positive balance on this account. Such short-term macroeconomic policy objectives may induce exchange rate and/or macroeconomic policies that are very costly from the perspective of economic growth.

A third reason to think of microeconomic efficiency separately, in transition economies in particular, is that macroeconomic policies may affect incentives for price adjustment and factor mobility. This issue is discussed in the next section. The chapters in this volume demonstrate that all of the objectives of exchange rate regime choice discussed above play a role in the decisions of policymakers. Their weights vary across countries as well as over time, although not necessarily primarily on economic grounds.

Issues in Exchange Rate Policy:
An Overview of this Volume

In this section we provide an overview of issues that appear frequently in the chapters of this volume. The first issue to be discussed is, does exchange rate adjustment work? Domestic and international price and wage adjustment play a crucial role in the answer to this question, regardless of the objective of exchange rate policy. The inflation-discipline issue, which underlies so much of the recent advocacy of fixed rates, is addressed next. Political economy considerations are particularly important for this issue. Finally, we turn to the issue of exchange rate stability, emphasizing foreign exchange-market behavior and expectations formation of market participants.

Do Exchange Rate Adjustments Work?

Some advocates of European Monetary Union have argued that there is little cost to giving up the exchange rate instrument since economies have become so internationalized that a change in the nominal exchange rate will have little effect on the real exchange rate; that is, a devaluation will quickly generate an almost equivalent increase in domestic prices and thus rob exchange rate changes of their usefulness in promoting balance of payments adjustment. The available empirical evidence does not support this view as a general proposition, and the country studies here confirm this view. The OCA literature, however, has long focused on domestic price effects as an important aspect of evaluating exchange rate regimes and demonstrates that the seriousness of this problem should vary substantially across countries depending on their size and openness and on their wage-setting practices. In Part V, Hrnčíř, Gáspár, Kowalski and Stawarska, and Banaian and Zhukov discuss real exchange rate adjustment in the Czech Republic, Hungary, Poland and Russia in the early days of transition.

Another type of argument focuses on the possible unresponsiveness of firms to changes in economic incentives. "Elasticity pessimism" was a common criticism of the usefulness of exchange rate adjustments during the early days of the Bretton Woods system. If elasticities were too low, exchange rate changes would have perverse effects on the trade balance. Experience showed, however, that while this effect often operated in the short run, it was not a problem over the medium term. This became characterized as the J-curve effect, with devaluation frequently leading to a small worsening of the trade balance for several quarters before improvements were generated. As Goldberg discusses in Chapter 2 in Part I, low responsiveness is likely to be a particularly serious problem in the initial stages of transition from command to market economies. She points out that this presents a strong case against attempting to use the exchange rate as a direct instrument for short-run macroeconomic stabilization. Instead, exchange rate arrangements should be designed to support institution building that contributes to price-level stability. The view Goldberg presents here is consistent with the views of those favoring fixed exchange rates such as currency boards (discussed in Part IV). Willett and Wihlborg argue, however, that the evidence suggests that exchange rate adjustments would still be useful to promote balance of payments adjustment over the medium term in most emerging market economies. Prolonged real exchange rate effects of exchange rate policy are, of course, a prerequisite for real exchange rate targeting as discussed by Arndt, and Siklos and Ábel in Part III.

The effectiveness of real exchange rate changes as an adjustment mechanism depends also on the types of disturbances that a country faces. Fixed exchange rates spread out disturbances internationally, while flexible exchange rates tend to confine them to the place of origin. Thus advocates of fixed exchange rates tend to focus on examples of the usefulness of fixed exchange rates in stabilizing the domestic economy by considering cases of domestic fluctuations whose domestic effects can be mitigated by spreading them abroad. Advocates of flexible exchange rates tend more often to discuss cases of foreign disturbances, where flexible exchange rates can help protect the domestic economy from the ravages of foreign inflation or from the need for domestic deflation to correct a balance of payments deficit. In much of the recent technical literature on exchange rate analysis, these source-of-disturbance arguments have received primary emphasis. The difficulty is that most countries are likely to be hit by many different types of shocks that have different implications for optimal exchange rate policies. Statistical studies of past patterns may offer a fairly limited ability to predict future patterns except where these can be linked to underlying structural characteristics such as a concentration of exports in raw materials that are subject to substantial market fluctuations or domestic political instabilities that make high inflation endemic.

The Inflation-Discipline Issue

Judgments differ greatly about the relationship between exchange rate regimes and inflation. The most common view is that flexible exchange rates tend to be inflationary whereas fixed exchange rates help restrain inflation. In particular circumstances this is true, but there are many counterexamples. As Willett and Wihlborg (Chapter 3) and Banaian and Zhukov (Chapter 18) discuss, with the high rates of inflation generated in Russia in the early days after the fall of communism, the only option for the former Soviet republics to protect themselves from quadruple-digit inflation was to adopt flexible exchange rates against the ruble.

The old discipline argument for fixed exchange rates has enjoyed a resurgence of popularity in recent years based on new theoretical models of credibility effects and the success of the members of the European Monetary System in disinflating. As argued in the contributions by Hochreiter (Chapter 1), Sweeney (Chapter 12), and Westbrook and Willett (Chapter 4), in such analysis it is crucial to distinguish between commitments to genuinely fixed exchange rates, i.e., those which would be abandoned only under the most extreme circumstances, and temporarily pegged exchange rates that are likely to be abandoned if pressures arise. No regime can be expected to survive, for example, the dissolution of a country. Nevertheless, if the commitment is strong enough, fixed exchange rates will provide true macroeconomic discipline, and the issue becomes whether this is worth the costs imposed by gearing the domestic economy to the behavior of the external sector. For the emerging market economies, the adoption of such genuinely fixed exchange rates requires stronger institutional arrangements than just pegging the exchange rate. Currency board arrangements, discussed in Part IV by Sweeney, Ross, Dubauskas, and Dubauskas, Wihlborg and Willett, have been adopted by Argentina, Estonia and Lithuania as an approach to the creation of strong institutional arrangements. Bulgaria is in the process of adopting such a scheme. Currency boards have also been recommended for large economies like Russia and Ukraine. Here the optimum currency area approach offers important insights. The attractiveness of seeking to provide macroeconomic discipline through external rather than internal means should be much less attractive for large than for small countries (see Wihlborg and Willett in Chapter 3, and Sweeney in Chapter 12). Such considerations would in turn affect the credibility of less formal commitments to fixed exchange rates (see Chapter 4 by Westbrook and Willett).

The country experiences analyzed in Parts II and V indicate that the record of programs using pegged as opposed to genuinely fixed exchange rates as instruments to fight inflation is quite mixed. In some instances pegging the rate has helped break the momentum of inflation, and in several cases within the European Monetary System commitments to defend the exchange rate developed considerable credibility over time. There are other cases, however, where pegging the rate created greater incentives for politically motivated demand expansions that set back disinflation efforts. Perhaps the strongest conclusion that can be drawn is that the focus of anti-inflation policy must be domestically based and that the key requirement of exchange rate policies is that they not become grossly inconsistent with domestic economic policies. Where there are mild inconsistencies exchange rate commitments can sometimes be used to force domestic economic policies into line. But where the inconsistencies are large, it is almost always exchange rate policies which give way, with the interim efforts to maintain the exchange rate peg ultimately leading to greater instability. The crisis of the Mexican peso in

1994–95 and the plunge of the Russian ruble on Black Tuesday in 1994 are prime examples.

One of the most interesting findings from our country studies in Parts II and V is that the adoption of strong institutional commitments to monetary discipline do appear to have aided the disinflationary process, but that most of the gains in credibility which occurred came gradually rather than instantaneously. For example, the success of Estonia's disinflationary policies bolstered by the adoption of a currency-board type monetary arrangement was not noticeably different from that of the Czech Republic, until the spring of 1997 when the pegged rate of the Czech Republic came under speculative pressure. The Czech central bank never made an official commitment to keep the parity unchanged, however. Thus it appears that institutional commitments can help countries gain credibility, but they do not substitute for the need to earn it through sustained, prudent, domestic monetary and fiscal policies. The evidence from the Baltic states presented in Parts II and IV by Dubauskas, Dubauskas, Wihlborg and Willett, and Ross indicates that the final judgment on currency boards is still out.

One compromise policy approach which initially received a great deal of favorable attention is the strategy of using a crawling peg to gradually reduce inflation. This strategy is discussed for Poland by Kowalski and Starwaska and for Hungary by Gáspár in Part V. For a country starting with a very high rate of inflation, it would be very difficult to make credible the adoption of a permanent peg. The idea of the crawling peg nominal anchor strategy is to precommit to a downward crawl which is less than the difference between the country's own rate of inflation and the average of its trading partners. Through this strategy the external sector would generate pressures against above-target wage and price increases and inflation would gradually fall. The historical record suggests that the most difficult part of disinflation policy is to bring inflation down from high to low double-digit (or single-digit) levels. In Mexico this strategy helped bring inflation down into the single-digit range, but ultimately resulted in a substantially overvalued peso which led to a balance of payments crisis. The plunge of the peso when Mexico was forced to let it float undermined much of the government's hard-earned gains on the inflation front. So far Hungary and Poland have operated their variants of this strategy in a much less disruptive manner, but also without succeeding in bringing their inflation rates down below the 20 percent level. In general we believe that the use of crawling peg regimes are viewed more realistically as methods of reducing the damage caused by high inflation than as effective methods of reducing inflation.

The Exchange Rate (In)Stability Issue

Another major source of controversy concerns the behavior of flexible exchange rates. Critics of flexible rates typically assume that large exchange rate movements are frequently caused by destabilizing speculation that imposes disruptions which could be avoided under pegged exchange rates. Advocates of flexible rates, on the other hand, typically see exchange rate fluctuations as being caused by reasonable market responses to changes in underlying economic fundamentals.

Much of the continuing dispute about speculation is due to the crucial role of expectations in the behavior of financial markets. In efficient financial markets prices are influenced not just by what has happened, but by expectations about what will happen. This makes it difficult to explain the behavior of exchange rate dynamics with ex post statistical data. For example, where a deadlock in the budget process raises fears of an acceleration of inflation, then in an efficient market the exchange rate should depreciate by more than could be explained by past inflation differentials. Likewise, many shocks may cause substantial changes in equilibrium real exchange rates, but with the amount of appropriate change being subject to considerable uncertainty. In such circumstances plausible shifts in expectations may lead to large, rapid exchange rate movements. Such behavior is consistent with both destabilizing speculation and with speculation in efficient markets. Because it is often difficult to clearly discriminate between these hypothesis, there is considerable scope for observers to cling to their prior beliefs.

The history of the fluctuations of the ruble highlights this problem. During the period of exchange rate flexibility the ruble has been substantially undervalued in terms of actual inflation differentials. This undervaluation can be explained by reference to expected future inflation, however. Likewise, many of the large movements in the ruble can be easily explained in terms of changing expectations about election outcomes and prospects for budget deficits and monetary accommodation. Yet it is hard to show that the amounts of these swings were fully justified in relation to the market's expectations or that these expectations did not suffer from excessive optimism or pessimism. To many, the dramatic fall of the ruble by 27 percent against the dollar in a single day, the infamous "Black Tuesday" in the summer of 1994, was a clear illustration of the dangers of destabilizing speculation and market overreaction. More correct is the conclusion drawn by Granville (1995) that Black Tuesday was a "response to serious failings in government policy" (p. 96) and "a proof that markets are working" (p. 93). In other words, the speculators were the messengers that government policy was unsustainable and not the causes of the crisis. The same conclusion applies to the Mexican peso crisis of 1994–95 and the Asian financial crisis of 1997–98.

More of a problem than overt destabilizing speculation is the thinness of financial and foreign exchange markets in the initial stages of transitions from command to market economies. For floating exchange rates to be reasonably stable in the short run, one needs not only the absence of destabilizing speculation but the presence of stabilizing speculation. Otherwise factors such as J-curve effects can cause short-term exchange rate movements that magnify the longer term effects of shocks. This is not an argument for pegged over flexible exchange rates but rather an argument for a managed rather than a free float; government's role here would be that of the missing stabilizing speculators. A crawling peg with wide enough bands could also be an intermediate regime solution. It is possible, however, that the fears of thinness for a floating exchange rate have been exaggerated. Kranjec (1995) argues that such a regime has worked well for Slovenia without seemingly excessive exchange rate volatility.

When recommending policies to compensate for such "market failures," it is also important to recognize the potential dangers of "government failures." While the magnitude of the drop of the ruble on Black Tuesday was due primarily to concerns about domestic economic policies, the timing and speed of the drop was due to bad management of exchange rate policy. The Russian authorities attempted to counter worsening expectations by increasingly heavy exchange market intervention to prop up the ruble. Reserve losses became unsustainable, forcing the authorities to pull out of the market and resulting in the sharp plunge of the ruble. Predictably, Russian officials blamed the plunge on greedy speculators who were destabilizing the market.

A virtually identical episode occurred in Bulgaria earlier in 1994. In several workshops connected with this project we heard reports from knowledgeable Bulgarian officials and members of the press that there had been a serious case of destabilizing private speculation which had brought down the lev. Upon investigation, however, we discovered that the Bulgarian authorities had been holding the nominal value of the lev virtually constant for well over a year while their inflation continued to run at levels well above the average of their trading partners. Not surprisingly, Bulgaria's international reserves began to fall. By the end of 1993 the government was virtually out of reserves and in early 1994 had to pull out of the market. A plunge of the lev followed. Under such circumstances it would not be surprising if the fall of the market rate overshot the equilibrium level, but clearly in this case the culprit was not market overreaction but a badly conceived government intervention policy.[11]

When overshooting is discussed, the "equilibrium" exchange rate is often defined by purchasing power parity (PPP). This parity holds when exchange rate changes over time compensate for inflation differentials among countries. When exchange rates deviate from PPP, exchange rate changes are "real." There are substantial disagreements about how to measure real exchange rates and about the long-run behavior of these rates.

Since the late 1970s, much empirical work, focused mainly on developed countries, has supported the view that countries do not have constant long-run equilibrium real rates to which the actual rates tend to return. This empirical work suggests instead that real exchange rates tend to wander aimlessly over time. In Chapter 9 Sweeney discusses recent evidence that real exchange rates do in fact have long-run equilibrium values to which they tend to return, but that these equilibrium values are also subject to change. This later evidence suggests that displacements of a real exchange rate from its equilibrium value are, ceteris paribus, eliminated gradually over time. Sweeney emphasizes that because the equilibrium real rate is itself subject to shocks, the signs of adjustment are often obscured in the data.

In transition economies the problems of measuring real exchange rates are particularly severe as discussed by Dubauskas (Chapter 14), Kowalski and Stawarska (Chapter 17), and Hrnčíř (Chapter 15). These chapters illustrate the difficulties of finding a sustainable level for a pegged rate and the problems of identifying cases of over- and undervalued currencies. In some cases there have been substantial differences in indices of real exchange rates as measured by wholesale versus consumer prices. This presented particularly great problems in Bulgaria. There is also strong reason to believe that many transition economies will enjoy above average rates of productivity growth and that this will lead to a gradual appreciation of their equilibrium real exchange rates over time. The magnitude of these trends is difficult to assess, however, and in several cases countries have faced severe exchange rate crises because their governments were overly optimistic about the amount of appreciation of the equilibrium real rate. Mexico is a prime example.

In recent years there has been considerable debate not only about the desirability of discretionary exchange rate management but also about its feasibility. Where international capital mobility is high, then under pegged exchange rates central banks cannot sterilize, i.e., neutralize, the effects of balance of payments surpluses or deficits on the domestic money supply. Thus, pegged rates would imply the loss of control over domestic monetary policy even in the short run. Similarly, sterilized intervention in the foreign exchange market would not affect the exchange rate. Under such circumstances, even if the authorities could easily identify cases of destabilizing private speculation, they could prevent undesirable exchange rate movements only at the cost of directing monetary policy to exchange rate rather than domestic objectives.

Recent analysis suggests that these policy ineffectiveness conclusions are too strong, however. Despite the growth in international capital mobility, empirical studies have found that many developing and industrial countries have the ability to sterilize a substantial portion of the domestic monetary effects of payments imbalances, at least in the short run. The analysis by Siklos and Ábel of the Hungarian experience presented in Chapter 11 suggests that this conclusion holds for many emerging market economies as well.

We are not aware of any studies which have been undertaken on the effectiveness of sterilized exchange market intervention by governments of emerging market economies, but in Chapter 9 Sweeney presents evidence that such intervention has had some degree of effectiveness for the industrial countries. This suggests that at present the best assumption to make is that, for better or worse, many governments in emerging market economies do have some scope for short-term discretionary exchange rate management. Thus, how management should be conducted is a relevant issue.

Conclusion

A major lesson we draw from the analysis presented in this volume is that it is difficult to do a good job of directing management of the exchange rate even when one is considering economic factors alone. When political pressures are added in, the job becomes even more difficult. Based on the experiences reviewed in the chapters in Parts II and V, it is difficult to draw conclusions about a clear ranking of desirability between heavily managed floating and adjustable or crawling peg systems. The key differences to date appear to have come primarily from how governments actually operate exchange rate policy rather than which of these regimes is adopted. In general, however, these compromise systems have not worked as well as many of their advocates had hoped.

The Asian currency crisis of 1997–98 presents the latest example of this problem. It appears that many countries will be better served by adopting either a lightly managed float or a genuinely fixed exchange rate. The compromise systems have great short-run attraction since they allow one to avoid this difficult choice. But too often over time they have tended to generate the worst rather than the best aspects of each extreme.

Notes

1. If capital mobility is high, then a fixed exchange rate will be credible only if the rate is irrevocably fixed. Irrevocability requires, in effect, a currency area, as noted in Goodhart (1995) and Wihlborg and Willett (1991).

2. See the analyses in Krugman (1995).

3. An exception is Minford (1995). Macroeconomic models incorporating a "representative" agent's utility function allow explicit welfare analysis. These models are invariably highly "stylized," with the purpose of analyzing welfare effects of exchange rate regimes under specific assumptions about market imperfections such as a cash-in-advance constraint or information availability. Their relevance for economic policy decisions is questionable, because economic policymakers usually face complex situations and uncertainty about the validity of any particular model.

4. See, for example, Gros and Thygesen (1990) and Emerson et al. (1992); the arguments are reviewed in, for example, de Grauwe (1992), Goodhart (1995) and Wihlborg (1996).

5. Many economists argue that the total uncertainty caused by macroeconomic factors is not related to exchange rate flexibility, because if a particular disturbance does not affect a pegged exchange rate, then it affects other variables. Only short-run exchange rate fluctuations can be considered relatively independent of macroeconomic shocks. There are often cheap ways of hedging such short-term risk, however.

6. See also Chapter 10 by Arndt in this volume.

7. On these issues, see the country studies in Parts II and V and the analysis by Westbrook and Willett in Chapter 4.

8. See Eliasson, Rybczynski and Wihlborg (1993).

9. For evidence and references, see Burdekin et al. (1995). Some have argued that such relationships do not apply to the former communist countries, but the evidence says otherwise.

10 In Hungary, the government has fluctuated between anti-inflation and trade promotion objectives in its exchange rate policy. See Gáspár, Chapter 16.

11. For data and analysis of this experience, see International Monetary Fund (1996).

References

Baldwin, Richard. 1989. "The Growth Effects of 1992." *Economic Policy*, October: 248–79.

Burdekin, Richard C.K., Suyono Salamon, and Thomas D. Willett. 1995. "The High Costs of Monetary Instability," in Thomas D. Willett, Richard C.K. Burdekin, Richard J. Sweeney, and Clas Wihlborg, ed., *Establishing Monetary Stability in Emerging Market Economies*. Pp. 13–33. Boulder, Colo.: Westview Press.

De Grauwe, Paul. 1992. *The Economics of Monetary Integration*. Oxford: Oxford University Press.

Eichengreen, Barry. 1992. *Should the Maastricht Treaty Be Saved?* Princeton Studies in International Finance No. 74. Princeton: Princeton University Press, December.

Eliasson, Gunnar, Tad Rybczynski and Clas Wihlborg. 1993. *The Necessary Institutional Framework to Transform Formerly Planned Economies*. Stockholm: The Industrial Institute for Economies and Social Research.

Emerson, Michael et al. 1992. *One Market, One Money*. Oxford: Oxford University Press.

Fisher, Stanley, Ratna Sahey, and Carlos Végh. 1991. "Stabilization and Growth in Transition Economies." *Journal of Economic Perspectives*, Spring: 45–66.

Goodhart, Charles. 1995. "The Political Economy of Monetary Union," in Peter B. Kenen, ed., *Understanding Interdependence: The Macroeconomics of the Open Economy*. Pp. 450–505. Princeton: Princeton University Press.

Granville, Briggitte. 1995. *The Success of Russian Economic Reforms*. London: Royal Institute of International Affairs.

Gros, Daniel, and Niels Thygesen. 1990. "The Institutional Approach to Monetary Union in Europe." *Economic Journal*, September: 925–35.

Hayek, Friedrich. 1977. *Denationalisation of Money.* London: Institute for Economic Research.

International Monetary Fund. 1996. *Bulgaria—Recent Economic Development.* IMF Staff Country Report No. 96113. Washington, D.C.: International Monetary Fund.

Kranjec, Marko. 1995. "Introduction of a New Currency: The Case of Slovenia." *Development and International Cooperation*, June/December: 127–47.

Krugman, Paul. 1995. "What Do We Need to Know About the International Monetary System?" in Peter B. Kenen, ed., *Understanding Interdependence: The Macroeconomics of the Open Economy.* Pp. 509–30. Princeton: Princeton University Press.

Minford, Patrick. 1995. "Other People's Money: Cash in Advance Microfoundations for Optimal Currency Areas." *Journal of International Money and Finance* 14(3): 427–40.

Wihlborg, Clas. 1996. "Macroeconomic Effects of Macroeconomic Exposure: Conceptional Issues and Estimation." *Rivista Di Politica Economica*, November/December: 195–218.

Wihlborg, Clas, and Thomas D. Willett. 1991. "Optimum Currency Areas Revisited on the Transition Path to a Monetary Union," in Clas Wihlborg, Michele Fratianni, and Thomas D. Willett, eds., *Financial Regulation and Monetary Arrangements After 1992.* Pp. 279–97. Amsterdam: North Holland.

Willett, Thomas D., Richard C.K. Burdekin, Richard J. Sweeney, and Clas Wihlborg, eds. 1995. *Establishing Monetary Stability in Emerging Market Economies.* Boulder, Colo.: Westview Press.

PART ONE

Fixed vs Flexible Exchange Rates: The Debate Continues

1

The Case for Hard Currency Strategies for Emerging Market Economies

Eduard Hochreiter

Introduction

There is almost universal agreement that the statutory prime objective of central bank policy is the maintenance of price stability. As has been pointed out elsewhere,[1] the basic policy problem facing the central banks of economies in transition is how to best achieve this objective, i.e., with the least economic cost in terms of *frictional* unemployment.[2]

Recall that government policymakers in the transitioning economies initially faced, inter alia, massively distorted relative price structures characterized by heavy subsidies and state monopolies. There were neither central banks nor monetary policy in the Western sense, and financial markets were nonexistent. The opening of these economies to market forces required very substantial changes in relative prices, which, in conjunction with downward stickiness of prices, initially implied a once-and-for-all jump in the general price level. This, in turn, led to an (economically warranted) dramatic decline in measured real wages, which subsequently made it difficult in many of these countries to contain renewed pressures to raise nominal wages.

There continues to be an urgent need for economic policymakers to devise policies that stabilize expectations and speed up economic adjustment, i.e., to make the supply side more flexible and responsive to market signals, and so increase the adaptability of the economy. Such considerations are also relevant for central bank policy.

The challenge for governments and central banks is, therefore, to select a monetary regime that is conducive to the achievement and maintenance of price stability, to define the intermediate target(s), and to devise effective operating procedures. In addition, and closely linked to these goals, the central bank should support the development of financial markets. The policies that support these goals critically depend on how the systemic reform process evolves. At the same time, it is my conviction that no new monetary policy theory has to be developed for economies in transition, but rather that the same economic principles of, say, exchange rate policy, apply both to market economies and transitioning economies.[3]

This chapter develops arguments for the adoption of a fixed peg by six selected transitional economies: Bulgaria, the Czech Republic, Hungary, Poland, Slovakia and Slovenia.[4] It interprets the likely occurrence of real appreciation and, in the context of fostering credibility for the peg, examines the role of currency convertibility in these countries. The final section presents my conclusions.

A Fixed Peg as Anchor for Monetary Policy

There is an abundant literature dealing with the choice of the exchange rate regime.[5] However, so far no consensus has emerged. In principle—taking the G-3 countries (the United States, Japan, and Germany) as a yardstick—one could argue that the larger, the less open, and the more diversified a country's trade links with the rest of the world (and thus in the absence of an obvious dominant economy with common policy aims which is politically acceptable as the center country), and the more developed the financial system, the more likely that policymakers will opt for a flexible exchange rate regime; that is, to employ a monetary aggregate as the intermediate target or anchor for monetary policy and let the market determine the exchange rate.

The recent experience of the European Monetary System has led to arguments that the lifting of exchange controls has advanced the case for greater exchange rate flexibility because of the ensuing rise in capital mobility. Increased capital mobility makes pegged exchange rates much more vulnerable to speculative attacks.[6] In a world with substantial economic interdependence, one cannot in general sustain a combination of pegged exchange rates, freedom of domestic monetary policy and freedom from capital controls. Eventually, at least one of these policies will have to go. My argument is that giving up the pegged exchange rate is generally not the least-cost solution for a small, open (reforming) economy.

It is my view that the substitution of other nominal anchors for the exchange rate peg—save in extreme circumstances—is not the best way to anchor monetary policy, at least for the smaller transitioning economies.[7] The use of monetary aggregates as the nominal anchor critically depends on the stability of the demand for money and the central bank's ability to control the money supply process. At this point, the transitioning economies lack the track record to empirically test if these conditions hold.[8] Moreover, the smooth operation of floating exchange rate regimes requires well-developed money and capital markets to offset short-term fluctuations in the demand for money. Finally, floating exchange rates tend to substantially over- and undershoot, even in countries such as the United States where money and capital markets are very well developed. The volatility and the tendency of floating exchange rates to overshoot is related to the fact that monetary aggregates do not provide such a clear, simple and transparent anchor for expectations as pegged exchange rates. As we learned a long time ago, the time lags in monetary policy are long and variable. Deviations from purchasing power parity are large and sustained, and the construction of monetary aggregates is complex and subject to change over time. For these and other reasons, floating exchange rates have not converged on purchasing power parity for extended periods, even in developed market economies (Hochreiter 1989:214). For countries undergoing the transition from planned to market economies the problems are all the greater. Consequently, floating exchange rates and the use of monetary aggregates as intermediate targets are—as a rule—not the preferred option, at least for the smaller transitioning economies.

This leaves us with the alternative of using the exchange rate as nominal anchor for macroeconomic policy.[9] Such a view has been echoed by Michael Bruno. He argues that Estonia, which is not covered in this study, is a textbook case of successful monetary stabilization using an immediate and credible fixing of the currency (CEPR 1993:4). Another interesting point in favor of a pegged exchange rate system has been made by Guitián (1994:24). He notes that "with a fixed exchange rate, an economy expresses its willingness to withstand the consequences of external shocks and disturbances."

The optimal choice of the peg remains an unresolved issue although, after the experiences with the European Exchange Rate Mechanism in the early 1990s, the majority opinion of policymakers and academia appears to lean to some form of limited flexibility; say, in the form of some sort of adjustable peg. But before setting a peg, several critical issues must be addressed: which currency or currencies to peg to; the speed of price liberalization and the initial degree of price distortions to be corrected; the degree of convertibility to be introduced and when, and the population's reaction to it (currency substitution); the existing and/or expected disequilibrium in the current account of the balance of payments, the (prospective) foreign reserve position and the level of foreign debt; the supply-side reaction of the economy to systemic change, etc.[10] All of these factors entail massive uncertainty with regard to the initial equilibrium level of the exchange rate and its likely evolution. As a consequence, a more flexible peg has generally been recommended for transitional economies.[11] A flexible peg is defined as a peg which is devalued or revalued at irregular intervals. Alternatively, the exchange rate may be adjusted according to some indicator (crawling peg) or not at all (fixed peg). Crawling pegs come in two varieties: the endogenous and the exogenous crawling peg. In the former case the nominal exchange rate is periodically adjusted to the *actual* inflation rate, while in the latter case the exchange rate is adjusted in steps related, among other things, to the *projected* rate of inflation.

In spite of the problems enumerated, my preference—drawing heavily on the Austrian experience—remains for a fixed peg to one or more of the stable Western currencies with no—or next to no—escape clauses after having taken into account the initial effects of price liberalization and of the (near) abolition of subsidies.[12] An initial devaluation of the currency to a somewhat undervalued level is desirable before pegging the rate, because an undervalued exchange rate will help support exports at a very difficult juncture of the economy. This will help sustain the fixed peg through the period when the development of the services sector and further liberalization measures drive the (overall) inflation rate above that of the center country(ies).

One decisive factor for a successful monetary policy and, indeed, for the sustainability of a pegged exchange rate, is the credible commitment of the central bank to price stability. In this respect a single-currency peg constitutes the simplest, and preferred, rule: it is transparent and easily understood by policymakers and the public alike. Since monetary policy in the Western sense is new to the transitioning economies, their central banks have no track record against which to evaluate their commitment to stated policy aims. Therefore, one of the central banks' first goals ought to be to build a reputation for policy steadfastness and to earn credibility as quickly as possible. Institutional design can aid or hinder the achievement of this goal; legal independence is important.[13] The creation of favorable expectations concerning price stability at home and a stable exchange rate with regard to the center country (or countries in the case of a basket peg) should positively influence investment and savings behavior and should, in particular, limit currency substitution.[14] In my view, an endogenous crawling peg risks the continuation (or even the acceleration) of inflation, while an exogenous crawling peg tends to work too slowly to reduce inflation expectations because of continuing devaluations, even when they are less than the current inflation rate.

The initial setting of the exchange rate is, however, an extremely difficult task. It appears that in Poland and the former Czechoslovakia policymakers did err as far as devaluation was concerned: the initial undervaluation of the exchange rate was more than was warranted by the (expected) jump in the price level due to the liberalization of prices and the sharp curtailment of subsidies. It is my judgment that in no case was the initial error so large that the peg had to be abandoned on this account later on.[15] Provided that the initial mistake in setting the exchange rate is not "too large," one can expect that—over time—the domestic economy will adjust to the exchange rate level chosen without undue economic cost. Within bounds, the commitment of the authorities is more important than the exchange rate level selected.

Indeed, the flexibility and adaptability of the micro side of the domestic economy in conjunction with consistent fiscal and incomes policies are crucial. Successful macroeconomic stabilization requires both stringent monetary and fiscal policy. Apart from making sure any initial error in setting the exchange rate level is not "too" large, the sustainability of the peg critically depends on the wage formation process. Therefore, it seems advisable to supplement the exchange rate anchor by a wage anchor.

There are several options available for such a (supplementary) anchor: administrative wage controls either in the form of a temporary wage freeze (Bruno 1991), longer term wage controls (e.g., taxing the marginal wage increase), or a productivity-oriented wage formation process, where nominal wage increases are determined by productivity advances, possibly plus an increment reflecting the (ex ante or ex post) inflation rate.

In practice, administrative wage anchors were in operation at some stage in both Poland and the former Czechoslovakia. The durability of such a secondary anchor may be substantially enhanced if social partnership institutions, e.g. of the Austrian type, exist.[16] The reason is that social partnership-type wage anchors do not amount to administrative wage controls but rather to productivity-oriented self restraint. This is a decisive difference. Administrative wage controls in practice only aim at temporarily reducing or halting wage growth per se. Wage control of a social partnership type, however, aims at bringing wage growth in line with productivity developments plus some measure of "unavoidable" inflation. Experience has shown that administrative wage controls generally do not work in the longer term because they do not take differential productivity growth into account and often are resisted by unions. Hence, wage earners attempt to "catch up" after the controls are lifted or relaxed. In contrast, wage control of the latter type has been successfully applied in Austria for over 30 years.

Real Exchange Rate Movements: An Interpretation

After setting the initial exchange rate, policymakers must project the likely evolution of the (unknown) equilibrium real exchange rate.[17] Such an estimate is decisive for assessing whether or not to adjust the exchange rate in view of observed real exchange rate changes (in general, real appreciations). Again, this is a timely topic both in the West, in particular in the context of the European Monetary System, and in the transitioning economies.

The (equilibrium) real exchange rate ultimately depends on the real wage.[18] The real wage itself depends in large part on nominal wages and labor productivity. The important point is that the development of the nominal wage be dependent on the development of productivity. If so, a rise in real wages is *not* a cause for concern but rather is the result of "good" policy.

If the above reasoning is correct, then countries like the transitioning economies, which have a technically rather well-trained workforce, should have significant productivity reserves that could be exploited once better management methods have been introduced and the capital stock has been renovated. A transitioning economy, if it is to catch up with the West, must raise productivity to enable it to pay higher real wages. Therefore, the (equilibrium) real exchange rate typically should appreciate over time. Thus, and contrary to standard reasoning, for the real exchange rate to appreciate following the initial devaluation is not a priori a cause for concern but, as noted above, may reflect sound economic policy.

This is not to deny that an appreciating real exchange rate can also result from overexpansionary macroeconomic policy and too-high wage increases. This is why a wage anchor as used—at least intermittently—in some of the countries under consideration is warranted. Judging the development of the real exchange rate by looking at its development as measured by the consumer price index is, however, very likely to be misleading. The problems are:

1. This index includes indirect taxes which are neutral with regard to international price competitiveness.
2. The CPI covers services whose prices, as the classic example of Japan in the 1960s demonstrated, tend to rise much faster than those of traded goods because of differing growth rates in productivity.
3. The meaning of inflation is not at all clear in transitioning economies as they liberalize prices and dismantle subsidies.
4. Starting levels might be rather different.

If this reasoning is correct, we may observe large differences between the rate of inflation as measured by consumer prices and producer prices or, put another way, between the prices of tradable and nontradable goods and hence in measured real exchange rate movements.[19] Figure 1.1 supports this view for a number of the countries under consideration.[20]

FIGURE 1.1 Real Effective Exchange Rates: Bulgaria and the Czech Republic

Bulgaria

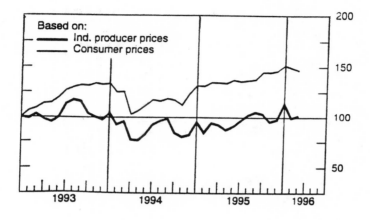

Czech Republic

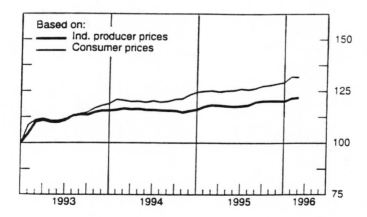

(*continued*)

FIGURE 1.1 (continued): Hungary and Poland

Hungary

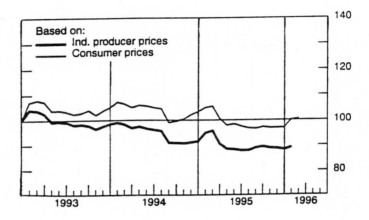

Poland

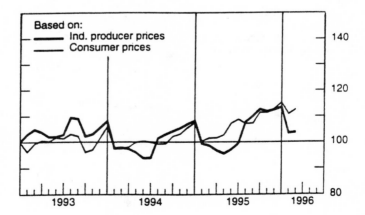

(continued)

FIGURE 1.1 (continued): The Slovak Republic and Slovenia

Slovak Republic

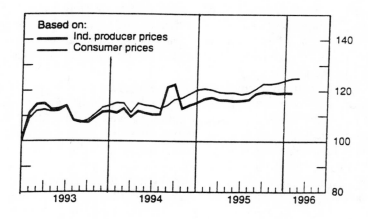

Slovenia

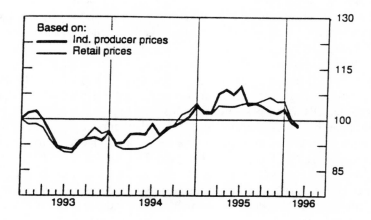

SOURCE: Bank for International Settlements

The Actual Practice of Exchange Rate Policy

In actual practice, a wealth of exchange rate regimes has been adopted in the countries considered here. Not only have different regimes been tried, but in some countries they have changed since the inception of the reforms, as can be seen in the Appendix.

Bulgaria and Slovenia opted for a flexible exchange rate at the start of their transformation process (the beginning of 1991 for Bulgaria and October 8, 1991, for Slovenia) and have maintained the regime ever since. Both countries resorted to flexible exchange rates because of their extremely tight external financial positions, which made it—in their view—impossible to defend a pegged exchange rate.

Czechoslovakia (beginning in 1991), and after the dissolution of the federation, the Czech Republic, not only chose a (sharp) devaluation-cum-basket-peg approach, but is the only country covered in this study that has also been successful in sustaining its peg. In addition, the Czech Republic potentially hardened its nominal anchor further by replacing the five-currency basket it had pegged the crown to (U.S. dollar, German mark, Austrian schilling, Swiss franc, and pound sterling) with a two-currency basket (German mark 65 percent, U.S. dollar 35 percent) in May 1993. Until the end of February 1996, the Czech monetary authorities pursued a "hard currency policy concept" that came close to a fixed peg, restricting the permitted exchange rate fluctuation margin to ± 0.5 percent. On February 28, 1996, the Czech National Bank increased the exchange rate band to ± 7.5 percent around parity to counter sustained and substantial (short-term) capital inflows. Slovakia devalued the Slovak crown by 10 percent in July 1993 but continued to peg the crown to the five-currency basket until July 1994 when it also switched to a two-currency basket (German mark 60 percent, U.S. dollar 40 percent).[21]

The "middle road" was taken by the remaining two countries, Poland and Hungary. Poland initially (at the beginning of 1990) opted for the sharp-devaluation-cum-peg approach, maintaining the peg against the dollar for 17 months. Since October 1991 an exogenous crawling peg against a basket of five currencies has been in operation.[22] The preannounced monthly devaluation rate has been gradually reduced (see the Appendix), except for two large devaluations of 12 and 8 percent in February 1992 and August 1993 respectively. More recently, Poland has had to cope (as have some other successful reform countries) with sizable capital inflows. In an attempt to stem such flows, in May 1995 the Polish National Bank broadened the exchange rate fluctuation band from 2 percent to 7 percent to enable the zloty (which was redenominated at a rate of 10,000:1 in January 1995) to appreciate. In addition, the zloty was revalued in December 1995 by 6 percent.

Hungary's exchange rate strategy is the most difficult to precisely classify, as it has undergone a number of changes. Up to 1991, the exchange rate was geared to managing the balance of payments, with periodic devaluations designed to more or less offset domestic inflation.[23] Thereafter, the policy emphasis shifted to using the exchange rate as an instrument to fight inflation by letting the real exchange rate appreciate; it was hoped this would reduce inflation expectations. More recently, in 1993, when Hungary's foreign trade performance deteriorated sharply, balance of payments considerations once again began to dominate. The number of mini-devaluations doubled between 1992 and 1993 from three to six, and the real exchange rate target seems to have shifted towards a real depreciation. This policy continued in 1994. Through July 1994, the forint was devalued four times for a total of 5.8 percent. Afterward the policy of fairly frequent mini-devaluations continued until October 1994, interrupted by a maxi-devaluation of 8 percent in August 1994 in response to continuing severe current account problems.[24] As theory predicts, exchange rate devaluations without parallel restrictive economic policies do not eliminate balance of payments problems. In recognition of this simple truth, the Hungarian authorities adopted a comprehensive stabilization package in March 1995 and, at the same time, devalued the forint by another 9 percent and replaced the adjustable peg with an exogenous crawling peg. In addition, an 8 percent import surcharge was introduced, implying a further devaluation on the import side.

Moreover, there were several changes in the composition of the currency basket. In August 1993, as a consequence of the crisis in the European Exchange Rate Mechanism, the German mark replaced the ECU in the basket of currencies to which the forint was pegged (the U.S. dollar and the German mark had equal weights of 50 percent). The composition of the basket changed again on May 16, 1994, when the ECU replaced the German mark again with a weight of 70 percent while the weight of the U.S. dollar was reduced to 30 percent.

Convertibility as an Instrument to Enhance Credibility

In Western terminology a currency is said to be fully convertible if it is exchangeable for another currency at a legal exchange rate for any purpose whatsoever. This exchangeability relates to both current account and capital account transactions of the balance of payments. The concept of convertibility that is enshrined in the Articles of Agreement of the IMF is restricted to current account transactions. Article VIII, section 2 (a) states that "no member shall without the approval of the Fund impose restrictions on the making of payments and transfers for current international transactions." This current account convertibility allows residents and nonresidents to buy and sell foreign exchange to settle current transactions (trade in goods and services, securities income, repatriation of profits, and unrequited transfers).

In Central and Eastern Europe (or, more precisely, in the former centrally planned economies) different concepts of convertibility have been in use: that of internal convertibility, where residents may buy and sell foreign exchange, and that of external convertibility, where this right is extended to nonresidents only.

In Western Europe the introduction of convertibility, even that of current account convertibility, was not accorded a high priority after World War II. Convertibility was not seen as an instrument of economic policy but as the crowning result of a long process of economic development. Indeed, full convertibility in many of the industrialized economies, e.g., Italy or France, was not achieved until 1990, and in Austria not until November 1991.

In contrast, Central and Eastern Europe have taken the opposite road. The early introduction of (partial) convertibility has been part and parcel of the reform process. Although none of the countries under consideration accepted the obligations under Article VIII of the IMF statutes until July 1994, their de facto status came close to the article's requirements.[25] Acceptance of Article VIII would, in my opinion, further raise the credibility of a country's monetary policy and the reputation of its central bank.

With the exception of Poland and Slovenia, the countries considered here restrict to varying degrees the foreign exchange that is available for tourism.[26] Restrictions on foreign exchange available for individual travel need not, in my opinion, be a reason for *not* accepting the obligations of Article VIII. This view is also held by Polak (1991:20) when he states that such a restriction is "a tolerable deviation from full convertibility."[27] Furthermore, there are still some restrictions on domestic companies, which are generally not allowed to keep foreign exchange accounts and are obliged to sell any foreign currencies acquired to domestic banks.[28] In May 1994, the Czech National Bank decided to lift the latter restriction. Finally, unrequited transfers, in general, need prior approval. It should soon be feasible to remove such restrictions, and so they should not prevent the adoption of the obligations of Article VIII if it were desired. The only remaining substantive restrictions on current transactions relate to the restrictions on debt service payments in Bulgaria and Poland. Lifting these restrictions has become possible because both Poland (March 1994) and Bulgaria (July 1994) have reached agreements with commercial banks in the London Club.

At the same time, these countries have liberalized some capital transactions of which the right of foreign investors to liquidate direct investments and transfer the receipts, as well as the right of private residents to hold foreign exchange accounts (although with domestic banks only), are the most important. While I consider the fast track to current account convertibility (as has happened) as vital for the transitional economies, capital account convertibility substantially beyond the level reached at present is a two-edged sword.[29] Full capital account convertibility would not by itself induce much more foreign direct investment or capital inflows to supplement domestic savings, while it would generate undue risks of currency substitution when (inevitably) political and economic setbacks in the transition occurred.[30] Yet, as Wihlborg and Willett (1997) argue, capital account liberalization may substantially raise the credibility of the reform process as a whole.

The early introduction of (partial) convertibility in transitioning economies as an instrument to foster systemic change has received broad support from economists both in the East and in the West.[31] The transitioning countries face the task of fundamentally changing the working of their economies, their incentive structures and their institutions under a severe time constraint. The frontloading of convertibility, it was argued, would go a long way toward replacing totally distorted price patterns with a rational relative price structure, would prevent (still existing) state monopolies from maximizing their monopoly rent after the liberalization of prices, and support the creation of a competitive climate. On the macroeconomic side it was hoped that the early adoption of convertibility would enhance the credibility of the reform process and that of government economic policy in general. Furthermore, more credible reform policies would attract much-needed foreign direct investment.

With the benefit of hindsight one may conclude that the introduction of convertibility was not so easy as Vaclav Klaus hoped when he said "there is no convertibility problem—all there is to do is declare it" (Nuti 1991:48).[32] The difficulties of forcing systemic change on the micro side and the time required to adapt have been seriously underestimated. Large, loss-making state enterprises still exist and price incentives are slow to work efficiently. Yet, as far as one can judge, the introduction of (partial) convertibility in the countries under consideration has raised the credibility of the reform process. The transitioning economies under study could further increase credibility by accepting the obligations of Article VIII of the IMF statutes in the near future.[33]

Summary and Conclusions

I favor—save in extreme circumstances—the adoption of a fixed single-currency peg for smaller transitioning economies immediately following an initial devaluation because of its simplicity and transparency. The credibility of such a regime, and hence its longer term sustainability, critically depends on the commitment of the authorities as well as consistent fiscal and incomes (e.g., of the Austrian social partnership type) policies. I argue that an appreci-ation of the real exchange rate need not necessarily be the result of "bad" economic policy, making the peg unsustainable. It may also reflect "good" economic policy, making the peg quite sustainable. The latter is the case if wage increases are determined by advances in productivity. In this case the rate of inflation predominantly reflects increases in the price of services. If the transitioning economies are to catch up with the West, they should strive for real exchange rate changes which are the result of productivity advances (and not of monetary laxness).

With regard to the question of convertibility in transitioning economies, I have argued that the economies examined here have opened up current account transactions enough to be in a position to formally accept the obliga-tions of Article VIII of the IMF's Articles of Agreement in the near future. Such a move would further raise the credibility of monetary policy and enhance the reputations of the central banks of these countries. Since this paper was first presented in February 1994, a number of the countries cov-ered in this study have either taken most of the remaining steps so that Article VIII convertibility is, in effect, around the corner or have accepted the obligations of Article VIII. As far as capital account convertibility is con-cerned, I argue that the risks connected with an early introduction outweigh conceivable gains. Therefore, I advocate a step-by-step approach as far as the capital account of the balance of payments is concerned.

Appendix
Selective Policy Indicators

Bulgaria

1. Exchange rate	Floating
2. Nominal anchors	Yes (money supply, incomes)
3. Internal convertibility for firms	Yes
4. Internal convertibility for households	Limited
5. Capital account convertibility	Limited

Czech and Slovak Federal Republic

1. Exchange rate	Devaluation; then peg against 5-cur-rency basket
2. Nominal anchors	Yes (exchange rate, wages and money supply)
3. Internal convertibility for firms	Yes
4. Internal convertibility for households	Limited
5. Capital account convertibility	Limited

Czech Republic

1. Exchange rate

Peg against 5-currency basket (see text for weights); since May 3,1993, basket is 65% DM, 35% US$

2. Nominal anchors

Yes (exchange rate, wages and money supply)

3. Internal convertibility for firms   Yes
4. Internal convertibility for households   Limited
5. Capital account convertibility   Increasingly liberalized

Slovak Republic

1. Exchange rate

Peg against 5-currency basket: US$ 49.07%, DM 36.15%, Austrian schilling 8.07%, CHF 3.79%, French franc 2.92%;10% devaluation on July 10, 1993; since July 15, 1994, basket is 60% DM, 40% US$

2. Nominal anchors   Yes (exchange rate and wages)
3. Internal convertibility for firms   Yes
4. Internal convertibility for households   Limited
5. Capital account convertibility   Very limited

Hungary

1. Exchange rate

Exogenous crawling peg since March 1995: monthly devaluations of 1.9% until June 1995;1.3% until December 1995 and 1.2% thereafter; before this a fixed but adjustable peg; basket composition changed over time: August 1993, 50% DM, 50% US$; since May 1994, 70% ECU, 30% US$; varying frequency of mini-devaluations; maxi-devaluations of 8% on August 5,1994, and of 9 % on March 13, 1995.

2. Nominal anchors   Yes (exchange rate, but not all the time)
3. Internal convertibility for firms   Yes
4. Internal convertibility for households   Limited
5. Capital account convertibility   Very limited

Poland

1. Exchange Rate

Sharp initial devaluation, US$ peg, since October 1991 exogenous crawling peg against 5-currency basket (45% US$, 35% DM, 10% pound sterling, 5% French franc, 5% Swiss franc); monthly devaluation until July 1993, 1.8%; from August 1993, 1.6 %; from September 1994, 1.5%; from November 1994, 4 %; from February 1995, 1.2%; from January 1996, 1.0%; revaluation of the zloty by 6% on December 22, 1995.

2. Nominal anchors — Yes (exchange rate and most of the time also wages)
3. Internal convertibility for firms — Yes
4. Internal convertibility for households — Limited
5. Capital account convertibility — Very limited

Slovenia

1. Exchange rate — Managed float
2. Nominal anchors — Money supply
3. Internal convertibility for firms — Yes
4. Internal convertibility for households — Limited
5. Capital account convertibility — Limited

Notes

Earlier versions of this paper were presented at conferences and workshops at Bocconi University, the University of Chicago, Claremont McKenna College, the Federal Reserve Bank of San Francisco and at the Annual Meetings of the Western Economic Association, San Diego, 1995. Helpful comments by Robert Z. Aliber, Richard Burdekin, Wayne Camard, Peter Dittus, Hans Genberg, Peter Havlik, Miroslav Hrnčíř, Elena Kohutikova, Ryszard Kokoszczynski, Kurt Mauler, George Neshev, Olga Radzyner, Sandra Riesinger, Pierre Siklos, Alfred Steinherr, Petr Vojtisek and Tom Willett are kindly acknowledged. Efficient research assistance was provided by Peter Backé. The views expressed in this paper are those of the author and do not necessarily represent the opinions of the Oesterreichische Nationalbank.

1. Hochreiter (1995).
2. It is quite interesting to see how the Western debate concerning the link between economic growth and price stability has been taken up in the transitioning economies. For example, Bod (1994:55) states that "price stability is the necessary precondition for maximizing output and income growth in the long run."
3. See also Guitián (1994).
4. Other reforming countries will be analyzed in a future study.
5. See, for example, Borensztein and Masson (1993) or Calvo and Kumar (1993) and the references contained therein.
6. Cf. Svensson (1994).
7. Bofinger (1991) argues in much the same way.
8. The transmission of monetary policy intentions in the West relies on giving interest rate signals. This in turn requires developed financial markets. Despite all

the efforts undertaken so far in the transitioning economies, money and bond markets remain relatively thin, which continues to hinder the use of indirect instruments of monetary control. Moreover, statistics are still inadequate, which makes it very difficult to track and interpret monetary policy actions. Finally, statistical series, when they exist at all, are rather new and thus brief, and so do not easily lend themselves to econometric investigation because of the lack of degrees of freedom.

9. Incidentally, there might also be a formal reason to argue for a pegged exchange rate in some of the transitioning economies. The central bank acts of Bulgaria and Hungary explicitly call for maintaining internal and external currency stability, while the acts of the Czech Republic, Slovakia and Slovenia call for currency stability in a more general sense that does not exclude a peg. It is only the Polish central bank act which explicitly calls for a "strengthening" of the national currency.

10. Initially, the size of the monetary overhang was also an important consideration. This aspect might still be important for countries from the former Soviet Union.

11. An interesting order of sequencing of various pegging regimes for transitioning economies has been advanced by Rosati (1993:225). He favors a fixed peg initially (about six months), which is to be followed by an exogenous crawling peg (three to four years) and finally he advocates the return to a fixed peg (indefinitely) once the rate of inflation has fallen into a range from 12 to 20 percent.

12. See, e.g., Hochreiter and Winckler (1995).

13. See, e.g., Burdekin and Willett (1995) or Hochreiter (1995).

14. Calvo and Végh (1994) specifically argue that a high degree of currency substitution favors use of the exchange rate as the nominal anchor.

15. Lutkowski (1991:202), while agreeing that a substantial initial devaluation of the Polish zloty was necessary, is of the opinion that the 50 percent devaluation was excessive and thereby contributed to making the cost of stabilization unnecessarily high.

16. For a discussion of the Austrian social partnership, see Handler and Hochreiter (1996), and in the context of transitioning economies see Hochreiter (1995). Basically, what I have in mind pertains to an informal and voluntary institutional forum not regulated by law which brings together the main social groups—e.g., entrepreneurial organizations, industry, agriculture, trade and employees' organizations, trade unions, etc.—to discuss economic and social policy issues and to devise means to achieve the aims agreed upon.

17. On this issue also see Halpern and Wyplosz (1995).

18. Terms-of-trade shocks may also be important for some economies. Their inclusion would not alter the qualitative arguments developed here.

19. Incidentally, such inflation differentials also exist in Western countries although the (absolute) difference between the two sectors tends to be less than one would expect in transitioning economies or rapidly growing countries (e.g., Portugal and Spain).

20. For a discussion of the divergences between real exchange rate indices based on consumer and producer prices see, for example, Oblath (1993) or Aghevli et al. (1991).

21. The basket consists of the following currencies (weights in brackets): U.S. dollar (49 percent), German mark (36 percent), Austrian schilling (8 percent), Swiss franc (3.8 percent), French franc (2.9 percent).

22. The basket consists of the following currencies (weights in brackets): U.S. dollar (45 percent), German mark (35 percent), pound sterling (10 percent), French franc (5 percent), Swiss franc (5 percent).

23. There were seven devaluations between 1989 and 1991, of which three amounted to 10 percent or more.

24. In addition, the room for maneuver in setting the exchange rate was raised by increasing the intervention margins from ± 0.5 percent to ± 1.25 percent in August 1994, to ± 2.25 percent in December 1994, and ± 5 percent in late 1995.

25. Note that the IMF classifies these countries as having (de facto) current account convertibility, while acknowledging that "there continue to be certain restrictions" (IMF 1993:66–67).

26. As of mid November 1994, the following annual tourist quotas were applied (approximate values expressed in US$ and converted at current exchange rates): Bulgaria, US$ 20; Czech Republic, US$ 430; Hungary, US$ 800, raised to Ft 200,000 (approximately US$ 1,400) on January 1, 1996; Slovakia, US$ 300. No quotas were in force in Poland and Slovenia. The Czech Republic increased the quota as of January 1, 1995, from Kc 12,000 to Kc 100,000, which already implied a de facto full liberalization for tourists, and abolished the quota altogether later in 1995. Slovakia has raised the quota from Sk 9,000 to Sk 16,000, and as of July 1, 1995, to Sk 30,000.

27. For the same view see also Williamson (1991:379).

28. This obligation was abolished in November 1995.

29. On the general issue of the pros and cons of capital controls, see Ries and Sweeney (1997).

30. An interesting counterexample up to now (end of 1994) has been Estonia, which was able—under very adverse initial conditions—to maintain the fixed peg of the Estonian kroon to the German mark from June 1992 under de facto full convertibility until the beginning of May 1994, and under de jure full convertibility as of May 4, 1994.

31. For a dissenting view, see Levcik (1991).

32. Compare this with the statement by Klaus three years later in early 1994 that there was no need for a "salto mortale" to achieve immediate (capital account) convertibility. A step-by-step approach is feasible (Austria Presse Agentur, February 10, 1994).

33. After the first draft of the paper (February 28, 1994) was written, Estonia (August 1994), Latvia (June 1994), Lithuania (May 1994), Poland (June 1995), Slovenia (September 1995), the Czech Republic (October 1995), Slovakia (October 1995) and Hungary (January 1996) formally accepted the obligations of Article VIII of the IMF Articles of Agreement.

References

Aghevli, Bijan B., Moshin S. Khan, and Peter J. Montiel. 1991. *Exchange Rate Policies in Developing Countries. Some Analytical Issues.* IMF Occasional Paper No. 78. Washington D.C.: International Monetary Fund.

Austria Presse Agentur. February 10, 1994.

Bod, Peter A. 1994. "Monetary Policy and Exchange Rate Policy in Hungary During the Years of Transition," in Dieter Duwendag, ed., *Geld - und Währungspolitik in Kleinen, Offenen Volkswirtschaften: Österreich, Schweiz, Osteuropa.* Pp. 55–70. Schriften des Vereins für Socialpolitik, Neue Folge Band 230. Berlin: Duncker & Humblot.

Bofinger, Peter. 1991. "The Transition to Convertibility in Eastern Europe: A Monetary View," in John Williamson, ed., *Currency Convertibility in Eastern Europe.* Pp. 116–138. Washington, D.C.: Institute for International Economics.

Borensztein, Eduardo, and Paul Masson. 1993. "Exchange Arrangements of Previously Centrally Planned Economies," in *Financial Sector Reforms and Exchange Arrangements in Eastern Europe.* IMF Occasional Paper No. 102, Part II. Washington, D.C.: International Monetary Fund.

Bruno, Michael. 1991. *High Inflation and the Nominal Anchors of an Open Economy.* Essays in International Finance No. 183. Princeton: Princeton University.

Burdekin, Richard C. K., and Thomas D. Willett. 1995. "Designing Central Bank Arrangements to Promote Monetary Stability," in Thomas D. Willett, Richard Burdekin, Richard Sweeney, and Clas Wihlborg, eds., *Establishing Monetary Stability in Emerging Market Economies.* Pp. 115–26. Boulder, Colo.: Westview Press.

Calvo, Guillermo A., and Manmohan S. Kumar. 1993. "Financial Markets and Intermediation," in *Financial Sector Reforms and Exchange Arrangements in Eastern Europe.* IMF Occasional Paper No. 102, Part I. Washington, D.C.: International Monetary Fund.

Calvo, Guillermo A., and Carlos A. Végh. 1994. "Inflation Stabilization and Nominal Anchors," in Richard C. Barth and Chorng-Huey Wong, eds., *Approaches to Exchange Rate Policy: Choices for Developing and Transitional Economies.* Pp. 91–102. Washington, D.C.: International Monetary Fund.

Centre for Economic Policy Research. 1993. *The Economics of New Currencies.* London.

Claassen, Emil-Maria, ed. 1991. *Exchange Rate Policies in Developing and Post-Socialist Countries.* San Francisco: ICS Press.

Davenport, Michael. 1992. *Exchange Rate Policy for Eastern Europe and a Peg to the ECU.* CEC Economic Papers No. 90. Luxembourg: Commission of the European Communities, March.

De Haan, Jacob, K. Knot and J. E. Sturm. 1993. "On the Reduction of Disinflation Costs: Fixed Exchange Rates or Central Bank Independence?" Banca Nazionale del Lavoro *Quarterly Review* 187 (December): 429–44.

Deszeri, Kalman. 1993. "First Practical Steps in Introducing Convertibility in the Eastern European Countries." Institute for World Economics Working Paper No. 22, Budapest, August.

Dimitrov, Emil. 1994. "The Exchange Rate Policy and the Exchange Rate Regime in Bulgaria." Mimeo. Bukarest: Bulgarian National Bank.

Duchatczek, Wolfgang, and Aurel Schubert. 1992. *Monetary Policy Issues in Selected East European Economies.* SUERF Paper No.11. Tilburg: Societe Universitaire Europeenne Recherches Financieres.

Duwendag, Dieter, ed. 1994. *Geld - und Währungspolitik in Kleinen, Offenen Volkswirtschaften: Österreich, Schweiz, Osteuropa.* Schriften des Vereins für Socialpolitik, Neue Folge Band 230. Berlin: Duncker & Humblot.

Flood, Robert P., and Nancy P. Marion. 1991. "Exchange Rate Regime Choice." IMF Working Paper 90. Washington, D.C.: International Monetary Fund, September.

Gáspár, Pál. 1994. "The Exchange Rate Policy in Hungary Between 1989 and 1993." Manuscript. Budapest: Institute of World Economics of the Hungarian Academy of Sciences.

Guitián, Manuel. 1994. "The Choice of Exchange Rate Regime," in Richard Barth and Chorng-Huey Wong, eds., *Approaches to Exchange Rate Policy.* Pp. 13–36. Washington, D.C.: International Monetary Fund.

Halpern, László, and Charles Wyploz. 1995. *Equilibrium Real Exchange Rates in Economies in Transition.* CEPR Working Paper No. 1145. London: Centre for Economic Policy Research, April.

Handler, Heinz, and Eduard Hochreiter. 1996. *The Austrian Economy in the Wake of Joining the EU.* CEPS Working Document No. 103. Bruxelles: Centre for Economic Policy Studies, June.

Havlik, Peter. 1994. "Exchange Rates, Wages and Competitiveness of Central and Eastern Europe." Mimeo. Vienna: Wiener Institut fur Internationale Wirtschaftsvergleiche.

Hochreiter, Eduard. 1995. "Central Banking in Economies in Transition," in Thomas D. Willett, Richard Burdekin, Richard Sweeney, and Clas Wihlborg, eds., *Establishing Monetary Stability in Emerging Market Economies.* Pp. 127–44. Boulder, Colo.: Westview Press.

————. 1994. "Reflections on Central Bank Independence and Monetary Policy—The Case of Austria," in Bernhard Böhm and Lionello F. Punzo, eds., *Economic Performance: A Look at Austria and Italy.* Pp. 198–207. Berlin: Physica-Verlag.

————. 1989. "Is a New International Monetary Order Needed?" in Gary Bertsch and Chrism Saunders, eds., *East-West Economic Relations in the 1990s.* Pp. 209–21. London: Macmillan.

Hochreiter, Eduard, and Sandra Riesinger. 1995. "Central Banking in Central and Eastern Europe—Selected Institutional Issues." *ECU-Journal* 22 (July): 17–22.

Hochreiter, Eduard, and Georg Winckler. 1995. "The Advantages of Tying Austria's Hands: The Success of the Austrian Hard Currency Policy." *European Journal of Political Economy* 11: 83–111.

Hrnčíř, Miroslav. 1994a. "Exchange Rate Regime in the Transition Period," in Christoph M. Schneider and Vit Bárta, eds., *Stabilization Policies at Crossroads?* Pp. 133–66. Laxenburg, Austria: International Institute for Applied Systems Analysis.

————. 1994b. "Economic Recovery and Foreign Exchange Rate Regime in the Transition Economies: The Case of Czechoslovakia," in Janos Gacz and Georg Winckler, eds., *International Trade and Restructuring in Eastern Europe.* Pp. 67–99. Laxenburg, Austria: International Institute for Applied Systems Analysis.

————. 1993. "Reform of the Banking Sector in the Czech Republic." Mimeo. Prague: Czech National Bank.

International Monetary Fund. 1993. *World Economic Outlook.* IMF Occasional Paper. Washington, D.C.: International Monetary Fund, May.

Kicinsky, Wojciech, and M. Golik. 1994. "Exchange Rate Policy and Exchange Reserves." Mimeo. Warsaw: National Bank of Poland.

Klier, Rudolf, ed. 1990. *From Control to Market—Austria's Experiences in the Post-War Period.* Internationale Schriftenreihe der Oesterreichischen Nationalbank, Vol. 4. Vienna: National Bank of Austria.

Kohutikova, Elena. 1993. "Some Issues Concerning Monetary Developments and Banking System Progress in the Slovak Republic." Mimeo. Bratislava: National Bank of Slowakia.

Kowalski, Tadensz. 1994. "Exchange Rate Policy in the Period of Transition—The Case of Poland." Mimeo. Poznań University of Economics.

Levcik, Friedrich. 1991. "The Place of Convertibility in the Transformation Process," in John Williamson, ed., *Currency Convertibility in Eastern Europe.* Pp. 31–47. Washington D.C.: Institute for International Economics.

Lutkowski, Karol. 1991. "Three Pioneers: Poland, Yugoslavia and East Germany: Comment," in John Williamson, ed., *Currency Convertibility in Eastern Europe.* Pp. 200–204. Washington D.C.: Institute for International Economics.

Maciejewski, Wojciech. 1994. "Current State of the Polish Economy and the Problem with the Reforms." Mimeo. Warsaw: Warsaw University.

Mencinger, Jose. 1993a. "The Birth and Childhood of a Currency: The Experience of Slovenia," in Janos Gacz and Georg Winckler, eds., *International Trade and Restructuring in Eastern Europe.* Pp. 101–19. Laxenburg: International Institute for Applied Systems Analysis.

————. 1993b. "The Experience with the Tolar in Slovenia," in *The Economics of New Currencies.* Pp. 137–60. London: Centre for Economic Policy Research.

Mogni, Andrea. 1994. "Current Exchange Rate Policies and Convertibility in Central and Eastern European Countries." Mimeo. Luxembourg: Commission of the European Communities.

————. 1993. "Monetary, Credit and Exchange Rate Policies in Central and Eastern European Countries in Transition: A First Assessment (1990–mid 1993)." Mimeo. Luxembourg: Commission of the European Communities.

Nuti, Mario D. 1991. "Comment," in John Williamson, ed., *Currency Convertibility in Eastern Europe.* Pp. 48–55. Washington D.C.: Institute for International Economics.

Nuti, Mario D., and Richard Porte, eds. 1993. *Economic Transformation in Central Europe: A Program Report.* London: Centre for Economic Policy Research and Commission of the European Communities.

Oblath, Gabor. 1993. "Exchange Rate Policy and Real Exchange Rate Changes in Economic Transition," in Janos Gacz and Georg Winckler, eds., *International*

Trade and Restructuring in Eastern Europe. Pp. 15–46. Laxenburg: International Institute for Applied Systems Analysis.

Pasztor, Csapa, and Ilona Baar. 1994. "Hungarian Exchange Rate Policy and Foreign Exchange Reserves." Mimeo. Budapest: National Bank of Hungary.

Polak, Jacques. 1991. "Convertibility: An Indispensable Element in the Transition Process in Eastern Europe," in John Williamson, ed., *Currency Convertibility in Eastern Europe*. Pp. 21–30. Washington, D.C.: Institute for International Economics.

Ries, Christine, and Richard D. Sweeney, eds. 1997. *Capital Controls in Emerging Market Economies*. Boulder, Colo.: Westview Press.

Rosati, Dariusz. 1993. "How to Make Inconvertible Currencies Convertible?" in *The Economics of New Currencies*. Pp. 222–26. London: Centre for Economic Policy Research.

Sarcinelli, Mario. 1992. "Eastern Europe and the Financial Sector: Where Are They Going?" Banca Nazionale del Lavoro *Quarterly Review* 183 (December): 463–92.

Schaffer, Mark. 1993. "Polish Economic Transformation: From Recession to Recovery and the Challenges Ahead." *Business Strategy Review* 3(3): 53–69.

Svensson, Lars E. O. 1994. "Fixed Exchange Rates as a Means to Price Stability: What Have We Learned?" *European Economic Review* 38(3–4): 447–68.

Tosovsky, Josef. 1994. "Exchange Rates and the Transition: The Case of the Czech Republic," in Dieter Duwendag, ed., *Geld - und Währungspolitik in Kleinen, Offenen Volkswirtschaften: Österreich, Schweiz, Osteuropa*. Pp. 71–86. Schriften des Vereins für Socialpolitik, Neue Folge Band 230. Berlin: Duncker & Humblot.

Wihlborg, Clas, and Thomas D. Willett. 1997. "Capital Account Liberalization and Policy Incentives: An Endogenous Policy View," in Christine Ries and Richard D. Sweeney, eds., *Capital Controls in Emerging Market Economies*. Pp. 111–135. Boulder, Colo.: Westview Press.

Willett, Thomas D., and Fahim Al-Marhubi. 1994. "Currency Policies for Inflation Control in the Formally Centrally Planned Economies: An Optimum Currency Area Approach." *The World Economy* 17(6): 795–815.

Willett, Thomas D., Richard C. K. Burdekin, Richard J. Sweeney, and Clas Wihlborg, eds. 1995. *Establishing Monetary Stability in Emerging Market Economies*. Boulder, Colo.: Westview Press.

Williamson, John. 1991. "Advice on the Choice of an Exchange Rate Policy," in Emil-Maria Claassen, ed., *Exchange Rate Policies in Developing and Post-Socialist Countries*. Pp. 395–407. San Francisco: ICS Press.

Williamson, John, ed. 1991. *Currency Convertibility in Eastern Europe*. Washington D.C.: Institute for International Economics.

Zahradnik, Jaromir. 1991. "Czechoslovakia," in John Williamson, ed., *Currency Convertibility in Eastern Europe*. Pp. 217–25. Washington D.C.: Institute for International Economics.

2

Is Optimum Currency Area Theory Irrelevant for Economies in Transition?

Linda S. Goldberg

Introduction

Countries view the establishment of an independent currency as an important element of national sovereignty. Beyond this nontrivial symbolism, the economics of independent currencies with fixed versus flexible exchange rates has long been debated. One influential line of reasoning is rooted in "optimal currency area" theory, originally associated with Robert Mundell (1961), Ronald McKinnon (1963) and Peter Kenen (1969). According to this approach, an independent currency and an independent monetary policy are potentially useful stabilization tools, especially when other stabilization instruments are lacking or inadequate. The arguments of optimal currency area theory and the indicators of which conditions make a country well-suited for an independent monetary policy were launched from a strong Keynesian tradition for the industrialized countries of the mid-twentieth century.

In general, the traditional optimal currency area approach presents a set of conditions under which a country stands the greatest chance of benefitting from having an independent currency with a flexible or adjustable exchange rate.[1] Exchange rates would be used for adjusting the relative price of two countries' goods either for the purpose of output stabilization or for freeing domestic macroeconomic policies from a balance of payments constraint. The idea is that exchange rate movements can adjust relative prices (and relative demand for a country's goods and workers) and be most useful when particular optimum currency area reference criteria are satisfied. These criteria include asymmetric shocks among countries, the inability of cross-border labor flows to contribute substantially to the smoothing of employment cycles, and the absence of other fiscal-based methods for achieving output or balance of payments stabilization in response to shocks.

The Keynesian traditions in which the optimal currency area arguments were developed allowed for a setting with highly elastic goods supply and internationally price-elastic demand for goods. In this climate, devaluation would elicit a positive adjustment in employment and income, along with an improvement in the trade balance, in the devaluing country. A nominal depreciation would, given a high degree of short-run price stickiness, be particularly useful when it led to rapid real exchange rate changes, and when output, employment, and the balance of payments were highly sensitive to relative price movements.

In this chapter I argue that the supply elasticities required for the exchange rate to be an effective stabilization tool simply may not be present during early stages of economic transition. Employment is not likely to rapidly adjust, and even the (foreign and domestic) elasticities of demand for goods are undetermined. In such an economic environment, the traditional optimal stabilization policy criteria applied to output and/or balance of payments targets may not be relevant for the decision about whether or not to implement or maintain an independent currency. Thus, it does not matter whether transition economies satisfy the reference criteria that point to optimum conditions for introducing independent currencies. The traditional optimum currency area criteria, interpreted in terms of optimal real stabilization policy, are only useful if *the exchange rate is able to effectively perform the task of short-term stabilization (output or balance of payments) to which it is assigned.*

Although I make an argument based on "elasticity pessimism," these reservations may be vitiated if economic reforms rapidly create market conditions that are contrary to (and more responsive to stimuli than) those stressed here. The short-term effectiveness of exchange rates in stabilization may increase in the future, at which time the optimal currency area criteria would warrant serious scrutiny as useful guides to the tradeoffs in exchange rate regime selection.

If the choice of exchange rate regime and degree of currency independence are not to be determined according to their functions as output and/or balance of payments stabilizers, are there other important criteria which should influence this potentially important decision? The issue of monetary discipline under alternative exchange rate regimes is often offered.[2] However, I argue that this criteria also is not convincing. The evidence that fixed exchange rates are associated with greater central bank discipline is mixed. It is not obvious that tendencies toward inflating are endogenous with respect to the exchange rate regime, especially in transition economies.

Instead, I argue that an exchange rate regime should be adopted with credibility and sustainability in mind. Since the symbolic importance of a national currency is nontrivial, a regime should be adopted which enables a currency to maintain its real value. An independent currency with a fixed nominal exchange rate or a crawling peg can be desirable for a country that is able to contain inflation. A country with strong inflation tendencies either would need to implement an independent currency with a more flexible exchange rate or relinquish monetary autonomy to a country with more conservative and credible monetary policies.[3]

Finally, an independent currency can support economic reform through its signaling function. This argument, initially expounded by Goldberg, Ickes, and Ryterman (1994, 1995) in relation to the countries of the former Soviet Union, emphasizes that there are conditions under which an independent currency can reinforce or can undermine the credibility of announced reform trajectories.

The Optimal Currency Area Approach

The early "optimal currency area" literature, following from the seminal work of Robert Mundell (1961), associates the importance of establishing an independent currency (with a flexible exchange rate) with the benefits of an independent money supply and the ability to adjust the relative price of a country's output for the purpose of employment and output stabilization. The merits of departing from a common currency area often are presented in terms of the use of exchange rate flexibility as an instrument so as to allow domestic macroeconomic policies to be used for economic stabilization.

The reasoning behind this approach is best expressed using an example. Consider a scenario where two countries are contemplating discarding their pre-existing unified currency and instead introducing monetary autonomy and flexible exchange rates.[4] Both countries are subject to output disturbances, due to natural forces or even imported from exogenous third countries. These disturbances may be expansionary or contractionary, and may be correlated across countries. Suppose one country receives a negative shock leading to unemployment. The issue is whether the exchange rate and independent monetary policy can be used to mitigate some of the negative effects of the shock. McKinnon (1963) adds that these issues are most relevant for open economies, so that the degree of openness to external trade also is an important factor in assessing the value of an independent currency with an adjustable exchange rate.

Tower and Willett (1976) argue that the potential importance of the exchange rate as an automatic stabilizer depends on whether the output disturbances affecting a country are positively correlated with those of its trading partners. If so, a depreciation of the first country's currency relative to the second country's will not be an effective tool for output stabilization. In periods of unemployment, neither country is able to benefit from the automatic stabilizer function of the exchange rate, since both countries have an incentive to devalue. Neither country would succeed at shifting the relative prices of goods in its favor in order to reallocate demand toward its goods and smooth its output and employment.

By contrast, if the output disturbances of the two countries are negatively correlated it is possible for a flexible exchange rate to shift relative bilateral prices and thereby reorient the demand for traded goods toward the more depressed economy. In this way, the flexible exchange rate and independent monetary policies can operate as effective stabilization tools. According to this approach, an independent currency imbues a country with an expanded capacity to respond to shocks, especially when shocks have varied impacts across countries. The commonalty and correlations among output shocks therefore are held as important indicators of whether independent currency policies should be pursued. Kenen (1969) also argues that regions with a highly diversified production base should be better equipped to maintain a currency union than regions with low production diversification. The rationale is that countries without a diversified production base are more likely to be subjected to macroeconomic shocks that could be mitigated or offset using the exchange rate tool.

According to the standard argument in the traditional optimal currency area paradigm, if nominal wages are rigid downward, nominal exchange rate flexibility may be desirable. For example, if an economy experiences a negative demand shock and nominal wage rigidity is absent, the real wage would fall and employment would remain the same. With nominal-wage rigidity, output and employment will fall since sticky real wages exceed the value added of the workers. By contrast, under exchange rate flexibility, a depreciation of the domestic currency increases domestic prices and lowers real wages, thereby alleviating the distortions that result from nominal wage rigidity. Thus, another optimum currency area criterion for independent currencies is the extent of downward real wage flexibility within a country.

The need for the exchange rate as a stabilization tool also depends on whether there exist other tools for output adjustment. In addition to the aforementioned point about wage rigidities, another possible mechanism for dealing with unemployment could be automatic intercountry transfers such as those that would be provided by a fiscal federalist entity. In the event of less than perfectly correlated transitory shocks, the country with the less favorable position could receive a transfer from its partner.[5] Alternatively, if workers from the adversely affected economy are willing and able to move across borders, this lessens the necessity of using the exchange rate as an instrument of stabilization.

In sum, even if the exchange rate is a potentially effective stabilization tool, if it is a redundant tool then the case for independent currencies is weakened. Redundancy can arise if alternative mechanisms lead to rapid adjustment following disturbances. Such alternative mechanisms include mobility of labor and other productive inputs or agreed upon mechanisms for cross-country transfers (such as a type of fiscal federalist system).

The "New" Optimal Currency Area Theory

The traditional optimal currency area approach draws its insights largely from an economic environment in which there exist short-run price stickiness and employment adjustment to shocks, accompanied by a longer run inflation-employment tradeoff. Supply is assumed to be highly elastic once demand is stimulated.

The fundamental advances in macroeconomics over the past three decades have, to some degree, been incorporated in the "new" optimal currency area theory. In general, the basic economic insights from the traditional optimal currency area approach withstand this modernization. Wihlborg and Willett (1991), De Grauwe (1992), and Tavlas (1993) survey the attempts to introduce into the optimum currency area literature recent advances, including expectations formation, incentive compatibility, and political economy tradeoffs. Mainly, these approaches modify and modernize the conditions used to evaluate the appropriateness of alternative exchange rate regimes.[6]

Aizenman and Flood (1992) go beyond the early literature by highlighting disturbances driven from the supply side, rather than the traditional Keynesian demand-side disturbances emphasized in much of the literature. When labor can move across regions (with some cost) and there are sticky nominal wages, the case against independent currencies with flexible exchange rates is even stronger than posited by Mundell. The result arises because supply-side shocks drive a wedge between the productivity of labor in different countries. This implies that there are strong efficiency reasons for labor to move across borders.

Efficiency gains possible under fixed exchange rates or a common currency area lead to monetary equilibrium in which labor moves across countries. By contrast, a flexible exchange rate will discourage labor mobility and provide an environment in which productivity differences are not exploited. Thus, Aizenman and Flood provide conditions under which foregoing currency independence can be welfare enhancing. In contrast to the more neutral result from Mundell, Aizenman and Flood show that the presence of labor mobility weakens the case for independent currencies with adjustable exchange rates.

Applying the Traditional Arguments
for Transition Economies

The broad historic appeal of the traditional optimal currency area arguments has led scholars to apply the reference criteria to recent debates over developed and transition economy exchange rate regime choice. For example, the appropriate form and size of a European common currency area was examined by Bayoumi and Eichengreen (1993) and Bean (1992). Other scholars have applied the optimal currency areas approach to transition economies.

I think that such applications are premature in economies in the early stages of transition. Both Gros (1993) and Willett and Al-Marhubi (1994) focus their analysis on the former Soviet Union. Gros undertakes an analysis of the mobility of labor, the incidence of shocks, and the rigidity of prices, i.e., the basic Mundellian criteria. Willett and Al-Marhubi emphasize a set of criteria which embed the view of using the exchange rate regime as a facilitator of monetary discipline. The criteria that they emphasize are country size, country openness and inflation histories. The data examined by Willett and Al-Marhubi suggest that the case for independent currencies and flexible exchange rates is weaker for small open economies (Estonia) than for large countries (Ukraine), and less appropriate for countries that have a stronger history of inflation than the core country of the union.

The premise that the exchange rate regime plays a useful role in aiding inflation stabilization is investigated further in the fourth section of this chapter. If, for now, we accept this premise, it still is essential to recognize that inflation histories of the transition economies in the early 1990s can yield very misleading rankings about future inflation tendencies. These countries historically could not engage in independent monetary policies and more recently have undergone price adjustments which need not reflect persistent tendencies toward inflation. Such inflation histories may generate misleading conclusions: it is more appropriate to carefully examine the country characteristics which generally are associated with inflation tendencies. Below I discuss methods for identifying a country's tendency toward using inflation as a means of budgetary finance.

Goldberg, Ickes, and Ryterman (1994, 1995) voice considerable skepticism about the optimal currency area criteria applied to countries at the stages of reform which characterize the republics of the former Soviet Union. Before turning to these arguments, first consider the conclusions that would arise from applying the full set of optimum currency area criteria to the former Soviet republics. One criteria focuses on the role of a stabilizing fiscal federalist center of a common currency area. If an effective center does not exist, the case for independent currencies is strengthened. Thus, in the integrated Soviet Union individual currencies were undesirable. In the dissolved union, Russia does not pursue the objective of stabilizing output in the non-Russian republics. This strengthens the justification for independent flexible exchange rate currencies.[7]

The desirability of independent currencies and flexible exchange rates among countries of the former Soviet Union is reinforced by the observation that there are impediments to broad inter-regional labor flows. Labor mobility is not likely to automatically stabilize output shocks either within large countries like Russia or across the former Soviet republics. Labor mobility will not serve the objective of equalizing real wages across countries.

However, labor mobility may not be important if there nonetheless exists real wage flexibility across the former Soviet Union. There appears to be evidence of substantial real wage flexibility across regions and across countries. *If* this real wage flexibility also leads to production and employment stabilization, an empirically open question at this point, the traditional optimal currency area approach would suggest that there is less reason to introduce independent currencies with freely floating exchange rates.

The natural diversity of the broad set of countries in the former Soviet Union might lead to the conclusion that the shocks affecting these countries will not be highly correlated or at least will be substantially different. In this case, independent currencies with adjustable or flexible exchange rates might be deemed attractive. However, the legacy of the Soviet system remains pervasive in these early years of transition, and the support of independent currencies is weakened to the extent that there remain strong dependencies among the more industrialized western countries—i.e., Ukraine, Belarus, and Russia—and the more agricultural economies of Central Asia. The vestiges of the Soviet infrastructure lead to a high degree of transmission of shocks throughout this region. If and when these countries establish more diversified customer and supplier networks, the optimal currency area case for independent currencies will receive stronger support.

On balance, the traditional optimal currency area criteria suggest that the countries of the former Soviet Union should have independent currencies with adjustable exchange rates between these currencies. An exception to this result may arise if the countries remain very closely intertwined through industrial ties so that the shocks to each country are highly and positively correlated.

Elasticity Pessimism for the Transition Economies

The application of optimal currency area criteria presented above is misguided unless it can first be established that the reference criteria are appropriate. The operating premise of the optimal currency area approach is that the case for independent currencies and flexible exchange rates is strengthened when other mechanisms for stabilization are lacking. This premise does not have global validity. The lack of alternative instruments or mechanisms for output and balance of payments stabilization does not demonstrate that the exchange rate is able to effectively aid in stabilization.[8] Before applying the optimal currency area criteria for optimal stabilization policy, a distinct necessary condition must be satisfied: *Will nominal exchange rate movements have timely and significant effects on a country's output and/or balance of payments?*

Two main issues therefore must be addressed on the issue of the applicability of optimum currency area criteria in the context of these objectives. First, is it the case that nominal exchange rate movements are associated with real exchange rate movements? Second, can it be established that real exchange rate movements, i.e., adjustments in a country's terms of trade, lead to demand adjustments which then are met by a timely supply-side response? The supply-side response is needed for real output effects and real export adjustment through the balance of payments. If the answers to these queries are negative, then issues other than output, employment, and balance of payments stabilization should receive considerably more weight than the optimal currency area themes in the exchange rate regime debate.

It is not at all apparent that the real exchange rate adjustment and the real output adjustment requirements will be satisfied in the early stages of reform in the former Soviet republics. First, consider the issue of whether real exchange rate movements are likely to elicit large and significant production adjustment. Given the structure of enterprises in these countries—and the early transition status of these enterprises—it is unlikely that real exchange rate movements will trigger rapid production responses. Ickes and Ryterman (1993 and forthcoming) argue that enterprises have been pursuing a pattern of behavior based on "survival" constraints which leads to a strong reluctance to dramatically alter their supplier and distribution networks or their production base.

In the face of an adverse terms-of-trade shock, such as can be induced by real exchange rate appreciation, survival behavior would limit the real output implications. Enterprises can provide their adversely affected trading partners with large volumes of interenterprise credit, with the hope that the government will bail out enterprises that are unable to collect debts in arrears.[9] Thereafter, the "creditor" enterprise will not readily shift its business to alternative partners: such a reorientation of a producer network could lower expected future paybacks from those enterprises in arrears. Overall, survival behavior will weaken the cross-country reorientation of demand for industrial and intermediate goods in response to exchange rate movements, and therefore weakens the exchange rate elasticity of the balance of payments.

The current status of transition and prevailing modes of enterprise behavior imply that producers have a reduced focus on their bottom line of profits and losses. Instead of undertaking real production and employment adjustments in response to stimuli, the enterprises may be more willing to adjust prices. The high "pass through" of nominal exchange rate movements implies that the effects of real exchange rate movements will be mitigated.

A weak link between nominal and real exchange rate movements also can be fostered by the competitive structure of production, which also is a vestige of the centrally planned system. Brown, Ickes, and Ryterman (1993) show that production in the former Soviet republics is characterized by enterprises that have large local market shares. Unlike the conventional case—where monopoly is achieved by having few competing firms throughout a country—concentration in the former Soviet Union arises mainly because of a poor distribution system which creates powerful local markets. Concentrated market power leads to monopolistic pricing behavior, with consequent low output sensitivity. The poor infrastructural networks which contribute to the monopolistic behavior are unlikely to facilitate the reallocation of demand by producers and consumers in the face of price changes that are passed through by enterprises. Again, these points underscore the theme that nominal exchange rate adjustments are unlikely to lead to a substantial real output response in the short to medium run.

These arguments, which yield an elasticity pessimism about the output and balance of payments stabilization value of exchange rates, could be substantially weakened if rapid industrial reform and demonopolization of industry occurred in the former Soviet Union. However, I doubt that the economic conditions emphasized above will disappear in the near future. The survival behavior and concentrated market power of large producers will persist as long as there are barriers to the entry of new firms and of existing firms into new markets, economic uncertainty, lack of information about potential suppliers and customers, absence of working real estate and capital markets, inadequate legal guidelines and instruments, and a poor system of communication and payments. These problems may be reinforced by the growth of local governments, which often enact local controls and further impede free domestic trade.

The problem of very low price elasticities remains acute for many countries of the former Soviet Union and the transition economies of Central and Eastern Europe. Problems in the payments system continue to hamper inter-republic and international trade. Bottlenecks in the payments systems have also sometimes hampered foreign exchange markets and real transactions in Central and Eastern Europe.[10]

The continued underdevelopment of the banking and financial system means that it is difficult to arrange payments across the countries of the former Soviet Union, Central Europe, Eastern Europe, and with Western trading partners. Such difficulties contribute to long and variable lags in the receipt of payments for goods, and also sometimes lead to the requirement that import transactions (for example) are paid in full before goods are shipped. This reduces the sensitivity of trade volumes to exchange rates. Efforts to circumvent the payments system using barter transactions also limit the effectiveness of the exchange rate instrument, since it reduces the sensitivity of the decision to export to fluctuations in the nominal exchange rate. These insensitivities are compounded in trade activities with those countries of the former Soviet Union that are immersed in ethnic and regional conflicts. Even though ongoing improvements in the payment and settlements systems are aiding foreign exchange transactions and market development in Bulgaria, the Czech Republic, and Poland, markets are not developed enough to facilitate the rapid response of trade and settlements to relative price movements.

As a final point, although I have argued that elasticity pessimism is relevant for transition economies, it also is important to note that the elasticity pessimism arguments may have broader relevance for other developing economies. Rose (1990), for example, based on data for 30 developing countries, finds that changes in the real exchange rate do not have a significant effect on the trade balance. Reinhart (1994), using data for 12 developing countries, shows that relative prices are a significant determinant of trade and income for the majority of developing countries, but the price elasticities of output are very low. The conclusion of these studies is that a very large devaluation would be required to elicit a large trade and output adjustment in most developing countries. This suggests that elasticity pessimism as a reason for doubting the relevance of the traditional optimal stabilization policy criteria may extend well beyond the transition economies.

The Exchange Rate Regime and
Inflation Control: Mixed Results

If the optimal degree of currency independence is not determined by the output value of the exchange rate tool, perhaps more modern arguments about the link between currency regime and central bank monetary discipline have greater relevance for transition economies. In both academic and policy circles a credibly fixed exchange rate system is often viewed as being able to provide a nominal anchor for an economy and to impose monetary discipline on potentially lax central bankers.[11] Whether or not the announcement of a pegged exchange rate enhances the degree of central bank commitment to a conservative monetary policy (and to the fixed exchange rate regime) depends on the specific institutional and political arrangements of the country making the exchange regime announcement.[12]

If history is a guide, the widespread studies and evidence surveyed by Quirk (1994) show that the choice of an exchange rate regime (fixed versus floating) per se does not give a clear indication of a government's likely success at controlling inflation. Edwards (1993) and Ghosh, Gulde, Ostry and Wolf (1995) find that fixed exchange rate regimes have been associated with financial discipline. However, Edwards demonstrates that this history of financial discipline preceded the exchange rate regime. Fajgenbaum and Quirk (1991) also find that the use of exchange rate anchors in the Western Hemisphere through 1990 was not successful in containing inflation, except in countries with pre-existing low-inflation situations. By contrast, a group of independently floating countries overwhelming experienced improvements in their balance of payments and inflation performance.

The national sovereignty symbolism of an independent currency is important to the population of a country. But, as noted above, the pride a country takes in its currency is likely to be related to the ability of this currency to maintain its value. This, in turn, depends on the likelihood that the new monetary authorities will resist pressures for printing money. A country must be able to deal with the inconsistencies between its expenditure plans and the availability of resources for financing this spending. By eliminating monetary autonomy, a government signals some optimism about its ability to exercise restraint. This optimism may be enacted into law with mechanisms such as currency boards. However, studies examining the inflation-exchange rate regime relationship suggest that, on balance, monetary discipline does not occur simply *because* a fixed exchange rate regime is implemented.

In a broader discussion of the lessons to be learned from fixed exchange rates, Svensson (1994) discusses regime credibility and the incentives for monetary discipline, or the lack of it, in the context of the European Monetary Union in its various stages. First, fixed exchange rate regimes can be particularly fragile, especially when there are asymmetric real shocks to the countries whose currencies are linked together. Second, conditions may arise wherein monetary discipline is procyclical and less under a fixed exchange rate regime than under floating. Third, real exchange rate variability from real shocks, combined with downward wage and price rigidity, may result in an inflation bias under fixed rates because nominal devaluation ultimately may be required. Ultimately, Svensson correctly argues that fixed exchange rates are not a shortcut to price stability and the only way to truly build policy credibility is by having a consistent, responsible and credible set of economic policies.

In assessing the appropriate choice of exchange rate and the conditions for policy credibility, one must take into account the political climate and commitment to reform on a country by country level. There are specific country features, some transitory and others more endemic, which are associated with a high reliance on inflation. These characteristics also may shed light on the conditions likely to be associated with success in sustaining a controlled exchange rate regime, if such a regime is implemented. Indeed, if it is likely from the inception that a controlled exchange rate regime will be unsustainable, implementing that exchange rate regime may be counterproductive: the very pride that having an independent currency was intended to foster will be eroded.

Is there any way to predict the inflation tendencies of a particular transition economy? An obvious approach is to examine the inflation histories of specific transition economies. But in East and Central Europe and the former Soviet Union this data is likely to give misleading results and be a flawed indicator of future tendencies to maintain monetary discipline and sustain controlled exchange rate regimes. First, observed inflation in the early 1990s reflects price reforms as well as excess money creation and therefore could yield misleading rankings of countries. Those countries which were most progressive in price liberalization and reforms could incorrectly appear to be most irresponsible in managing their money supply. Second, the ability of a country to internally cover its budgetary needs will become evident only after the country implements and stabilizes a system of taxation, achieves a tax base, establishes a position in private international capital markets, and realizes a less transitory regime of government-to-government transfers.

An alternative approach to statistically identifying likely candidates for undisciplined money creation uses data from other countries all over the world. Empirical results on cross-country reliances on seignorage may provide useful lessons about the potential inflationary tendencies of the transition economies.[13] Government reliance on seignorage has been quite widespread. Between the 1960s and the 1980s, evidence from countries around the world shows that the ratio of seignorage to total government revenues was substantial for some countries, sometimes in excess of 10 percent. Fischer (1982) identifies two types of countries that relied heavily on inflationary finance: those with "active" and "passive" seignorage collection. "Seignorage use is active in the high inflation countries, such as Argentina, Uruguay, Chile and Brazil. It is passive in the rapidly growing countries, such as many members of OPEC. In the passive case, seignorage is obtained by providing high-powered money to meet the rapidly growing demand, without necessarily having high inflation" (Fischer 1982:301). Cukierman, Edwards and Tabellini (1992) found that between 1971 and 1982, of the 79 economies examined, 35 percent relied on seignorage for more than 10 percent of their total government revenues.

There are particular country characteristics associated with tendencies toward using inflation finance. Cukierman, Edwards and Tabellini (1992) have shown inflation and a reliance on seignorage to be strongly, inversely related to the efficiency of tax collection systems, and positively correlated with political instability. Transition economies have inherited very inefficient tax collection systems. Moreover, the observed turnover of governments and battles for power in newly formed governments grappling with young democratic institutions will increase pressures for populist fiscal spending. At least for the early years of transition and reform, these key characteristics suggest that monetary conservatism will be relatively difficult to achieve in economies with significant budgetary demands.

Cross-country differences in the likely reliance on seignorage will also depend upon the sectoral composition of production and the ability of a government to collect taxes in particular sectors. A country's reliance on seignorage significantly increases with the share of agricultural output in an economy, with the degree of urbanization, and with observed political polarization and instability. It declines with the extent of industrialization and the dependence of an economy on foreign trade. The agricultural sector is viewed as a more difficult target for collecting taxes than, for example, mining and manufacturing sectors. The degree of urbanization is viewed as reflecting the ease with which market activities can move underground and evade taxes.[14] Of course, the need for seignorage as a source of budget finance also depends on the extent to which other countries provide independent financial support and transfers to the transition economy. In the former Soviet Union, countries which were formerly the recipients of large net transfers from Russia are most likely to be financially strapped in the early transition years (Goldberg, Ickes and Ryterman 1994, 1995).

For those countries with tendencies toward inflating, controlled exchange rate regimes will be neither viable and sustainable nor—based on historical lessons—lead to central bank discipline. If a country is in pursuit of a sustainable regime, it is left with the choice between some degree of flexibility in exchange rates (such as that which a floating rate regime or adjustable peg would provide) or almost complete abandonment of monetary autonomy as arises with a currency board.[15]

Concluding Remarks

Despite my pessimism about the real effects of the exchange rate on output and inflation, there still remains a potentially important reason for having an independent currency and a flexible exchange rate regime. If the new currency is properly managed, it can reinforce a desired reform trajectory. Goldberg, Ickes, and Ryterman (1994) emphasize that control over the money supply can serve as a signal of commitment to an economic reform agenda and therefore aid current agendas for stabilization. This theme is also taken up by other authors in this volume. The discussion of currency boards, in particular, indicates that such considerations are important.

Monetary independence is important in order to signal that a comprehensive economic reform will be undertaken. This decision begins to address a key problem in the transition: governments have difficulty making their reform programs credible. Adopting a new currency signifies a break with the past. If combined with a comprehensive reform package, the independent currency can improve the country's situation. Overall gains can arise if the new currency is successful in enhancing the credibility of the reform package.

Notes

The views expressed in this paper are those of the author and do not necessarily reflect the position of the Federal Reserve Bank of New York or the Federal Reserve System.

1. Quirk (1994) provides a useful and thoughtful discussion of the classification of exchange rate systems into various headings of fixity and flexibility.

2. Willett and Al-Marhubi (1994) argue that the case against independent currencies with flexible rates can be grouped under four broad headings: (1) exchange rate adjustments will not work to promote economic adjustments; (2) fixed exchange rates are needed to provide a nominal anchor for controlling domestic inflation; (3) destabilizing speculation and shifts in capital flows will generate exchange rate misalignments and excessive volatility, thus hurting international trade and distorting resource allocation; and (4) flexible exchange rates promote economic warfare and make economic integration impossible.

3. For insights into which country characteristics are associated with reduced monetary discipline, see the work by Cukierman, Edwards and Tabellini (1992).

4. Alternatively, the initial situation may be one of distinct currencies with non-discretionary monetary policy and fixed exchange rates.

5. Transfers are less likely to be sustained in the event of permanent shocks, and provide more scope for competitive devaluation.

6. Bayoumi (1994), for example, embeds the traditional Mundellian insights into a general equilibrium model with regionally differentiated goods.

7. The exception to this discussion of transition economies is East Germany. Since the former East Germany is stabilized by the former West Germany, this Mundellian criterion suggests that a single currency could exist between East and West Germany.

8. This section draws on material from Goldberg, Ickes, and Ryterman (1994).

9. For a detailed discussion of survival constraints on enterprises and the evolution of interenterprise arrears in Russia see the working paper by Ickes and Ryterman (1993).

10. See Baliño, Dhawan, and Sundarajan (1994).

11. For recent discussions see Edwards (1993), Calvo and Végh (1993), and Chapter 4 in this volume by Westbrook and Willett.

12. Currency boards, wherein there is full foreign exchange backing of the domestic currency, are intended to provide credibility to a fixed exchange rate regime while imposing a strict rule-based monetary policy. Such regimes have been implemented in Argentina (1992), Estonia (1993), and Lithuania (1994). Currency boards provide a country with the symbolism of a national currency, but almost completely eliminate monetary autonomy. Most of the studies of nominal anchors and inflation predate these recent experiences with currency boards.

13. Seignorage is often called the inflation tax because it taxes existing holders of money balances. When a country prints money to pay for its expenditures, it generates inflation, lowering the real value of the payments.

14. Cukierman, Edwards, and Tabellini (1992).

15. See Bennett (1993) and Chapter 13 by Ross and Chapter 14 by Dubaskas in this volume on the operation of currency boards in Estonia and Lithuania.

References

Aizenman, Joshua, and Robert Flood. 1992. "A Theory of Optimum Currency Areas Revisited." IMF Working Paper No. 92/39. Washington, D.C.: International Monetary Fund, May.

Baliño, Tomás, Juhi Dhawan and V. Sundarajan. 1994. "Payments System Reforms and Monetary Policy in Emerging Market Economies in Central and Eastern Europe." *IMF Staff Papers* 41(3): 383–410.

Bayoumi, Tamim. 1994. "A Formal Model of Optimum Currency Areas." *IMF Staff Papers* 41(4): 537–54.

Bayoumi, Tamim, and Barry Eichengreen. 1993. "Shocking Aspects of European Monetary Union," in Francisco Torres and Francesco Giavazzi, eds., *Adjustment and Growth in the European Monetary Union.* Pp. 193–229. Cambridge: Cambridge University Press.

Bean, Charles. 1992. "Economic and Monetary Union in Europe." *Journal of Economic Perspectives* 6 (Fall): 31–52.

Bennett, Adam. 1993. "The Operation of the Estonian Currency Board." *IMF Staff Papers* 40(2): 451–70.

Brown, Annette, Barry Ickes, and Randi Ryterman. 1993. "The Myth of Monopoly: A New View of Industrial Structure in Russia." Manuscript. Washington, D.C.: The World Bank.

Calvo, Guillermo, and Carlos Végh. 1993. "Exchange Rate-Based Stabilization Under Imperfect Credibility," in Helmut Frisch and Andreas Worgotter, eds., *Open Economy Macroeconomics.* Chapter 1. London: Macmillan Press.

Cukierman, Alex, Sebastian Edwards and Guido Tabellini. 1992. "Seignorage and Political Instability." *American Economic Review* 82(3): 537–55.

De Grauwe, Paul. 1992. *The Economics of Monetary Integration.* Oxford: Oxford University Press.

Edwards, Sebastian. 1993. "Exchange Rates as Nominal Anchors." *Weltwirtschaftliches Archiv* 129(1): 1–32.

Fajgenbaum, Jose, and Peter Quirk. 1991. "Experiences in Western Hemisphere Developing Countries with Exchange Rate Anchors." Mimeo. Washington, D.C.: International Monetary Fund.

Fischer, Stanley. 1982. "Seigniorage and the Case for a National Money." *Journal of Political Economy* 90(2): 295–313.

Ghosh, Atish, Anne-Marie Gulde, Jonathan Ostry and Holger Wolf. 1995. "Does the Exchange Rate Regime Matter?" Manuscript. Princeton University, June.

Goldberg, Linda, Barry Ickes and Randi Ryterman. 1995. "The Political Economy of Introducing New Currencies in the Former Soviet Union," in B. Crawford, ed., *Markets, States and Democracy: The Political Economy of Post-Communist Transformation.* Pp. 246–66. Boulder, Colo.: Westview Press.

———. 1994. "Departures from the Ruble Zone: The Implications of Adopting Independent Currencies." *The World Economy* 17(3): 293–322.

Gros, Daniel. 1993. "Costs and Benefits of Economic and Monetary Union: An Application to the Former Soviet Union," in Paul Masson and Mark Taylor, eds., *Policy Issues in the Operation of Currency Unions.* Pp. 55–74. Cambridge: University of Cambridge Press.

Ickes, Barry, and Randi Ryterman. 1993. "Inter-Enterprise Arrears and Financial Underdevelopment in Russia." IMF Working Paper. Washington, D.C.: International Monetary Fund, August.

————. Forthcoming. "The Organization of Markets and its Role in Macroeconomic Stabilization During Transition." *Post Soviet Affairs*.

Kenen, Peter. 1969. "The Theory of Optimum Currency Areas: An Eclectic View," in Robert Mundell and Alexander Swoboda, eds., *Monetary Problems of the International Economy*. Pp. 41–60. Chicago: University of Chicago Press.

McKinnon, Ronald. 1963. "Optimum Currency Areas." *American Economic Review* 53 (September): 717–25.

Mundell, Robert. 1961. "A Theory of Optimal Currency Areas." *American Economic Review* 51 (September): 657–65.

Quirk, Peter. 1994. "Fixed or Floating Exchange Regimes: Does It Matter for Inflation?" IMF Working Paper No. 94/134. Washington D.C.: International Monetary Fund.

Reinhart, Carmen. 1994. "Devaluation, Relative Prices, and International Trade: Evidence from Developing Countries." IMF Working Paper No. 94/140. Washington D.C.: International Monetary Fund, November.

Rose, Andrew. 1990. "Exchange Rates and the Trade Balance: Some Evidence from Developing Countries." *Economics Letters* 34(3): 271–75.

Svensson, Lars E. O. 1994. "Fixed Exchange Rates As a Means to Price Stability: What Have We Learned?" *European Economic Review* 38(3–4): 447–68.

Tavlas, George. 1993. "The New Theory of Optimal Currency Areas." *World Economy* 16(6): 663–85.

Tower, Edward, and Thomas D. Willett. 1976. *The Theory of Optimum Currency Areas*. Princeton Studies in International Finance. Princeton: Princeton University.

Wihlborg, Clas, and Thomas D. Willett. 1991. "Optimum Currency Areas Revisited," in Clas Wihlborg, Michale Fratianni, and Thomas D. Willett, eds., *Financial Regulation and Monetary Arrangements After 1992*. Pp. 274–97. Amsterdam: Elsevier.

Willett, Thomas, and Fahim Al-Marhubi. 1994. "Currency Policies for Inflation Control in Formerly Centrally Planned Economies. *The World Economy* 17(6): 795–815.

3

The Relevance of the Optimum Currency Area Approach for Exchange Rate Policies in Emerging Market Economies

Thomas D. Willett and Clas Wihlborg

Introduction

Few debates have claimed economists' attention more persistently than that over the merits of adopting fixed versus flexible exchange rates. In the 1960s the cogency of the debate was enhanced substantially by the development of optimum currency area (OCA) theory, which emphasized that there are costs and benefits to both fixed and flexible exchange rate regimes and that these may vary substantially across countries based on a number of economic characteristics.[1] Recognition that one type of exchange rate would not be optimal for all countries substantially elevated the practical usefulness of economists' analyses of exchange rate issues.

Despite this fundamental contribution, the relevance of optimum currency area theory has been questioned in recent years. We evaluate several of the most important of these criticisms and conclude that they do not seriously undermine the usefulness of the optimum currency area approach.

The early literature on optimum currency areas focused on criteria for the choice between an irrevocably fixed exchange rate—in effect joining a currency area—and a flexible rate adjusting either to market forces or to policy-induced realignments. In general, the choice between the exchange rate regimes was viewed as a trade-off between the microeconomic benefits of extending a currency area and the macroeconomic costs associated with the inability to change the exchange rate in order to achieve external and internal balance. The analytical contributions of optimum currency area

analysis have focused on the macroeconomic aspect while the microeconomic benefits of establishing a currency area have been asserted or taken for
granted.[2]

Originally macroeconomic effects were viewed primarily in terms of
Keynesian models, but today economists look at macroeconomic policy quite
differently. Neither modern theory nor empirical evidence supports the old
Phillips curve idea that a country can permanently trade a higher rate of
inflation for more rapid growth and lower unemployment. Indeed, today we
understand that over the longer run higher inflation hurts growth.[3]

Furthermore, although Keynesian economists thought macroeconomic
policies could be used to stabilize the economy by offsetting the effects of
shocks originating in the private sector, practical experience and public
choice analysis of macroeconomic policy have shown instead that government policies are often a major source of macroeconomic instability. This
instability sometimes reflects direct government manipulation for expected
political gain or, more often, insufficient political strength to constrain the
forces pushing for higher spending and lower taxes.[4]

Today the watchword is discipline rather than maximum discretion for
macroeconomic policy. This shift in views has led a number of economists
to argue that optimum currency area theory has become a Keynesian relic that
should be abandoned. It has been suggested that the appropriate role of
exchange rate policy for all countries is as a nominal anchor for monetary
policy.[5] Other economists have argued that traditional optimum currency area
theory does not apply to the special conditions of the emerging market
economies.[6] We argue that none of these three propositions is correct.

In the following section we offer a brief overview of the optimum currency area approach. We make no attempt here to offer a full survey of all the
relevant considerations that have been developed in the technical literature.
Our purpose, rather, is to offer some examples of the relevance of modern
optimum currency area theory for the choice of exchange rate regimes in
emerging market economies and in the process challenge arguments that
"question the relevance of using optimum currency area arguments for
considering the adoption of independent currencies in the FSU [former Soviet
Union]" (Goldberg, Ickles and Ryterman 1994:295). In the third section we
focus on conditions for promoting price level stability rather than the more
traditional Keynesian concerns with unemployment. We show that elements
of traditional optimum currency area theory are quite relevant for such
analysis. They show that flexible exchange rates are in some circumstances
more helpful than fixed exchange rates in pursuing price level stability. In the
fourth section we consider effects on output and employment and argue that
some recent criticism of the relevance of traditional optimum currency area
analysis for the choice of exchange rate policies in the emerging market
economies has missed the mark because it failed to distinguish between the

automatic stabilizer and balance-of-payments adjustment functions of exchange rate changes. We then consider the recent arguments made for currency competition approaches to monetary reform in the former centrally
planned economies and argue that optimum currency area theory highlights
some important difficulties with this approach. The final section concludes
with a short list of propositions from optimum currency area analysis which
we believe are especially relevant for the choice of exchange rate policies in
emerging market economies.

The Optimum Currency Area Approach

Developments in macroeconomic analysis have led to important improvements in optimum currency area theory. Some traditional criteria have been
dropped, modified or de-emphasized, while a number of new criteria have
been added.[7] But despite the strong conclusions offered by some new classical economists that optimum currency area theory should be abandoned as a
relic of Keynesian analysis, balanced assessments of modern optimum
currency area theory must concur with Paul De Grauwe's assessment that
"the hard core of the optimum currency area analysis still stands" (1992:59).

The traditional optimum currency area approach looked at the choice of
whether or not to peg the exchange rate as a question of balancing the increased microeconomic benefits derived from fixing the exchange rate
against the macroeconomic costs that this would impose.[8] More recent
analysis has suggested caveats to both sides of this equation. As will be
discussed in the third section, flexible exchange rates may help protect
domestic price stability in the face of foreign instability and hence enhance
rather than reduce the microeconomic benefits generated from the issue of
money. Likewise, under some conditions fixed exchange rates may generate
net macroeconomic benefits rather than costs. Overall, it seems fair to
conclude that developments in economic analysis over the last several
decades suggest that the net macroeconomic costs of fixed exchange rates are
somewhat less than would have been thought in the 1960s when optimum
currency area theory was pioneered, while there is little strong basis for a
substantial shift in views on the microeconomic benefits in one direction or
the other.[9]

Bean (1992) identifies the major costs of a fixed exchange rate as "a loss
of seignorage [inflation tax] in high inflation countries and the loss of the
exchange rate as an instrument of macroeconomic management" (p. 33).[10]
Seigniorage considerations were not included in the initial optimum currency
area literature but rose to considerable prominence during the 1980s. More
recent analysis, however, suggests that the costs of using the inflation tax are
much greater than was assumed in the original literature on the optimal
inflation tax, and that, as a consequence, while seigniorage considerations

remain relevant for many countries in a political economy context, they are much less relevant for the determination of optimal economic policies.[11]

There are two aspects to the possible use of the exchange rate as an instrument of macroeconomic policy. Recent literature has focused a great deal on the direct use of exchange rate adjustments as an element of short-run macroeconomic stabilization policy. Despite its popularity in the recent technical literature, we view this role as being of relatively limited importance and, as we discuss below, think that emphasis on it has led to serious confusion in some cases.

The original optimum currency area literature focused more on the use of the exchange rate as an instrument for balance of payments adjustment, i.e., to achieve external balance. If the exchange rate is fixed, then other mechanisms must be relied upon. As Robert Mundell (1961) noted in his original contribution to optimum currency area theory, "A system of flexible exchange rates is usually presented, by its proponents, as a device whereby depreciation can take the place of unemployment when the external balance is in deficit, and appreciation can replace inflation when it is in surplus" (p. 657). Mundell's focus was on the role of factor mobility as an adjustment mechanism where wages and prices were sticky. Where wage and price flexibility and/or factor mobility is high, the costs of the restrictive macroeconomic policies required to correct a balance of payments deficit will be relatively low, and hence the macroeconomic costs of adopting a fixed exchange rate would typically be modest.

Likewise, the less is the need for balance of payments adjustment, the lower would be the costs of maintaining a fixed exchange rate. Thus the patterns and origins of economic shocks and differences in countries' policy objectives became factors to be considered in optimum currency area analysis of both short-run stabilization policy and longer run balance of payments adjustment.

Optimum currency area theory suggested that the smaller and more open an economy, the greater would be the microeconomic costs of maintaining an independent national currency while the less cost effective would be the exchange rate as an instrument of balance of payments adjustment because of the high feedback effects of exchange rate changes on the domestic price level. Note that the argument about the declining effectiveness of exchange rate adjustments as openness increases rests entirely on the effects of the resulting change in traded goods' prices on the overall domestic price level, including the pressures generated for wage increases. Sticky nominal wages not only increase the cost of downward adjustment through macroeconomic policies but may increase the effectiveness of exchange rate adjustments.

There is no presumption, however, that the quantity of trade adjustment to a given change in relative prices between traded and nontraded goods will be less in a small open economy. Indeed, the long-run export elasticities in such a country are likely to be quite high, facilitating balance of payments adjustment. In addition, where short-run wage and price stickiness makes the Keynesian model relevant, the higher is a country's marginal propensity to import, the less is the decline in domestic income which would be needed to restore payments balance. For all these reasons the conclusion that a smaller and more open economy benefits from a fixed exchange rate rests on the assumption that the nominal wage level will be less sticky in response to changes in exchange rates in such an economy. Optimum currency area analysis concludes that the smaller and more open is the economy, the stronger is the case for it to adopt fixed exchange rates, and the larger and more closed the economy the stronger is the case for adopting flexible exchange rates.

Economists disagree about the extent to which increased economic interdependence has reduced the effectiveness of exchange rate adjustments by increasing the openness of the economy. We believe that the answer is "not a great deal" and see considerable scope for currencies with a fairly small domain, while some see most of Europe as forming a desirable, even if not fully optimal, currency area. Differences of opinion come both from differing analysis of the operation of specific economic mechanisms and from differing judgments about the relative weights which should be given to various criteria.

Commonly optimum currency area theory is applied from the standpoint of an industrial country deciding to fix its exchange rate or join a monetary union with another country or group of countries. The classic case is that of a small country fixing its rate to a large country's. Some attention, however, has been given to the effects on the large country and on third countries.[12] Different patterns of shocks can give rise to any combination of welfare effects. In general we believe that there is a presumption that if a currency union is advantageous for its members, any net adverse economic effects on nonmembers are likely to be small. Concerns with the possibility of multi-speed European Monetary Union appear to have much more to do with politics than economics.

The larger a country's trade is with its prospective currency area partners, the stronger is the case for joining. This is because the balance of payments constraint imposed on its domestic macroeconomic policymaking will be equally binding, however much is its trade with the currency area, while the microeconomic benefits of a fixed exchange rate or common currency will be greater, the higher is the proportion of trade covered. One implication of this is that there may be benefits from a multicountry negotiation to form a currency area which would not naturally evolve from individual countries' decisions on exchange rate policy. Such negotiated currency areas also raise the issue of how the common monetary policy would be determined, while in the traditional small country–large country case the small country recognizes that it must accept the monetary policies of the large country. This analysis highlights the conflicts generated for a small open economy that does not have a dominant stable trading partner. As is discussed below, this has been a major problem for a number of the countries that were formerly republics of the Soviet Union.

It is important to note with respect to discussions of openness and trade patterns that these are the results of a combination of "natural" factors such as size, location, transportation costs, historical and cultural ties, etc., as well as government policies. Thus trade patterns are partially endogenous, and it is the expected export trade patterns after new policies are adopted that should be most relevant in determining exchange rate policy and currency area formation. There has already been a substantial alteration of trade patterns for many of the formerly communist countries. While experts generally agree that small open economies are better candidates for adopting fixed exchange rates or joining a currency area than are large ones, they disagree about the optimal size for currency domains. The greater is the inefficiency of exchange rate adjustment among currencies under either floating or pegged rates, the larger would be optimal domains. For example, flexible exchange rates have tended to be considerably more volatile than most advocates would have predicted back in the 1970s. However, this volatility does not appear to have depressed levels of international trade as much as critics feared.[13] A possible reason is that exchange rate uncertainty has also been large under pegged rates, although for different reasons.

To some critics the failure to identify any single quantifiable criterion on which to base exchange rate decisions is taken as a fatal deficiency of optimum currency area theory. In our judgment this is a misguided inference. Tower and Willett (1976) argue that optimum currency area analysis should be thought of as an approach, not a specific theory, and that its greatest value lies in its emphasis on the sterility of debates over the virtues of fixed versus flexible exchange rates in the abstract. There are costs and benefits to both regimes, and the ratio of the costs to benefits varies systematically depending upon a number of considerations. It is this vision of how to think about exchange rate regimes that gives the optimum currency area approach its power. This power is not diminished by the multiplicity of considerations which have been shown to be relevant.

Non-Keynesian Optimum Currency Area Theory: Conditions for Achieving Price Level Stability

Much of the recent controversy over the Keynesian legacy of optimum currency area theory concerns the argument that a country can correct a balance of payments deficit with less transitional unemployment through a devaluation than through the use of restrictive domestic monetary and fiscal policies alone (see Corden 1993). Strong believers in new classical macro-economic models with fully flexible wages and prices and no money illusion or coordination problems challenge this argument.[14]

The empirical evidence does not support the strong forms of these price and wage flexibility assumptions, but even if these assumptions held, optimum currency area theory would still be relevant to the choice of exchange rate regime.[15] For the sake of argument, in this section we abstract from short-run output and employment stabilization objectives and take price stability as our only macroeconomic objective.

The process of monetary reform in the former centrally planned economies—along with the push for monetary union in Western Europe—has greatly increased economists' and policymakers' interest in the use of the exchange rate as a nominal anchor for domestic monetary policy. As is discussed in by Westbrook and Willett in Chapter 4 of this volume, to be a true anchor the exchange rate must be credibly fixed, not just adjustably pegged. This can be done either through collective action to adopt a common currency, as is envisioned in the Maastricht Treaty on European Monetary Union, or unilaterally through the adoption of a currency board based on some hard currency.[16]

As discussed above, one of the major conclusions of optimum currency area theory is that the smaller and more open the economy, the stronger is the case for adopting a fixed exchange rate. One of the major reasons for this is the feedback effects of exchange rate changes on domestic prices and wages. Where the economy is very open, the effects of an exogenous exchange rate change on domestic wages and prices will be substantial, implying that a nominal exchange rate change will have little impact on the real exchange rate.[17] Some global monetarists have argued that the world economy has become so highly integrated that even large countries like the United States and Russia are functionally small, open economies. The empirical evidence does not support this view.[18] In fact, the opposite argument can be made, namely that even very small economies typically produce a large proportion of nontraded goods. Therefore, when Estonia, population less than two million, chose to institute a currency board arrangement, and Russia, population approximately 150 million, did not, there is no presumption that one of these countries made a mistake.

A major necessary condition for the use of a fixed exchange rate as a nominal anchor to promote price stability is that there be a stable currency or group of currencies to which to peg. Over and above the political considerations underlying their wish to establish independent national currencies, the rampant inflation in Russia made staying in the ruble zone an extremely unattractive option for those former Soviet republics which had some reasonable expectation for bringing domestic inflation under control.[19] Thus despite their initial heavy dependence on trade with Russia, all three of the Baltic states soon established new currencies which they allowed to appreciate against the ruble.

What is clear is that considerable exchange rate flexibility is essential if a country wishes to protect itself from rapid inflation abroad.[20] Note that these propositions hold regardless of the openness of the economy. This may not be self-evident since, as noted above, one important strand of optimum currency area theory focuses on the inflationary effect of exchange rate changes and shows that this is an increasing function of the openness of the economy. However, that conclusion holds with respect to a discrete change in the nominal exchange rate which has the purpose of promoting balance of payments adjustment through a change in the real exchange rate.[21] Where the purpose of the exchange rate change is to offset differences in inflation rates, however, the changes in the nominal exchange rate serve to keep international prices from changing in terms of domestic currency. For this purpose, openness defined as the ratio of domestic to internationally traded goods and services does not matter. Indeed, Presley and Dennis (1976) go so far as to argue that "more open economies should have flexible exchange rates to protect them from changes in world prices" (p. 22).

The essential point is that the case for creating a nominal anchor for monetary policy does not imply that the exchange rate is necessarily the appropriate anchor. In many respects the appropriate criteria for the choice of a nominal anchor parallel those for the formation of an optimum currency area. The pattern of shocks is important. Where there is substantial inflation abroad or major changes in equilibrium real exchange rates, then the maintenance of a fixed nominal exchange rate can lead to the importation of price level instability rather than stability. In the case of changes in the equilibrium real exchange rate, the size and openness of the economy are also important considerations. When conflicts develop between the requirements for the stability of traded and nontraded goods prices, which should take precedence?[22] Clearly this should be determined in large part by the relative sizes of the traded and nontraded goods sectors and this, of course, varies tremendously across countries.

A major problem with domestically based nominal anchors is the potential variability in the demand for money and velocity of various monetary aggregates. As a number of writers have pointed out, this is likely to be a serious problem for the former centrally planned economies. Given these conditions, some economists (for example, Bofinger 1991 and Havrylyshyn and Williamson 1991) have suggested that the balance of payments could be used in a fixed exchange rate regime as an indicator of domestic monetary conditions, thus allowing an exchange rate anchor to approximate an optimal monetary rule in response to shocks in the demand for money.

A necessary assumption for this conclusion to hold, however, is that there be no changes in the equilibrium real exchange rate, i.e., that there be no conflicts in the requirements for the stability of the aggregate prices of traded and of nontraded goods. While this assumption is commonly made in analysis based on purchasing power parity and in monetary models of the exchange rate, the empirical evidence suggests that substantial changes in equilibrium real exchange rates are not uncommon. (See Chapter 9 by Sweeney.) With the economic restructuring taking place in the former centrally planned economies, uncertainty about and variability in equilibrium real exchange rates seems likely to be particularly high.[23] Given the rapid changes taking place in the emerging market economies, neither simple exchange rate nor money supply growth rules will typically be very satisfactory. This means that more sophisticated forms of targeting and disciplining monetary policies are likely to be desirable but, of course, these are also harder to implement.[24]

Balance of Payments Adjustment
vs. Automatic Stabilization

In their section on "Rejecting the Traditional Arguments [of optimum currency area theory] in the Current Context of the FSU," Goldberg, Ickles, and Ryterman (1994:298) argue that "to apply the traditional optimum currency area arguments, one must assume that exchange-rate changes will trigger rapid production responses."[25] We agree with much of their discussion of why the responsiveness of production to changed price incentives is likely to be low in the early stages of the transformation of the former centrally planned economies. We strongly disagree, however, with their assumption that traditional optimum currency area theory depends upon there being rapid production responses.

Much of the recent technical literature on optimum currency area theory and optimal exchange rate regimes has focused on the properties of fixed versus flexible exchange rates as automatic stabilizers in the face of different types of shocks.[26] The concern that output responses need to be fairly rapid is relevant for the application of much of this automatic stabilization literature, but this is only one type of optimum currency area criterion and one which several economists have argued is relatively unimportant.[27]

The much more important roles of exchange rate changes in optimum currency area theory are to protect countries from inflation or deflation abroad and to provide an instrument for balance of payments adjustment which gives a country freedom to use its monetary and fiscal policy for domestic purposes rather than to adjust the balance of payments. Neither of these purposes require rapid production responses to exchange rate changes.

The case of insulation from foreign price level movements was discussed in the previous section. For balance of payments adjustment, what is important is the total response of quantities demanded and supplied in the foreign exchange market. For this question, the standard elasticities analysis is

relevant. While the simplified Marshall-Lerner conditions for stability do
rely on the assumption of infinite supply elasticities, lower supply elasticities
reduce rather than increase the critical value of the sum of the demand
elasticities necessary for a devaluation to improve the trade balance.[28]

Even in the industrial countries, the elasticities are sufficiently low in the
short run that devaluation will often lead to an initial worsening of the trade
balance before improvement begins to set in. This is the well-known J-curve
effect. It is quite relevant for the economies in transition. Exchange-rate
related trade balance adjustment will take some time, and in the interim
private capital inflows or official financing will be necessary.[29] But this does
not undercut the case for using exchange rate changes to correct balance of
payments disequilibria. Over the several years time horizon typically applied
to macroeconomic policy analysis there is little reason to believe that the sum
of relevant elasticities is not sufficiently high in the former centrally planned
economies for real exchange rate changes to produce balance of payments
adjustment.[30] The crucial issue is to what extent changes in nominal exchange
rates will produce substantial changes in real exchange rates. As we have
discussed above, this relationship will vary greatly across countries as is
emphasized in traditional optimum currency area theory.

Currency Competition and
Optimum Currency Area Theory

Another approach favored by some economists to constrain governments
from inflationary tendencies is to allow competition among privately issued
monies or among different national currencies. Some go so far as to recommend that government production of money should be prohibited and the
creation of monies left to the private market.[31] Advocates of private money
correctly point out that some of the traditional arguments for government
production of money do not make sense. Money, for example, is not a public
good as is sometimes claimed.[32] There may be important externalities,
however, which make purely private provision of monies a potentially costly
arrangement.[33]

One key aspect of traditional optimum currency area theory is its focus on
the reduction in the microeconomic benefits of money caused by the use of
multiple currencies. Thus, with equally effective adjustment mechanisms
under fixed and flexible exchange rates, a single currency is optimal. Multiple currencies increase transaction costs and reduce the information value of
prices quoted in any one currency.

These same considerations weigh against the optimality of private
competitive monies. These might be a superior alternative to a highly inflationary government's currency, but they are not a first-best solution. Even if

a purely private system of competitive money issue did prove to be stable (and we believe there is considerable risk that it would not), the monitoring by private agents that would be necessary to provide incentives against the overissue of currencies would require substantial amounts of information gathering and processing. This is a costly allocation of scarce resources that the former communist countries are in an especially poor position to make.

The less extreme currency competition proposals argue that monetary instability could be reduced in high-inflation emerging market economies such as Russia through competition from foreign currencies and/or the introduction of a new parallel currency backed, for example, by a currency-board type arrangement to limit its supply.[34] The basic idea is that competition would reduce the scope for government seigniorage through expansion of the money supply and hence lower the country's optimum and revenue-maximizing rates of inflation. There is some logic to such arguments, but where the cause of high inflation is a politically weak government with a short effective time horizon and little ability to reduce the government budget deficit, a reduction in the potency of the inflation tax caused by currency competition may force the government to resort to its use even more.[35] Thus currency competition cannot be relied upon to hold a weak government's inflationary tendencies in check. The standard analysis of currency substitution implies also that it strengthens the case for fixed exchange rates because a flexible exchange rate tends to become volatile if currency substitution is strong.[36]

Concluding Remarks

We have argued that the recent challenges to the optimum currency area approach, while often contributing to improved analysis, have not damaged the fundamental core of the approach. It still gives us a basically correct way to frame the issues. Many, sometimes conflicting, criteria have been identified, and some of these are extremely difficult if not impossible to make operational. Acceptance of this approach does not provide us with an easy way to always get the right answers, but it offers a sound conceptual basis and asks the right questions. From this standpoint the optimum currency area approach has proven its value over and over again.

Another important issue is that as traditionally developed, optimum currency area theory analyzed the choice of adopting a genuinely fixed exchange rate or common currency versus unspecified forms of exchange rate flexibility. On optimum currency criteria relatively few countries of substantial size are likely to want to adopt genuinely fixed exchange rates. In traditional optimum currency area theory all other forms of exchange rate regime such as adjustable pegs and crawling pegs as well as managed floats are variants of a flexible rate regime. Yet it is the choice among these forms of "flexible rates" that is the most relevant issue for most medium-sized countries. While the traditional form of the analysis does not speak directly to these issues, optimum currency area theory provides a valuable starting point for the analysis of these questions. We believe that one of the most fruitful areas for research on exchange rate issues will prove to be the systematic application of optimum currency area theory to the analysis of the variety of intermediate exchange rate regimes which lie between the extremes of genuinely fixed and freely floating exchange rates.

Furthermore, while the technical literature on exchange rate regimes does offer a potentially confusing array of often conflicting criteria and conclusions, there are some simple but powerful propositions to be extracted from the theory of optimum currency areas that are highly relevant for exchange rate policy. We briefly summarize some of these.

The smaller and more open are economies, the greater is the weight which should be given to external (traded goods) versus internal (nontraded goods) aspects of price stability. Furthermore, for small open economies nominal exchange rate adjustments tend to be less effective in changing real exchange rates. For such counties fixing their exchange rate to an important, stable trading partner will typically be the ideal policy. When global inflation is high, however, even relatively small open economies may benefit from exchange rate flexibility.

Where changes in equilibrium real exchange rates are relatively modest, fixed exchange rates can provide a useful monetary anchor. This could be particularly valuable for economies in transition where restructuring of the monetary and financial systems is likely to make the demand for money unstable and difficult to estimate. Unfortunately, the transition process is also likely to make equilibrium real exchange rates quite variable and difficult to estimate. Therefore, it is not clear on balance whether these considerations would tend to favor pegged or flexible exchange rates for the transitioning economies.

Finally, the efficiency of internal adjustment mechanisms should be an important determinant of exchange rate choice. There is still a strong case for exchange rate flexibility where low factor mobility and sticky wages and prices would require the use of deflationary domestic macroeconomic policies to correct balance of payments deficits, since this would also generate considerable transitional unemployment. This case becomes stronger, the larger is the economy and the lower is the ratio of international trade to GDP.

The essential case for using exchange rate adjustment is that it works to promote balance of payments adjustment at a lower cost than internal adjustment mechanisms. Furthermore, exchange rate adjustment allows internal considerations, such as the domestic price level, to dominate external considerations (for example, the external price level, the prices of traded goods) in the formulation of macroeconomic policies. The theory of optimum currency areas shows that the ratio of costs to benefits for such freedom varies from one country to another.

While these propositions do not exhaust the list of potentially relevant considerations for the choice of exchange rate regimes, they give us a useful starting point for such analysis.

One of the greatest difficulties in applying the optimum currency area approach is the lack of a large stable trading partner to which small open economies may fix their exchange rates. This has been a particular problem for the Baltic states. Even apart from political considerations, because of its high inflation Russia is not an appropriate anchor despite its large share in the Baltic countries' trade. One alternative possibility is for the Baltic states to adopt a common currency. Over and above the lack of political and cultural identity which is typically an important requirement for forming a currency union (see Cohen 1994 and Goodhart 1995), there are good economic reasons why such a currency area does not make sense. Despite their geographic proximity, the economies of the three Baltic states are not closely integrated with one another. They rank relatively far down on each other's list of major trading partners. Not only would they score badly on Mundell's criteria of cross-national factor mobility, but the differences in these economies' structures suggests there will be substantial changes in their cross-national real exchange rates. This would require domestic price level movements relative to the group average if they formed a currency area.

Ultimately Estonia chose to fix its currency to the German mark and Lithuania chose to fix to the U.S. dollar. In each case the proportion of their trade flows with their key currency partner is relatively low, and while the United States and Germany are two of the more stable countries in terms of their domestic inflation rates, each has had major real exchange rate variations against other currencies. This in turn subjects a high proportion of Estonia's and Lithuania's traded goods sector to considerable exchange rate variability relative to their trading partners.

Perhaps Latvia made a wiser choice by fixing its exchange rate to the SDR—a weighted average of a large number of currencies.[37] While this would be likely to carry less favorable initial credibility effects than fixing to a hard currency (see Willett and Al-Marhubi 1994, and Dubauskas, Wihlborg and Willett in Chapter 6), it would seem likely to subject the domestic economy to fewer international shocks over time.

Notes

1. The term optimum currency area was coined by Robert Mundell (1961). In the 1960s the theory was extended in important ways by McKinnon (1963) and Kenen (1969). For a history of the evolution of the literature on optimum currency areas,

including references to many precursors of Mundell's work, see Tower and Willett (1976). For surveys of more recent contributions which incorporate the rational expectations and political economy revolutions in macroeconomic analysis, see Bofinger (1994), De Grauwe (1992), Masson and Taylor (1993, 1994), Melitz (1995a, 1995b), Tavlas (1993, 1994), and Wihlborg and Willett (1991).

2. See the analysis in Krugman (1992) and (1995).

3. On these issues see the analysis and references in Burdekin et al. (1995).

4. See, for example, the analysis and references in Hibbs (1987), Persson and Tabellini (1994) and Willett (1988).

5. On the first point, see Bofinger, Svindland, and Thanner (1993). On the second, see Bofinger (1991). The literature on the exchange rate as a nominal anchor is reviewed in Chapter 4 by Westbrook and Willett in this volume.

6. See Goldberg, Ickles and Ryterman (1994) and Chapter 2 by Goldberg in this volume.

7. Recent surveys of this literature include Bofinger (1994), De Grauwe (1992), Masson and Taylor (1993, 1994), Melitz (1995a, 199b), Tavlas (1993, 1994), and Wihlborg and Willett (1991).

8. On the microeconomic effects of fixed compared to flexible exchange rates, see the analysis and references in Eichengreen (1992), Krugman (1992, 1995), Tavlas (1993), and Wihlborg (1995).

9. For similar judgments see Krugman (1992) and Tavlas (1993).

10. Seigniorage is the profit earned by the central bank as a result of interest-free borrowing when it issues money. It increases with the nominal interest rate and, therefore, with the level of inflation.

11. On these issues see the analysis and references in Banaian, McClure and Willett (1994), Banaian (1995) and Willett and Banaian (1996).

12. For a recent discussion of third-country effects, see Bayoumi (1994).

13. See the surveys in Edison and Melvin (1990), Eichengreen (1992) and Willett (1986).

14. Note that the case for the effectiveness of exchange rate adjustment need not rest on money illusion. On these issues see Corden (1993).

15. For an interesting sketch of the outlines of a monetarist approach to optimum currency area theory, see Bofinger et al. (1993). On the relevance of some of the major optimum currency area criteria even in a new classical flexible price model, see Minford (1995).

16. In Part IV of this volume, currency boards are discussed. The point is made by Sweeney in Chapter 12 of this volume that currency board arrangements are not always credible.

17. See Mundell (1961) and McKinnon (1963).

18. For an analysis of the global monetarists' view, see Whitman (1975). For recent empirical evidence on this issue, see the analysis and references in Edwards (1994), Mast (1996), and Papell (1994), and specifically on Central Europe see Branson and de Macedo (1995).

19. Unfortunately, some of the former Soviet republics ran even higher rates of inflation than Russia. See Willett, Burdekin, Sweeney and Wihlborg (1995) and Chapter 18 by Banaian and Zhukov in this volume.

20. Of course a flexible exchange rate cannot offer complete insulation from inflationary disturbances occurring abroad. In a world of international capital mobil-

ity, changes in monetary policy may induce substantial movements in real exchange rates which may have direct effects on prices. On this issue see Arndt, Sweeney and Willett (1985), Bordo and Schwartz (1988), and Sweeney and Willett (1977).

21. For a small open economy, much of the effectiveness of an exogenous change in the nominal exchange rate would be lost due to induced changes in domestic prices, resulting in little change in the real exchange rate. This is one of the most powerful facets of the case for fixed exchange rates for small open economies.

22. It is interesting to note that Keynes himself formulated the case for exchange rate flexibility in this way in his *Tract on Monetary Reform* (1923).

23. See Halpern and Wyplosz (1995).

24. See the analysis and references in Burdekin and Willett (1995), Hochreiter (1995), and Willett (1995).

25. See also the contribution by Goldberg in this volume.

26. See, for example, Aghevli, Kahn and Montiel (1991), Bayoumi and Eichengreen (1994), Masson and Taylor (1993, 1994) and Tavlas (1994).

27. See Guitián (1994).

28. See Yeager (1996, Ch. 8).

29. While arguments that emerging market economics are particularly likely to be subject to destabilizing speculation do not appear to have been confirmed by recent experience, there are reasons to be concerned about possible shortages of stabilizing speculation while financial markets are in early stages of development. As is discussed in Willett and Al-Marhubi (1994), such conditions present a strong case against the use of completely freely floating exchange rates, but not against a considerable degree of exchange rate flexibility. They do point to a potential need for greater official financing in the early stages of transition.

30. Note that if the long-run elasticity conditions are not met, this implies that instability would result not just from exchange rate changes, but also from price level changes under fixed exchange rates.

31. See, for example, the analysis and references in Anderson (1995) and Carrington (1992).

32. See Vaubel (1984) and White (1988) for critiques of sloppy arguments for the necessity of public provision of money.

33. See Friedman and Schwartz (1986).

34. Again, see, for example, Anderson (1995).

35. See Willett and Banaian (1996).

36. See the analysis and references in Mahdavi and Kazemi (1996).

37. Williamson (1982) discusses the literature on the choice of pegs.

References

Anderson, Annelise. 1995. "Alternative Approaches to Monetary Reform in the Former Communist Countries," in Thomas D. Willett, Richard C. K. Burdekin, Richard J. Sweeney, and Clas Wihlborg, eds., *Establishing Monetary Stability in Emerging Market Economies*. Pp. 145–63. Boulder, Colo.: Westview Press.

Aghevli, Bijan B., Mohsin S. Khan and Peter J. Montiel. 1991. "Exchange Rate Policy in Developing Countries: Some Analytical Issues." IMF Occasional Paper No. 78. Washington, D.C.: International Monetary Fund.

Arndt, Sven W., Richard J. Sweeney, and Thomas D. Willett. 1985. *Exchange Rates, Trade, and the U.S. Economy.* Cambridge, Mass.: Ballinger Publishing Co.

Banaian, King. 1995. "Inflation and Optimal Seigniorage in the CIS and Eastern Europe," in Thomas D. Willett, Richard C. K. Burdekin, Richard J. Sweeney, and Clas Wihlborg, eds., *Establishing Monetary Stability in Emerging Market Economies.* Pp. 63–80. Boulder, Colo.: Westview Press.

Banaian, King, J. Harold McClure, and Thomas D. Willett. 1994. "Inflation Uncertainty and the Optimal Inflation Tax." *Kredit und Kapital* 27(1): 30–42.

Bayoumi, Tamim. 1994. "A Formal Theory of Optimum Currency Areas." *IMF Staff Papers* 41(4): 537–54.

Bayoumi, Tamim, and Barry Eichengreen. 1994. *One Money or Many? Analyzing the Prospects for Monetary Unification in Various Parts of the World.* Princeton Studies in International Finance No. 76. Princeton: Princeton University Press.

Bean, Charles R. 1992. "Economic and Monetary Union in Europe." *Journal of Economic Perspectives*, Fall: 31–52.

Bofinger, Peter. 1994. "Is Europe an Optimum Currency Area?" in Alfred Steinherr, ed., *30 Years of European Monetary Integration.* Pp. 38–56. London: Longman.

———. 1991. "The Transition to Convertibility in Eastern Europe: A Monetary View," in John Williamson, ed., *Currency Convertibility in Eastern Europe.* Pp. 116–38. Washington D.C.: Institute for International Economics.

Bofinger, Peter, Eirik Svindland, and Benedikt Thanner. 1993. "Prospects of the Monetary Order in the Republics of the FSU," in Bofinger et al., *The Economics of New Currencies.* Pp. 10–33. London: Centre for Economic Policy Research.

Bofinger, Peter, et al. 1993. *The Economics of New Currencies.* London: Centre for Economic Policy Research.

Bordo, Michael, and Anna J. Schwartz. 1988. "Transmission of Real and Monetary Disturbances under Fixed and Floating Exchange Rates." *Cato Journal*, Fall: 451–72.

Branson, William, and Jorge Braga de Macedo. 1995. "Macroeconomic Policy in Central Europe." CEPR Working Paper No. 1195. London: Centre for Economic Policy Research, August.

Burdekin, Richard C. K., Suyono Salamun, and Thomas D. Willett. 1995. "The High Costs of Monetary Instability," in Thomas D. Willett, Richard C. K. Burdekin, Richard J. Sweeney, and Clas Wihlborg, eds., *Establishing Monetary Stability in Emerging Market Economies.* Pp. 13–32. Boulder, Colo.: Westview Press.

Burdekin, Richard C. K., and Thomas D. Willett. 1995. "Designing Central Bank Arrangements to Promote Monetary Stability," in Thomas D. Willett, Richard C. K. Burdekin, Richard J. Sweeney, and Clas Wihlborg, eds., *Establishing Monetary Stability in Emerging Market Economies.* Pp. 115–26. Boulder, Colo.: Westview Press.

Carrington, Samantha. 1992. "The Remonetization of the Commonwealth of Independent States." *American Economic Review*, May: 22–26.

Cohen, Benjamin J. 1994. "Beyond EMU: The Problem of Sustainability," in Barry Eichengreen and Jeffry Frieden, eds., *The Political Economy of European Monetary Integration.* Pp. 149–66. Boulder, Colo.: Westview Press.

Corden, W. Max. 1993. "European Monetary Union: The Intellectual Pre-History," in *The Monetary Future of Europe.* Pp. 1–26. London: Centre for Economic Policy Research.

De Grauwe, Paul. 1992. *The Economics of Monetary Integration.* Oxford: Oxford University Press.

Edison, Hali, and Michael Melvin. 1990. "The Determinants and Implications of the Choice of an Exchange Rate Regime," in William Haraf and Thomas D. Willett, eds., *Monetary Policy for a Volatile Global Economy.* Pp. 1–44. Washington, D.C.: American Enterprise Institute for Public Policy Research.

Edwards, Sebastian. 1994. "Exchange Rate Misalignment in Developing Countries," in Richard C. Barth and Chorng-Huey Wong, eds., *Approaches to Exchange Rate Policy.* Pp. 45–64. Washington, D.C.: International Monetary Fund.

Eichengreen, Barry. 1992. *Should the Maastricht Treaty Be Saved?* Princeton Studies in International Finance No. 74. Princeton: Princeton University Press.

Eichengreen, Barry, and Jeffry Frieden, eds. 1994. *The Political Economy of European Monetary Unification.* Boulder, Colo.: Westview Press.

Friedman, Milton, and Anna Schwartz. 1986. "Has Government Any Role in Money?" *Journal of Monetary Economics,* January: 37–62.

Giovannini, Alberto, and Bart Turtelboom. 1994. "Currency Substitution," in Frederick van der Ploeg, ed., *The Handbook of International Macroeconomics.* Pp. 390–436. Cambridge: Blackwell.

Goldberg, Linda S., Barry W. Ickes, and Randi Ryterman. 1994. "Departures from the Ruble Zone: The Implications of Adopting Independent Currencies." *World Economy* 8(1): 293–322.

Goodhart, Charles. 1995. "The Political Economy of Monetary Union," in Peter B. Kenen, ed., *Understanding Interdependence: The Macroeconomics of the Open Economy.* Pp. 450–505. Princeton: Princeton University Press.

Guitián, Manuel. 1994. "The Choice of an Exchange Rate Regime," in Richard D. Barth and Chorng-Huey Wong, eds., *Approaches to Exchange Rate Policy: Choices for Developing and Transition Economies.* Pp. 13–36. Washington, D.C.: International Monetary Fund.

Halpern, László, and Charles Wyplosz. 1995. "Equilibrium Real Exchange Rates in Transition." CEPR Working Paper No. 1145. London: Centre for Economic Policy Research, April.

Havrylyshyn, Oli, and John Williamson. 1991. *From Soviet Disunion to Eastern Economic Community?* Policy Analyses in International Economics No. 35. Washington, D.C.: Institute for International Economics.

Hibbs, Douglas. 1987. *The Political Economy of Industrial Democracies.* Cambridge, Mass.: Harvard University Press.

Hochreiter, Eduard. 1995. "Central Banking in Economies in Transition," in Thomas D. Willett et al., eds., *Establishing Monetary Stability in Emerging Market Economies.* Pp. 127–44. Boulder, Colo.: Westview Press.

Kenen, Peter. 1969. "The Theory of Optimum Currency Areas: An Eclectic View," in Robert A. Mundell and Alexander K. Swoboda, eds., *Monetary Problems of the International Economy.* Pp. 41–60. Chicago, Ill.: University of Chicago Press.

Keynes, John Maynard. 1923. *A Tract on Monetary Reform,* vol. 4 of the *Collected Works of John Maynard Keynes.* London: Macmillan, 1971.

Krugman, Paul. 1995. "What Do We Need to Know About the International Monetary System?" in Peter B. Kenen, ed., *Understanding Interdependence.* Pp. 509–30. Princeton: Princeton University Press.

————. 1992. "Second Thoughts on EMU." *Japan and the World Economy* 4:3.

Mahdavi, Mahnaz, and Hossein Kazemi. 1996. "Indeterminancy and Volatility of Exchange Rates under Imperfect Currency Substitution." *Economic Inquiry*, January: 168–81.

Masson, Paul, and Mark P. Taylor. 1994. "Optimal Currency Areas: A Fresh Look at the Traditional Criteria," in Pierre Siklos, ed., *Varieties of Monetary Reform.* Pp. 23–44. Boston: Kluwer.

————. 1993. "Currency Unions: A Survey of the Issues," in Paul Masson and Mark P. Taylor, eds., *Policy Issues in the Operation of Currency Unions.* Pp. 3–51. Cambridge: Cambridge University Press.

Mast, Tamara. 1996. *The Impact and Feedback Effects of Nominal Exchange Rates on Real Exchange Rates: New Evidence from the European Monetary System.* Ph.D. Thesis, Claremont Graduate School, Claremont, Calif.

Mayer, Thomas, and Thomas D. Willett. 1988. "Evaluating Proposals for Fundamental Monetary Reform," in Thomas D. Willett, ed., *Political Business Cycles: The Political Economy of Money, Inflation, and Unemployment.* Pp. 400–23. Durham, N.C.: Duke University Press.

McKinnon, Ronald I. 1982. "Currency Substitution and Instability in the World Dollar Standard." *American Economic Review* 72(3): 474–76.

————. 1963. "Optimum Currency Areas." *American Economic Review* 53 (September): 717–25.

Melitz, Jacques. 1995a. "The Current Impasse in Research on Optimum Currency Areas." *European Economic Review* 39(3): 492–500.

————. 1995b. "A Suggested Reformulation of the Theory of Optimum Currency Areas." *Open Economies Review* 6(3): 281–98.

Minford, Patrick. 1995. "Other People's Money: Cash-in-Advance Microfoundations for Optimal Currency Areas." *Journal of International Money and Finance* 14 (3): 427–40.

Mundell, Robert A. 1961. "A Theory of Optimum Currency Areas." *American Economic Review* 51 (September): 657–65.

Papell, David. 1994. "Exchange Rates and Prices: An Empirical Analysis." *International Economic Review*, May: 397–410.

Persson, Torsten, and Guido Tabellini. 1994. *Monetary and Fiscal Policy: Politics.* Cambridge, Mass.: MIT Press.

Presley, John R., and Geoffrey Dennis. 1976. *Currency Areas: Theory and Practice.* London: Macmillan.

Richards, Anthony, and Gunnar Tersman. 1995. "Growth, Nontradables, and Price Convergence in the Baltics." IMF Working Paper 95/45. Washington D.C.: International Monetary Fund, April.

Sweeney, Richard J., and Thomas D. Willett. 1977. "The International Transmission of Inflation." *Kredit and Kapital* 10(4): 441–517.

Tavlas, George S. 1994. "The Theory of Monetary Integration," *Open Economies Review* 5(2): 211–30.

————. 1993. "The New Theory of Optimum Currency Areas." *The World Economy* 16(6): 663–85.

Tower, Edward, and Thomas D. Willett. 1976. "The Theory of Optimum Currency Areas and Exchange Rate Flexibility." Special Papers in International Economics No. 11. Department of Economics, Princeton University.

Vaubel, Roland. 1984. "The Government's Money Monopoly: Externalities or Natural Monopoly?" *Kyklos* 37(1): 27–58.

White, Lawrence H. 1988. "Depoliticizing the Supply of Money," in Thomas D. Willett, ed., *Political Business Cycles: The Political Economy of Money, Inflation, and Unemployment*. Pp. 460–78. Durham, N.C.: Duke University Press.

Whitman, Marina. 1975. "Global Monetarism and the Monetary Approach to the Balance of Payments." *Brookings Papers on Economic Activity*, No. 3: 491–555.

Wihlborg, Clas. 1995. *Searching for the Gains from a Monetary Union*. Helsinki: Yrjö Jahnsson European Integration Lectures No. 9, September.

Wihlborg, Clas, and Thomas D. Willett. 1991. "Optimal Currency Areas Revisited," in Clas Wihlborg, Michele Fratianni, and Thomas D. Willett, eds., *Financial Regulation and Monetary Arrangements After 1992*. Pp. 279–97. Amsterdam: North Holland.

Willett, Thomas D. 1995. "Guidelines for Constructing Monetary Constitutions," in Thomas D. Willett, Richard C. K. Burdekin, Richard J. Sweeney, and Clas Wihlborg, eds., *Establishing Monetary Stability in Emerging Market Economies*. Pp. 103–14. Boulder, Colo.: Westview Press.

———. 1988. *Political Business Cycles: The Political Economy of Money, Inflation, and Unemployment*. Durham, N.C.: Duke University Press.

———. 1986. "Exchange Rate Volatility, International Trade, and Resource Allocation: A Perspective on Recent Research." *Journal of International Money and Finance* 5 (Supplement): S101–12.

Willett, Thomas D., and Fahim Al-Marhubi. 1994. "Currency Policies for Inflation Control in the Formerly Centrally Planned Economies." *The World Economy*, November: 795–815.

Willett, Thomas D., and King Banaian. 1996. "Currency Substitution and Seigniorage Considerations in the Choice of Currency Policies," in Paul Mizen and Eric Pentecost, eds., *The Macroeconomics of International Currencies*. Pp. 77–96. Cheltenham, England: Edward Edgar.

Willett, Thomas D., Richard C. K. Burdekin, Richard J. Sweeney, and Clas Wihlborg, eds. 1995. *Establishing Monetary Stability in Emerging Market Economies*. Boulder, Colo.: Westview Press.

Williamson, John. 1982. "A Survey of the Literature on the Optimal Peg." *Journal of Development Economics*, August: 39–61.

Yeager, Leland. 1996. *International Monetary Relations*, 2nd ed. New York: Harper and Row.

PART TWO

Exchange Rate Pegging as an Anti-Inflation Strategy

4

Exchange Rates as Nominal Anchors: An Overview of the Issues

Jilleen R. Westbrook and Thomas D. Willett

Introduction

Discipline arguments for fixed exchange rates have a long history. While such arguments were championed by only a small minority of economists during most of the postwar period, after the inflationary excesses of the 1970s interest increased dramatically. The role of pegged exchange rates in the European Monetary System was widely cited as a major cause of the successful European disinflations of the 1980s, and there have been widespread efforts to export this strategy to other countries by economists, national governments, and influential institutions such as the IMF.[1] For example, in discussing exchange rate policies of the former communist countries, IMF economists Stanley Fischer, Ratna Sahay, and Carlos Végh report that "based on our reading of previous experience, we expected growth to be higher and inflation lower in countries with a fixed exchange rate" (1996:60).

A typical statement by advocates of exchange rate based stabilization policy is given by Dani Rodrik (1995:293):

> In most of the successful stabilization of the past decade, and certainly in all of those involving triple digit or higher levels of inflation, fixing the exchange rate has played an important role in coordinating expectations around a low inflation equilibrium and in achieving a quick break in the inflationary cycle.

Similarly, Jeffrey Sachs (1997:251) argues, "Most successful stabilizations in the past decade have relied on a pegged exchange rate for at least a short period after the start of stabilization."[2] Some economists even go so far as to argue that "floating exchange rates are not very compatible with stabilization" (Fanelli and McMahon 1996:19).

The experiences surveyed in the chapters in this section strongly suggest that such conclusions are substantially overstated. While genuinely fixed exchange rates such as currency boards have demonstrated an enviable record of promoting monetary discipline, the theory of optimum currency areas suggests that this approach makes sense only for relatively small, open economies. When one compares the track record of pegged versus flexible exchange rates during stabilization efforts, the superiority of pegged rates is far from evident

In this chapter we discuss the reasons why we believe that support for the use of pegged exchange rates as nominal anchors has been excessive. Careful analysis suggests that the role the exchange rate system plays in facilitating disinflation is more complex than suggested by popular theoretical models. Those models demonstrate the possibility of instant credibility gains from adopting exchange rate commitments. However, in discussions of exchange rates as nominal anchors advocates often fail to distinguish between temporarily pegged exchange rates and rates which are more genuinely fixed. Not only do the former fail to provide the full discipline and credibility effects of the latter, but they may actually create perverse incentives for domestic macroeconomic policies.

Another difficulty is that advocates of exchange rate pegging often seem to imply that pegging has general applicability. This overlooks the basic point of the theory of optimum currency areas. There are both costs and benefits to any exchange rate regime, and the net benefits will vary across countries. Thus, no exchange rate regime is best for all countries.[3] In a situation where optimal currency area criteria point strongly toward flexibility because the unemployment and output costs of focusing macroeconomic policy on balance of payments equilibrium would be high, efforts to follow a pegged strategy are unlikely to be seen as credible.[4] Yet it is such credibility effects that are at the core of the recent advocacy of pegging as an anti-inflation strategy.

In this regard it is important to distinguish clearly between the case for using a temporary peg to attempt to break the momentum of inflationary expectations and the case for using a longer run commitment to a pegged rate as a constraint on domestic macroeconomic policies.[5] Only the latter should be considered a nominal anchor strategy which has the potential of bringing substantial gains in credibility. Of course, in neither case will the exchange rate peg be effective in lowering inflation expectations unless combined with more fundamental policy reform.[6]

The following section discusses the meaning of nominal anchors. It argues that while the term has often been applied to short-run policy targets, it should be reserved to refer only to long-term institutional commitments which are quite costly to break. In the third section we consider exchange rate pegs that may be temporary. We discuss some of the practical issues of implementation and review ways in which temporary pegs may have destabilizing rather than stabilizing effects. In the fourth section we discuss the problem of establishing the credibility of exchange rate pegs and review the experience of the EMS in this regard. Following this we turn to a more general discussion of the major factors likely to affect the credibility and desirability of choosing the exchange rate as a long-run nominal anchor. We argue that to a substantial degree these will rest on the same factors as identified in the theory of optimum currency areas as influencing the costs and benefits of fixed versus flexible exchange rates. Most analyses suggest that many countries do not closely approximate the optimum currency conditions for adopting fixed exchange rates (see Chapter 3 by Wihlborg and Willett in this volume). Such countries should adopt domestically rather than internationally based anchors. The final section offers brief concluding remarks.

What Is a Nominal Anchor?

The term nominal anchor is used in two ways in the literature. Anchors are described as (1) long term, fixed, and nonadjustable, or (2) short term, temporary, and adjustable. In both cases, nominal anchors are viewed as targets for monetary policy (Flood and Mussa 1994). If the definition of an anchor is a target for monetary policy, then both descriptions are consistent. If a government hopes to gain long-run discipline and credibility from an anchor, then only the first description is appropriate.

In the debate surrounding the use of exchange rates as nominal anchors, analysts often fail to explain whether they view the exchange rate anchor as temporary or permanent. Quite frequently reference is made to nominal anchors without definition or discussion of their meanings. Because the emphasis is often on discipline and credibility effects, the idea of anchors as long-run constraints is usually strongly implicit (Corden's 1994 paper is an exception in that he explicitly discusses the time dimension). Frankel is quite explicit in describing the nominal anchor argument as "a prescription to peg exchange rates firmly as a credible precommitment on the part of monetary authorities not to inflate" (1996:153). Clearly such a definition is not consistent with treating a temporary peg as part of a nominal anchor strategy, yet one frequently encounters references to changeable or temporary nominal anchors (see, for example, Bruno 1991b, Claassen 1991, Cooper 1991, Edwards 1997, and Paredes and Sachs 1991). Indeed, policies are often implemented in which the exchange rate is used as a short-term nominal anchor, meant to be abandoned at some unspecified future date, and yet credibility effects are often assumed. For example, Sachs (1997:250) argues that an important argument in favor of temporary pegging at the beginning of a stabilization program is its symbolic value: "the commitment to a pegged exchange rate is a very visible signal of the government, that may increase confidence and stop a flight from the currency." Likewise, Bofinger et al. (1997:19) argue that "if a central bank adopts an exchange rate target, this reflects a strong commitment to macroeconomic stabilization." Exchange rate pegging is certainly a strong indicator that the government is undertaking a major stabilization effort, but we question whether it should convey a credible signal to economic agents that the stabilization programs will be sustained long enough to succeed. Indeed, writers such as Calvo and Végh (1994) and Kiguel and Liviatan (1992, 1991) offer imperfect credibility as an explanation for why exchange rate based stabilization in chronic high inflation countries often leads to an initial boom.[7]

As is reviewed in Chapter 7 in this volume by Martin, Westbrook and Willett, the Latin American experience with pegging during stabilization efforts hardly gives reason for optimism on this score. While some did succeed, a substantial majority of programs taking this approach failed. Why should a peg that may be only temporary, such as the one adopted in the Polish stabilization program, carry credibility and generate confidence any more than temporary wage and price controls?[8] In many cases discussions of exchange rates as nominal anchors are reminiscent of the tendency during the Bretton Woods system to fail to distinguish clearly between adjustably pegged and more genuinely fixed exchange rates.

In some cases the nominal anchor terminology has been broadened so far that it appears to include any aspect of anti-inflation policy. An example is the statement by Sachs, Tornell and Velasco that "central bank independence, publicly announced inflation targets, flexible labour markets and solid fiscal policies are all forms of nominal anchors that can keep inflation low even with a floating exchange rate" (1996:54). With such a broad definition, reference to nominal anchor strategies would retain little meaning. Thus we argue that the use of the term should be limited to cases where the anchor is expected to constrain government behavior for a substantial period of time.

In order for credibility to be permanently enhanced by an exchange rate anchor, the anchor must act as a long-run constraint, rather than a short-run policy target. In other words, the commitment to the fixed exchange rate must be viewed as a long-term commitment to give up an independent domestic macroeconomic policy and let the domestic money supply adjust to the dictates of the balance of payments as under the rules of the game of the gold standard. To be fully credible such a commitment also requires that capital and trade controls not be used to insulate domestic monetary policy from developments in the external sector (see Janáčková 1996). Thus, this is quite a different type of strategy from efforts to stabilize the exchange rate for short periods of time. There is a natural tendency for officials to hope that the market will confuse a weak commitment of the second type for a strong commitment of the first type, and at times this has occurred. The Mexican peso and several of the currencies in the European Monetary System provide examples in the 1990s.[9] These examples also illustrate, however, the dangers to which credibility illusion can give rise. The Mexican case shows that markets can punish harshly when they discover that they've been fooled.[10]

This having been said, it should be acknowledged that at times temporary pegs—like temporary wage and price controls—are useful in helping to break the inertia of inflationary expectations. Furthermore, temporary price controls may help create political support for stabilization efforts. They may create immediate political gains with their major economic and political costs coming later, just the opposite time pattern of the cost-benefit ratios of restrictive macroeconomic policies. Thus while temporary controls may be part of a politically optimal stabilization package, there are incentives for election cycles in controls which should reduce their credibility.[11] Similar arguments would apply to exchange rate pegging.

It is interesting that despite their analytic similarities, at present there seems to be much greater support among economists for temporary exchange rate pegging than for temporary wage and price controls. Both types of policies may make a modest positive contribution, but only if they are backed by fundamental reforms and the political temptations to prolong them excessively are avoided.

The crucial point for our purposes is that the analytical distinction between the two types of pegged rate strategies be clearly understood despite the frequency with which the distinction is blurred in official statements and economic commentaries. Of course the distinction between temporarily and permanently pegged exchange rates cannot be made airtight. Countries did eventually go off the gold standard and even common currencies are sometimes split apart, as the recent cases of Czechoslovakia, Yugoslavia and the Soviet Union illustrate. The lesson from history is that a fixed or pegged exchange rate regime can never be thought of as unalterable.[12] Still, while no fixed exchange rate can be completely credible over a long time frame, there is a tremendous variation in the degree of institutional commitment made to preserving the exchange rate and in perceptions about the likely durability of different pegs. In this regard, we would expect fixed exchange rates that are backed by currency board arrangements (which make it quite difficult to change the parity) would establish credibility more quickly and firmly than would a peg which can be changed at the discretion of the executive branch. The Estonian adoption of a currency board offers some evidence in support of this view.[13]

A prime example of an apparently successful use of an exchange rate based stabilization policy is the Israeli program of 1985. Leonardo Leiderman (1993:7) concludes that the use of an exchange rate anchor and temporary wage and price controls "probably resulted in faster and less costly disinflation than otherwise." He stresses, however, that this was because these heterodox measures were accompanied by tough monetary and fiscal restraint. He argues that earlier Israeli efforts to use the exchange rate to slow inflation had failed because they were not backed by the necessary adjustments of monetary and fiscal fundamentals.[14]

Temporary Pegging and Disinflation

Indeed, to some governments one of the attractions of pegging is the hope that markets can be fooled into ascribing to pegs greater credibility than is objectively warranted. A new government may use a peg as a signal about its intentions, hoping to attain long-term credibility without having to endure the pain of policy restraint. This desire to get credibility on the cheap is quite understandable, but it doesn't take perfect foresight to make one doubt that such a strategy would work consistently. Further, the possibility of the cheap purchase of credibility in the early stages of stabilization should be balanced against the potential cost to the long-term credibility of a governments' economic reforms—especially if market realities later force the abandonment of a peg perceived as a policy centerpiece. The devaluation of the Mexican peso in late 1994 exemplifies this point.[15]

While Fischer, Sahay and Végh (1996) report econometric estimates showing a statistically significant association of fixed exchange rates with lower inflation in the former communist countries, we question the extent to which causation is at work here. Countries with runaway inflation obviously have no option but to adopt considerable exchange rate flexibility. We suspect that if a greater number of domestic determinants of inflation had been taken into account the positive correlation between inflation and flexible rates would have been substantially weakened.[16] (Furthermore, Fischer et al. (1996) treat all crawling pegs as fixed exchange rate systems. We think this is a questionable practice.)

There is no reason to believe that short-run nominal anchors like those regularly used by Argentina and Brazil in the 1980s—or under the Southern Cone experiments of the 1970s—should by themselves enhance credibility. Short-run nominal anchors will increase discipline at best only in the very short run. But this is of little help. Governments are frequently willing to initiate policies of monetary and fiscal restraint. At least as important as the problem of delaying the adoption of stabilization programs is the problem of sustaining them to completion. One of the reasons why announcements of stabilization programs often have so little effect on expectations is the frequency with which such efforts have been abandoned before disinflation is completed. As Bruno (1993:7) has pointed out, "The aftermath of a failed shock stabilization is not the same as a fresh start or a first major stabilization, because the credibility problem worsens."

In this regard, the timing of the recessionary effects of disinflation policies under pegged exchange rates is not favorable. Calvo and Végh (1994) and Kiguel and Liviatan (1992) present empirical evidence for developing countries that the recessions associated with disinflation are delayed with pegged as opposed to flexible exchange rates.[17] As Lachler (1985) has argued, this pattern should reduce the credibility of disinflation efforts under pegged rates. The sooner the recession associated with disinflation ends, the greater are the chances of completing the stabilization. By deferring the recession costs of disinflation, pegged rates transfer the costs from a time when they could more easily be handled politically to a time when these costs are politically higher.[18] In other words, pegging will typically lower the political costs of the disinflation package over the first year or two, but it is during this period these costs are normally most manageable. The costs climb in later years when the dangers of policy reversals are usually greater.

The timing of these costs must be balanced against the need for public perception that the stabilization program is working, meriting the costs. This perception is likely to be primarily a function of whether a noticeable reduction in inflation occurs within a reasonably short time. Again, the comparative effects of pegged- versus flexible-rate based strategies are not entirely clear. To the extent that a pegged rate approach avoids exchange rate depreciation, this may lead to a more rapid fall in inflation, helping build support for the program. On the other hand, to the extent that stabilizing speculation in response to credible stabilization efforts leads to currency appreciation under flexible rates, this will generate a faster drop in inflation than would occur under pegged rates. For example, flexible rates appear to have increased the speed of disinflation under Paul Volcker and Ronald Reagan in the early 1980s (see Arndt, Sweeney, and Willett 1985). In such cases the initial costs and benefits of stabilization under flexible rates will both be higher. In the U.S. case the stabilization effort under flexible exchange rates in the early 1980s was carried through to a successful conclusion while the previous effort in the early 1970s under a pegged exchange rate (and another Republican president, Richard Nixon) was abandoned due to political concerns as election time drew near.

In the short run it is possible, so long as one has adequate foreign exchange reserves, to maintain an exchange rate target while following expansive macroeconomic policies. For example, the growth of the Italian money supply outstripped devaluations of the lira during the early part of the 1980s. But this led to real exchange rate appreciation and, ultimately, a large devaluation in the early 1990s. In fact, the possibility of maintaining an exchange rate peg in the short run which is inconsistent with other policy choices over the long run can undermine the success of stabilization efforts. As Begg

(1996:20) concludes, "Another Latin American lesson is that dogged pursuit of an exchange rate peg (or predetermined crawl) unmatched by credible fundamentals rapidly leads to a grossly overvalued exchange rate that impedes continuing success."

Alternatively, when the exchange rate peg is backed by strong fundamentals an undervalued currency may result. While this is typically less of an immediate problem than overvaluation, over the longer term undervaluation can generate a serious problem of imported inflation. For example, Argentina and Brazil both faced rapid endogenous increases in their money supplies during stabilization attempts as capital flowed in from abroad. To the extent that these capital inflows reflected an increase in money demand associated with disinflation, this is not a problem (indeed it is a benefit),[19] but in a number of cases capital flows have been much greater than this and have generated a serious problem of imported inflation.[20] As is discussed in the chapters in this section, imported inflation proved to be a problem for the Czech Republic, Estonia, Poland and a number of Asian nations.[21]

Temporarily pegged exchange rates can also increase incentives to generate political business cycles before elections which later destabilize the economy. This possibility is highlighted by the recent Mexican experience.[22] More generally, in a study of 35 developing countries, Schuknecht (1996) finds that political business cycles were much more common in countries with pegged than with flexible exchange rates.

For the EMS countries, pegged exchange rates did not stimulate a strong tendency for governments to engage in political business cycles. High capital mobility, however, helped reduce the interest costs of financing large budget deficits in countries such as Italy and thus tended to undermine rather than increase discipline over fiscal policies. As De Cecco and Giavazzi (1994:21-3) argue, capital inflows

> ...reduced the urgency with which the Italian political leaders had to address the structural problems of the Italian economy...a fool's paradise was created in Europe with foreign short term capital flows validating the virtuousness of monetary authorities and the profligacy of political authorities, putting fiscal and monetary policies on collision courses which foreign capital inflows temporarily managed to hide from view.[23]

A further problem with pegging as part of a disinflation program is picking the right exchange rate. Typically, countries initiating stabilization programs have needed to begin with a substantial initial devaluation. Too small a devaluation will quickly lead to balance of payments deficits and speculation against the currency. Too large a devaluation will raise the price of tradable goods by too much and create additional pressures for cost-push inflation. Picking an initial level of the exchange rate which avoids these two problems is particularly difficult for countries suffering from high inflation. One must estimate not only the equilibrium real exchange rate but also the amount of cumulative inflation that will occur during the disinflation process. As is discussed in the following chapter by Burdekin, Nelson and Willett, when Poland initiated an exchange rate based stabilization program in 1991, estimates of the equilibrium level of the exchange rate varied by over 50 percent. Hrnčíř reports (see Chapter 15 of this volume) that estimates of the appropriate new rate for the Czech koruna against the dollar ran from 16 to 38.

To some extent these problems can be attenuated by using a crawling instead of a fixed peg.[24] The idea is that while maintaining a fixed peg for a substantial period of time might not be feasible, the use of a crawling peg with a declining rate of depreciation could help slow inflation while avoiding serious balance of payments problems. Often the rate of crawl is pre-announced, the so-called tablita approach. The track record of this strategy is not impressive, however. While it did appear to work well for Mexico for several years, this experience ultimately ended in the crisis of 1994–1995. Bruno (1993) judges efforts by Chile and Israel to have been failures. For Poland, the record is mixed. Inflation was rapidly brought down from near hyperinflation, but five years were required to bring it down to below 20 percent per year. Hungary, under a discretionary crawling peg, also made slow progress in reducing inflation and, indeed, 1994 saw an acceleration of inflation, prompting a new stabilization program in 1995 which included a preannounced crawl. The acceleration of inflation was halted, but progress in reducing inflation is quite slow. In some cases, however, the strategy of moving from an initial narrow peg to wider crawling bands in a second stage of stabilization has been reasonably successful. In the cases of Chile, Israel, and Mexico, "the shift toward more flexible exchange rate regimes, under a relatively tight fiscal discipline, was not associated with a rise in inflation. On the contrary, the rate of inflation exhibit[ed] a downward trend" (Helpman, Leiderman, and Bufman 1994:291–92). In the Mexican case this strategy did work well for several years, but the flexibility provided was not sufficient to avoid the major speculative crisis of 1994–1995.

While some crawling peg regimes have been designed to depreciate by less than the inflation differential and hence force some domestic price discipline, many have operated more flexibly. Although the adoption of pegged rates was helpful for the disinflation efforts of a number of the former communist counties, some of the most successful disinflations, such as those in Latvia, Lithuania, and Slovenia, occurred under flexible exchange rates. As Corden (1994:83) concludes from his comparison of a number of examples from Asia and Latin America, "The true anchor is the policymakers' conviction—usually rooted in and backed by widespread community conviction—that inflation is undesirable." He goes on to note that:

Perhaps a fixed exchange rate has a role in signaling the government's anti-inflationary commitment to private agents. But they will always be alert...to the possibility that the signal is a false one. If they are rational, they will look for the underlying commitment. (P. 83)

In summary, the case for temporarily pegging the exchange rate as part of a stabilization program needs to be clearly distinguished from the case for a permanent peg. While we have pointed to a number of dangers associated with exchange rate based disinflation strategies, the verdict should not be entirely negative. Sachs (1996b:147), for example, argues that "there are good reasons for countries at the start of stabilization and liberalization programs to adopt a pegged exchange rate regime for part of the initial policy, even if the countries should then move to flexible-rate systems after one or two years of stabilization and liberalization." To the extent these strategies are useful, however, they should be viewed as counterparts to temporary wage and price controls to try to break the momentum of inflationary expectations, not as true anchors.

Earning Credibility: The Lessons from the EMS

While the EMS experience is frequently cited as strong evidence of the value of exchange rate based stabilization policy, careful analysis suggests that the lessons to be drawn are more complex.[25] While the pegged rates of the EMS did not prove to be an engine of inflation such as operated in the last days of the ruble zone,[26] neither was disinflation by the EMS members particularly more successful than for comparable industrial countries outside the EMS. If anything, the EMS countries tended to disinflate less rapidly in the 1980s than the other industrial countries,[27] and it appears that the output costs of disinflation may have been higher.[28]

While there is some evidence that a combination of policies in support of the exchange rate lowered inflation expectations (Burdekin, Westbrook and Willett 1994; Westbrook 1995), stabilizations based upon exchange rate pegs did not have substantial immediate credibility effects. This is particularly so for countries that have had persistent inflation problems in the past. When a government announces an exchange rate based stabilization, it has to earn a reputation for "sticking to" its new anti-inflation policy stance before it is fully believed by the public. If the credibility of the pegging arrangement is low, economic agents will not immediately adjust their inflation expectations downward by a substantial amount.

Indeed, in the case of the EMS one should not have expected to see instant credibility effects, since the system was initially based on the idea of avoiding the speculative problems of the Bretton Woods adjustable peg by having a wider band for exchange rate fluctuations and more frequent adjustments in parities. In its early period parity adjustments were frequent.[29] As de Cecco and Giavazzi (1994:228) emphasize, "the EMS was at its inception not yet seen as a way for inflationary countries to borrow credibility from less inflationary ones... Nor had the 'advantage of tying one's hands' been yet appreciated by the authorities of profligate countries or by analytical economists."

Within the EMS, different countries began to view defending the exchange rate as an important priority at different times. In the case of the Netherlands, a hard currency peg to the German mark was adopted early on, and the comparable experience of Austria's unilateral hard currency peg to the German mark (see Hochreiter and Winckler 1995) suggests that the EMS per se played a relatively small role with respect to the credibility of the guilder. In some cases, such as France in 1983, there was a clear decision point where a hard currency strategy was adopted.[30] In other countries, such as Italy, the increase in commitment was more gradual (and less complete).[31]

As the exchange rate arrangements within the EMS hardened in the mid and late 1980s, there is some suggestion in the evidence that credibility effects accrued to new entrants into the system more quickly than it had for the original members. For example, Kapopoulos (1995) points out that the sacrifice ratios associated with the substantial disinflation for Portugal and Spain (entry 1985) and Greece (entry 1986) were quite low. However, in his regressions of credibility effects as measured by long-term interest differentials, the coefficients on the ERM membership dummy are insignificant. After the U.K.'s entry in 1990, its one-month and twelve-month interest differentials began to fall steadily for about a year, suggesting a more rapid than usual, although not instantaneous, gain in credibility.[32]

While pegging in and of itself appears to have only a limited effect upon credibility, other types of anti-inflation policies appear to be more potent. Sargent (1986) provides support for the idea that fiscal austerity will substantially lower inflationary expectations.[33] Westbrook (1995) finds evidence that fiscal austerity did indeed enhance the credibility of countries within the EMS. However, the fiscal austerity undertaken in France and Italy was intended to support those countries' currencies within the ERM bands. Within the EMS it appears that fiscal austerity and pegging worked as complements. For example, in 1983 the French government had to choose between abandoning the peg or dramatically altering fiscal spending. They chose the later and inflation expectations (as measured by the expected change in the spot exchange rate) declined.

Hochreiter (1997) suggests that the corporatist policy between government and labor was important to credibility in Austria. In Austria, the government sought an agreement with unions on wages in order to battle inflation. Mexico followed a similar plan with the PACTO of 1986, whereby unions agreed to coordinate their wage demands with the government's stabilization efforts. Within the EMS there is some support for this idea. Coupled with monetary austerity and the pegged exchange rate, an announcement of wage, price and incomes policies reduced interest differentials between Denmark and Germany and reduced inflation expectations (as measured by survey data) in Belgium. Unlike Denmark, Belgium did not undertake fiscal austerity, but rather instituted a general price freeze in February of 1982 and announced plans to de-index wages. While a formal agreement with labor was not necessary in the Belgian case, labor did not actively oppose the government's plan.

It may have been the perception that credibility had been won at a cost that led many EMS member nations to maintain the pegging arrangement after 1990, when it became clear that exchange rate changes were needed because of German reunification. Faced with the shock of German unification, France (and others) chose to raise interest rates during a recession in order to defend the French franc. In clinging to the exchange rate arrangement, and its perceived hard-won credibility gains, the French government increased the severity of the recession at home, lost reserves and competitiveness abroad, and had to endure months of speculative pressure until finally, in 1993, substantial exchange rate flexibility was introduced by widening the bands around central parity values from 2.5 percent to 15 percent.[34] On the other hand, when Italy and the U.K. left the system in 1992 inflation rates in the U.K. and Italy did not surge as some expected, and export-led growth was important for both economies.[35]

At the very least, the experience of the EMS members suggests that as a criterion for choosing an exchange rate regime, credibility gains should be examined with extreme care. While it is not clear whether the EMS's members would have been able to disinflate successfully without the system, it does not appear that the regime made disinflation any less costly. There are exceptions such as the U.K., which joined the system when it was much more rigid and when the perceived costs of devaluing were significantly higher.

It is unclear how long a nation must remain committed to an exchange rate anchor before it can successfully "borrow" its anchor's reputation. For example, the perceived gains in credibility attained by France between 1987 and 1992, when it successfully pegged the franc to the German mark, did not save the franc from speculative attack during 1992 and 1993, when strains developed in the mark-franc exchange market. Yet the Netherlands, an EMS member, was clearly able to borrow German credibility when it undertook a hard-pegging strategy in the early 1980s, as was a non-EMS member, Austria, before it. Interest differentials between Germany and the Netherlands were very small throughout the 1980s, and even reversed after 1990. Of course, on optimum currency area criteria Austria and the Netherlands are much stronger candidates to join in a currency area with Germany than is

France, perhaps lending credibility to the perceived permanence of the exchange rate peg between the guilder and the mark and diminishing the credibility of the franc/mark peg.

Credibility and the Costs and Benefits of Using the Exchange Rate as a Long-run Nominal Anchor: The Relevance of Optimum Currency Area Theory

An exchange rate commitment increases discipline and credibility by increasing the cost to a government of abandoning this commitment. The cost to government occurs through multiple channels, both economic and political. If, for example, abandoning a fixed exchange rate is more visible to the public than abandoning a monetary aggregate, politically sensitive governments will strive more vigorously to maintain the fixed exchange rate arrangement.[36] The cost of maintaining a peg will be greater, the greater the balance of payments or exchange rate disequilibrium and the greater the cost of adjusting the domestic economy, as opposed to the exchange rate, to the disequilibrium. Thus, the traditional optimum currency area criteria (discussed in Chapter 3 by Willett and Wihlborg in this volume) should be quite relevant to evaluating the credibility of the peg. For example, the smaller and more open is the economy, the less will be the costs of using domestic macroeconomic policy to adjust to balance of payments disequilibrium, while the more inflationary would be exchange rate adjustments. Similarly, if domestic prices are highly flexible, this reduces the costs of adjusting domestic policy to external deficits.

Patterns of disturbances will also be important. If the domestic demand for money is highly variable due to international currency substitution, then fixed exchange rates will reduce financial instability compared with flexible exchange rates. For example, Bruno (1993:243) argues that "Given the inherent instability of the demand for money, preference should probably be given to the exchange rate over monetary aggregates as a nominal anchor."[37] On the other hand, where the majority of shocks are due to foreign inflation or changes in equilibrium real exchange rates, then the maintenance of fixed exchange rates could prove to be quite costly. For the transition economies of Central and Eastern Europe and the former Soviet Union, it appears that such real shocks and the pressures of imported inflation from Russia have been quite important. Velocity also has been quite variable for many of these countries. However, in a study of 10 states that were former members of the Soviet Union, Anderson and Citrin (1995:50) conclude that "the relationship between inflation and exchange rate behavior in these countries does not suggest that shifts in money demand in favor of foreign currency were significant in explaining increases in inflation and velocity."

While optimum currency area theory has traditionally focused only on economic costs and benefits, analysis of the credibility of policies must adopt a broader political economy perspective and examine not only aggregate economic effects, but also distributional effects and the political salience of economic effects. For example, a devaluation could generate net economic benefits for a country and still impose great political costs on the government because of rational ignorance and political activity by the losers from devaluation. Furthermore, these political effects may differ considerably depending upon the timing of devaluation in relation to elections. The credibility effects from an exchange rate anchor also will be affected by the full range of institutional arrangements (including announcements) surrounding the regime. For example, if a central banker will lose his or her job if the peg is abandoned, credibility will be enhanced. Alternatively, if the central bank is subject to electoral politics, the initial credibility gains may be minimal.[38]

It is typically assumed that devaluations are viewed by the public as an admission of failure and that the political costs of devaluations are quite substantial, but there has been relatively little systematic research on this issue.[39] Certainly the majority of exchange rate based stabilization efforts have been unsuccessful in maintaining a fixed exchange rate for an extended period of time.[40] Thus we should not expect typical unilateral pegs to carry much initial credibility.

It is possible, however, that credibility can be enhanced where exchange rate commitments are part of a multilateral agreement. If nothing else, this would raise the cost to the reputations of officials presiding over a devaluation. With respect to the reputations of officials within their country and their ability to sell policies to defend currency commitments, the broader project of European integration appears at times to have played a major role (see Andrews and Willett 1997). In developing countries, the International Monetary Fund often plays a positive role in tipping the balance of domestic policy debates toward stabilization, and the IMF's seal of approval often enhances the credibility of those efforts.[41] On the other hand, the credibility of the IMF began to suffer from poor compliance records and domestic opposition to programs perceived to be externally imposed.[42] Perhaps more important would be quasi-constitutional institutional measures which would directly limit the government's discretionary authority to change the exchange rate; currency board arrangements are attractive on this score.

To overcome the political incentives to adopt destabilizing macroeconomic policies, there is a strong case for rules over discretion. Typically, however, to be politically feasible monetary rules need to be simple, such as maintaining a fixed exchange rate or rate of money growth. The problem is that any particular monetary rule is optimal only in the face of particular types of disturbances. In general, economies face a wide range of disturbances. Variability in the demand for money undercuts the efficiency of Friedman's simple monetary rule just as shocks to equilibrium real exchange rates raise the cost of following an exchange rate rule. Most simulation studies find that a rule of constant nominal income growth typically performs much better than either a simple money supply or exchange rate rule.[43] The difficulty is that a nominal income rule does not fit on a bumper sticker and cannot be implemented directly. Thus, in general, efficient monetary constitutions are likely to require multipart procedures.[44]

One attractive approach is illustrated by New Zealand's Reserve Bank Law, which requires the central bank to achieve inflation rates in a mandated low range unless an override is provided in the case of major shocks.[45] A contingent commitment should not always carry less credibility than an unconditional commitment since the former may be viewed as being more realistic and the likelihood of default could, therefore, be perceived as being reduced. As Sachs, Tornell and Velasco (1996:54) point out, "Unrealistic 'toughness' on the exchange rate does not increase credibility...devaluing in the face of a clear exogenous shock (e.g. political assassination) reduced the loss of credibility attendant upon a move of the exchange rate."[46]

Shocks that are difficult to clearly identify in a timely manner, however, can pose severe problems for contingent commitment strategies. This problem would seem to be particularly likely to apply to simple exchange rate and money supply rules. Designing an effective set of monetary rules or institutions is extremely difficult under stable conditions. It is even more difficult where rampant inflation must first be brought under control. As Obstfeld (1997:62) concludes, "while well designed rules with escape clauses can raise welfare in principle, limited credibility makes it difficult for governments to implement them in practice."[47]

Frenkel (1991:402) makes the interesting argument that

> since credibility is one of the key factors governing the success of stabilization programs, it is important that the program should allow for mid-course corrections that do not destroy its credibility...The public should be informed on the basic contribution that the nominal anchors make but, at the same time, be aware that in an uncertain world occasional corrections might be necessary. With such transparency and clarity, mid course corrections might actually enhance the credibility of the stabilization effort rather than signify its failure.[48]

Again, on this count it seems that exchange rate anchors would typically not score well. Certainly the Mexican crisis illustrated the potential dangers of attempting midterm corrections to an anchor which was widely thought to be firm. Of course, this problem can be countered by making only weak commitments, but as we argued in the second section, in such a case it does not really seem appropriate to talk of anchors.

Concluding Remarks

While credibility effects have captured the imagination of economists concerned with policy reform and inflation control, most commitments to pegged exchange rates lack the degree of credibility typically assumed in theoretical models. The overstatement of the importance of exchange rate pegs as nominal anchors comes from ascribing long-run benefits to policies that are often intended to be followed only in the short run. For commitments to pegged rates to enjoy a good deal of credibility, the perceived feasibility of maintaining the peg should be high as should the costs of breaking the commitments.

As is illustrated in the following chapters, typically the initial credibility effects from pegging exchange rates have not been great and vary depending on the degree of institutionalized commitments. Thus, for example, the adoption of a currency board arrangement like Estonia's, which makes it impossible for the executive branch to unilaterally change the exchange rate parity, rationally carries much more credibility than the typical decision of a government to peg. Likewise an exchange rate peg backed by large stabilization loans and international commitments should carry greater credibility than unilateral national actions backed by a low level of international reserves and continuing domestic political instability. However, the experiences of Argentina, Estonia, and Lithuania suggest that even with the adoption of strong institutional arrangements—such as currency boards —full credibility may still require a considerable time to develop.[49]

Within the European Monetary System the evidence suggests that successful defenses of pegged rates did help increase the credibility of countries' anti-inflation efforts, but this more closely approximated earning credibility through sustained policy actions than creating it through institutional reforms. Furthermore, the crises of 1992 and 1993 demonstrated that the credibility earned was far from complete. In addition, there is the danger, so vividly illustrated in the recent Mexican case, that if too much emphasis is put on the exchange rate as the centerpiece of a government's policy strategy, rather than the need to adjust the exchange rate with substantial disequilibrium, this emphasis can undercut the credibility of the whole policy strategy, even after sustained macroeconomic restraint that lowered inflation from triple to single digits.

In general the available evidence suggests that the case for exchange rates as nominal anchors rests much more heavily on the ability of governments to use such commitments to defend restrictive macroeconomic policies in the face of domestic political pressures than through the effects in enhancing credibility that have been stressed in the recent theoretical literature. In other words, it is the old-fashioned discipline argument rather than the new-fangled credibility effects that should be given more weight.[50]

While we believe that the case against the general use of exchange rates as nominal anchors is overwhelming, for small open economies a genuinely fixed exchange rate against a low-inflation trading partner can make a great deal of sense. However, adjustable pegged exchange rates can create substantial incentive-compatibility problems that run counter to the discipline and credibility arguments made for pegged rates. The balance of these contending considerations seems likely to vary substantially across cases depending upon a number of factors, including the past reputation of the government, the sources of macroeconomic disturbances and budget issues.

Furthermore, many small open economies face the problem of not having a satisfactory partner for this purpose. The ideal partner is both highly stable and a major trade partner. Such conditions are only rarely met, causing potentially serious problems. For example, while Estonia ultimately decided to fix its currency to the German mark and Lithuania to the dollar, neither has a high proportion of trade with these countries. Thus Estonia is in a less advantageous position than Austria, for example, which has a large amount of trade with Germany. Furthermore, while Germany and the U.S. have both maintained low average rates of inflation by international standards, both "anchors" have also at time followed macroeconomic policy mixes which have generated substantial changes in equilibrium real exchange rates. Concerns with the effects of substantial changes in real exchange rates are clearly not just hypothetical. To some extent such problems can be reduced by fixing to a basket of currencies rather than to a single currency. While fixing to a basket would likely make it more difficult to gain substantial initial credibility, we have argued that experience suggests that such instantaneous credibility effects are difficult to achieve in any case. Thus Latvia with its basket peg may have made a wiser choice than Estonia with its peg to the German mark and Lithuania with its peg to the dollar.[51]

Perhaps the best simple generalization is that the use of pegged exchange rates as an anti-inflationary device is fraught with potentially severe economic and political difficulties. These should be carefully evaluated on a case-by-case basis before such strategies are adopted. We concur with David Begg's (1996:21) suggestion that "In giving advice on the form of nominal anchor during initial stabilization, it may be more costly mistakenly to classify a country as suitable for an exchange rate peg than mistakenly to classify it as unsuitable for an exchange rate peg." While differences of view have been expressed about the costs of doing so, even the very small, open economies of Latvia and Slovenia brought inflation under control without the use of exchange rate pegs. While a number of economists have pointed to the short-term advantages of a temporary peg in helping to break inflationary inertia, less attention has been paid to the substantial difficulties involved in moving from a pegged to a more flexible exchange rate regime. There are substantial political pressures to delay the transition for much longer than would be consistent with a smooth transition. As Sachs (1995:185) has noted,

> moving from an initially pegged rate to a flexible rate (e.g., a crawling band) is easier said than done. We still don't have an agreed approach to announcing, at the start of stabilization, that a peg will be temporary, to be followed by some sort of band or float.

In general, strategies based on central bank independence combined with inflation or nominal income targeting appear much more attractive than using the exchange rate as the centerpiece of anti-inflation policy.[52]

Notes

1.   On the tendency of the IMF to recommend pegging on anti-inflation grounds, see Edwards (1993) and for an earlier expression see Frenkel et al. (1991). After (inappropriately in our view) advising the continuation of the fixed exchange rate based ruble zone for the countries of the former Soviet Union, the IMF did switch to advocating flexible exchange rates for a number of former communist countries. See Sachs (1996b).

2.   See also Bruno (1991b) and Rebelo and Végh (1995).

3.   Our analysis assumes that exchange rate adjustments do work to correct the balance of payments. Typically, observers are no longer concerned that elasticities in the foreign exchange market are too low to promote adjustment; see, however, the discussion by Linda Goldberg in this volume concerning the possibility of low elasticities for economies in the initial stages of transition from central planning to the market. More frequently, criticisms of the effectiveness of exchange rate adjustments focus on arguments that induced inflation will keep changes in nominal exchange rates from having policy relevant effects on real exchange rates. While this is likely true for very small open economies—a point emphasized in the theory of optimum currency areas—the empirical evidence suggests that nominal exchange rate changes are generally an effective method of changing real exchange rates: see Edwards (1994), Mast (1996), Papell (1994) and, for specific evidence in the case of Central Europe, see Branson and de Macedo (1995).

4.   By credibility we mean the extent to which government announcements of policy intentions are believed by the public. According to this definition, a government is also credible if the public believes a policy change has occurred after the government announces it, even if the government has no intention of following through. That government will quickly lose credibility, however.

5.   As Maurice Obstfeld has recently argued, "A pegged or even fixed exchange rate may be useful in the early stages of disinflation...But leaving an exchange rate

in place for long...invites trouble" (1995:171). Sachs, Tornell, and Velasco (1996:19) argue similarly that "pegged exchange rates are often helpful in ending very high inflation...but they become dangerous if they are maintained long after stabilization has been achieved."

6. For a valuable review of the Israeli experience which dramatically demonstrated the differences in effects when pegging-based stabilization programs were backed by fundamental changes in monetary and fiscal policies and when they were not see, see Bruno (1993) and Leiderman (1993), and on the Latin American experiences, see Chapter 7 by Martin, Westbrook, and Willett.

7. Végh (1992) argues that stabilization efforts under hyperinflation will be much more credible than those under chronic inflation, so that in the former case inflation can be quickly eliminated with little cost in terms of employment and output. On the imperfect credibility explanation of initial booms under exchange rate based stabilization, see also Rebelo and Végh (1995).

8. In the Polish case, see the analysis and references in Chapter 5 by Burdekin, Nelson, and Willett, and Chapter 17 by Kawalski and Stawarska in this volume.

9. In these cases there was a strong interaction between perceptions of the credibility of the exchange rate commitment and the reputation earned by governments following conservative monetary policies. There is an important question concerning whether the markets, often characterized as being too pessimistic about the credibility of government policies, in these cases became too optimistic. We are inclined to believe that this was so, at least in the Mexican case.

10. The credibility costs imposed on the countries which dropped out of the exchange rate mechanism of the EMS in the early 1990s was much less than in the Mexican case. Several of the Southeast Asian countries forced off of their pegs in 1997 also appeared to face substantial credibility costs.

11. See Aǵenor (1995) and Aǵenor and Asilis (1997).

12. The presumption that one nation can borrow another's reputation is based upon it relinquishing control of domestic monetary policy. A nation can certainly choose to do so, but rarely have there been cases where a nation permanently chooses to relinquish control of this policy tool. For a valuable discussion of the political economy characteristics that led countries to stick to the gold standard for a longer or shorter time period, see Simmons (1994).

13. See Hansson and Sachs (1994), Saavalainen (1995), Sachs (1996b) and Chapter 6 in this volume by Dubuskas, Wihlborg and Willett.

14. On the Israeli stabilization efforts see also Bruno (1993). On the key role of fiscal adjustments, see also Burdekin (1995) and Sargent (1986) and the discussion in the following section on the EMS experience.

15. See, for example, Calvo and Mendoza (1996), Gil-Díaz and Carstens (1996), Sachs, Tornell and Velasco (1996), and Willett (1995a).

16. On the selection bias involved in simple correlations of inflation and exchange rate regime, see also Begg (1977). Buina and Wijnbergen (1997) find that once the sustainability of fiscal policy is taken into account, "the eastern European experience...suggest no clear link between exchange-rate regime and inflation track record" (p. 53). The recent statistical literature on the association between exchange rate regimes and inflation reaches mixed results. See also Edwards (1993), Ghosh et al. (1996), Quirk (1994, 1996) and Siklos (1997). Indeed, in a recent empirical study

of the industrial countries, Al-Marhubi and Willett (1997) find that the association between exchange rate regimes and inflation depends strongly on the countries' degree of openness—one of the major variables in optimum currency area theory. Fixed rates are associated with lower rates of inflation in more open economies and higher rates of inflation in less open ones. Across all countries there is a strong positive simple correlation between pegged exchange rates and lower inflation, but clearly this is due in part to the infeasibility of maintaining pegged rates in the face of high inflation. When attempts are made to take casual factors into account, the results are mixed. See Al-Marhubi (1996), Edwards (1993), Ghosh et al. (1996), Quirk (1994) and Siklos (1997).

17. A number of contending hypotheses have been offered to explain this pattern. After a detailed examination, Rebelo and Végh (1995) conclude that the most promising explanations require wage and price stickiness and expectations that the exchange rate peg and overall stabilization program will prove to be only temporary. For questions about the frequency of such delayed recessions see Easterly (1996) and Gould (1996). Khamis (1996) finds that in the Argentine, Chilean and Mexican, but not the Israeli, stabilization programs reductions in inflation were associated with substantial increases in private sector credit and suggests that this may be one of the factors generating initial booms often associated with exchange rate based stabilizations.

18. As Balerowicz et al. (1997:135) note, "Gradual reform would also mean wasting political capital...This sort of political capital is a typical benefit of any large scale political breakthrough, but it quickly vanishes, giving way instead to 'normal' politics conducted by political parties, a game of special interests." The same point applies to the output and employment costs associated with disinflation. See also the discussion by Boone and Fedorov (1997).

19. In order to minimize the output costs of disinflation, one would ideally combine a reduction in the rate of money growth with a one-time increase in the level of the money supply, since lower inflation rates will lead to increases in demand for real money balances. Such a strategy is difficult to make credible, however. In some circumstances the adoption of a non-sterilization policy with a pegged exchange rate could bring about the desired pattern of behavior of the money supply. See Bruno (1991a), Fischer (1986) and Pikoulakis (1990). Bini-Smaghi and Micossi (1990) argue that to minimize output costs, disinflation should be accompanied by both fixed rates and capital controls.

20. See Martin, Westbrook and Willett in this volume for further discussion of this issue.

21. For a valuable analysis of capital inflow problems in Central and Eastern Europe, see Calvo et al. (1995).

22. On the incentives under pegged rates to generate political business cycles, see Svensson (1994), Wihlborg and Willett (1991) and Willett and Mullen (1982).

23. For further analysis of this issue, see also Giavazzi and Spaventa (1990) and Bini-Smaghi and Micossi (1990).

24. Step devaluations are also an option, but one which does not appear to work well. Reporting on a study of 15 developing countries in the Caribbean and Latin America between 1960 and 1990, Quirk (1996:44) concludes that step devaluations as "exchange rate anchor policies were not successful in the region."

25. Strictly speaking one should refer to the ERM (Exchange Rate Mechanism) since European Union members such as the U.K. were by definition members of the EMS even when not pegging their exchange rates.

26. See the analysis in Chapter 18 by Banaian and Zhukov in this volume.

27. See Burdekin, Westbrook and Willett (1994), Christensen (1987a, 1987b), Collins (1988), Fratianni and von Hagen (1992), Giavazzi and Giovannini (1988), and Westbrook (1995).

28. See Fratianni and von Hagen (1992).

29. See Fratianni and von Hagen (1992).

30. On the French case, see the analysis and references in Andrews and Willett (1997). On the long time required for the French disinflation, see Blanchard and Muet (1993).

31. See de Cecco and Giavazzi (1994).

32. See Rose (1993).

33. See also Burdekin (1995).

34. On the EMS crisis of 1992 and 1993, see De Grauwe (1994) and Eichengreen and Wyplosz (1993).

35. The evidence on the loss of credibility generated by countries dropping out of the EMS in 1992 and the substantial widening of the band of permissible exchange rate fluctuations in 1993 was less clear. Masera argues that for Italy, "the traumatic steps to more flexible exchange rates in the EMS have caused a significant loss in the central bank's credibility" (1994:285). For the U.K., however, any loss of credibility was insufficient to keep long-term bond rates from falling from 10 to 7 percent over the following year. See Gilibert (1994).

36. This potential advantage of exchange rate anchors has been stressed by a number of writers. See, for example, Bruno (1991b) and Bofinger et al. (1997). If devaluation is expected to be contractionary rather than expansionary, then this should also increase the credibility of a peg. See the analysis and references in Welch and McLeod (1993).

37. See also Bofinger et al. (1997). On the role of international currency substitution in increasing the case for exchange rate anchors, see Calvo and Végh (1994).

38. On the role of political instability in reducing the credibility of exchange rate commitments, see Al-Marhubi (1996) and Edwards (1996).

39. See, for example, Bean (1992) and Corden (1994). Somewhat surprisingly, Bloomberg and Hess (1997) find that exchange rate movements have no systematic effect on government approval ratings in Germany, the United Kingdom and the United States over the last two decades. Of course, devaluations would likely have greater political costs than depreciations under flexible rates.

40. See Chapter 7 by Martin, Westbrook and Willett.

41. Citing Poland as a successful case, Sachs (1996a) has criticized the IMF for not doing more to provide currency stabilization loans for other former communist countries. On the IMF's external assistance in the former Soviet Union, see Brau (1995). On the role of external assistance in stabilization policy see also Karagodin (1996) and on the successful role of the League of Nations in the 1920s, see Santabello (1993).

42. The political economy of these issues is a fertile area for future research. See, for example, Kahler (1992).

43. See, for example, Flood and Mussa (1994).

44. See Willett (1987) and (1995b).

45. See the analysis and references in Burdekin and Willett (1995).

46. Blanchard et al. (1991:5) make an important related point. "A tough package would seem more credible, but the effects on economic activity may be so drastic as to be unnecessarily painful, and more important, to force withdrawal of the program. This implies that tough programs may not be politically sustainable, and hence risk not being credible."

47. For additional analysis of the credibility effects of different degrees of commitment versus flexibility see Cukierman, Kiguel, and Liviatan (1995), Dixit (1996:65–80), Eichengreen (1994:31–5) and Lohmann (1992).

48. On the importance of clear explanations of policy to the public, see also Bruno (1993) and Leiderman (1993).

49. See, for example, Saavalainen (1995) and the following chapters by Dubauskas, Wihlborg and Willett. Some currency board advocates might argue that this is because these were not true full-fledged currency boards. On this issue, see the chapters in Part IV of this volume.

50. Williamson (1991) offers an interesting explanation for this. He argues that continuing inflationary pressures may be due more to the inconsistency of real income claims, stressed by writers such as Hirsch and Goldthorpe (1978), rather than to rational inflationary expectations and that the former cause is less influenced by precommitment strategies. Thus he is critical of the use of exchange rates as nominal anchors. For a recent treatment of the inconsistent claims approach, see Burdekin and Burkett (1996).

51. On the issues involved in selecting a basket versus a single-currency peg, see Argy (1990). Bofinger et al. (1997) emphasize that the published figures suggest that the output cost of stabilization was considerably higher for Latvia under flexible rates than for Estonia under fixed rates, and criticize Zettelmeyer and Citrin's (1995) conclusion that the published figures overstate the actual difference. On the other hand, Begg (1996:16) concludes that "comparison of Estonia and Latvia offers no easy confirmation of the general superiority of exchange rate based stabilization," while Saavalainen (1995:14) argues that "the Baltic experience does not appear to support the commonly held hypothesis that the use of a fixed exchange rate is more successful in reducing inflation than the use of money-based stabilization policies." This is obviously an important topic for further research.

52. On central bank independence see the analysis and references in Willett et al. (1995). On recent research and discussion of policy experiences with inflation targeting see Bernanke and Mishkin (1997), Panizza (1997), Mishkin and Posen (1997), and Svensson (1997).

References

Agénor, Pierre-Richard. 1995. "Credibility Effects of Price Controls in Disinflation Programs." *Journal of Macroeconomics*, Winter: 161–71.

Agénor, Pierre-Richard, and Carlos Asilis. 1997. "Price Controls and Election Cycles." *European Journal of Political Economy*, February: 131–42.

Al-Marhubi, Fahim. 1996. "Cross-Country Evidence on the Link Between Exchange Rate Fixity and Inflation." Mimeo. Sultan Qaboos University, Oman.

Al-Marhubi, Fahim, and Thomas D. Willett. 1997. "Exchange Rate Pegging versus Central Bank Independence to Control Inflationary Biases: The Relevance of Optimum Currency Area Theory." Working Paper, Claremont Graduate School.

Anderson, Jonathan, and Daniel Citrin. 1995. "The Behavior of Income and Velocity," in Daniel Citrin and Ashok Lahiri, eds., *Policy Experiences and Issues in the Baltics, Russia, and other Countries of the Former Soviet Union*. Pp. 44–62. IMF Occasional Paper No. 133. Washington, D.C.: International Monetary Fund.

Andrews, David, and Thomas D. Willett. 1997. "Financial Interdependence and the State." *International Organization* 51(3): 470–511.

Argy, Victor. 1990. "Choice of Exchange Rate Regime for a Smaller Economy," in Victor Argy and Paul De Grauwe, eds., *Choosing an Exchange Rate Regime*. Pp. 6–81. Washington, D.C.: International Monetary Fund.

Arndt, Sven, Richard Sweeney, and Thomas D. Willett, eds. 1985. *Exchange Rates, Trade, and the U.S. Economy*. Cambridge, Mass.: Ballinger.

Balcerowicz, Leszek, Barbara Blaszczyk and Marek Dabrowski. 1997. "The Polish Way to the Market Economy 1989–1995," in Wing Woo, Stephan Parker, and Jeffrey Sachs, eds., *Economies in Transition*. Pp. 131–60. Cambridge, Mass.: MIT Press.

Banaian, King, and Eugenue Zhukov. 1995. "The Collapse of the Ruble Zone," in Thomas D. Willett et al., eds., *Establishing Monetary Stability in Emerging Market Economies*. Pp. 209–30. Boulder, Colo.: Westview Press.

Bean, Charles. 1992. "Economic and Monetary Union in Europe." *Journal of Economic Perspectives*, Fall: 31–52.

Begg, David. 1997. "Monetary Policy During Transition: Progress and Pitfalls in Central and Eastern Europe, 1990–96." *Oxford Review of Economic Policy* 12 (Summer): 33–46.

———. 1996. "Monetary Policy in Central and Eastern Europe." IMF Working Paper No. 96–108. Washington, D.C.: International Monetary Fund, September.

Bernanke, Ben, and Frederic Mishkin. 1997. "Inflation Targeting: A New Framework for Monetary Policy?" *Journal of Economic Perspectives*, Spring: 97–116.

Bini-Smaghi, Lorenzo, and Stefano Micossi. 1990. "Monetary and Exchange Rate Policy in the EMS with Free Capital Mobility," in Paul De Grauwe and Lucas Papdemos, eds., *The European Monetary System in the 1990s*. Pp. 120–55. London: Longman.

Blanchard, Olivier, Rudiger Dornbusch, Paul Krugman, Richard Layard, and Lawrency Summers. 1991. *Reform in Eastern Europe*. Cambridge, Mass.: MIT.

Blanchard, Olivier, and Pierre Muet. 1993. "Competitiveness Through Disinflation: An Assessment of the French Macroeconomic Strategy." *Economic Policy,* April: 12–44.

Blomberg, S.B., and Gregory D. Hess. 1997. "Politics and Exchange Rate Forecasts." *Journal of International Economics,* August: 189–205.

Bofinger, Peter, Heiner Flassbeck, and Lutz Hoffman. 1997. "Orthodox Money-Based Stabilization (OMBS) versus Heterodox Exchange Rate-Based Stabilization (HERBS): The Case of Russia, the Ukraine and Kazakhstan." *Economic Systems*, March: 1–33.

Boone, Peter, and Boris Fedorov. 1997. "The Ups and Downs of Russian Economic Reforms," in Wing Woo, Stephan Parker, and Jeffrey Sachs, eds., *Economies in Transition.* Pp. 161–88. Cambridge, Mass.: MIT Press.
Branson, William H., and Jorge Braga de Macedo. 1995. "Macroeconomic Policy in Central Europe." CEPR Working Paper No. 1195. London: Centre for Economic Policy Research, August.
Brau, Eduard. 1995. "External Financial Assistance," in Daniel Citrin and Ashok Lahiri, eds., *Policy Experiences and Issues in the Baltics, Russia, and other Countries of the Former Soviet Union.* Pp. 103–116. IMF Occasional Paper No. 133. Washington, D.C.: International Monetary Fund.
Bruno, Michael. 1993. *Crisis, Stabilization, and Economic Reform.* Oxford: Oxford University Press.
———. 1991a. "Introduction and Overview," in Bruno et al., eds., *Lessons of Economic Stabilization and Its Aftermath.* Pp. 1–14. Cambridge, Mass.: MIT Press.
———. 1991b. "High Inflation and the Nominal Anchors of an Open Economy." Essays in International Finance No. 183. Princeton: Princeton University.
Bruno, Michael, Stanley Fischer, Elhanan Helpman and Nissan Liviatan, eds. 1991. *Lessons of Economic Stabilization and Its Aftermath.* Cambridge: MIT Press.
Burdekin, Richard C. K. 1995. "Budget Deficits and Inflation: The Importance of Budget Controls for Monetary Stability," in Thomas D. Willett, Richard C. K. Burdekin, Richard J. Sweeney and Clas Wihlborg, eds., *Establishing Monetary Stability in Emerging Market Economies.* Pp. 33–61. Boulder, Colo.: Westview Press.
Burdekin, Richard C. K., and Paul Burkett. 1996. *Distributional Conflict and Inflation.* New York: St Martin's Press.
Burdekin, Richard C. K., Jilleen Westbrook, Thomas D. Willett. 1998. "The Political Economy of Discretionary Monetary Policy: A Public Choice Analysis of Proposals for Reform," in Richard Timberlake and Keven Dowd, eds., *Money and the Nation State: The Financial Revolution, Government and the World Monetary System.* New Brunswick, N.J.: Transaction Publishers.
———. 1994. "Exchange Rate Pegging as a Disinflation Strategy: Evidence from the European Monetary System," in Pierre Siklos, ed., *Varieties of Monetary Reform: Lessons and Experiences on the Road to Monetary Union.* Pp. 42–72. Boston: Kluwer.
Burdekin, Richard, and Thomas D. Willett. 1995. "Designing Central Bank Arrangements to Promote Monetary Stability," in Thomas D. Willett, Richard C. K. Burdekin, Richard Sweeney, and Clas Wihlborg, eds., *Establishing Monetary Stability in Emerging Market Economies.* Pp. 115–26. Boulder, Colo.: Westview.
Budina, Nina, and Sweder Van Wijnbergen. 1997. "Fiscal Policies in Eastern Europe." *Oxford Review of Economic Policy* 13 (Summer): 47–64.
Calvo, Guillermo, and Enrique Mendoza. 1996. "Petty Crime and Cruel Punishment: Lessons from the Mexican Debacle." *American Economic Review*, May: 170–75.
Calvo, Guillermo, Ratnay Sahay, and Carlos Végh. 1995. "Capital Flows in Central and Eastern Europe: Evidence and Policy Options." IMF Working Paper No. 95/57. Washington, D.C.: International Monetary Fund, May.

Calvo, Guillermo, and Carlos Végh. 1994. "Inflation Stabilization and Nominal Anchors," in Richard C. Barth and Chorng-Huey Wong, eds., *Approaches to Exchange Rate Policy: Choices for Developing and Transition Economies.* Pp. 90–102. Washington, D.C.: International Monetary Fund.

Christensen, Michael. 1987a. "Disinflation, Credibility and Price Inertia: A Danish Exposition." *Applied Economics,* October: 1353–66.

———. 1987b. "On Interest Rate Determination, Testing for Policy Credibility and the Relevance of the Lucas Critique—Some Danish Experiences." *European Journal of Political Economy* 3: 369–88.

———. 1990. "Policy Credibility and the Lucas Critique—Some New Tests with an Application to Denmark," in Patrick Artus and Yves Barroux, eds., *Monetary Policy: A Theoretical and Econometric Approach.* Pp. 79–95. Boston: Kluwer Academic Press.

Claasen, Emile-Maria, ed. 1991. *Exchange Rate Policies in Developing and Post-Socialist Countries.* San Francisco: ICS Press.

Coles, Melvyn, and Apostolis Philippopoulos. 1997. "Are Exchange Rate Bands Better than Fixed Exchange Rates? The Imported Credibility Approach." *Journal of International Economics,* August: 133–53.

Collins, Susan. 1988. "Inflation and the European Monetary System," in Francesco Giavazzi, Stefano Micossi and Marcus Miller, eds., *The European Monetary System.* Pp. 112–36. Cambridge: Cambridge University Press.

Cooper, Richard N. 1991. "Opening the Soviet Economy," in Merton J. Peck and Thomas J. Richardson, eds., *What Is to Be Done? Proposals for the Soviet Transition to the Market.* Pp. 116–32. New Haven: Yale University Press.

Corden, W. Max. 1994. "Exchange Rate Policy in Developing Countries," in Richard C. Barth and Chorng-Huey Wong, eds., *Approaches to Exchange Rate Policy: Choices for Developing and Transition Economies.* Pp. 65–89. Washington, D.C.: International Monetary Fund.

Cukierman, Alex, Miguel Kiguel, and Nissan Liviatan. 1995. "How Much to Commit to an Exchange Rate Rule: Balancing Credibility and Flexibility," in Pierre Siklos, ed., *Varieties of Monetary Reforms: Lessons and Experiences on the Road to Monetary Union.* Pp. 73–94. Boston: Kluwer.

De Cecco, Marcello, and Francesco Giavazzi. 1994. "Italy's Experience within and without the European Monetary System: A Preliminary Appraisal," in J. de Beaufort Wijnholds, Sylvester Eijffinger and Lex Hoogdvin, eds., *A Framework for Monetary Stability.* Pp. 221–38. Boston: Kluwer.

De Fontenay, Patrick. 1995. "Using Exchange Rate Anchors in Adjustment Programs: When and How?" *IMF Survey,* November 20: 361–63.

De Grauwe, Paul. 1994. "Towards EMU without the EMS." *Economic Policy,* April: 149–74.

Dixit, Avinash. 1996. *The Making of Economic Policy: A Transactions Costs Politics Perspective.* Cambridge, Mass.: MIT Press.

Easterly, William. 1996. "When Is Stabilization Expansionary? Evidence from High Inflation." *Economic Policy,* April: 67–98.

Edwards, Sebastian. 1997. "Trade Liberalization Reform and the World Bank." *American Economic Review,* May: 43–8.

————. 1996. "Exchange Rates and the Political Economy of Macroeconomic Discipline." *American Economic Review*, May: 159–63.

————. 1994. "Exchange Rate Misalignment in Developing Countries," in Richard C. Barth and Chorng-Huey Wong, eds., *Approaches to Exchange Rate Policy.* Pp. 45–64. Washington, D.C.: International Monetary Fund.

————. 1993. "Exchange Rates as Nominal Anchors." *Weltwirtschaftliches Archiv* 129(1): 1–32.

Eichengreen, Barry. 1994. *International Monetary Arrangements for the 21st Century.* Washington, D.C.: Brookings Institute.

Eichengreen, Barry, and Charles Wyplosz. 1993. "The Unstable EMS." *Brookings Papers on Economic Activity*: 51–143.

Fanelli, José María, and Gary McMahon. 1996. "Economic Lessons for Eastern Europe from Latin America," in Gary McMahon, ed., *Lessons in Economic Policy for Eastern Europe from Latin America.* Pp. 1–42. New York: St. Martin's Press.

Fisher, Stanley. 1986. "Exchange Rates versus Monetary Targets in Disinflation," in Stanley Fisher, ed., *Indexing, Inflation, and Economic Policy.* Pp. 247–62. Cambridge: MIT Press.

Fisher, Stanley, Ratna Sahay, and Carlos Végh. 1996. "Stabilization and Growth in Transition Economies: The Early Experience." *Journal of Economic Perspectives*, Spring: 45–66.

Flood, Robert P., and Michael Mussa. 1994. "Issues Concerning Nominal Anchors for Monetary Policy," in Tomás J. T. Baliño and Carlo Cottarelli, eds., *Framework for Monetary Stability.* Pp. 42–80. Washington, D.C.: International Monetary Fund.

Frankel, Jeffrey. 1996. "Recent Exchange Rate Experience and Proposals for Reform." *American Economic Review*, May: 153–58.

Fratianni, Michele, and Jürgen von Hagen. 1992. *The European Monetary System and European Monetary Union.* Boulder, Colo.: Westview Press.

Frenkel, Jacob. 1991. "Panel Discussion," in Michael Bruno et al., eds., *Lessons of Economic Stabilization and Its Aftermath.* Pp. 400–3. Cambridge: MIT Press.

Frenkel, Jacob, Morris Goldstein and Paul R. Masson. 1991. "Characteristics of a Successful Exchange Rate System." IMF Occasional Paper No. 82. Washington, D.C.: International Monetary Fund.

Ghosh, Atish, Ann-Marie Gulde, Jonathan D. Ostry, and Holger Wolf. 1996. "Does the Exchange Rate Regime Matter for Inflation and Growth?" IMF Economic Issues Series No. 2. Washington, D.C.: International Monetary Fund.

Giavazzi, Francesco, and Alberto Giovannini. 1988. "The Role of the Exchange-Rate Regime in Disinflation: Empirical Evidence on the European Monetary System," in Francesco Giavazzi, Stefano Micossi and Marcus Miller, eds., *The European Monetary System.* Pp. 85–107. Cambridge: Cambridge University Press.

Giavazzi, Francesco, and Marco Pagano. 1988. "The Advantage of Tying One's Hands: EMS Discipline and Central Bank Credibility." *European Economic Review* 32 (June): 1055–82.

Giavazzi, Francesco, and Luigi Spaventa. 1990. "The New EMS," in Paul De Grauwe and Lucas Papademos, eds., *The European Monetary System in the 1990's.* Pp. 65–85. London: Longman.

Gil-Díaz, Francisco, and Agustín Carstens. 1996. "One Year of Solitude: Some Pilgrim Tales about Mexico's 1994–1995 Crisis." *American Economic Review*, May: 164–69.

Gilibert, Pier Luigi. 1994. "Living Dangerously: The Lira and the Pound in a Floating World," in Alfred Steinherr, ed., *Thirty Years of European Monetary Integration*. Pp. 105–42. London: Longman.

Gould, David. 1996. "Does the Choice of Nominal Anchor Matter?" Mimeo. Federal Reserve Bank of Dallas.

Hansson, Ardo, and Jeffrey Sachs. 1994. "Monetary Institutions and Credible Stabilization: A Comparison of Experience in the Baltics." Mimeo, Harvard University.

Helpman, Elhanan, Leonardo Leiderman and Gil Bufman. 1994. "A New Breed of Exchange Rate Bands: Chile, Israel, and Mexico." *Economic Policy*, October: 260–306.

Hirsch, Fred, and John Goldthorpe, eds. 1978. *The Political Economy of Inflation*. Cambridge, Mass.: Harvard University Press.

Hochreiter, Eduard. 1997. "Necessary Conditions for a Successful Hard Currency," this volume.

Hochreiter, Eduard, and Henry Winckler. 1995. "The Advantages of Tying Austria's Hands: The Success of the Austrian Hard Currency Policy." *European Journal of Political Economy* 11(1): 83–111.

Janáčková, Stanislava. 1996. "Certain Specific Features of Monetary Policy in the Czech Republic." *Eastern European Economics*, January/February: 60–74.

Kahler, Miles. 1992. "External Influence, Conditionality, and the Politics of Adjustment," in Stephan Haggard and Robert Kaufman, eds., *The Politics of Economic Adjustment*. Pp. 90–138. Princeton: Princeton University Press.

Kapopoulos, Panayotis. 1995. "Disinflation and Credibility in Small Open European Economies in the 1980s." *European Journal of Political Economy* 11(1): 157–70.

Karagodin, Nikolay. 1996. "Lessons of Monetary Policy in Latin America," in Gary McMahon, ed., *Lessons in Economic Policy for Eastern Europe from Latin America*. Pp. 146–80. New York: St. Martin's Press.

Khamis, May. 1996. "Credit and Exchange Rate Based Stabilization." IMF Working Paper No. 96-51. Washington, D.C.: International Monetary Fund, May.

Kiguel, Miguel, and Nissan Liviatan. 1992. "The Business Cycle Associated with Exchange Rate Based Stabilization Programs." *The World Bank Economic Review* 6(2): 279–305.

———. 1991. "Stopping Inflation: The Experience of Latin America and Israel and the Implications for Central and Eastern Europe," in Vittorio Corbo, Fabrizio Coricelli and Jan Bossak, eds. *Reforming Central and Eastern European Economies: Initial Results and Challenges*. A World Bank Symposium. Pp. 85–100. Washington, D.C.: World Bank.

Lachler, Ulrich. 1985. "Credibility and the Dynamics of Disinflation in Open Economies." *Journal of Development Economics*, May: 285–307.

Leiderman, Leonardo. 1993. *Inflation and Disinflation: The Israeli Experiment*. Chicago: University of Chicago Press.

Lohmann, Susanne. 1992. "Optimal Commitment in Monetary Policy: Credibility v. Flexibility." *American Economic Review*, March: 273–86.

Masera, Rainer. 1994. "Single Market, Exchange Rates, and Monetary Unification," in Alfred Steinherr, ed. *Thirty Years of European Monetary Integration.* Pp. 266–87. London: Longman.

Mast, Tamara. 1996. *The Import and Feedback Effects of Nominal Exchange Rates on Real Exchange Rates.* Ph.D. Dissertation, Claremont Graduate School.

McMahon, Gary, ed. 1996. *Lessons in Economic Policy for Eastern Europe from Latin America.* New York: St. Martin's Press.

Mishkin, Fredric, and Adam Posen. 1997. "Inflation Targeting." *Economic Policy Review*, Federal Reserve Bank of New York, August: 9–110.

Obstfeld, Maurice. 1997. "Destabilizing Effects of Exchange-Rate Escape Clauses." *Journal of International Economics*, August: 61–77.

———. 1995. "International Currency Experience." *Brookings Papers on Economic Activity* 1: 119–96.

Papell, David. 1994. "Exchange Rates and Prices: An Empirical Analysis." *International Economic Review*, May: 397–410.

Panizza, Ugo. 1997. "Optimal Contracts for Central Bankers: Inflation versus Money Supply and Exchange Rate Targets." *Open Economies Review*, January: 5–29.

Paredes, Carlos E., and Jeffrey D. Sachs. 1991. *Peru's Path to Recovery. A Plan for Economic Stabilization and Growth.* Washington, D.C.: Brookings Institution.

Pikoulakis, Emanual. 1990. "Efficient and Credible Exchange Rate and Monetary Policies for Stabilizing the Economy," in Anthony S. Courakis and Mark P. Taylor, eds., *Private Behavior and Government Policy in Interdependent Economies.* Pp. 355–372. Oxford: Clarenden Press.

Quirk, Peter J. 1996. "Exchange Rate Regimes as Inflation Anchors." *Finance and Development*, March: 42–45.

———. 1994. "Fixed or Floating Exchange Rate Regime: Does It Matter for Inflation?" International Monetary Fund Working Paper No. 94/134. Washington, D.C.: International Monetary Fund, November.

Rebelo, Sérgio, and Carlos A. Végh. 1995. "Real Effects of Exchange-Rate-Based Stabilization: An Analysis of Competing Theories," in Ben Bernanke and Julio Rotemberg, eds., *NBER Macroeconomics Annual.* Pp. 125–74. Cambridge Mass.: MIT Press.

Rodgers, John H., and Ping Wang. 1995. "Real Exchange Rate Movements in High Inflation Countries." International Finance Discussion Papers No. 501. Washington, D.C.: Board of Governors of the Federal Reserve System, February.

Rodrick, Dani. 1995. "Trade Liberalization in Disinflation," in Peter Kenen, ed., *Understanding Interdependence.* Pp. 291–312. Princeton: Princeton University Press.

Rogoff, Kenneth. 1985. "Can International Monetary Cooperation Be Counterproductive?" *Journal of International Economics*, May: 199–217.

Rose, Andrew. 1993. "Sterling's ERM Credibility." *Economic Letters* 41(4): 419–27.

Saavalainen, Tapio O. 1995. "Stabilization in the Baltics: A Comparative Analysis." IMF Working Paper No. 95/95. Washington, D.C.: International Monetary Fund.

Sachs, Jeffrey. 1997. "An Overview of Stabilization Issues Facing Economies in Transition," in Wing Woo, Stephan Parker, and Jeffrey Sachs, eds., *Economies in Transition.* Pp. 243–56. Cambridge, Mass.: MIT Press.

———. 1996a. "The Transition at Mid Decade." *American Economic Review*, May: 128–33.

———. 1996b. "Economic Transitions and the Exchange Rate Regime." *American Economic Review*, May: 147–52.

———. 1995. "Comment" on Rebelo and Végh in Ben Bernanke and Julio Rotemberg, eds., *NBER Macroeconomics Annual.* Pp. 180–85. Cambridge, Mass.: MIT Press.

Sachs, Jeffrey, Aaron Tornell and Andris Velasco. 1996. "The Collapse of the Mexican Peso: What Have We Learned?" *Economic Policy*, April: 15–56.

Santabello, Julio. 1993. "Stabilization Programs and External Enforcement." *IMF Staff Papers*, September: 584–621.

Sargent, Thomas J. 1986. *Rational Expectations and Inflation.* New York: Harper and Row.

Schuknecht, Ludger. 1996. "Fiscal Cycles and the Exchange Rate Regime in Developing Countries." Mimeo, International Monetary Fund, Washington, D.C.

Siklos, Pierre. 1997. "The Connection between Exchange Rate Regimes and Credibility: An International Perspective," in *Exchange Rates and Monetary Policy.* Pp. 73–121. Ottawa: Bank of Canada.

Simons, Beth. 1994. *Who Adjusts?* Princeton: Princeton University Press.

Svensson, Lars E. O. 1997. "Inflation Forecast Targeting: Implementing and Monitoring Inflation Targets." *European Economic Review*, June: 1111–46.

———. 1994. "Fixed Exchange Rates as a Means to Price Stability: What Have We Learned?" *European Economic Review*, April: 447–68.

Végh, Carlos. 1992. "Stopping High Inflation: An Analytical Overview." *IMF Staff Papers*, September: 626–95.

von Hagen, Jürgen. 1990. "Policy-Delegation and Fixed Exchange Rates." Mimeo, Indiana University, February.

Welch, John, and Darryl McLeod. 1993. "The Costs and Benefits of Fixed Dollar Exchange Rates in Latin America." *Economic Review*, Federal Reserve Bank of Dallas, First Quarter: 31–44.

Westbrook, Jilleen R. 1997. "Tests of Credibility Effects from EMS Membership Using Survey Data." Unpublished manuscript, Temple University.

———. 1995. "Does Exchange Rate Pegging Enhance Credibility? Evidence from the EMS." *Applied Economics,* December: 1153–66.

Wihlborg, Clas, and Thomas D. Willett. 1991. "Optimum Currency Areas Revisited," in Clas Wihlborg, Michele Fratianni, and Thomas D. Willett, eds., *Financial Regulation and Monetary Arrangements After 1992.* Pp. 274–97. Amsterdam: North-Holland.

Willett, Thomas D. 1995a. "The Plunge of the Peso: The Danger of Exchange Rate Based Stabilization Policy." Claremont Policy Briefs No. 95–01. Claremont, Calif.: Lowe Institute for Economic Policy Studies.

———. 1995b. "Guidelines for Constructing Monetary Constitutions," in Thomas D. Willett, Richard C. K. Burdekin, Richard J. Sweeney, and Clas Wihlborg, eds., *Establishing Monetary Stability in Emerging Market Economies.* Pp. 103–14. Boulder, Colo.: Westview Press.

———. 1987. "A New Monetary Constitution," in James Dorn and Anna Schwartz, eds., *The Search for Stable Money.* Pp. 145–60. Chicago: University of Chicago.

Willett, Thomas D., and Fahim Al-Marhubi. 1994. "Currency Policies for Inflation Control in the Formerly Centrally Planned Economies." *The World Economy*, November: 795–815

Willett, Thomas D., Richard C. K. Burdekin, Richard J. Sweeney, and Clas Wihlborg, eds. 1995. *Establishing Monetary Stability in Emerging Market Economies*. Boulder, Colo.: Westview Press.

Willett, Thomas D., and John Mullen. 1982. "The Effects of Alternative International Monetary Systems on Macroeconomic Discipline and Inflationary Biases," in Raymond E. Lombra and Willard E. Witte, eds., *Political Economy of International and Domestic Monetary Relations*. Pp. 143–55. Ames, Iowa: Iowa State University Press.

Willett, Thomas D., and Clas Wihlborg. 1991. "International Capital Flows, the Dollar, and U.S. Financial Policies," in William Haraf and Thomas D. Willett, eds., *Monetary Policy for a Volatile World Economy*. Pp. 51–88. Washington, D.C.: American Enterprise Institute.

Williamson, John. 1991. "Comment" on Miguel Kiguel and Nissan Liviatan "Stopping Inflation: The Experience of Latin America and Israel and the Implications for Central and Eastern Europe," in Vittorio Corbo, Fabrizio Coricelli and Jan Bossak, eds. *Reforming Central and Eastern European Economies: Initial Results and Challenges*. A World Bank Symposium. Pp. 101. Washington, D.C.: World Bank.

Woo, Wing, Stephan Parker, and Jeffrey Sachs, eds. 1997. *Economies in Transition*. Cambridge, Mass.: MIT Press.

Zarazaga, Carlos. 1995. "Argentina, Mexico and Currency Boards." *Economic Review*, Federal Reserve Bank of Dallas, Fourth Quarter: 14–24.

Zettelmeyer, Jeromin, and Daniel Citrin. 1995. "Stabilization: Fixed versus Flexible Rates," in Daniel Citrin and Ashok Lahiri, eds., *Policy Experiences and Issues in the Baltics, Russia and Other Countries of the Former Soviet Union*. Pp. 93–102. IMF Occasional Paper No. 133. Washington, D.C.: International Monetary Fund.

5

Central European Exchange Rate Policy and Inflation

Richard C. K. Burdekin, Heidi Nelson,
and Thomas D. Willett

Introduction

The Central European economies of the former Czechoslovakia (since 1993 the Czech Republic and Slovakia), Hungary and Poland provide interesting examples of alternative exchange rate policies during the transition from centrally planned to market-based economies. Many of the Eastern European economies, such as Bulgaria, Romania, Slovenia and Russia itself, had little choice but to opt for flexible exchange rates because of low levels of international reserves and limited access to international credit.[1] The Central European economies were able to adopt pegged exchange rates due to a combination of their own international reserve positions and (importantly) support from the International Monetary Fund and other stabilization programs. The forms of pegged rate systems adopted, however, were quite different.[2]

In this chapter, we discuss the rationale for the different choice of exchange rate systems among the Central European economies. We also contrast the durability of the Czech fixed peg, which held until the summer of 1997, with the more transitory Polish attempts at exchange rate fixity in 1990. We argue that optimum currency area (OCA) considerations combine with different domestic macroeconomic conditions to account for the different outcomes in Poland and the former Czechoslovakia. The Polish case, in our view, highlights the difficulties of using a pegged exchange rate as a nominal anchor to attempt to stabilize high rates of inflation. The Czech Republic, on the other hand, illustrates the danger of how even a "successful" peg can lead to imported inflationary pressures from abroad and also how quickly a strong balance of payments position can sometimes turn into a weak one.

The Hungarian Experience

Of the three Central European economies, Hungary began with the largest market-based component to its economy as well as the highest level of international reserves. But the Hungarian authorities did not attempt to defend a fixed exchange rate peg. Rather, they followed a policy of adjusting the peg from time to time. Typically the devaluations of the forint were small—in the 1 to 3 percent range—and changes were sufficiently frequent that we label this adjustable peg system a discretionary crawling peg system. As discussed by Pál Gáspár in Chapter 16, the initial Hungarian stabilization program was based upon monetary targeting rather than exchange rate targeting—with exchange rate policy geared more toward improving the trade balance. As monetary policy turned more expansionary in the early 1990s, greater weight was given to the exchange rate in fighting inflation. The form of the crawling peg was changed in March 1995, when the Hungarian authorities followed Poland's lead and adopted a preannounced crawl for the exchange rate following a substantial 9 percent devaluation.

Thus although Hungary is sometimes classified as having had an exchange rate based anchor program, this does not appear to actually have been the case until the mid-1990s. Krzak (1996:62) concludes that the crawling peg "failed to provide a nominal anchor for inflationary expectations." Exchange rate considerations did not prevent the Hungarian government from adopting a loose fiscal stance and the monetary authorities from following generally accommodative policies.

After three years of gradually slowing inflation from a peak of 35 percent in 1991 to below 20 percent, inflation began to accelerate, prompting financial crises and the adoption of a new stabilization program in March 1995. After a step devaluation of 8 percent in August 1994 proved insufficient to stabilize the foreign exchange market, the new stabilization program included another step devaluation of 9 percent, but also switched the exchange rate to a preannounced crawl similar to the regime which had been earlier adopted by Poland. Initially the credibility of this regime (with a downward crawl set at approximately 14 percent a year) was suspect in the foreign exchange market with forward rates suggesting a much greater expected depreciation than would be permitted by the preannounced crawl. Within a year, however, the forward discount had fallen to a level consistent with the announced rate of crawl. OECD (1997b) gives a mixed evaluation of the success of the new exchange rate regime. OECD (1997b:30) notes that with the 1995 program price stability became the official aim of monetary policy and argues:

As an integral element in the overall stabilization programme, the Hungarian authorities adopted a crawling peg regime, with fairly narrow bands, to serve as a nominal anchor against speculative attacks on the currency. Success has been achieved in this regard ...The crawling-peg exchange rate regime has acted as an effective anchor for inflation expectations, and makes for a more predictable policy environment.

OECD (1997b:4) also notes, however, that there is

a persisting contradiction between the central bank's aim of price stability and an exchange rate/interest rate stance which is effectively assigned to preserving external competitiveness and hence cushioning output and employment ... [T]he high costs of inflation call for a faster rate of disinflation.

The Polish Experience

Facing far greater initial problems of macroeconomic stabilization and transformation, both Czechoslovakia and Poland opted for fixed pegs that, it was hoped, would act as a nominal anchor for domestic prices.[3] Based on optimum currency area criteria, Poland would not otherwise have been considered a likely candidate for a fixed exchange rate peg. In terms of economic openness as measured by the total share of exports and imports in gross domestic product, Poland was the most closed of these economies in 1992 with a ratio of 32.1 percent compared to Hungary's 61.8 percent and the Czech Republic's 76 percent. Optimum currency area theory suggests that countries with lower degrees of openness are better suited to flexible, rather than fixed, exchange rate systems.[4] Moreover, Polish liberalization favored the import side, which helped to fuel a growing balance of payments deficit. Though the large initial devaluation prior to pegging the exchange rate in January 1990 temporarily boosted the trade balance, the scale of this devaluation may itself have contributed significantly to the growing inflationary pressures which led to the zloty having to be devalued again in May 1991 (see Chapter 17 by Kowalski and Stawarska in this volume).

We do not seek here to provide a full account of why the Polish authorities decided to adopt a temporarily fixed exchange rate peg as part of their anti-inflationary policies in January 1990. But particular emphasis seems to have been attached to the direct role of price competition from international traded goods to help break inflationary momentum. As discussed in Chapter 4 by Westbrook and Willett, exchange rate pegging can, in this way, be a potentially useful complement to domestic stabilization policies. A major problem lies, however, in calculating how large an initial devaluation is needed to put the exchange rate on a sufficiently competitive level for its maintenance to be credible, at least for the short term. Despite its inflationary effects, the general rule of thumb is that one should err on the side of over-devaluation—as the Poles did—since underdevaluation, insofar as it spurs an early speculative run on the currency, is likely to undercut efforts to establish the credibility of the overall stabilization program.[5]

In the Polish case, given the combination of uncertainty about the course of domestic inflation and the level of the equilibrium real exchange rate, the range of opinion about the appropriate level at which to peg the zloty was especially great. Wolf (1994:251) reports a range of expert estimates for the correct zloty exchange rate running from 6,500 zlotys to 13,000 zlotys per U.S. dollar; Kowalski and Stawarska report an even wider range. Ultimately, the initial rate was set at 9,500 zlotys per dollar, close to the black market rate. It has been commonly argued that this was an excessive devaluation and contributed to the continuation of high inflation in the initial stages of the stabilization program.

Imposition of the exchange rate peg requires, of course, not only the will to adopt the policy but also some modicum of financial resources with which to defend it. In this respect, a critical element was surely the provision of a $1 billion stabilization fund from the International Monetary Fund which, together with a $215 million loan from the Bank for International Settlements, augmented Poland's own meager level of exchange reserves (see Kowalski and Stawarska, Chapter 17, for further discussion). This new-found supply of hard currency may, in turn, help explain why the announcement of currency convertibility induced Polish citizens to rush to the banks not to sell zlotys but rather to buy zlotys with their dollar savings. In any event, the announcement of the stabilization program is claimed to have boosted Poland's foreign exchange reserves owing to growing, albeit short-lived, confidence in the zloty (see Sachs 1993:54). It still seems that foreign assistance played a critical role, however.

In part because of restrictive fiscal policy and wage curbs, Poland's inflation continued to decline rather than accelerate after the initial January 1990 devaluation, and the government was able to hold the new level of the zloty for almost a year and a half, far longer than had been initially hoped. The discount on the parallel market relative to the official rate remained low throughout most of 1991. Toward the end of the year the discount began to mount, however, in line with worries over the balance of payments. The zloty was devalued by 15 percent on May 17, 1990. The peg was also switched from the dollar to a basket of currencies at that time. In October a pre-announced crawl was initiated, with the zloty depreciating at a rate of 1.8 percent per month. The rationale for this strategy was to give short-run certainty for international trade and investment while avoiding a secular decline in competitiveness.

The rate of preannounced crawl for the zloty was selected to less than fully offset the current inflation differential so that the exchange rate, even while adjusting, could still play a role in lowering inflation over time. (In the European Monetary System exchange rate adjustments were supposed to be less than inflation differentials on similar grounds.) Such a strategy has merit as a sensible compromise between gearing exchange rate policy exclusively to domestic stabilization or to external balance. It is very difficult to implement successfully, however. Poland's policy has quite appropriately been labeled successful (see, for example, Otker 1994) to the extent that the hyperinflation was contained and the inflation rate substantially lowered. The preannounced crawl has not been successful, however, in terms of the more stringent criterion of continued progress toward lowering inflation to single-digit levels.[6]

Even though the new preannounced crawling peg policy was itself preceded by a sharp devaluation in October 1991, further step devaluations were imposed in February 1992 and August 1993. Krzak (1996:56) concludes that the "one-off devaluations...compromised the anchoring feature of the preannounced crawl." This trend was finally reversed, however, as Poland's relative stability and renewed economic growth began to attract substantial capital inflows. The new upward pressure on the exchange rate was met, first, by widening the band for permissible exchange rate fluctuations from 2 percent to 7 percent in May 1995 and then by revaluing the zloty by 6 percent in December 1995 (see Hochreiter's Chapter 1 in this volume). Still, the need for repeated devaluations in the first half of the 1990s raises some interesting questions. It is hardly surprising that the initial exchange rate peg of January 1990 could not be maintained for very long. But why did the zloty continue to be under pressure long after the initial "shock" and threat of hyperinflation had passed?

Krzak (1996) suggests that once the initial burst of accelerating inflation was brought to a halt, the priorities of the Polish authorities switched and further reductions in inflation were given low priority. In line with a good deal of standard macroeconomic analysis both the Hungarian and Polish governments decided that the "costs of rapid disinflation outweigh its benefits" (Krzak 1996:64). While we disagree with this judgement as an issue of normative economics, we believe that this belief is an important part of the explanation for why disinflation has been so slow in both these countries.[7] In both countries the continuation of inflation at substantial, albeit generally declining, levels has generated considerable stickiness in inflationary expectations. Krzak (1996:52) concludes that the

> inertia of Polish inflation is caused by entrenched expectations relative to price adjustment [i.e., gradual price liberalization], the widespread indexation of contracts, and the crawling peg system of exchange rates. Monetary policy tends to accommodate aggregate demand and the fiscal deficits are still partially financed by means of monetization.

While the primary causes of continuing inflation were clearly domestic pressures and policies, the preannounced crawl has quite possibly hurt the disinflation process more than it has helped. Krzak (1996:54) argues that the "preannounced rate of depreciation of the domestic currency sets the floor for inflationary expectations, as the pass-through of a devaluation to import prices is believed by the public to be high." As Krzak (1996:57) further notes: "A general weakness of a gradual strategy lies in its vulnerability to various macroeconomic shocks." Where a crawling peg regime tends to set the floor rather than the ceiling for inflationary expectations, its usefulness in aiding disinflation must be called into question.

Furthermore, as the Polish balance of payments turned into a strong surplus in the mid 1990s, this generated substantial pressures for imported inflation. As noted above, these pressures eventually led the Polish authorities to a substantial widening of the exchange rate band and a discrete revaluation of the parity level, but not before international reserves had almost tripled over only a two-year period. The OECD (1997a:30) concludes that, despite a considerable amount of sterilization, "an increasingly important inflationary factor in 1994–95 was the rapid accumulation of foreign exchange reserves which caused the money supply to grow much faster than projected."

In general, a nation's competitiveness can be sustained either through wage and price adjustment (in the case of a pegged rate) or exchange rate adjustment (under a flexible regime). Here, there again appears to be a marked contrast between Poland on the one hand and the Czech Republic on the other.[8] Domestic political conditions tended to make substantial wage reductions infeasible in Poland as a substitute for devaluation—except as a short-term component of the initial 1990 stabilization package. In contrast, the former Czechoslovakia was able to maintain a policy of tight wage controls even in the midst of increasing inflation in the early reform years. Influenced in part by the history of active political protest leading to the establishment of Solidarity in 1980, worker strikes and demands for wage increases continued to be more prevalent in Poland than in either the Czech Republic or Hungary. In the initial stages of reform, Polish workers got the parliament to pass a law promising full wage indexation, a settlement unheard of in Hungary or Czechoslovakia. In the 1993 elections, coal miners, teachers and emergency-service workers successfully pressed a divided parliament into further wage negotiations.

We should acknowledge that the demands by Polish workers for higher nominal wages were fueled, in part, by the serious reduction in real wages that accompanied Poland's "shock therapy" program. Kabaj and Kowalik (1995:8) argue that average monthly food consumption per capita declined precipitously between 1989 and 1994 in Poland, with double-digit declines in most major categories. Nevertheless, during the early post-Communist years, real wages in Poland did keep pace with increases in inflation to a much greater extent than in the former Czechoslovakia. Between 1990 and 1992 the real wage index for Poland fell by only 6 percent as compared to a 22 percent drop in the former Czechoslovakia (*PlanEcon* 1992). In comparing Poland and the former Czechoslovakia, it is interesting to note that Czechoslovakia, the country with the more fixed exchange rate, had the more flexible real wage rate. Constancy in the exchange rate would surely not have been as feasible if real wages had been more rigid.

As it is, Poland not only had the greatest rate of increase in inflation in the early 1990s of the Central European countries but also the highest measured unemployment rates. While unemployment rose sharply in all three countries, Poland's 1992 unemployment rate of 12.87 percent can be compared to rates of 10.30 percent in Hungary and 3.05 percent in the former Czechoslovakia (*PlanEcon* 1992). There are admittedly too many difficulties with the unemployment statistics for us to draw any meaningful inferences from these numbers about differences between Poland and Hungary. But the available evidence strongly suggests that Czech unemployment was much lower. Since the breakup of the Czechoslovak Federation, the Czech portion of the region has maintained its superior inflation performance as well as keeping unemployment at low levels.[9]

The Czech and Slovak Republics

While the Polish authorities did prove able to maintain a fixed exchange rate with the U.S. dollar for 17 months before being forced to devalue, the Czech Republic, until late 1996, continued to face more pressure for revaluation than for devaluation. As noted above, the Czech Republic—as a relatively small, open economy with a population of approximately 10 million—seems inherently much better suited to a fixed exchange rate regime than does Poland. The Czech pegged rate policy of 1991–1997 was bolstered by domestic political and institutional factors that allowed the government to quickly get its budget situation under control and promote stable economic policies. The Czechs' ability to avoid devaluation pressures for such a long period was accompanied by a near balanced budget in contrast to the more substantial budget deficits in Hungary and Poland (see Burdekin 1995). The Czechoslovak Federation's budget surpluses of 1991 and 1992 were followed by further surpluses under the Czech Republic. Meanwhile, by the mid 1990s, consumer price inflation in the Czech Republic had fallen below 10 percent—whereas it appeared to remain stuck in the 20 percent range in Hungary and Poland.

It should be added that the initiation of the pegged rate in the Czech case was not accompanied by strong policy statements committing the government to its defense. As Hrnčíř (1994:233) emphasizes, at the initiation of the peg the government felt that there were too many uncertainties and the possibility of future shocks was too high for it to realistically attempt to "irrevocably fix" the exchange rate. Whereas Estonia, for example, adopted a currency board that pegged the kroon to the German mark, neither the Czech Republic nor the former Czechoslovakia attempted to set such a commitment mechanism in place. Consequently, strong initial credibility effects were not to be expected. Nevertheless, the central bank's ability to maintain the peg over a number of years without a major balance of payments crisis, not surprisingly, led to a substantial increase in the credibility with which the market viewed the peg. This suggests, however, that it was primarily the course of domestic policies that gave credibility to the exchange rate peg rather than vice versa (as is consistent with the evidence on the European Monetary System provided by Burdekin, Westbrook and Willett 1994). This also allowed the Czechs to abandon the peg in 1997 without nearly as adverse consequences on confidence as accompanied Mexico's abandonment of its crawling peg regime in 1994.

The success of the Czech pegged exchange rate policy was evidenced by that country's ability to maintain its exchange rate unchanged for over six years without facing any severe balance of payments deficits. As in the Polish case this policy was preceded by an initial devaluation—but the scale of the Czech devaluation was substantially less in relation to the prevailing black market rate at the time (see Chapter 15 by Hrnčíř in this volume). The Czechs nevertheless ran substantial balance of payments *surpluses* until 1996—with their international reserves growing from just over $1 billion at the beginning of 1993 to over $4 billion at the beginning of 1994, over $8 billion at the beginning of 1995, and more than $12 billion in mid 1996. This reserve growth initially resulted from roughly balanced trade and current accounts combined with substantial capital inflows of the type also recently enjoyed by Poland.[10] During 1995 the trade and current account balances moved into substantial deficits, but these continued to be more than covered by capital inflows until mid 1996. As in the Polish case, the Czech National Bank reacted to its balance of payments surpluses by widening the exchange rate band (from ±0.5 percent to ±7.5 percent on February 28, 1996).

One factor allowing the Czech exchange rate to be held steady was the lack of convertibility in the current account of the balance of payments. Limitations on capital mobility helped the Czech National Bank to formulate a relatively independent monetary policy in spite of the quite rigid exchange rate peg (Janáčková 1996).[11] But cracks began appearing in this benign scenario after 1993. Growing capital inflows created increasing dangers of imported inflation through the pressures they created for acceleration in the rate of domestic money growth. Dĕdek (1995:43–44) assessed the post-1993 situation as follows:

The growth of the money supply tended to overshoot monetary targets despite the accelerated sterilization efforts of the Czech National Bank ... The obligation to support the fixed exchange rate resulted in accumulating external reserves ... The economy simply ceased to fit in any more with the open-current-account-closed-capital-account paradigm. Many observers were caught unawares by the already entrenched easiness with which some capital flows could cross national borders.

In early 1996, the Czech government resolved this dilemma—at least for the short term—by substantially widening the band of permissible exchange rate movements around parity and allowing the koruna to appreciate. A similar shift was made by the Slovak Republic later in 1996. We believe that this was a much wiser move than accepting the acceleration of imported inflation that would inevitably have been generated by maintenance of the old value of the exchange rate. Furthermore, by 1996, the degree of fixity implied by the old narrow band had arguably already served its purpose in providing an anchor for the early transition stage. Hrnčíř (1994) points to the exchange rate peg's role in disciplining private market behavior through import competition during this period. Janáčková (1996:63) adds that

the pressure of wage growth is stronger in a climate of repeated devaluations of the exchange rate. A stable exchange rate doubtless provided a proper framework for structural changes in the economy and helped to ameliorate the bad influence of the loss of traditional markets, as well as helping to introduce rapid reorientation to the markets of developed countries.

Surprisingly, the Czech Republic's strong balance of payments position began to reverse itself not long after the widening of the exchange rate band. The level of international reserves reached a peak of almost $13 billion in July 1996 but, by January 1997, had dipped below $12 billion. A growing trade deficit, and monetary concerns about political stability and some of the policies of the coalition government led by Václav Klaus, contributed to a substantial loss of confidence in the koruna. In the spring of 1997, reserve losses accelerated in the face of political infighting among the coalition partners and worsening economic statistics.

In response to these growing pressures in the foreign exchange market, the koruna was freed in late May, 1997, and promptly fell in value by some 10 percent. As reported in the *Financial Times* (Boland 1997:2), with the (possibly temporary) floating of the koruna, the "currency subsequently plunged on foreign exchange markets, and brought Mr. Klaus's political crisis to a head." Clearly it was the underlying political situation that prompted the foreign exchange crisis, rather than vice versa.

Concluding Comments

Notwithstanding the 1996 widening of the exchange rate band aimed at warding off the threat of imported inflation and the eventual floating of the koruna in 1997 as the result of a deteriorating political situation, it is hard to deny that the Czech Republic benefitted from the stability imparted by its pegged exchange rate during the early stages of its transformation into a market-orientated economy. The Polish experience, though, provides a clear warning that attempts to impose such a policy under less favorable conditions will, at best, offer nothing more than a short-term fix. The fixed rate enacted in Poland in 1990 may well have helped contain short-run hyperinflationary pressures. However, the Polish authorities' ability to sustain this peg in the short run did not alter the fact that neither domestic conditions nor optimum currency area criteria favored a fixed exchange rate regime. Indeed, it could be argued that the short-run benefits came at the expense of considerable dislocation as the initial shock of exchange rate fixity was followed by the repeated shifts in policy in 1991 and the devaluations of 1992 and 1993.

The adoption of a crawling peg exchange rate regime has many attractions. It allows countries to avoid the stark choice between genuinely fixed and flexible exchange rates. The experiences of the Central European economies in the late 1990s, however, highlight the substantial difficulties involved in managing such a regime effectively. Too slow a rate of crawl can precipitate foreign exchange market crisis. Neither Hungary nor Poland was able to operate their crawling peg regimes without adding major step changes in the value of their currencies. Where such step changes may still be required, the potential role of crawling pegs in stabilizing expectations is sharply compromised.

One important issue in the management of crawling pegs is the choice of discretionary versus preannounced rates of crawl. If we stopped our analysis in early 1994, we would likely have concluded that the Hungarian discretionary crawl had worked better than the Polish preannounced crawl since Hungary had avoided major step changes while Poland had not. Over the following year, however, Hungary made two step devaluations, while Poland made a step revaluation. Overall, the Central European experience does not offer evidence of the clear superiority of one type over the other.

The evidence on the issue of wide versus narrow bands seems much stronger. All of the Central European economies with the exception of Hungary have moved to widen bands of ±5 to 7 percent of parity. While international capital mobility facing these countries is not so high that they cannot engage in a substantial amount of sterilization of the domestic monetary effects of capital flows, the magnitudes of payments imbalances have been large enough to make such sterilization operations quite costly. Krzak and Schubert (1997) report estimates that for the Czech Republic the costs of sterilization reached 0.3 percent of GDP in 1994 and 0.5 percent of GDP in 1995. These costs were also quite substantial for the Slovak Republic in 1995 and 1996. Wider bands should help reduce the development of short-term speculative crisis, but whether they will be sufficient to substantially reduce the costs of protecting the domestic money supply from capital flows under pegged exchange rates is open to question.[12] Despite their crawling peg, the cost of Polish sterilization was approximately 0.6 percent of GDP in 1995 and 0.8 percent in 1996.

Simply correlating rates of inflation and exchange rate regimes across the four Visegrad countries would suggest a strong argument in favor of pegged rates. By 1995 inflation had fallen to high single-digit levels in both the Czech and Slovak Republics, while it was still running in the high twenties in Hungary and Poland. By 1997 the story looks not quite so strong, with the Czech Republic being forced to abandon its peg and inflation rates in Hungary and Poland dropping into the teens. A deeper analysis suggests, however, that in all of the countries under study the exchange rate regime has played a relatively minor role in determining the course of inflation. Considering a broader range of geographically proximate countries, Slovenia with a managed float also achieved single-digit inflation by 1996. And even the higher rates of inflation in Hungary and Poland have been running a little below those of Estonia and Lithuania despite those countries' fixed exchange rates backed by currency boards. (These countries' experiences are considered in the following chapter by Dubaskas, Wihlborg and Willett.)

Basically, the inflationary experiences of the major Central European countries have been influenced primarily by their domestic policy actions. While the full story is considerably more complex, the strong correlation across the countries in the size of their budget deficits and their progress in controlling inflation is indicative of the importance of domestic political economy considerations.[13] It is possible for the exchange rate regime to make a marginal contribution to increasing the ease or difficulty of bringing and keeping inflation under control, but it is difficult to draw confident conclusions about the direction of the net effects for any of the countries in our sample. For each country one can point to episodes where each country's regime was likely helpful, and to other episodes where it likely hurt.

The experiences of these countries does suggest that whatever disciplining effects exchange rate targets may have on domestic macroeconomic policy choices, they are relatively weak.[14] Even the long-sustained fixed peg of the Czech krona was insufficient to force policy consistency in the face of political dissent within the governing coalition. These experiences also highlight the importance of the credibility of government policies and illustrate a sad asymmetry: While a good reputation takes a long time to earn, high political uncertainty and poor policy choices can destroy a government's hard-earned reputation almost overnight. As the Czech Republic's experience demonstrates, pegged exchange rates or exchange rate targets provide little protection against this harsh fact.

Notes

The authors thank Pierre Siklos and the editors for helpful comments and are grateful to Ida Huang for research assistance.

1. See, for example, Bélanger (1994) and Wolf (1994).

2. For more detailed treatments of the Czech, Hungarian, and Polish experiences, see the later chapters by Hrnčíř, Gáspár, Siklos and Ábel, and Kowalski and Stawarska. For overviews of the experiences of the Slovak koruna after the Czechoslovakia divorce, and of the managed float of Slovenia's tolar, see Radzyner and Riesinger (1996).

3. For discussion of the initial conditions and early stages of the stabilization policies in the countries under review, see Sachs (1993) and the contributions in Blanchard, Froot and Sachs (1994) and Herr, Tober and Westphal (1994).

4. The size of the economy also plays an important role in OCA theory. On this count, the larger size of the Polish economy again points toward flexible exchange rates, whereas the smaller size of the Czech economy strengthens the case for a fixed exchange rate.

5. See, for example, Bruno (1993:223)—who also concludes that Czechoslovakia and Hungary initially devalued by about the right amount.

6. Mexico is one of the rare examples of success by this criterion over a period of several years. The experiment ultimately ended in the forced devaluation of 1994 and renewed inflationary pressures, however.

7. See Burdekin et al. (1995). Specifically on the growth depressing effects of inflation in the former communist countries, see Fischer et al. (1996) and Loungani and Sheets (1997).

8. See also Bruno (1993:Chapter 7).

9. The Czech unemployment rate was 3.2 percent in 1994, for example. Slovakia has not fared as well and, influenced by its disproportionate share of Czechoslovakia's old heavy industry and contracting sectors, measured unemployment there stood at 14.8 percent in 1994—falling between Hungary's 10.8 percent level and Poland's 16 percent level (see Åslund, Boone and Johnson 1996). Slovakia, however, has achieved an even lower inflation rate than the Czech Republic.

10. For an analysis of capital inflows into the Central European economies and the implications for monetary and exchange rate policy, see Calvo, Sahay and Végh (1995).

11. In September 1995, the new Czech foreign exchange law "practically fully liberalized capital flows" (OECD 1996a:40). Note that, while yielding greater short-run domestic monetary autonomy, capital controls—for this very reason—tend to undermine the use of the exchange rate peg as a nominal anchor.

12. Perhaps somewhat surprisingly, despite having a managed float Slovenia also engaged in a considerable amount of sterilization. This implies very heavy management of the exchange rate, which may be quite justified given the small, open nature of Slovenia's economy.

13. The major exception to this correlation is the Slovak Republic, which quite surprisingly—given its substantial budget deficits, slowness of movement toward a full market system and inability or lack of desire to attract sizeable amounts of direct foreign investment—still recorded in 1996 the lowest rate of inflation of any of the former communist countries (5.8 percent). As OECD (1996b:26) notes, despite their unfavorable underlying conditions, "The NBS [National Bank of Slovakia] appears to have obtained a high level of credibility in the domestic and international financial community, with its independence and policy stance widely respected and supported." How this has come about should be a fruitful topic for research.

14. A similar conclusion is reached by Zettermeyer and Citrin (1995) in their review of the experiences of the states of the former Soviet Union.

References

Åslund, Anders, Peter Boone and Simon Johnson. 1996. "How to Stabilize: Lessons from Post-communist Countries." *Brookings Papers on Economic Activity* 1: 217–313.

Bélanger, Gérard. 1994. "Comments," in Richard C. Barth and Chorng-Huey Wong, eds., *Approaches to Exchange Rate Policy: Choices for Developing and Transition Economies*. Pp. 253–57. Washington, D.C.: International Monetary Fund.

Blanchard, Olivier, Kenneth Froot and Jeffrey Sachs. 1994. *The Transition in Eastern Europe*. Chicago, Ill.: University of Chicago Press.

Boland, Vincent. 1997. "Czech Government Troubles Come to a Head." *Financial Times*, June 9, p. 2.

Bruno, Michael. 1993. *Crisis, Stabilization and Economic Reform*. Oxford: Clarendon Press.

Burdekin, Richard C. K. 1995. "Budget Deficits and Inflation: The Importance of Budget Controls for Monetary Stability," in Thomas D. Willett, Richard C. K. Burdekin, Richard J. Sweeney and Clas Wihlborg, eds., *Establishing Monetary Stability in Emerging Market Economies*. Pp. 33–61. Boulder, Colo.: Westview Press.

Burdekin, Richard C. K., Syuono Salamon, and Thomas D. Willett. 1995. "The High Cost of Monetary Instability," in Thomas D. Willett, Richard Burdekin, Richard Sweeney, and Clas Wihlborg, eds., *Establishing Monetary Stability in Emerging Market Economies*. Pp. 13–32. Boulder, Colo.: Westview Press.

Burdekin, Richard C. K., Jilleen R. Westbrook and Thomas D. Willett. 1994. "Exchange Rate Pegging as a Disinflation Strategy: Evidence from the European Monetary System," in Pierre L. Siklos, ed., *Varieties of Monetary Reforms: Lessons and Experiences on the Road to Monetary Union*. Pp. 45–72. Boston, Mass.: Kluwer Academic Publishers.

Calvo, Guillermo, Ratna Sahay and Carlos Végh. 1995. "Capital Flows in Central and Eastern Europe: Evidence and Policy Options." IMF Working Paper No. 95/57. Washington, D.C.: International Monetary Fund, May.

Dědek, Oldřich. 1995. "Currency Convertibility and Exchange-Rate Policies in the Czech Republic." *Eastern European Economics* 33 (November/December): 26–64.

Fischer, Stanley, Ratna Sahay, and Carlos Végh. 1996. "Stabilization and Growth in Transition Economies." *Journal of Economic Perspectives*, Spring: 45–66.

Herr, Hansjörg, Silke Tober and Andreas Westphal, eds. 1994. *Macroeconomic Problems of Transformation: Stabilization Policies and Economic Restructuring*. Brookfield, Vt: Edward Elgar.

Hrnčíř, Miroslav. 1994. "The Exchange Rate and Transition: The Case of the Former Czechoslovakia," in Hansjörg Herr, Silke Tober and Andreas Westphal, eds., *Macroeconomic Problems of Transformation: Stabilization Policies and Economic Restructuring*. Pp. 228–35. Brookfield, Vt: Edward Elgar.

Janáčková, Stanislava. 1996. "Certain Specific Features of Monetary Policy in the Czech Republic." *Eastern European Economics* 34 (January/February): 60–74.

Kabaj, Mieczyslaw, and Tadeusz Kowalik. 1995. "Who Is Responsible for Postcommunist Successes in Eastern Europe?" *Transition* 6 (July/August): 7–8.

Krzak, Maciej. 1996. "Persistent Moderate Inflation in Poland and Hungary." Österreichische National Bank, *Focus on Transition*, No. 2: 46–67.

Krzak, Maciej, and Auriel Schubert. 1997. "The Present State of Monetary Governance in Central and Eastern Europe." Österreichische National Bank, *Focus on Transition*, No. 1: 28–56.

Loungani, Prakash, and Nathan Sheets. 1997. "Central Bank Independence, Inflation, and Growth in Transition Economies." *Journal of Money, Credit, and Banking*, August: 381–99.

OECD. 1997a. *Economic Surveys: Poland*. Paris: Organisation for Economic Co-operation and Development.

———. 1997b. *Economic Surveys: Hungary*. Paris: Organisation for Economic Co-operation and Development.

———. 1996a. *Economic Surveys: The Czech Republic*. Paris: Organisation for Economic Co-operation and Development.

———. 1996b. *Economic Surveys: The Slovak Republic*. Paris: Organisation for Economic Co-operation and Development.

Otker, Inci. 1994. "Exchange Rate Policy," in Liam P. Ebrill, Ajai Chopra, Charalambos Christofides, Paul Mylonas, Inci Otker, and Gerd Schwartz, eds., *Poland: The Path to a Market Economy*. IMF Occasional Paper No. 113. Pp. 43–55. Washington, D.C.: International Monetary Fund, October.

PlanEcon. 1992. "Economic Recovery in Eastern Europe." December 28.

Radzyner, Olga, and Sandra Riesinger. 1996. "Exchange Rate Policy in Transition—Developments and Challenges in Central and Eastern Europe." Österreichische National Bank, *Focus on Transition*, No. 1: 20–38.

Sachs, Jeffrey. 1993. *Poland's Jump to the Market Economy*. Cambridge, Mass.: MIT Press.

Wolf, Thomas A. 1994. "Comments," in Richard C. Barth and Chorng-Huey Wong, eds., *Approaches to Exchange Rate Policy: Choices For Developing and Transition Economies*. Pp. 250–53. Washington, D.C.: International Monetary Fund.

Zettermeyer, Jeromin, and Daniel Citrin. 1995. "Stabilization: Fixed versus Flexible Exchange Rates," in Daniel Citrin and Ashok Lahiri, eds., *Policy Experiences and Issues in the Baltics, Russia, and other Countries of the Former Soviet Union*. IMF Occasional Paper No. 133. Pp. 93–102. Washington, D.C.: International Monetary Fund.

6

The Baltic States: Alternative Routes to Credibility

Gediminas Dubauskas, Clas Wihlborg
and Thomas D. Willett

Introduction

In this chapter we compare exchange rate policies in the three Baltic states—Estonia, Latvia and Lithuania—and evaluate their success in reducing inflation and establishing the credibility of their anti-inflationary strategies. A comparison of these countries is interesting because they chose different paths towards macroeconomic stabilization despite their similarities as very small, rapidly opening, transition economies. Estonia has been strongly committed to a currency board since June 1992, fixing the kroon to the German mark, while Lithuania, pegging the litas to the dollar, is more of a latecomer and has adopted a weaker currency board arrangement. Latvia initially chose to adopt a floating exchange rate, but switched to a "soft" SDR peg in February 1994. Thus, the three countries differ not only in terms of regime choice, but also in terms of the anchor currency to which they chose to peg.

In the next section we provide an overview of exchange rate and inflation developments in the three countries. In the third section the credibility of the currencies and inflation performance under different regimes is evaluated using the differential between interest rates in domestic and foreign currencies within each country as a proxy for credibility. In the fourth section we discuss the problems that political risk can generate for using this proxy, and argue that the differences between the interest rate on foreign currency deposits in each of the countries and a world market interest rate are a better measure of exchange rate credibility. Using this proxy, differences in the exchange rate credibility generated by the different strategies of the Baltic states appear to be much less. We argue that this finding combined with the superior inflation performance in Latvia and severe data problems with respect to output raise serious doubts about concluding, as several recent studies have, that the experience of the Baltic states illustrates the superiority of exchange rate based stabilization programs.

Overview of Exchange Rate Regimes in the Baltic States[1]

Estonia

The first proposals for a separate Estonian currency appeared in 1987, during the Gorbachev years. After Estonia gained independence in 1991 and the Estonian central bank—the Bank of Estonia—was formally re-established, currency reform became a priority. The ruble was losing value at a near-hyperinflation rate, and there was a shortage of cash within the ruble zone. The new Estonian kroon notes were printed at the beginning of 1992, and it was agreed that 11.3 tonnes of gold deposited in the West before the Soviet occupation would be restored to Estonia. Thus, Estonia was technically prepared for reform. The strategy adopted by Estonia was similar to that adopted by Germany in 1948. Like the Slovenian experience of 1991, the new money would be introduced within a few days.

Estonian citizens who had registered at special conversion points obtained the right to change 500 cash rubles at a rate of ten rubles per kroon between the 20th and the 22nd of June, 1992. Additional cash rubles could be converted at a rate of 50 rubles per kroon. All rubles on deposit were converted at a rate of ten to one, the prevailing exchange rate at that time. The kroon was then pegged to the German mark at eight kroons per mark, a substantially undervalued rate that was picked to generate credibility (see Lainela and Sutela 1994).

Estonia's central bank was made politically independent and given responsibility for managing the money supply under a currency board arrangement (as explained in Chapter 13 of this volume). Thus, changes in the monetary base were tied to changes in foreign exchange reserves. Only under specific circumstances associated with bank-rescue operations would the central bank be allowed to inject liquidity into the banking system. To enhance the credibility of the arrangement, the Bank of Estonia was divided into an Issue Department and a Banking Department. The Issue Department operates the currency board, and its foreign exchange assets have to match its liabilities: bank notes and kroon deposits with the Bank of Estonia. Revenues from seigniorage are passed on to the Banking Department, which is responsible for supervision and control of the banking system. The 1992 Foreign Currency Law of Estonia does not allow the use of foreign currency for domestic transactions, but does guarantee substantial capital account convertibility.

After the introduction of a currency board, foreign currency deposits were initially not allowed in Estonia; but this and other restrictions were eliminated in December 1993. Since the board's introduction, the kroon has remained fixed at eight kroon to the German mark.

The inflation rate in Estonia averaged 6 percent per month in 1993 and followed a falling trend until April 1994 when it reached 3 percent. Thereafter, the CPI inflation rate fluctuated at around 2 percent per month. Beginning in April 1996, the inflation rate has come down further to around 1 percent per month.

The inflation figures for producer prices (PPI) are similar but somewhat lower. Over a three-year period from January 1994 through December 1996 the CPI-price level increased 70 percent while the increase in producer prices was less than 60 percent. Nontraded goods are included to a greater extent in the CPI than in the PPI. Thus, nontraded goods prices have increased by more than 70 percent.

The exchange rate of eight kroon/mark was chosen in 1992 to allow for a doubling of prices on Estonian goods without creating a cost disadvantage for Estonian exporters. This estimated margin for real appreciation was covered by late 1993. Reforming economies with high productivity growth are expected to show an appreciation of the equilibrium real exchange rate, but only by a few percent a year. Thus, the substantial increase in prices of Estonian goods generated a real appreciation that by conventional reasoning would reduce the international competitiveness of Estonian firms. If so, we would not expect the currency board arrangement to remain credible for long. On the other hand, if the price increases in Estonia correspond to improvements in the quality of Estonian goods and an ability to substitute domestic production for imports at the fixed exchange rate, then the real appreciation is sustainable. Evidence of the peg's credibility is analyzed below.

Latvia

Latvia, like Estonia, was committed to the introduction of its own currency when it obtained independence in August 1991. The Latvian authorities implemented the monetary reform in two stages: in the first stage, in June 1997, a freely floating, independent, partially convertible Latvian "ruble" was introduced. In the second stage the Latvian ruble was exchanged for the lat, which is fully convertible.

The new Latvian national currency entered circulation on March 5, 1993, under a floating exchange rate regime. Lats circulated alongside the Latvian ruble until June 28, 1993. Thereafter, only lats were backed by the central bank. The lat was freely convertible on both the current and capital accounts from its introduction. To ensure free convertibility of lats, the Bank of Latvia officially promised to buy and sell any amount of hard currency to commercial banks upon request (*Monetary Review of the Bank of Latvia*, vol. 3, 1994). For tax reasons, Latvian enterprises and companies must declare every month all cash transactions worth more than one thousand lats.

In February 1994 a crawling peg to an SDR-basket was introduced following a period of sizable appreciation of the lat due to foreign capital inflows. The rate of crawl was not pre-announced; it was, therefore, similar to a managed float. The rate was set at 0.7997 lats to the SDR in February 1994. Under this arrangement, the appreciation of the lat initially decreased.

Figure 6.1 shows the development of the Latvian currency relative to the U.S. dollar from January 1993 through mid 1997. Its substantial appreciation during the float is evident. The appreciation that began at an exchange rate of lat .85/U.S. dollar in January 1993 continued until one dollar could be purchased for half a lat in April 1994.

By January 1994, the inflation rate in Latvia had fallen a little (but faster than in Estonia) to 4 percent. The rate fluctuated around a level of 1.5 percent per month through 1995 before falling further to between zero and 1.5 percent through 1996. Over the three-year period 1994 through 1996, consumer prices rose 50 percent in Latvia while producer prices rose only 30 percent. Both figures are substantially below the Estonian figures, but during the first half of this period the lat appreciated 15 percent. Thereafter, the lat depreciated slowly, as noted above. On the whole, the real appreciation of the lat appears slightly lower than the real appreciation of the kroon over this three-year period.

Lithuania

The monthly inflation rate in Lithuania, as in the other Baltic states in the ruble zone, reached 225 percent in 1991. Lithuania, like Estonia and Latvia, found currency reforms necessary. A temporary currency, the talonas, was introduced in May 1992. A memorandum with the IMF was signed in the fall of 1992, promising constraints on monetary policy and macroeconomic stabilization.

The talonas, which was not fully convertible, depreciated by over 500 percent against the dollar between its introduction in May 1992 and May 1993, when the litas was introduced. The litas was initially allowed to float and quickly appreciated 20 percent. At the same time, the monthly inflation rate fell from 25 percent in April 1993 to a low point of 1 percent in August. Thereafter, inflation rose again in the final months of 1993, to over 5 percent in January 1994. After some fluctuations of between 2 and 6 percent per month in 1994, inflation came down to around 2 percent per month in 1995 and 1 percent per month in 1996.

FIGURE 6.1 Bank of Latvia's Lats/U.S. Dollar Exchange Rate

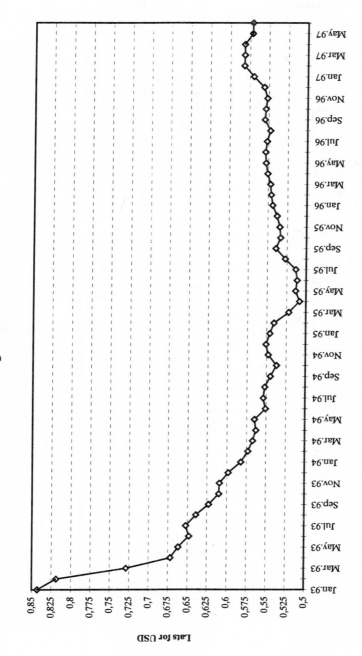

SOURCE: Bank of Latvia, 1993–1997.

Lithuanian monetary policy was at a critical stage in mid 1993. The flexible exchange rate seemed attractive because of Lithuanians' memories and expectations of a strong central bank and a credible currency as experienced before the war.

After an initial appreciation following its introduction in mid 1993, the litas depreciated in September 1993. Thereafter, it depreciated through November to a level of litas 3.9/U.S. dollar, where it stabilized.

On April 1, 1994, Lithuania followed Estonia's example and adopted a currency board arrangement. Unlike Estonia, Lithuania pegged its currency to the U.S dollar at a rate of 4 litas/dollar. (Lithuania's currency board arrangement is described by Dubauskas in Chapter 14 of this volume.) The currency board was introduced when the monthly inflation rate had already fallen to just above 1 percent, a level similar to rates in Estonia and Latvia. During the last two months of 1996, the inflation rate increased again to a level between 2 and 3 percent per month.

The Lithuanian inflation rate over the period 1994 to 1996 is comparable to the rate for Estonia and slightly higher than that for Latvia. Consumer prices increased 75 percent while producer prices increased about 60 percent. Both figures are very close to those for Estonia. Inflation in producer prices in both Estonia and Lithuania exceeded the corresponding inflation rate in Latvia by nearly 30 percentage points during this three-year period. The difference in consumer price inflation was smaller.

As Baliño et al. (1997:6) conclude, "there is no clear evidence that disinflation was achieved faster in Estonia and Lithuania than under a monetary rule and later a conventional peg in Latvia." (See also Saavalainen 1995). Nor did the rate of disinflation accelerate in Lithuania after its currency board began operation. Furthermore, over the medium term inflation rates did not converge to lower levels in the currency board countries.

With this background we turn to a comparison of interest rates in the three countries in order to evaluate whether the differences in inflation rates are reflected in differences in the credibility of monetary policy and exchange rates.

Interest Rates and Credibility

Interest rates on short-term time deposits (less than one year) in domestic currencies in the three Baltic states are presented in Figure 6.2. The period shown is January 1993 through March 1997. Through September 1994 the developments of the interest rates are quite different. Thereafter the patterns are similar, but the Estonian rate follows a path about ten percentage points below the others. This difference closed to about five percentage points during the last few months of 1996.

FIGURE 6.2 Average Annual Interest Rates for Time Deposits in Domestic Currencies

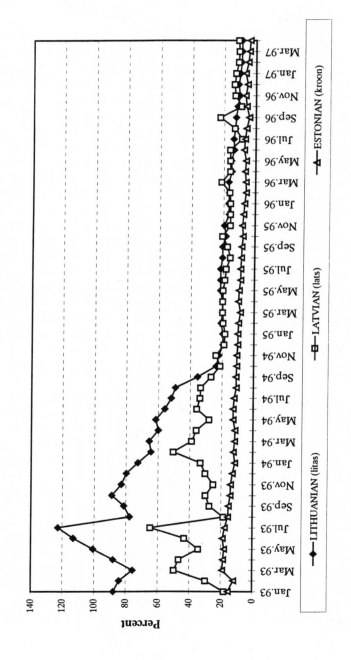

SOURCES: Bulletin of the Bank of Lithuania, Latvian Bank Bulletin, Estonian Bank Bulletin, 1993–1997.

The interest rates after the introduction of the currency board in June 1992 suggest that Estonia established, at the least, a stable level of credibility at an early stage. This is consistent with substantial, rapid, albeit not complete credibility effects.

The interpretation of the initial credibility effects of the introduction of the Lithuanian currency board in April 1994 is difficult because interest rates had started a sharp downward trend in December 1993. Interest rates fell sharply from over 60 percent just before the currency board was introduced to a little over 20 percent within six months, but there was no noticeable acceleration of the rate of decline until the two sharp declines in September and October of 1994. Expectations of the introduction of the currency board may have helped contribute to the downward trend that began before its implementation. Thus we are hesitant to draw strong conclusions about the very short-term credibility effects of the implementation of the Lithuanian currency board. The evidence, while ambiguous, is not inconsistent with strong initial credibility effects.

Latvia switched from a floating rate to a soft or crawling peg to the SDR in February 1994. It seems that the regime shift contributed to a reversal of the rising interest rate path which began in August 1993, but for several months the rate remained relatively high. In August Latvia's interest rate fell from over 30 percent to around 20 percent, and remained at that level for some time before beginning a slow downward trend. The declines in interest rates in Latvia and Lithuania were not achieved by regime shifts alone, but by consistent restrictive monetary policies. The declines in interest rates lagged the declines in inflation rates by about half a year in these two countries, while Estonian interest rates fell before the decline in inflation in early 1994.

In summary, based on the evidence from the behavior of interest rates the early adoption by Estonia of a currency board appears to have contributed to a lowering of the costs of disinflation. We concur with Zettermeyer and Citrin (1995), who argue that "interest rate differentials suggest that Estonia's exchange rate strategy may have commanded greater credibility than Latvia's, which may have reduced the real cost of stabilization" (p. 99), and our analysis suggests that the same conclusion likely applies with respect to Lithuania as well.

Hansson and Sachs (1994) likewise ascribe the lower interest rates in Estonia than in Latvia and Lithuania to the credibility effects of the Estonian currency board. Saavalainen (1995), however, notes several other important factors that may help explain this differential interest rate behavior. Slower restructuring in both the enterprise and financial sectors in Latvia and Lithuania meant that credit risks were higher in these countries. Needs to increase capital ratios would also lead banks to raise their lending rates, and on the deposit rate side perceptions of greater risks of defaults by the banks kept rates high. Saavalainen reports that for October 1994 there was a 5 to 6 percentage point differential between bank deposit rates and treasury bill rates in both Latvia and Lithuania.

As Saavalainen (1995) notes, time deposit rates alone do not reveal changes in exchange rate expectations. These expectations are better approximated by calculating the differences between the time deposit rate in each currency and the foreign currency deposit rate on deposits held in the same country. Figure 6.3 shows the foreign currency rates while the differences—proxing for exchange rate expectations—are shown in Figure 6.4.[2]

Initially there were quite substantial differences in the implied exchange rate expectations, with Lithuania's peg having much less credibility than Latvia's, which in turn was much less credible than Estonia's. The differentials tell essentially the same story about the time path of credibility gains as the interest rate levels discussed above, suggesting that the major cause of the substantial decline in interest rates in Lithuania was the increase in credibility. Figure 6.4 shows that by September 1994 exchange rate expectations in the three countries had converged to the same level—about 5 percent depreciation per annum. Thereafter Latvia, with the lowest inflation rate, had the lowest differential between domestic and foreign currency rates for almost a year. From September 1995 through most of 1996, Estonia's differential was two to three percentage points below the others.

These proxies for exchange rate expectations indicate that while substantial credibility for the Estonia currency was established much more rapidly over the medium term, the levels of credibility for the three countries' exchange rate arrangement were perceived to be very similar, in spite of the differences in their exchange rate arrangements. Estonia may have gained a slight edge in credibility, although its inflation rate has been a little bit above Latvia's. Given the lesser commitment to the currency board in Lithuania (as described in Chapter 14 of this volume), it is perhaps surprising that expected exchange rate changes as well as inflation rates were so similar in Estonia and Lithuania.

Country Risk Premia

It was noted above that most of the differences in time deposit interest rates after September 1995 can be explained by differences in foreign currency deposit interest rates in the three countries.

The interest rate levels for foreign currency deposits in Latvia and Lithuania were substantially higher than the corresponding interest rates in Germany and the United States throughout the period. The Estonian foreign currency rates reached levels close to levels in these countries as early as the

136

FIGURE 6.3 Average Annual Interest Rate for Time Deposits in Foreign Currency

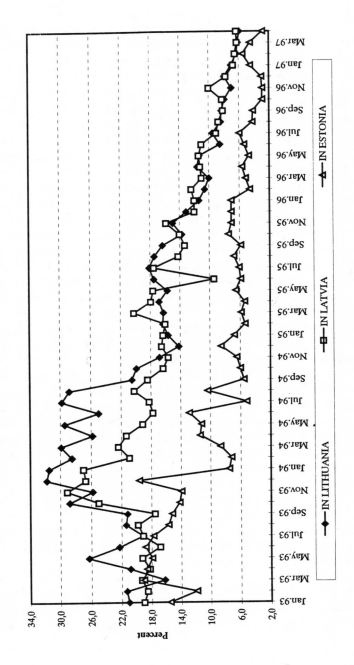

SOURCES: Bulletin of the Bank of Lithuania, Latvian Bank Bulletin, Estonian Bank Bulletin, 1993–1997.

FIGURE 6.4 Average Annual Interest Rate Differential for Time Deposits in Domestic Currency and FCC

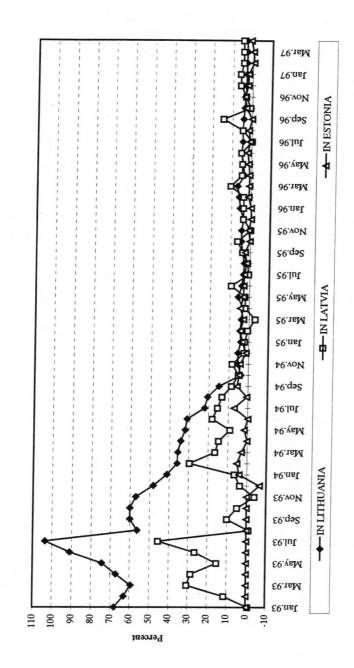

SOURCES: Bulletin of the Bank of Lithuania, Latvian Bank Bulletin, Estonian Bank Bulletin, 1993–1997.

second half of 1994. At this time, Latvia's and Lithuania's rates were 10 percentage points higher those of Estonia. Towards the end of 1996 the difference had declined to around five percentage points.

Differences between domestic currency interest rates and domestic foreign currency interest rates are usually interpreted as a country or political risk premium. As Lainela and Sutela (1997:138) argue, "even in the Baltics, which are similar in many respects, country risk not connected with currencies might well vary significantly." Thus, we must ask on what grounds Estonia's political risk premium has been substantially lower than the premia of Latvia and Lithuania.

One source of political risk premia for the three Baltic states was the probability that Russia would invade or that political instability in Russia would affect the three countries in a serious manner. It is hard to believe, however, that there is any difference between these three countries in their exposure to Russian instability.

More likely explanations are perceived risks of the imposition of capital controls or of defaults by commercial banks. Given the stronger commitment to reform in Estonia, lower risk of capital controls was likely a factor in the interest rate differential among the Baltic states.

After late 1994 such country risk factors appear to have been a more important determinate of differences between the home interest rates in the Baltic states and those in Germany and the U.S. This suggests that interest differentials between emerging market and industrial economies are much worse proxies for exchange rate expectations than are differentials among industrial countries.[3]

Conclusions

Latvia had the lowest inflation rate during the period 1994 to 1996, especially when measured by changes in producers' prices. The real appreciation of Latvia's currency has also been slightly lower under a crawling peg (or managed float) arrangement anchored to the SDR than under the floating regime. Inflation rates and real currency appreciation in Estonia and Lithuania have been similar in spite of the stronger currency board arrangements in Estonia (because of the requirement of a high majority vote to change the parity).[4] Interest rates in Estonia have been substantially lower than in the other countries, but not because of higher exchange rate credibility, except in the early transition years. The lower Estonian interest rates were explained by lower foreign currency deposit rates reflecting a lower political risk premium. The currency board may have contributed to perceptions of lower risk of the reintroduction of exchange controls in Estonia.

In studies covering a large number of former communist countries, both Bofinger et al. (1997) and Fischer et al. (1996) conclude that the output costs of disinflation were much lower in countries using exchange-rate based stabilization strategies. Saavalainen (1995) focuses on the three Baltic states and finds that both the initial output losses and sacrifice ratios were much lower in Estonia. While noting that differential policy credibility cannot be excluded as an explanation, Saavalainen notes that a number of other factors many also have been at work. Zettermeyer and Citrin (1996) also note that the data on output for Estonia and Latvia are not comparable. The official national accounts data for Estonia include an estimate of private sector activity, while the Latvian numbers do not contain any such estimate. Therefore, the stated difference in output performance almost certainly overstates the actual difference.

Our analysis casts some doubts on the conclusions of, for example, Bofinger et al. (1997) who argue that by enhancing the credibility of government policies, "exchange rate based stabilization as in Estonia tends to be less costly in terms of output than money based stabilization" as in Latvia, and in Lithuania (before the currency board arrangement was introduced in April 1994).

Notes

1. For additional details, see Chapters 13 and 14 in this volume, Lainelu and Sutela (1994), and Viksnins and Rimshevitchs (1995).

2. The foreign currency interest rates in each country are averages of interest rates in different foreign currencies. Thus, for exact comparability across countries the portfolios of foreign currency deposits should be the same.

3. For limitations on the use of interest differentials to measure exchange rate expectations even among the industrial countries, see the analysis and references in Burdekin, Westbrook and Willett (1994).

4. Interestingly, while Baliño and Enoch (1997) report that "the Lithuanian CBA [currency board arrangement] came under attack at the end of 1994 and beginning of 1995, following rumors of an impending devaluation and incipient banking system difficulties" (p. 9), we find no substantial widening of the domestic versus foreign interest rate differential on Lithuanian bank deposits (nor increase in the level of Lithuanian interest rates).

References

Baliño, Tomás, and Charles Enoch 1997. *Currency Board Arrangements: Issues and Experiences*. IMF Occasional Paper No. 151. Washington, D.C.: International Monetary Fund.

Bannerjee, B., V. Koen, T. Krueger, M. S. Lutz, M. Marrese, and Tapio O. Saavalainen. 1995. *Road Maps of the Transition: The Baltics, the Czech Republic, Hungary and Russia*. IMF Occasional Paper No. 127. Washington, D.C.: International Monetary Fund.

Bofinger, Peter, Heiner Flassbeck, and Lutz Hoffman. 1997. "Orthodox Money-Based Stabilization (OMBS) versus Heterodox Exchange Rate Based Stabilization (Herbs): The Case of Russia, the Ukraine, and Kazakhstan." *Economic Systems*, March: 1–33.

Burdekin, Richard C.K., Jilleen Westbrook and Thomas D. Willett. 1994. "Exchange Rate Pegging as a Disinflation Strategy: Evidence from the European Monetary System," in Pierre Siklos, ed., *Varieties of Monetary Reform: Lessons and Experiences on the Road to Monetary Union*. Pp. 42–72. Boston: Kluwer.

Fisher, Stanley, Ratna Sahay, and Carlos Végh. 1996. "Stabilization and Growth in Transition Economies: The Early Experience." *Journal of Economic Perspectives*, Spring: 45–66.

Hansen, Ardo, and Jeffrey Sachs. 1994. "Monetary Institutions and Credible Stabilization: A Comparison of Experience in the Baltics." Mimeo, Harvard University.

Lainela, Seija, and Pekka Sutela. 1994. "Institutional Choice in Transition Economies: The Baltic Monetary Reforms," in Randall Kindley and David Good, eds., *The Challenge of Globalization and Institution Building*. Pp. 123–42. Boulder, Colo.: Westview Press.

Saavalainen, Tapio O. 1995. "Stabilization in the Baltic Countries: Early Experience," in *Road Maps of the Transition: The Baltics, the Czech Republic, Hungary and Russia*. IMF Occasional Paper No. 127. Pp. 93–102. Washington, D.C.: International Monetary Fund.

Viksnins, George, and Ilmors Rimshevitchs. 1995. "The Latvian Monetary Reform," in Thomas D. Willett et al., eds., *Establishing Monetary Stability in Emerging Market Economies*. Pp. 231–6. Boulder, Colo.: Westview Press.

Zettermeyer, Jeromin and Daniel A. Citrin. 1995. "Stabilization: Fixed versus Flexible Exchange Rates," in Daniel A. Citrin and Ashok K. Lahiri, eds., *Policy Experiences and Issues in the Baltics, Russia, and Other Countries of the Former Soviet Union*. IMF Occasional Paper No. 133. Washington, D.C.: International Monetary Fund.

7

Exchange Rate Based Stabilization Policy in Latin America

*Pamela Martin, Jilleen R. Westbrook
and Thomas D. Willett*

Introduction

Successful exchange rate based stabilization programs in Europe, Israel and elsewhere have led many economists and policymakers to advocate the use of pegged exchange rates as an integral part of stabilization programs in the emerging market economies.[1] Although a number of economists have challenged the view that the reduction of inflation to low single-digits during the 1980s under the pegged exchange rate regime of the European Monetary System[2] strongly supports the case for exchange rate based stabilization policy, the experiences of developing countries have received much less critical analysis.[3] The current conventional wisdom is illustrated by José Fanelli and Gary McMahon's (1996) recent contention that "the main lessons Eastern Europe can learn from the experience of Latin America with ortho-dox programmes [include that] floating exchange rates are not very compatible with price stabilization" (p. 19),[4] while, "a persistently fixed exchange rate lends credibility to a government's commitment to a stable monetary policy (Welch and McLeod 1993:31). Likewise, Michael Bruno (1990) concludes that "the cumulative history of sharp disinflations in open economies seems to point to a dominant use of the exchange rate as a key nominal anchor" (p. 21).

Our examination of the Latin American experience suggests that the clear superiority of pegged over flexible exchange rates for developing countries during stabilization attempts has not been established. The recent fixed rate regime of Argentina's currency board has been quite successful so far, as has the fixed peg rate cum crawling peg strategy of Brazil's Plano Real; but so also have been Bolivia's and Peru's stabilizations under floating rates. The notable difference between experiences with pegged versus floating or flexible crawling peg rate regimes in our sample was the much greater number of failures under pegged rates. We find that the use of a pegged exchange rate often leads to balance of payments difficulties and exchange market crises that undercut the credibility and the sustainability of stabilization efforts, and that these problems are less likely to occur under a flexible rate regime.

As we discuss in the following section, there are many gray areas in evaluating the success of stabilization programs and in classifying exchange rate regimes. The standards applied by economists for judging the success of stabilization efforts have varied substantially. Likewise, while it is relatively simple to classify unified regimes of fixed and floating exchange rates, systems which use crawling pegs, wide bands and multiple exchange rates require much more judgment in classification. We found that the most common exchange rate policy adopted during stabilization efforts was the crawling peg, often operating within a sizable band. Crawling pegs which depreciate at less than the inflation rate differential can be a form of nominal anchor. While providing less short-term price discipline than a fixed rate, they are also likely to prove more durable. Alternatively, crawling pegs may function primarily to offset price differentials and other disturbances to the balance of payments and provide no nominal anchor at all. As a consequence, it is not always clear how to classify crawling peg regimes. However, in most of the cases in our Latin American sample, we can differentiate fairly confidently between these two types of crawling peg regimes. For example, the tablita form, where the rate of depreciation is announced in advance for a substantial period of time, is clearly meant to act as a nominal anchor.

As is discussed in Chapter 4 by Westbrook and Willett, the term nominal anchor is used to describe a variety of arrangements, ranging from short-run targets for monetary policy to "permanent" commitments which should provide strong discipline over domestic monetary and fiscal policies. For the purposes of this chapter we adopt Mecagni's (1995) broad definition that "A nominal anchor is a nominal variable that by policy decision is fixed or set on a predetermined and announced path to help stabilize the price level" (p. 67). We do not distinguish between short and longer term versions of anchoring.[5]

Even allowing for considerable ambiguity in classifications, both of stabilization success and of exchange rate regimes, the Latin American experience amply demonstrates that use of the exchange rate as a nominal anchor is neither a necessary nor a sufficient condition for successful stabilization policy. Crawling peg regimes do appear to be a promising compromise between fixed and flexible rates and may be an attractive option for many countries. Their successful operation requires high standards for the management of economic policy, however, and the political will to maintain those policies in spite of domestic political pressures. Thus we conclude that there is significant uncertainty about the best exchange rate regime to accompany stabilization efforts, and that countries will need to weigh the potential costs against the potential benefits from each regime, given their economic and political environments.

In the following section we discuss the ambiguous concept of "success" in stabilization. Recognizing the wide range of views among economists about the meaning of success, we apply both a tight and a looser set of criteria. We then examine the role of the exchange rate regime and other policies in stabilization programs in Argentina, Bolivia, Brazil, Chile, Ecuador, Mexico, Peru and Uruguay. The conclusion summarizes our findings.

Classification of Stabilization

The classification of a stabilization program as a success or failure is necessarily a matter of judgment. There is a wide range of opinions among economists and policymakers about what constitutes "acceptable" levels of inflation and how long inflation must be held at acceptable levels for stabilization to have occurred. Some economists would add criteria beyond the control of inflation; Morales (1991), for instance, adds the resumption of normal economic growth to his criteria. An even more stringent criteria would be that the program not only brings down inflation, but does so at less cost than alternative strategies. While determining the least-cost methods of stopping inflation may be the ultimate goal, the analysis in this chapter is limited to the first step of determining what works in reducing inflation.[6]

Definition of Success

While the idea of a long-run tradeoff between inflation and output has been generally discredited, the level at which inflation begins to hurt economic growth in developing and industrial countries is still unclear. Most economists would agree that single-digit inflation in developing countries indicates stabilization success, but some would argue that double-digit inflation up to 20 percent or 30 percent is a moderate and reasonable goal for developing countries to achieve.[7] Bruno and Easterly (1995) consider two or more years below 40 percent annual inflation following two or more years above 40 percent as constituting a successful stabilization episode. Bruno (1993) would accept even higher rates, remarking of Uruguay that it has "kept inflation at moderate levels" (p. 252); this moderate level ranged between 50 percent and 80 percent in the second half of the 1980s.

Durability is another important aspect of the criteria for success. There have been numerous instances where the adoption of wage and price controls in conjunction with other stabilization measures has led to dramatic declines in measured inflation rates over short periods of time but had little sustained effect: notable examples are the Austral Plan in Argentina in 1985–86 and Brazil's Cruzado Plan in 1986. Such programs we can easily classify as failures. There are other cases, however, in which there was substantial genuine short- and medium-run success, but the program became derailed over the longer term. Mexico in the 1990s is a prime example: Following implementation of the PACTO at the start of 1988, inflation was reduced from triple-digit levels to around 20 percent by mid 1991 and single-digit levels by mid 1993; thus we classify the PACTO as a success. But just as the single-digit objective was met, an exchange market and financial crisis in late 1994 forced Mexico to abandon its exchange rate anchor and sent inflation soaring again. Thus we have broken the Mexican experience into two parts. The first part through 1994 is classified as a success. The latter portion of Mexico's crawling peg regime, from late 1994, is classified as a failure.

While recognizing the inevitable arbitrariness of our choice, for the purposes of this chapter we define a clearly successful stabilization program as the reduction of annual inflation rates to the low double- to single-digit range (below 25 percent per annum), without price and wage controls, and maintenance of low rates for at least three years. We do not believe that this criteria is too strong; nonetheless, some economists take a more permissive attitude toward acceptable levels of inflation and, not wanting our conclusions to rest on the use of a single controversial criterion, we also consider a second looser definition of success that requires only that there be a substantial reduction in inflation from previous years that is not due to wage and price controls.

Classification of Exchange Rate Regimes

In Tables 7.1 and 7.2 we classify exchange rate regimes as (1) fixed rates, (2) crawling pegs, (3) floating rates and (4) multiple rate systems, and identify their role in a stabilization program as either a nominal anchor or not an anchor. Fixed rates are always classified as nominal anchors for prices or as a constraint on policymakers in connection with stabilization programs. Some crawling peg regimes may also act as a nominal anchor. We include preannounced schedules of exchange rate devaluation (called tablitas in Latin America), exchange rate bands, and adjustable pegs which depreciate at less than the rate of inflation in this category.[8] Other crawling peg arrangements do not seem to be intended to act as an anchor; these include rates which are adjusted according to an indicator or rule that takes into account such factors

TABLE 7.1 Successful Latin American Stabilization Programs

Country	Policy	Date	Exchange Rate Regime	Nominal Anchor	Inflation Before (annualized rate)	Inflation After (annualized rate)	12-Month Inflation Rate[a]
Tight Definition							
Argentina	Cavallo Plan	4/91–present	Fixed (Currency Board)	yes	March 1991 251.36	July 1996 6.12	July 1995–1996 0.0
Bolivia	New Economic Policy	9/85–present	Float	no	Sept. 1985 20000.00	June 1996 6.33	June 1995–1996 12.25
Chile	Orthodox	6/82–present	Crawling Peg	no	July 1982 26.53	June 1996 6.01	June 1995–1996 8.42
Mexico	PACTO	12/87–11/94	Crawling Pegc	yes	Dec. 1987 422.24	Nov. 1994 6.57	Aug. 1994–1995 28.89
Peru	Fujimori	8/90–present	Float	no	July 1990 35804.00	June 1996 6.19	June 1995–1996 11.92
Looser Definition							
Brazil	Plano Real	12/93–present	Fixedb	yes	Dec. 1993 4777.48	June 1996 20.81	June 1995–1996 18.42
			Crawling Peg	?	June 1996 20.81	March 1997 7.16	March 1996-1996 9.57
Chile	Orthodox	9/73–1/78	Crawling Peg	no	Sept. 1973 550.18	Jan. 1978 46.64	Jan. 1978–1979 30.85

(continued)

146

TABLE 7.1 (continued)

Country	Policy	Date	Exchange Rate Regime	Nominal Anchor	Inflation Before (annualized rate)	Inflation After (annualized rate)	12-Month Inflation Rate[a]
Ecuador	Emergency Plan	08/88–09/92	Multiple Rate[d]	?	Aug. 1988 96.82	Sept. 1993 35.74	Sept. 1993–1994 26.24
		09/93–present	Multiple Rate/ Float[e]	no	Sept. 1993 35.74	June 1996 19.47	June 1995–1996 22.76
Uruguay		3/72–9/78	Multiple Rate[f]	no	March 1972 145.00	Sept. 1978 61.34	Sept. 1978–1979 73.42
		10/78–11/82	Crawling Peg	yes	Oct. 78 55.50	Nov. 82 11.27	Nov. 1982–1983 62.79
	Atraso Cambiario	9/90–present	Crawling Peg[g]	yes	Sept. 1990 413.07[h]	June 1996 16.67	June 1995–1996 29.19

SOURCE: Inflation rates calculated by author from CPI data in International Monetary Fund, *International Financial Statistics*, various years.
NOTES:

a. This is the rate for the year following the end of the program or for the last available 12 months.

b. In 1994 the Brazilian central bank set a floor for the real at a rate of $R1 = $US1 and committed itself to use its reserves to support the floor for an "indefinite period." Since January 1996, the commercial rate has fluctuated within a band set at $R .97 to $R 1.06 to the dollar; since the first quarter of 1995 the commercial (official) rate has gradually depreciated. The tourist rate floats.

c. In November 1991, Mexico introduced a sliding exchange rate band, within which the exchange rate floated. This band was gradually enlarged, making the exchange rate more flexible over time.

d. Ecuador had three exchange rates: an official rate used for accounting purposes; a free market rate; and the central bank's intervention rate, which was adjusted weekly on the basis of a preannounced rate of depreciation.

(continued)

TABLE 7.1 (continued)

e. Beginning September 1, 1993, the central bank's intervention rate was set weekly at a rate equal to the previous week's average selling rate in the free market. All private transactions were conducted through the free market. In 1994 the number of exchange rates was reduced to two: the free market rate and the intervention rate.

f. Under the dual exchange market there was a commercial market in which the exchange rate was fixed, although adjusted periodically, and a financial market, in which the exchange rate fluctuated. In practice, the fixed rate was devalued several times, especially in 1974, when the commercial rate gradually depreciated from UR$928/US$1 to UR$1,640 (the financial rate went from UR$925 to UR$2150). In this it more resembled a crawling peg or a managed rate than a fixed rate.

g. In September 1990 Uruguay established an exchange rate band within which the exchange rate freely floats. The band has been gradually enlarged from 2% in 1990 to 7% since October 1992. In January 1991 the rate of depreciation was reduced to 2% a month as part of a new stabilization program, the Atraso Cambiario.

h. Monthly inflation usually ran about 6–9% in 1990 (130% annual rate), but jumped to over 14% in September.

Description of Stabilization Policy Components

Argentina: Cavallo Plan - Wage/Price agreement negotiated with business, extensive privatization, tax reform and clamp-down on evasion, cut in government payroll, rescinded subsidies, exchange controls removed, indexation banned, price controls removed, austral made fully convertible and pegged to the dollar.

Brazil: Plano Real - No price freeze, fiscal adjustment to balance budget; created a basic index, adjusted daily, with the aim of coordinating prices. The unit of real value was first applied to wages and as a reference for the exchange rate; later to private sector prices and contracts. Introduction of a new currency, the real. Indexing of financial contracts prohibited and wages adjustments limited to once a year.

Bolivia: New Economic Policy - Price controls dismantled, public sector wage freeze/jobs cut in public sector, wage indexation abolished, fiscal deficit reduced, tax reform, VAT introduced, property taxes introduced, import quotas eliminated, tariffs reduced, exchange rate unified and managed float implemented.

(continued)

TABLE 7.1 (continued)

Chile: Price controls removed, privatization, tax reforms, including the introduction of a VAT, subsidies cut to public sector, real public sector wages cut, budget deficit eliminated, import licenses and quotas eliminated, tariffs cut, backward indexation (introduced 1978, eliminated in 1982). Chile currently has a dual exchange rate: an official rate and a market-determined floating rate for private transactions. The official rate and market rate move closely together.

Ecuador: Prices of public goods and services raised, subsidies eliminated, controls imposed on expenditures. Tax reform begun, including simplification of tax system and introduction of withholding. Reduction of tariffs and gradual elimination of quantitative restrictions. Price controls revised.

Mexico: PACTO - Wage/price controls with social pact (agreement with labor and business regarding controls), tax reform, privatization, capital controls eliminated, trade liberalization culminating in NAFTA.

Peru: Fujimori government - Subsidies and price controls eliminated, tax code reform, vigorous privatization, public sector employment cut, capital controls simplified or eliminated, controls on imports lifted (import duties remain), exchange rate let float.

Uruguay: Orthodox stabilization policies and structural reforms; capital controls removed; prudent fiscal policy. Privatization has been beset by political difficulties, and more or less halted in 1993. Began to implement trade reforms in 1978 to open economy to competition; efforts gather strength after 1986.

TABLE 7.2 Unsuccessful Latin American Stabilization Programs

Country	Policy	Date	Exchange Rate Regime	Nominal Anchor	Inflation Before (annual rate)	Inflation After (annual rate)	12 Month Inflation Rate
Argentina	De Hoz Tablita	12/78–3/81	Crawling Peg	yes	Dec. 1978 183.35	March 1981 101.07	March 1981–1982* 149.70
	Austral Plan I	6/85–9/86	Fixed	yes	June 1985 2346.35	Sept. 1986 131.15	Sept. 1986–1987 157.45
	Austral Plan II	10/86–11/87	Crawling Peg	yes	Oct. 1986 102.39	Nov. 1987 205.59	Nov. 1987–1988* 493.66
Brazil	Cruzado Plan	2/86–11/86	Fixed	yes	Feb. 1986 967.01	Nov. 1986 28.65	Nov. 1986–1987* 1369.01
	Summer Plan	1/89–2/90	Fixed	yes	Jan. 1989 5137.91	Feb. 1990 48,749.53	Feb. 1990–1991* 325.48
	Collor Plan	6/90–10/91	Float	no	June 1990 322.24	Oct. 1992 1600.58	Oct. 1992–1993* 2335.69
Chile	Exchange Rate Anchor	2/78–6/79	Crawling Peg	yes	Feb. 1978 33.18	June 1979 34.60	June 1979–1980 30.30
	Exchange Rate Anchor	7/79–5/82	Fixed	yes	July 1979 53.11	May 1982 5.85	May 1982–1983 48.01
Mexico	PACTO	12/94–present	Float	no	Jan. 1995 56.18	Feb. 1997 21.95	Feb. 1996–1997 21.95

(continued)

TABLE 7.2 (continued)

				Aug. 1985 242.39	Aug. 1988 960.66	Aug. 1988–1989 10286.15
Peru	Garcia Govt.	7/85–8/88	Fixed	yes		
Uruguay		12/82– 8/90	Float	no	Dec. 82 169.46	Aug. 1990 93.28	Aug. 1990–1991 106.2

Description of Stabilization Policy Components

Argentina: De Hoz Tablita: Exchange rate anchor based on a declining rate of devaluation according to a preannounced monthly schedule of mini-devaluations. Attempted to gradually introduce market discipline into the Argentine economy by reducing the fiscal deficit, privatizing public firms and opening the economy. Price controls temporarily lifted but reimposed in 1982; wages controlled. Fiscal discipline faltered quickly.

Austral Plan I & II- Wage, price and exchange rate freeze following devaluation. A new currency was introduced and pegged to the dollar. Regulated interest rates were cut sharply. Taxes raised to reduce deficit. A fiscal correction was envisioned but proved to be short-lived (and due primarily to the Olivera-Tanzi effect of the price freeze). By mid 1986 price and wage controls were relaxed. In September 1986 a crawling peg was reintroduced and new price and wage controls announced.

Brazil: Cruzado Plan/Summer Plan - No significant fiscal correction, a new currency was introduced and pegged to the dollar, price controls introduced to combat inflationary inertia. In November 1986 went to a crawling peg to offset inflation, returned to fixed rate in January 1989.

Collor: Attempt to tighten fiscal policy, cut subsidies and reduce public workforce; price freezes; froze individual and company assets above a minimum level; attempts to promote privatization largely frustrated; heavily managed exchange rate; monetary policy aimed at maintaining positive real interest rates. Gradual relaxation of price controls followed by rise in inflation.

Chile: See Table 7.1.

Peru: Garcia government - New currency introduced and pegged to the dollar, fiscal and monetary expansion and wage increases.

Uruguay: From the end of 1985 the central bank intervened heavily in the market. The inflation rate leaped in December 1982 and January 1983, probably as a consequence of the large depreciation of the currency when it was let float, before falling to about 40% in February.

as inflation differentials, market conditions, the level of reserves, and balance of payments considerations. More difficult to classify are the multiple-rate regimes in which an official rate(s) covers certain transactions and a free-market rate others. We judged the anchor nature of these arrangements on a case-by-case basis, depending on descriptions of how the official rate(s) was set. Obviously, the classification of regimes is an inexact science, as is estimating their relative flexibility. A floating rate may be "stabilized" by heavy market intervention, while a crawling peg which is supposed to provide a nominal anchor may be subject to repeated large devaluations.

In two cases, Ecuador's multiple rate regime from 1988 to 1992 and Brazil's Plano Real, we were not able to make a classification with confidence. The Brazilian Plano Real is particularly hard to classify. In the earliest days it was probably best considered as a nominal anchor strategy. Popular discussion often referred to the Plano Real as providing a fixed rate. In fact, it began as an asymmetrical peg with only a minimum dollar price for the real being set. Substantial capital inflows led to a double-digit appreciation, and it is unclear what net effect this appreciation had on inflationary expectations. While providing additional domestic price discipline, these developments also implied that there could be a substantial short-term depreciation within the current exchange rate regime. In any event, the asymmetric peg was later replaced with a more conventional wide band crawling peg regime in which there is no explicit nominal exchange rate (or inflation) commitment.[9] We have bravely put a "?" for this episode in the nominal anchor column in Table 7.1.

Discussion of Country Experiences

The successful cases are summarized in Table 7.1 and Table 7.2 presents information on programs judged to have been failures. Among the examples of long-run success we have a floating exchange rate in Peru and a more managed float in Bolivia.[10] Uruguay also stabilized its inflation rate, although at a relatively high level, under first a market-determined floating exchange rate and then an exchange rate band.[11] Ecuador has also substantially reduced inflation since the late 1980s using a multiple rate system of varying flexibility (see notes to Table 7.1). Argentina's currency board represents a fully fixed exchange rate. A preannounced crawling peg and a fixed exchange rate were also associated with Chile's disinflation from 1978 to 1982 and a crawling peg with short-run success in Mexico.

To date Argentina's current program has provided the best example of success with a rigidly fixed exchange rate. This is likely due in part to the strong form of Argentina's commitment to a fixed rate. By adopting a currency board, which limits the allowable amount of domestic monetary expansion to the level of international reserves available to back the currency, the Argentinian regime provides for automatic balance of payments adjustment and makes abandonment of the fixed rate more difficult and politically costly than if the exchange rate were fixed by discretionary policy. The operation of the currency board has not been without serious strains, however. While the success in stabilizing inflation has been quite impressive, unemployment has been high and the institutional arrangements of the currency board were not sufficient to provide full credibility to the fixed rate of the peso against the dollar. Due in part to the strengthening of the dollar on the world market, Argentina has been running a sizable trade deficit, and in the wake of the crisis of the Mexican peso, Argentina faced a large speculative run on its currency. Success in weathering this crisis appears to have provided a substantial boost to the credibility of Argentina's fixed rate regime.

The Chilean experience since the late 1970s summarizes many of the problems associated with categorizing whether a country had a successful or unsuccessful disinflation under various exchange rate regimes. Chile's government experimented with a number of exchange rate regimes during its attempts to restructure and stabilize the economy, and the outcomes typify the risks and benefits inherent in each type of exchange rate arrangement.[12] The first stage from 1974–78 was a largely orthodox stabilization based on fiscal and monetary restraint with a depreciating exchange rate. In this period the government began a program of structural reforms to restore price and labor market flexibility, cut the fiscal deficit and liberalize financial markets. This approach succeeded in pulling inflation down from about 350 percent to about 40 percent, but at the cost of high unemployment. In early 1978 the government attempted to speed the rate of disinflation and lower the costs of adjustment by employing an exchange rate anchor to combat inflationary inertia and shift inflationary expectations downward. This anchor, the *tablita*, was a preannounced, decreasing rate of crawl below the rate of inflation that was supposed to lead to a rapid convergence of the domestic with the global inflation rate through Purchasing Power Parity. By mid 1979 inflation had inched down to the mid-30 percents. In June 1979 the exchange rate was fixed, and the following three years under a pegged rate saw a continued decline in inflation to around 6 percent by May 1982. Thus the exchange rate anchor policy was initially quite successful. Between 1978 and 1982 inflation was brought down from double-digit to single-digit levels. But by mid 1982 this policy had produced a large real appreciation (on the order of 25 to 30 percent[13]), a ballooning of the current account deficit and a financial and balance of payments crisis which forced a devaluation of the currency in mid June. The peso was then pegged to a basket of currencies and a schedule was announced under which the peso would depreciate by .8 percent a month. This failed to end expectations of further devaluations and in August the peso was allowed to float, but this quickly turned into a "dirty" float that resulted in a continued loss of central bank reserves. In late September 1982 the continued drain on reserves and pressure on the exchange rate led the government to establish a crawling exchange rate, pegged to the dollar, to be adjusted daily according to domestic and foreign inflation differentials with a maximum permitted fluctuation of 2 percent above and below the official daily rate. Thus, we categorize this period as an unsuccessful one.

The breakout of the debt crisis and the shrinking of capital inflows in late 1981 had much to do with the outcome of Chile's exchange rate strategy, since these volatile conditions would likely require a more flexible exchange rate regardless of other factors. In 1982, 1984 and 1985 the government implemented a series of devaluations that more than offset the inflation rate, effecting a real devaluation to correct the current account deficit. The inflation rate came down to the 20–25 percent annual level around 1985–86, accompanied by a recovery of GDP growth. Inflation fell into the low double-digit level by the mid 1990s, and in 1992 the peg was shifted from the dollar to a basket of currencies. The Chilean peso's value continues to be adjusted daily according to market conditions and the differential between domestic and foreign inflation.[14] Thus, this period we classify as a successful stabilization.

Chile's experiment with the tablita illustrates a common difficulty with the use of an exchange rate anchor. Unless inflation is brought down rapidly, substantial real appreciation typically follows even under crawling peg versions of nominal anchor strategies. On the one hand, such real appreciation helps hold down domestic price increases and may be consistent with government objectives to promote inflation stabilization and economic efficiency. On the other hand, real appreciation is usually associated with a substantial worsening of the trade balance, which may result in balance of payments deficits, exchange market crisis and the abandonment of the exchange rate regime, often with serious adverse consequences for the continuation of stabilization efforts.

Fixed or preannounced crawling exchange rate regimes have not, in fact, usually lasted very long. The Latin American experience shows that fixed exchange rates are more likely to give way in the face of continued inflation than for inflation to be constrained by a fixed rate. Typically the peg (or a crawl below the rate of inflation) holds for two or three years and then overvaluation accompanied by a loss of competitiveness, balance of payments deficits, and market perceptions of an overvalued currency lead to speculative attacks or international reserve losses that frequently compel devaluation in order to adjust the real exchange rate and improve the external balance.[15] This pattern of overvaluation and speculative attack was exactly what happened in Argentina in 1981 when perceived overvaluation of the peso and falling reserves led to a devaluation in February, followed by a continued drain on reserves until the currency was let float, ending Martinez de Hoz's tablita policy. In the first quarter of 1989 a run on the currency and depletion of reserves combined with incipient hyperinflation to unseat the Alfonsin administration in Argentina. Similarly, Brazil's Cruzado Plan pegged the cruzado to the dollar, to be "fixed for an unlimited time":[16] seven months later a policy of minidevaluations was begun to restore trade competitiveness. The followup Summer plan in January 1989 pegged the new cruzado to the dollar; continued inflation forced the government to return to a crawling peg later that year and in early 1990 to float the currency. The Peruvian inti was pegged to the dollar in 1986, and devalued almost 40 percent in 1987. Chile pegged the peso to the dollar in June 1979 to provide an anchor for its anti-inflation program. The peso was subject to massive speculative attack in 1981 and early 1982 after two years of fixed exchange rates had led to a much overvalued peso—20 percent according to Kiguel and Liviatan (1988). In June 1982, following months of widespread expectations of devaluation and large reserve losses defending the peso, the Chilean government devalued the currency and adopted a policy of substantial real devaluation.

The exception to this pattern was Mexico, which maintained a preannounced crawling or pegged rate from 1988 to 1994—a period of seven years. To a large extent the relatively stable peso was made possible by the consistency of Mexico's economic policies: under the PACTO—the social pact between business, labor and the government—mutually consistent wage, price and exchange rate targets were negotiated which were strongly supported by the government's economic policies. It should also be noted that beginning in November 1991 the Bank of Mexico allowed the peso to float within a preset but widening exchange rate target zone, gradually increasing the flexibility of the exchange rate. The target zone arrangement allowed exchange rate variations rather than changes in international reserve levels to offset some of the massive capital inflows Mexico was experiencing, easing the central bank's task of conducting an anti-inflationary monetary policy. The band was gradually widened in the face of continued appreciation of the real exchange rate in an effort to maintain the credibility of the exchange rate anchor and Mexico's stabilization policy. But even this regime proved unsustainable. A major devaluation at the end of 1994 was followed in early 1995 by the large depreciation of a floating peso in an atmosphere of great uncertainty. Thus, Mexico was not able to escape the problem of overvaluation of the currency over the longer term. We break the Mexican case into two parts—one part is deemed a success because of the early reforms and inflation record, but the second part is deemed unsuccessful and the pattern of exchange rate rigidity and overvaluation is quite similar to that of other unsuccessful cases.

Because Mexican officials had made the crawling peg regime such an integral part of their economic policy strategy, the forced abandonment of the exchange rate strategy generated a loss in confidence which carried over to the government's whole economic policy. The hard-won credibility which had been built up over years of prudent domestic monetary and fiscal policies was destroyed overnight. By 1997 the Mexican economy was moving back on track, but the costs during 1995 and 1996 were enormous. Mexico's GDP plunged 6.9 percent in 1995 and annual inflation surged from 6.5 percent in November 1994, before the December crisis, to 56 percent in January and hit 151 percent in April. This quickly fell to double-digit levels, but inflation remained high and volatile, ranging from 20 to 50 percent in 1996 and early 1997.

There have been many analyses of the causes of the Mexican crises.[17] The proximate causes were reductions in capital inflows coupled with a widening trade deficit. Higher interest rates in the United States, political uncertainties in Mexico (including the assassination of the leading candidate for the presidency), and election-inspired expansions in both monetary and fiscal policy were the short-run causes of these movements in the trade and capital accounts. The severity of the crisis once it developed was multiplied by an initial devaluation which was much too small (as well as long overdue) and the denomination of large amounts of short-term government debt in dollars rather than pesos.

These developments illustrate the sensitivity of pegged rate regimes to major shocks and certainly reflect in part bad luck. But the Mexican experience also illustrates the difficulties of managing a crawling peg system. A major rationale of the use of a crawling peg as a nominal anchor is the hope that slowing the downward crawl can help to hold down domestic wage and price pressures. In Mexico the PACTO negotiations each year simultaneously set major wage increases and the rate of downward crawl. These negotiations tended to result in rates of depreciation which were too low to maintain a competitive exchange rate. Large capital inflows helped mask this problem for a number of years, but resulted in a situation in which the exchange rate regime was quite vulnerable to any disturbance which caused a sizable reduction in capital inflows. In 1994, Mexico was hit by several such disturbances. It is at least as much to the development of this vulnerability as to the specific disturbances that we should ascribe the ultimate breakdown of Mexico's crawling peg regime

Summarizing the Lessons from Latin America

Looking at the successful stabilization efforts in Latin America listed in Table 7.1, it is true that floating exchange rates usually were not adopted. But when they were used, their track record compared favorably with that of other types of exchange rate regimes. Of the five clear successes, two, Bolivia and

Peru, used floating rates. One used a fixed rate, Argentina's currency board. When we examine the countries included under our looser definition of success we add another floating case, Ecuador since 1993 (Ecuador has a multiple-rate system in which the intervention rate is based on a market rate), and a semi-fixed rate, Brazil's Plano Real, which began as an asymmetrical fixed rate which evolved into an exchange rate band. Thus there are three successes with a floating rate compared to two fixed rate programs. Looking at the failures in Table 7.2, in our sample there were only three clear failures associated with floating rates while there were five with fixed rates.

Evaluating the multiple rate and crawling peg regimes is more complex. We find there was one case of success with a nominal anchor-type crawling peg under our tight definition—Mexico in the first seven years of the PACTO. With the looser definition this regime scores another success, Uruguay from 1978 to 1982 (and possibly Brazil since 1996). This is compared with three failures. For non-anchor crawling peg regimes, there was one clear success, Chile from 1982 to the present. There was one definite success by the looser definition, Chile between 1973 and 1978, and possibly Uruguay from 1972 to 1978 and since 1990. The case of Uruguay is unclear: between 1972 and 1978 it had a multiple rate system which behaved to some degree like a frequently adjusted or crawling peg. There were no failures for non-anchor crawling peg regimes in our sample. Among the failures we find three crawling pegs, all of which attempted to serve as nominal anchors. In fact, if we examine the failures (Table 7.2) just in terms of whether the exchange rate was used as a nominal anchor, we find eight programs (70 percent) were based on some type of exchange rate anchor and three were not. Of the successful programs (including loose definition successes), five (41 percent) used an exchange rate anchor and six (50 percent) did not (a multiple-rate regime and Brazil's crawling peg were not classifiable). Overall, just over a third of the programs using a nominal anchor were successful; of those not using an exchange rate anchor, two-thirds were successful.

Concluding Remarks

The simple comparisons undertaken in this paper cannot tell us which type of exchange rate regime is the most effective for stabilizing economies. In most cases the major causes of success and failure lay in underlying domestic factors such as budget and monetary policies, and we cannot fairly judge the success of alternative exchange rate regimes without systematically taking the effects of these domestic policies into account. This is an important topic for further research.[18]

Our analysis clearly shows, however, that contrary to often expressed views, exchange rate based stabilization is neither a necessary nor sufficient condition for success. Despite the recent successes of Argentina and Brazil, a substantial majority of stabilization efforts based on fixed exchange rates were clear failures. The success rate of crawling peg systems (whether acting as an anchor or not) was much higher. These clearly are a type of regime which deserves serious consideration, but to make them operate effectively is not easy. The initial years of the Mexican crawling peg system illustrate the potential usefulness of this approach, just as its breakdown in 1994 equally well illustrates its perils.

Given the frequency with which exchange rate flexibility is criticized as being incompatible with the control of inflation,[19] perhaps the most surprising conclusion of our analysis is that flexible exchange rates—floating rates or non-anchor crawling pegs—were associated with the highest success rate in our sample. Taken as a group, these two types of flexible regimes had a slightly higher success rate than the exchange rate based stabilization plans—three to three in the tight definition groups and three to two in the looser definition group, or seven to four overall. More revealingly, the overwhelming majority of failures involved a fixed rate or a nominal anchor crawling peg.

This, of course, does not show that exchange rate based stabilization strategies are always inappropriate. For example, a recent review of countries with IMF sterilization programs between 1988 and 1991 found a much better comparative rate of success for exchange rate based anchor programs than occurred in our sample (see Mecagni 1995). We strongly agree with the conclusions drawn by Mecagni, however, that while exchange rate anchors likely can provide some enhancement of credibility where domestic monetary and fiscal policy already has a good deal of credibility, where these conditions are absent, they are more likely to end in crisis than in stability.[20] This suggests that exchange rates should be used as nominal anchors only with great care. The recent flirtation of President Suharto with the idea of establishing a currency board for Indonesia provides a good example of a case where the necessary preconditions for the successful establishment of an exchange rate anchor were not present. Exchange rates do sometimes provide useful nominal anchors, but they don't produce miracles.

Notes

Pamela Martin is a Ph.D. Candidate at The Claremont Graduate University, Jilleen Westbrook is Assistant Professor, Temple University, and Thomas D. Willett is Horton Professor of Economics, Claremont McKenna College and Claremont Graduate University.

1. See the discussions and references in Bruno (1993, 1990); Helpman, Leiderman and Bufman (1994); Koragodin (1996); and Fanelli and McMahon (1996). Sachs, Tornell and Velasco (1996b) also argue that a pegged exchange rate is helpful

in the early stages of stabilization from high inflation, but express some reservations about its use over the medium or longer term. They advocate a crawling band or crawl based on expected inflation, noting the need to leave some flexibility to respond to shocks (p. 52).

2. See the analysis and references in Chapter 4 by Westbrook and Willett in this volume.

3. Major cross-country comparisons include Calvo and Végh (1994), Corden (1993) and Little et al. (1993). The latter study, based on 18 developing countries across a number of regions, concludes, as do we, that the case for using exchange rates as a nominal anchor for stabilization programs has been overstated, as does Corden (1993). Large-scale statistical comparisons include Edwards (1993), Ghosh et al. (1995) and Quirk (1994). Ghosh et al. (1996) interpret their results as supporting the view that pegged rates help reduce inflation while Quirk (1996) stresses the limited success of pegged relative to flexible rates.

4. See also the study by Karagodin (1996) on which their analysis draws and Rodrik (1995).

5. Doing so is an important area for future research.

6. The relative costs of disinflation under different exchange rate regimes is a subject of current debate. Calvo and Végh (1994), Easterly (1996), Gould (1996), Hoffmaister and Végh (1996), and Kiguel and Liviatan (1992) offer conflicting views and evidence on this question.

7. See Burdekin, Salamun and Willett (1995) for a discussion and calculations of the threshold level at which inflation begins to adversely affect economic growth for developing and industrial counties.

8. Our classification differs from the IMF's, which calls exchange rate bands and other crawling peg arrangements a managed float. In many cases this covers regimes in which the exchange rate clearly was meant to serve as a nominal anchor, for instance Mexico in the mid and late 1980s. We prefer not to call these regimes floating rates in this chapter, reserving the term floating for market-based rates or rates determined by rules that mimic market forces.

9. See Dornbusch (1997) and the comment by William Cline for a discussion of the strengths and vulnerabilities of the Plano Real. Since January 1996 the real has floated within a narrow band. Although the IMF calls this a managed float, we call it a crawling peg, although a fluctuating peg might be more accurate.

10. Bernholz (1995:247). One of the first steps in Bolivia's 1985 stabilization program was to unify the foreign exchange market. This was accomplished by legalizing the black foreign exchange market and then letting the exchange rate float, which resulted in a huge de facto devaluation of the currency. The currency was made fully convertible and the official rate is now determined by a daily auction. Prior to the sale, the central bank decides the amount of Bolivianos to be auctioned and sets a price floor below which bids will not be accepted. Peru also scrapped a multi-tier exchange system in its 1990 reforms and let the unified exchange rate float, with the government intervening to smooth currency movements and speculation. As in Bolivia, inflation has somewhat exceeded currency depreciation resulting in some real appreciation. See the IMF's *Exchange Arrangements and Exchange Restrictions* for details of exchange rate regimes.

11. Uruguay's annual inflation rate has stabilized in the range of 40–50 percent.

12. The discussion below draws mainly on Bruno et al. 1991, Chapter 6.

13. Inter-American Development Bank, *Economic and Social Progress in Latin America*, 1983, p. 288.

14. IMF, *Exchange Arrangements and Exchange Restrictions: Annual Report*, 1995.

15. Faced with reserve losses, countries have sometimes taken recourse to tightened currency controls, as Brazil did in 1990. So did Chile in September 1982 in the face of continued reserve losses following devaluation.

16. Feijo and de Carvalho (1992).

17. See, for example Calvo and Mendoza (1996a,199b), Carstens (1994), Cole and Kehoe (1996), Gil-Diaz and Carstens (1996), Helpman, Leiderman and Bufman (1994), Kamin and Rodgers (1996), Willett (1995), and more recently, Edwards (1996a, 1996b) and Sachs, Tornell and Velasco (1996a, 1996b).

18. Such research should also consider the output costs of alternative strategies and the extent to which exchange rate regimes may themselves influence domestic monetary and fiscal policies through discipline effects. Also of importance appear to be the removal of indexation, the extent of trade liberalization, and possibly also the degree of privatization. On these issues see the analysis and references in Chapter 4 by Westbrook and Willett in this section.

19. As, for example, in the quote from Fanelli and McMahon (1996) in the introduction to this chapter.

20. See also Begg (1997).

References

Atkeson, Andrew, and Jose-Victor Rios-Rull. 1996. "The Balance of Payments and Borrowing Constraints: An Alternative View of the Mexican Crisis." *Journal of International Economics* 41(3-4) Supplement: 331–49.

Barro, Robert. 1995. "Latin Lessons in Monetary Policy." *Wall Street Journal*, 1 May, sec. A, p. 14, col. 3.

Begg, David. 1997. "Monetary Policy During Transition." *Oxford Review of Economic Policy* 13(2): 33–46.

Bernholz, Peter. 1995. "Hyperinflation and Currency Reform in Bolivia: Studied from a General Perspective," in Pierre Siklos, ed., *Great Inflations of the 20th Century: Theories, Policies and Evidence*. Pp. 227–54. Brookfield, Vt.: Edward Edgar.

Bruno, Michael. 1993. *Crisis, Stabilization, and Economic Reform: Therapy by Consensus.* Oxford: Clarendon Press.

_____. 1990. *High Inflation and the Nominal Anchors of an Open Economy.* NBER Working Paper Series No. 2518. Cambridge, Mass.: National Bureau of Economic Research, November.

Bruno, Michael. 1988. *Inflation Stabilization : The Experience of Israel, Argentina, Brazil, Bolivia, and Mexico.* Cambridge, Mass.: MIT Press.

Bruno, Michael, Stanley Fischer, Elhanan Helpman and Nissan Liviatan, eds. 1991. *Lessons of Economic Stabilization and Its Aftermath.* Cambridge: MIT Press.

Bruno, Michael, and William Easterly. 1995. "Inflation Crises and Long-Run Growth." NBER Working Paper. Cambridge, Mass.: National Bureau of Economic Research.

Burdekin, Richard C. K. 1995. "Budget Deficits and Inflation: The Importance of Budget Controls for Monetary Stability," in Thomas D. Willett, Richard C. K. Burdekin, Richard J. Sweeney and Clas Wihlborg, eds., *Establishing Monetary Stability in Emerging Market Economies*. Pp. 33–61. Boulder, Colo.: Westview Press.

Burdekin, Richard C. K., Suyono Salamun and Thomas D. Willett. 1995. "The High Cost of Monetary Instability," in Thomas D. Willett, Richard C. K. Burdekin, Richard J. Sweeney and Clas Wihlborg, eds., *Establishing Monetary Stability in Emerging Market Economies*. Chapter 1. Boulder, Colo.: Westview Press.

Calvo, Guillermo A., and Enrique G. Mendoza. 1996a. "Mexico's Balance-of-Payments Crisis: A Chronicle of a Death Foretold." *Journal of International Economics* 41(3–4) Supplement: 235–64.

Calvo, Guillermo A., and Enrique G. Mendoza. 1996b. "Petty Crime and Cruel Punishment: Lessons from the Mexican Debacle." *American Economic Review* 86(2): 170–75.

Calvo, Guillermo A., and Carlos A. Végh. 1994. "Inflation Stabilization and Nominal Anchors," in Richard C. Barth and Chorng-Huey Wong, eds., *Approaches to Exchange Rate Policy: Choices for Developing and Transitional Economies*. Pp. 91–102. Washington, D.C.: International Monetary Fund.

Cavallo, Domingo. "Lessons from the Stabilization Process in Argentina, 1990–1996." Kansas City Federal Reserve Symposium on Achieving Price Stability, Jackson Hole, Wyoming, August 29-31.

Cavallo, Domingo F., and Joaquin A. Cottani. 1997. "Argentina's Convertibility Plan and the IMF." *American Economic Review*, May: 17–22.

Choksi, Armeane M., Michael Michaely, Demetris Papageorgiou. 1991. "The Design of Successful Trade Liberalization Policies," in Andras Koves and Paul Marer, eds., *Foreign Economic Liberalization: Transformations in Socialist and Market Economies*, Pp. 37–56. Boulder and Oxford: Westview Press.

Cline, William R. "Comment." *Brookings Papers on Economic Activity* 1: 395–401.

Cole, Harold L., and Timothy J. Kehoe. 1996. "A Self-fulling Model of Mexico's 1994–1995 Debt Crisis." *Journal of International Economics* 41(3–4): 309–30.

Corden, W. Max. 1993. "Exchange Policies for Developing Countries." *The Economic Journal* 103(416): 198–207.

Dornbusch, Rudiger. 1997. "Brazil's Incomplete Stabilization and Reform." *Brookings Papers on Economic Activity* 1: 367–94.

Easterly, William. 1996 "When Is Stabilization Expansionary? Evidence from High Inflation." *Economic Policy*, April: 67–98.

Edwards, Sebastian. 1997. "Trade Liberalization Reforms and the World Bank." *American Economic Review*, May: 42–48.

Edwards, Sebastian. 1996a. "Exchange Rates and the Political Economy of Macroeconomic Discipline." *American Economic Review* 86(2):159–63.

Edwards, Sebastian. 1996b. "Exchange-rate Anchors, Credibility, and Inertia: A Tale of Two Crises, Chile and Mexico." *American Economic Review* 86(2): 176–80.

————. 1995. *Crisis and Reform in Latin America: From Despair to Hope.* New York: Oxford University Press for the World Bank.

————. 1993. "Exchange Rates as Nominal Anchors." *Weltwirtschaftliches Archiv* 129(1): 1–32.

Edwards, Sebastian, and Alejandra Cox Edwards. 1987. *Monetarism and Liberalization: The Chilean Experience.* Cambridge, Mass.: Ballinger.

Falk, Pamela S., ed. 1990. *Inflation: Are We Next? Hyperinflation and Solutions in Argentina, Brazil, and Israel.* Boulder: Lynne Rienner.

Fanelli, José María, and Gary McMahon. 1996. "Economic Lessons for Eastern Europe from Latin America," in Gary McMahon, ed., *Lessons in Economic Policy for Eastern Europe from Latin America.* Pp. 1–42. New York: St. Martin's Press.

Federal Reserve Bank of Kansas City. 1996. *Achieving Price Stability: A Symposium Sponsored by the Federal Reserve Bank of Kansas City.* Jackson Hole, Wyoming, August 29–31.

Feijo, Carmem, and Carpim de Carvalho. 1992. "The Resilience of High Inflation: Recent Brazilian Failures with Stabilization Policies." *Journal of Post Keynesian Economics* 15(1): 109–24.

Flood, Robert P., Peter M. Garber and Charles Kramer. 1996. "Collapsing Exchange Rate Regimes: Another Linear Example." *Journal of International Economics* 41(3–4): 223–34.

Frankel, Jeffrey. 1996. "Recent Exchange-rate Experience and Proposals for Reform." *American Economic Review* 86(2): 153–58.

Ghosh, Atish R., Ann-Marie Gulde, Jonathan D. Ostry and Holger Wolf. 1996. "Does the Exchange Rate Regime Matter for Inflation and Growth." IMF Economic Issues Series No. 2. Washington, D.C.: International Monetary Fund.

Gil-Diaz, Francisco, and Agustin Carstens. 1996. "One Year of Solitude: Some Pilgrim Tales About Mexico's 1994–1995 Crisis." *American Economic Review* 86(2): 164–69.

Gould, David M. 1996. "Does the Choice of Nominal Anchor Matter?" Manuscript. Federal Reserve Bank of Dallas.

Helpman, Elhanan, Leonardo Leiderman and Gil Bufman. 1994. "A New Breed of Exchange Rate Bands: Chile, Israel, and Mexico." *Economic Policy*, October: 260–306.

Hoffmaister, Alexander W., and Carlos A. Végh. 1996. "Disinflation and the Recession-Now-Versus-Recession-Later Hypothesis: Evidence from Uruguay. IMF *Staff Papers* 43(2): 355–94.

Inter-American Development Bank. various years. *Economic and Social Progress in Latin America.* Washington, D.C.: Inter-American Development Bank, annual issue.

International Monetary Fund. various years. *Exchange Arrangements and Exchange Restrictions: Annual Report.* Washington, D.C.: International Monetary Fund, annual issue.

Kamin, Steven B., and John H. Rogers. 1996. "Monetary Policy in the End-game to Exchange-rate Based Stabilizations: The Case of Mexico." *Journal of International Economics* 41(3–4) Supplement: 285–307.

Karagodin, Nikolay. 1996. "Lessons of Monetary Policy in Latin America," in Gary McMahon, ed., *Lessons in Economic Policy for Eastern Europe from Latin America.* Pp. 146–80. New York: St. Martin's Press.

Kiguel, Miguel A., and Nissan Liviatan. 1992. "The Business Cycle Associated with Exchange Rate-Based Stabilizations." *World Bank Economic Review* 6(2): 270–306.

———. 1991. "Stopping Inflation: The Experience of Latin America and Israel and the Implications for Central and Eastern Europe," in Vittorio Corbo, Fabrizio Coricelli and Jan Bossak, eds. *Reforming Central and Eastern European Economies: Initial Results and Challenges.* A World Bank Symposium. Pp. 85–100. Washington, D.C.: World Bank.

———. 1988. "Inflationary Rigidities and Orthodox Stabilization Policies: Lessons from Latin America." *World Bank Economic Review* 2(3): 273–98.

Krueger, Anne. 1978. *Liberalization Attempts and Consequences.* Cambridge, Mass: Ballinger.

Leiderman, Leonardo. 1993. *Inflation and Disinflation: The Israeli Experiment.* Chicago: University of Chicago Press.

Little, Ian, et al. 1993. *Boom, Crisis, and Adjustment: The Macroeconomic Experience of Developing Countries.* Oxford: Oxford University Press for the World Bank.

McMahon, Gary, ed. 1996. *Lessons in Economic Policy for Eastern Europe from Latin America.* New York: St. Martin's Press.

Mecagni, Mauro. 1995. "Experience with Nominal Anchors" in Susan Schadler, ed., *IMF Conditionality,* Part II. IMF Occasional Paper No. 129. Washington D.C.: International Monetary Fund.

Morales, Juan Antonio. 1991. "The Transition from Stabilization to Sustained Growth in Bolivia," in *Lessons of Economic Stabilization and Its Aftermath* edited by Michael Bruno, Stanley Fischer, Elhanan Helpman, Nissan Liviatan and Leora Rubin Meridor. Pp. 16–56. Cambridge, Mass.: MIT Press.

Quirk, Peter. 1996. "Exchange Rate Regimes as Inflation Anchors." *Finance and Development,* March: 42–45.

———. 1994. "Fixed or Floating Exchanging Regimes: Does It Matter for Inflation?" International Monetary Fund Working Paper No. 94134. Washington D.C.: International Monetary Fund, November.

Rodrik, Dani. 1995. "Trade Liberalization in Disinflation," in Peter Kenen, ed., *Understanding Interdependence.* Pp. 291–312. Princeton: Princeton University Press.

Sachs, Jeffrey, Aaron Tornell, and Andrés Velasco. 1996a. "The Mexican Peso Crisis: Sudden Death or Death Foretold?" *Journal of International Economics.* 41(3–4) Supplement: 265–83.

———. 1996b. "The Collapse of the Mexican Peso: What Have We Learned?" *Economic Policy,* April: 15–56.

Sachs, Jeffrey, and Alvaro A. Zini, Jr. "Brazilian Inflation and the Plano Real." *World Economy,* January: 13–37.

Sargent, Thomas J. 1986. *Rational Expectations and Inflation.* New York: Harper & Row.

Siklos, Pierre L. "The Connection Between Exchange Rate Regimes and Credibility: An International Perspective." Paper prepared for the Bank of Canada Conference on Exchange Rates and Monetary Policy, Ottawa, October 1996.

Ter-Minassian, Teresa, and Gerd Schwart. 1997. "The Role of Fiscal Policy in Sustainable Stabilization: Evidence from Latin America." IMF Working Paper. Washington, D.C.: International Monetary Fund.

United Nations. Various years. *Economic Panorama of Latin America.* Santiago, Chile: Economic Commissions for Latin America and the Caribbean, annual issues.

Végh, Carlos A. 1992. "Stopping High Inflation." *IMF Staff Papers*, September: 626–95.

Welch, John H., and Darryl McLeod. 1993. "The Costs and Benefits of Fixed Dollar Exchange Rates in Latin America." Federal Reserve Bank of Dallas *Economic Review* (First Quarter): 31–44.

Westbrook, Jilleen. 1995. "Does Exchange Rate Pegging Enhance Credibility? Evidence from the European Monetary System." *Applied Economics*, December: 1153–66.

Willett, Thomas D. 1995. "The Plunge of the Peso: The Dangers of Exchange Rate-Based Stabilization Policy." Claremont Policy Briefs. No. 95-01, February.

Willett, Thomas D., Richard C. K. Burdekin, Richard J. Sweeney and Clas Wihlborg, eds. 1995. *Establishing Monetary Stability in Emerging Market Economies.* Boulder, Colo.: Westview Press.

8

Is Pegging the Exchange Rate a Cure for Inflation? East Asian Experiences

Reuven Glick, Michael Hutchison, and Ramon Moreno

Introduction

A common argument for pegging the exchange rate is that linking to a stable foreign currency enforces discipline on domestic monetary and fiscal policy which in turn stabilizes inflation expectations. Presumably the same result could also be achieved under a floating exchange rate regime if the domestic central bank is able to convince private agents of its ability to maintain low monetary growth. The argument for exchange rate pegging in this case is that it serves as a "precommitment mechanism" that increases the credibility of the central bank's announced low-inflation goal. Through commitment to a fixed exchange rate arrangement, policy makers may import some of the credibility for stable monetary control associated with foreign policies.

To varying degrees, East Asian economies have pegged their currencies to the U.S. dollar.[1] Most have also achieved relatively low inflation, certainly by the standards of developing countries. In the 1980s inflation in the region averaged 7 percent, close to the average for the industrial countries, but well below the average of nearly 30 percent for developing countries as a group, or the average of more than 50 percent for Latin America. Can the relatively successful performance of East Asian economies be attributed to their exchange rate policies?

We argue that the exchange rate pegging policies of East Asia economies are *not* the explanation for their low inflation. To the contrary, in most cases pegging hindered adjustment of the real exchange rate in response to external shocks. Since 1985, those economies whose currencies have appreciated relatively less against the U.S. dollar in nominal terms have tended to experience higher inflation. This inflation experience has been generally associated with policymakers' efforts to stabilize the exchange rate in the face of large current account surpluses or capital inflow surges and related increases in money base growth.

Factors other than pegging the exchange rate appear to account for Asia's low inflation, in particular, relatively stable domestic political institutions and independent fiscal policy processes. The conclusion we draw from the East Asian experience is that exchange rate pegging has not led to lower inflation and, in some cases, has created difficulties in macroeconomic management.

The organization of the paper is as follows. The second section describes the nature of the exchange rate regimes in selected East Asian economies. The third section discusses the complications of monetary management in East Asian countries when they have attempted to limit adjustment of their exchange rates. It also discusses how for most countries pegging has not worked as a mechanism to dampen inflation. In the fourth section we explain how the low inflation achieved by East Asian countries can be attributed to other factors. The fifth section concludes the paper.

Exchange Rate Regimes in East Asia

The exchange rate regimes of East Asian economies have varied widely. (See the Appendix for a description of each country's policies.) They have ranged from unilateral pegs to the U.S. dollar (Thailand until 1984, Hong Kong since 1983), to fixed or adjustable pegs to a currency basket (Indonesia, Malaysia, and Singapore; Korea until 1990, and Thailand since 1984), to managed floats (Taiwan up to 1989, Korea since 1990).

In spite of such differences in stated exchange rate policies across the region, policymakers in almost all economies have tended to limit adjustment of their currencies against the U.S. dollar. This is suggested by Figure 8.1 showing indices of monthly nominal bilateral exchange rates against the U.S. dollar over the period January 1985 to April 1995 (for the new Taiwan dollar to December 1994). The indices are constructed so that an increase implies an appreciation of the local currency. The top panel presents indices for economies whose currencies on average appreciated against the dollar; the lower panel shows indices for economies whose currencies have not appreciated or on average depreciated. The yen/dollar exchange rate index is included as a benchmark.

Two main observations may be made from Figure 8.1. First, in comparison to the yen, all East Asian currencies appreciated by much less against the dollar over this period. Between 1985 and 1989, the cumulative appreciation

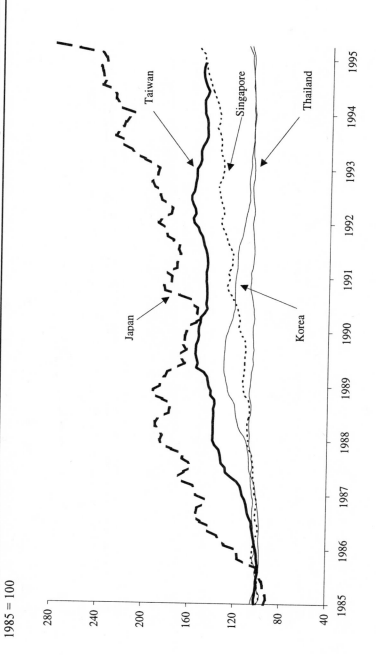

FIGURE 8.1 Nominal Bilateral Exchange Rate Indices (US$/local currency): Japan, Korea, Singapore, Taiwan and Thailand

1985 = 100

(continued)

FIGURE 8.1 (continued): Hong Kong, Indonesia, Malaysia, and the Philippines

1985 = 100

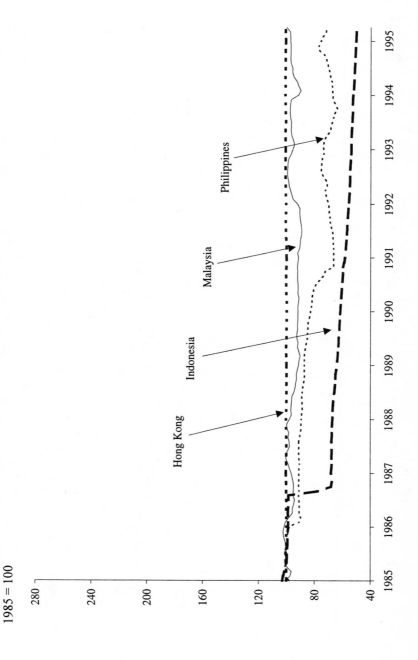

of the yen against the dollar was almost 275 percent. Over the same period only the New Taiwan dollar and Singapore dollar appreciated significantly, but by less than 50 percent. Other East Asian currencies either remained relatively flat or depreciated against the dollar.

Second, with the exceptions of the Singapore dollar, which has appreciated more or less steadily, and the Indonesian rupiah, which has depreciated relatively steadily, clear trends in exchange rate movements for most countries are not evident. The Hong Kong dollar[2] and the Thai baht have been relatively stable against the U.S. dollar, and while the currencies of Taiwan, Korea, Malaysia, and the Philippines have displayed more volatility, they have tended to return to their previous level against the U.S. dollar or settled on new plateaus. Moreover, for all of these currencies (including those of Singapore and Indonesia) monthly fluctuations in exchange rates against the dollar appear to be smaller than those against the Japanese yen. The dampened trends and the relative smoothness of the series appear to reflect policies designed to stabilize the value of these currencies against the U.S. dollar.

The relative importance of the dollar in the exchange rate policies of East Asian countries is supported by research by Frankel and Wei (1994). Because policymakers typically do not disclose the weight placed on individual basket currencies, Frankel and Wei infer the implicit weights from regressions of local currency values against the U.S. dollar, Japanese yen, and German mark, using the Swiss franc as a numeraire. Table 8.1, based on Frankel and Wei's findings, indicates that over the period 1979 to 1992 the weight of the U.S. dollar in estimated currency baskets averaged over 90 percent for East Asian economies, compared to a 6 percent weight for the yen, and 3 percent weight for the German mark. Singapore and Malaysia tended to assign the lowest weight (71 and 73 percent, respectively) to the U.S. dollar, and responded significantly to fluctuations in the yen and the German mark. The other currencies assigned weights of 90 percent or higher to the U.S. dollar, and responses to yen or German mark fluctuations were small or insignificant.

What are the motivations for attempting to limit exchange rate movements against the dollar? One consideration is the impact of exchange rate fluctuations on international trade flows, arising from the high degree of openness of most East Asian economies. Given the historical importance of the United States as a trading partner and as a source of capital for most East Asian countries, pegging to the U.S. dollar is not surprising. As can be seen in Table 8.2, the United States historically accounts for the largest share of the exports of East Asian economies to the three major industrial countries (the United States, Japan, and Germany). The sole exception is Indonesia, which exports large quantities of oil to Japan. The U.S. also accounts for a significant proportion of the imports of East Asian economies, second to Japan.

Reuven Glick, Michael Hutchison and Ramon Moreno

TABLE 8.1 Average Implicit Weights for Dollar, Yen and DM (1979–1992)

	U.S. Dollar	Yen	German Mark
Hong Kong dollar	0.89***	-.01	.02
Indonesian rupiah	1.01***	.17**	-.00
Korean won	0.96***	-.01	-.00
Malaysian ringgit	0.73***	.06**	.12**
Philippine peso	1.09***	-.01	-.05
Singapore dollar	0.71***	.12***	.14***
New Taiwan dollar	0.94***	.04***	.05
Thai baht	0.92***	.05*	.03
Average weights	0.91	.06	.03

***denotes significant at 1 percent; **denotes significant at 5 percent; *denotes significant at 10 percent. Insignificant coefficients set to zero when averaging. All currencies are in terms of units of Swiss francs.
SOURCE: Frankel and Wei (1994).

In many developing countries, particularly those experiencing hyperinflation, exchange rate pegging is an essential part of a stabilization program involving government efforts to enhance the credibility of its commitment to a disinflation (at least initially). In East Asia, concern about inflation credibility appears to have played some role only in the exchange rate policies of Indonesia and the Philippines, both with historically high inflation. Indonesia, however, by following a crawling peg, sought to balance its inflation credibility concern with the desire to maintain international competitiveness.

Pegging to the dollar has had certain drawbacks for East Asian economies. Pegging has exposed them to foreign disturbances, particularly nominal shocks, against which they might have better insulated themselves by allowing greater exchange rate flexibility. Among the major shocks to East Asian economies in the last decade was the strong depreciation of the U.S. dollar against major currencies beginning in 1985 and the lowering of U.S. interest rates between 1989 and 1993. Difficulties may also arise with factors requiring equilibrium adjustment of the real exchange rate. In the case of some East Asia economies, relatively higher productivity growth than in the United States and significant economic and financial liberalization measures have created long-run pressures for real appreciation against the dollar.[3] Given this likely tendency for real appreciation, pegging to the dollar forced the real exchange rate adjustment to occur through more rapid inflation in these

TABLE 8.2 Shares in East Asian Trade

	Exports 1980	Exports 1995	Imports 1980	Imports 1995	Exports + Imports 1980	Exports + Imports 1995
Indonesia						
U.S.	20	17	13	10	17	13
Japan	49	30	31	28	43	29
Germany	2	4	6	8	3	6
Korea						
U.S.	27	19	22	22	24	21
Japan	17	14	27	24	23	19
Germany	5	5	3	5	4	5
Malaysia						
U.S.	16	22	15	16	16	19
Japan	23	13	23	28	23	21
Germany	4	3	5	5	4	4
Philippines						
U.S.	28	36	24	18	25	25
Japan	27	16	20	23	23	20
Germany	4	4	4	4	4	4
Singapore						
U.S.	12	18	14	15	13	17
Japan	8	8	18	21	14	15
Germany	3	3	3	3	3	3
Thailand						
U.S.	13	18	14	11	14	14
Japan	15	17	21	30	19	24
Germany	4	3	4	5	4	4

SOURCE: IMF, *Direction of Trade Statistics.*

economies. For these reasons, pegging to the dollar can complicate, rather than enhance, monetary control and efforts to curb inflation.

Shocks and Monetary Control [4]

To illustrate how pegging to the dollar has complicated monetary control and led to inflationary pressures, consider the impact of two major shocks to East Asian economies: the strong downward movement beginning in 1985 of the U.S. dollar against major currencies, such as the Japanese yen and the German mark, and the decline of U.S. (nominal) interest rates between 1989 and 1993. The dollar depreciation of 1985 to 1987 created a competitive export advantage for economies in the region, particularly the newly industrialized economies of Korea, Taiwan, and Singapore, leading to significant increases in their trade balances. To the extent that the forces moving the value of the U.S. dollar against major currencies were largely unrelated to the economic fundamentals facing the newly industrialized East Asian economies, this created pressure for some real appreciation of their equilibrium real exchange rates against the dollar. Given sticky prices, pegging of nominal exchange rates implied that their currencies were undervalued in real terms. The lower U.S. interest rates encouraged investors to look for foreign investment opportunities, including in East Asia, and spurred capital inflows to countries in the region. Such inflows were particularly large in those cases where market participants felt that pegging had produced an undervalued currency that would eventually have to appreciate. These shocks thus resulted in significant changes in capital and current account flows in the various economies in the region that, as a result of efforts to peg through intervention, posed significant challenges for monetary control.

Capital and Current Account Flows

To examine the impact of these developments on monetary policy in East Asia, Figure 8.2 plots annual data on net capital inflows (CAP) and current account deficits (CA) for seven East Asian economies over the years 1984 to 1993.[5] Net capital flows are defined to include balance-of-payments errors and omissions; the current account includes private and official transfers. To facilitate comparison across economies the data for each are scaled by GDP.[6]

While the magnitudes of observed capital flows do not fully reflect ex ante pressures to the extent that policy changes such as monetary restraint, currency appreciation, or the imposition of capital controls limit incipient inflows, they nevertheless capture broad trends. Observe that the mid- and late 1980s witnessed dramatic changes in capital flows for all of these countries. Capital inflows rose significantly in Thailand in 1988, in Malaysia in 1989, and in Indonesia, the Philippines, and Singapore in 1990. At their respective peaks, capital inflows as a percentage of GDP were above 13 percent for Thailand and Malaysia, above 10 percent for Singapore, 6 percent for the Philippines, and almost 5 percent for Indonesia. Korea and Taiwan have had periods of both large capital outflows and capital inflows since the mid 1980s. Korea experienced significant net capital outflows in the period 1986 to 1989, peaking at 6 percent of GDP in 1987, followed by net inflows beginning in 1990. Taiwan experienced large capital inflows in 1986 and 1987, amounting to almost 10 percent of GDP in 1987; net capital outflows of a roughly equal magnitude occurred from 1989 to 1990.

It may also be observed that net capital inflows (outflows) have generally been associated with current account deficits (surpluses). Along with the increases in their capital inflows in the late 1980s, Thailand, Malaysia, Indonesia, and the Philippines have recorded larger current account deficits.

FIGURE 8.2 Net Capital Inflow and Current Account Deficit: Korea, Indonesia, Singapore and Malaysia (percentage of GDP)

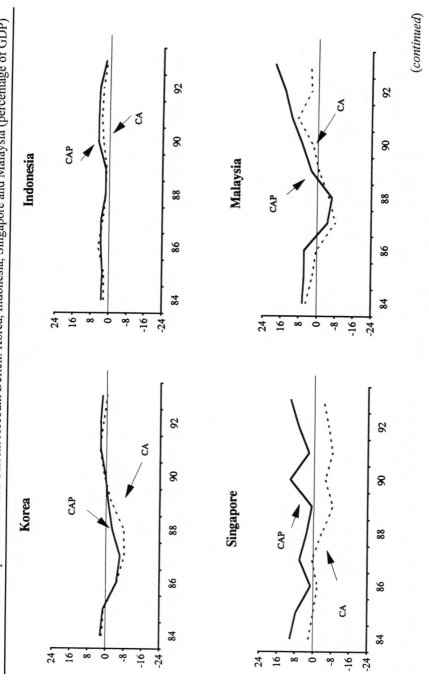

(continued)

174

FIGURE 8.2 (continued): Taiwan, the Philippines and Thailand

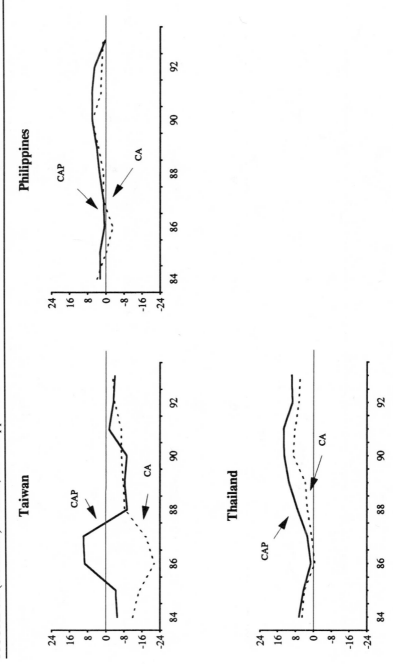

Korea experienced current account surpluses along with its capital outflows in the 1980s and deficits along with its net capital inflows in the 1990s. Taiwan and Singapore represent exceptions to this pattern. Taiwan experienced enormous current account surpluses in the mid 1980s (on the order of 20 percent of GDP) at the time of its large capital inflows; these surpluses declined significantly as capital outflows increased. Singapore's net capital inflows have also been associated with current account surpluses.

By the logic of balance of payments accounting, the gaps between capital inflows and current account deficits imply an accumulation of official foreign reserve assets.[7] In Thailand and Malaysia, the gap between capital inflows and the current account deficits that emerged in the late 1980s financed increases of official reserve assets that peaked at over 7 percent of GDP in Thailand in 1989 and over 11 percent of GDP in Malaysia in 1992. Reserve accumulation in Indonesia amounted to 2 percent of GDP in 1990; in the Philippines it peaked at almost 4 percent of GDP in 1991. In Korea, with current account surpluses exceeding net capital outflows beginning in 1985, reserve accumulation rose to more than 5 percent of GDP in 1988. In Taiwan and Singapore, capital inflows and current account surpluses combined to push reserve accumulation above 30 percent of GDP in the former in 1986 and above 15 percent of GDP in the latter in 1990.[8]

The sharp increases in official reserves in East Asian economies indicate that the balance of payments surpluses were met with a heavy degree of foreign exchange intervention by monetary authorities as they sought to limit upward pressure on their nominal exchange rates by increasing their holdings of foreign reserve assets. With this goal of moderating exchange rate movements, policymakers faced the choice of whether to allow the reserve accumulation associated with the capital inflows to stimulate demand and growth, or whether to restrain this possibly destabilizing effect by sterilization. Without sterilization, the capital inflows would tend to raise the money supply by raising the net foreign reserve component of the money base, thereby lowering interest rates.

Sterilization

Sterilized intervention was pursued to varying degrees in most East Asian countries to curb the upward pressure on monetary aggregates. One indirect indication of sterilization is the extent to which changes in net foreign assets are accompanied by offsetting changes in domestic credit. If net foreign asset increases are offset by declines in net domestic credit by the monetary authorities, the monetary base is unaffected. Table 8.3 presents data for particular capital flow episodes of each economy on annual money base growth and annual changes in the net foreign asset and domestic credit components of the base, each as a ratio of the previous year's monetary base level. (The two ratios sum to the rate of annual money base growth by construction.)

TABLE 8.3 Contributions to Monetary Base Growth (in percent)

		Year of Capital Inflow Episode[a]			
	Average of Two Prior Years	0	1	2	3
Indonesia (1990)					
Monetary Base	10.8	16.3	3.3	19.6	-
Foreign Reserves	-3.0	58.1	62.3	74.0	-
Domestic Credit	13.7	-41.8	-59.4	-54.4	-
Korea (1986)					
Monetary Base	2.7	16.2	48.9	30.2	31.8
Foreign Reserves	6.0	4.3	18.0	81.0	19.5
Domestic Credit	-3.3	11.8	30.9	-50.8	12.3
Malaysia (1989)					
Monetary Base	10.0	28.5	23.7	19.1	12.2
Foreign Reserves	11.0	28.6	36.0	18.6	76.4
Domestic Credit	-0.8	-0.0	-12.4	0.5	-64.1
Philippines (1990)					
Monetary Base	27.6	17.7	20.1	13.0	10.1
Foreign Reserves	18.6	-33.6	63.7	44.8	36.7
Domestic Credit	9.0	51.3	-43.6	-31.8	-26.6
Singapore (1990)					
Monetary Base	14.2	7.2	10.6	10.6	8.9
Foreign Reserves	47.8	96.1	65.9	81.6	89.3
Domestic Credit	-33.6	-88.9	-55.2	-71.0	-80.4
Taiwan (1986)					
Monetary Base	13.6	29.1	27.5	25.7	32.5
Foreign Reserves	64.3	187.8	111.4	-4.6	-19.9
Domestic Credit	-50.6	-158.8	-83.9	30.4	52.4
Thailand (1988)					
Monetary Base	16.3	14.9	16.9	18.6	13.3
Foreign Reserves	30.4	48.4	74.6	62.5	56.2
Domestic Credit	-14.2	-33.6	-57.7	-43.9	-43.0

[a] First year of episode noted in parentheses next to country name.
SOURCE: Glick and Moreno (1995).

Observe that in the first year of capital inflow surges, the associated increases in net foreign assets were accompanied by declines in domestic credit in Thailand, Indonesia, Taiwan, and Singapore. Significant declines in domestic credit occurred in Malaysia a year after the onset of its surge in 1989, and in Korea two years after foreign asset reserves began rising in 1986. In the Philippines the capital inflow surge was initially accompanied by a loss of official reserves because of an accompanying large current account deficit; domestic credit was raised to accommodate increased fiscal surpluses. When the capital inflows continued in the following two years and foreign reserves rose, the authorities sterilized by reducing domestic assets.

The relative development of financial markets influenced the way that sterilization policies were implemented among individual East Asian countries. Most countries sought to limit the serious distortions in their financial markets that would have resulted from the broad use of direct credit controls. However, in many cases, open market sales were limited by the absence of marketable government securities in the portfolios of the monetary authorities. As a result, monetary authorities resorted to a number of alternative devices for curbing money growth.

Some central banks issued their own liabilities to absorb excess domestic credit (Korea, Taiwan, the Philippines, Indonesia). However, sterilization through open market sales was costly since it typically involved the simultaneous purchase of low-yielding foreign assets and sale of high-yielding domestic assets. In other cases, the monetary authorities made pragmatic use of public institutions such as social security funds, state banks, and public enterprises as monetary instruments (Singapore and Malaysia). In some economies sterilization was implemented through changes in reserve requirements and liquidity ratios, as well as through direct credit constraints that affect the capacity of commercial banks to lend and thus the money multiplier between broad money and the monetary base. Korea, Taiwan, and Malaysia all relied heavily on reserve requirements as a monetary policy instrument after the onset of foreign reserve asset surges. However, using reserve requirements as a sterilization tool is also costly. Increasing requirements, by raising the cost of commercial banking, promotes disintermediation over time as new financial institutions and instruments arise to bypass controls.

Apart from attempting to sterilize the monetary impact of capital inflow surges, monetary authorities in the region have from time to time responded to balance of payments surpluses through changes in financial regulations designed to encourage capital outflows or discourage inflows. For example, Taiwan introduced a major liberalization of controls on capital outflows in July 1987. The outward movement of capital in 1988 offset a large part of the ongoing current account surpluses and dampened the magnitude of reserve accumulation. At the same time, Taiwan responded to capital inflow surges by freezing the foreign liabilities of domestic banks. Partly in an effort to curb the effect of currency speculation, Taiwan also restricted foreign access to domestic equity markets. In response to persistent capital inflows, in 1994 Malaysia's central bank limited commercial banks' holdings of foreign funds that were not trade related or intended for investment in plant, equipment, or inventory stocks. It also took measures that effectively raised reserve requirements on foreign deposits, set a ceiling on the net external liabilities of domestic banks, and prohibited the sale of short-term financial instruments to foreigners.[9]

Impact on Money Aggregates

The efforts to sterilize the potential effects of net foreign asset changes on the monetary base met with mixed success.[10] Because sterilization was not always implemented immediately and not always effectively, in a number of countries the reserve accumulations were accompanied by a significant increase in monetary base growth, as shown in Table 8.4. Korea, Taiwan, Malaysia, and Indonesia experienced the most difficulty in limiting increases in monetary base growth. In Korea, annual monetary base growth rose to 16 percent in 1986, fivefold above the average for 1984 and 1985. It rose to almost 50 percent in 1987, before slowing in 1988 and 1989, and falling sharply in 1990. In Taiwan, monetary base growth increased sharply in 1986, more than doubling the average growth rate of the previous two years, and peaked at more than 30 percent per annum in 1989, before declining sharply in 1990. Taiwan's net accumulation of foreign reserves ceased in 1988. However, the rate of monetary base growth remained high, because of open market purchases by the central bank of liabilities sold in sterilization operations in the previous two years. In the case of Malaysia, the growth rate of the monetary base rose from 10 percent in 1987–1988 to almost 30 percent in 1989, and remained relatively high thereafter. (Malaysia appeared to be more successful in sterilizing a second surge of net foreign reserve assets in 1992, with monetary base growth slowing to 12 percent.) In Indonesia, the monetary base growth rate rose from 11 percent in 1988–1989 to 16 percent in 1990.

Thailand and Singapore appeared to be somewhat more successful in limiting the impact of foreign reserve accumulation on their monetary base growth. In Thailand, monetary base growth fell from 16 percent in 1986–1987 to 15 percent in 1988, the first year of the capital inflow surge, and was not much higher in succeeding years. In Singapore, base growth was significantly lower in 1990 than in previous years, despite an increase in reserve assets almost equal in magnitude to its entire monetary base.

Observe in Table 8.4 that in association with the greater growth of the monetary base, broad money growth was higher during the capital inflow period than previously in all countries, with the exception of Singapore.[11] Although Korea, Taiwan, and Malaysia had relatively less success in curbing the growth of the monetary base, as noted above, these countries increased reserve requirements on bank deposits to limit broad money growth and inflationary pressures. This explains why money growth (and inflation) in Malaysia, for example, was in fact lower than in Thailand despite the former's higher rate of base growth. From 1989 to 1993, broad money growth averaged over 20 percent a year in Thailand and 17 percent a year in Malaysia.

TABLE 8.4 Selected Monetary Indicators (in percent)

	Average of Two Prior Years	Year of Capital Inflow Episode[a]			
		0	1	2	3
Indonesia (1990)					
Monetary Base Growth	10.8	16.3	3.3	19.6	-
Broad Money Growth	31.6	44.6	17.5	19.8	-
Currency Appreciation	-0.2	-8.7	-3.8	-1.0	-0.8
Price Inflation	5.8	9.4	9.9	5.0	10.2
Korea (1986)					
Monetary Base Growth	2.7	16.2	48.9	30.2	31.8
Broad Money Growth	11.6	18.4	19.0	21.5	19.8
Currency Appreciation	-4.9	-5.7	-2.2	18.8	9.7
Price Inflation	2.8	1.3	6.0	7.2	5.1
Malaysia (1989)					
Monetary Base Growth	10.0	28.5	23.7	19.1	12.2
Broad Money Growth	6.9	16.1	12.8	14.5	19.1
Currency Appreciation	-7.1	6.4	-3.5	-0.4	10.1
Price Inflation	2.0	2.1	3.3	4.2	4.9
Philippines (1990)					
Monetary Base Growth	27.6	17.7	20.1	13.0	10.1
Broad Money Growth	27.4	22.5	17.3	13.6	-
Currency Appreciation	0.9	-22.1	7.0	8.7	-7.1
Price Inflation	12.3	16.2	13.1	8.1	8.4
Singapore (1990)					
Monetary Base Growth	14.2	7.2	10.6	10.6	8.9
Broad Money Growth	18.0	20.0	12.4	8.9	8.4
Currency Appreciation	6.4	8.2	6.8	2.7	4.8
Price Inflation	2.4	3.9	2.8	1.8	3.0
Thailand (1988)					
Monetary Base Growth	16.3	14.9	16.9	18.6	13.3
Broad Money Growth	16.8	18.2	26.2	26.7	19.8
Currency Appreciation	-9.0	2.3	6.5	-1.2	1.0
Price Inflation	2.6	3.2	6.1	6.6	4.7
Taiwan (1986)					
Monetary Base Growth	13.6	29.1	27.5	25.7	32.5
Broad Money Growth	21.6	26.0	26.4	18.5	16.1
Currency Appreciation	1.5	3.7	13.4	4.4	15.2
Price Inflation	0.2	2.8	1.8	1.1	3.2

[a] First year of episode noted in parentheses next to country name.
SOURCE: Glick and Moreno (1995)

Exchange Rate Adjustment and Inflation

How successful were exchange rate policies in simultaneously maintaining exchange rate stability and curbing inflation? Figure 8.3 shows how the nominal and real bilateral exchange rates of East Asian countries behaved against the dollar from 1985 up to the mid 1990s. The real exchange rates are constructed from consumer price indices; the exchange rate indices are constructed so that an increase implies an appreciation of the domestic currency in either nominal or real terms. It is apparent that in those countries where the nominal exchange rate did not appreciate, domestic price increases tended to exceed U.S. price increases. In contrast, those countries which allowed some nominal appreciation experienced smaller price increases or greater price declines relative to the United States. This is confirmed by Figure 8.4, a scatter diagram relating cumulative nominal exchange rate appreciation and domestic consumer price inflation relative to the United States over the period January 1985– December 1994; it displays a distinct negative relationship.

The negative relationship between nominal currency appreciation and relative domestic inflation rates suggests that pegging to the dollar by and large led to undervalued real exchange rates. Since the tendency to peg limited the equilibrium adjustment through changes in the nominal exchange rate, adjustment occurred instead through changes in relative inflation over time.

The contrast between adjustment through the nominal exchange rate or relative prices is best illustrated by Hong Kong and Singapore. Hong Kong has had a rigidly fixed exchange rate parity against the dollar since 1983 and real appreciation was effected entirely by a rise in the price level relative to the U.S. exceeding 50 percent since early 1985.[12] Singapore, by contrast, has allowed its nominal exchange rate to appreciate by about 50 percent against the U.S. dollar, limiting cumulative price increases to 20 percent less than the U.S. over the decade from 1985 to 1994.

Korea and Taiwan provide less extreme contrasts. The real appreciation of the Korean won was effected both by nominal exchange rate appreciation and, similarly to Hong Kong, by a rise in the relative price level. As in Singapore, nominal exchange rate appreciation in Taiwan exceeded real appreciation, implying that the price level rose about 8 percent less than in the United States since 1985.

Thailand's experience is similar to that of the more advanced newly industrialized East Asian economies. It has experienced a 17 percent real appreciation since 1985, most of which was effected through nominal appreciation (9 percent) and the remainder through a relative price level rise (8 percent). The Philippines, by contrast, experienced a substantial nominal exchange rate depreciation since 1985 (21 percent) so that the real apprecia-

181

FIGURE 8.3 Nominal and Real Bilateral Exchange Rate Indices (US$/local currency): Korea, Indonesia, Singapore and Malaysia

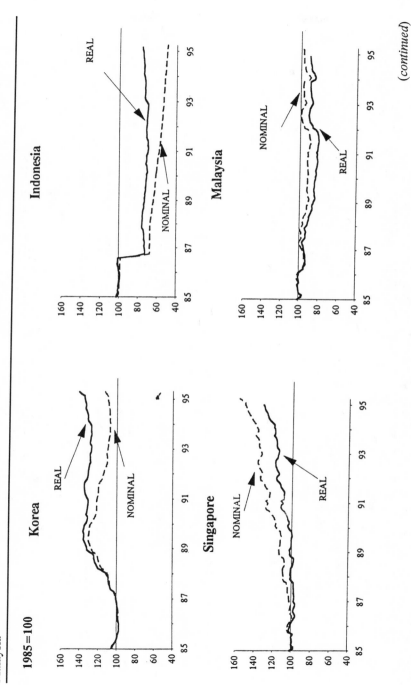

(continued)

FIGURE 8.3 (continued): Taiwan, the Philippines, Thailand, and Hong Kong

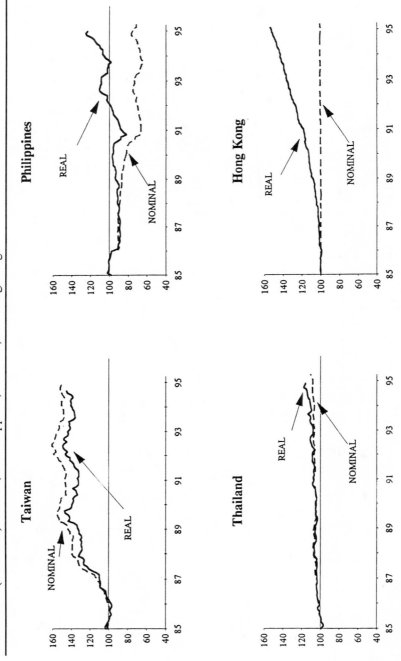

FIGURE 8.4   Bilateral Nominal Exchange Rate and Relative Price Changes Against the Dollar, 1985–1994 (cumulative percent)

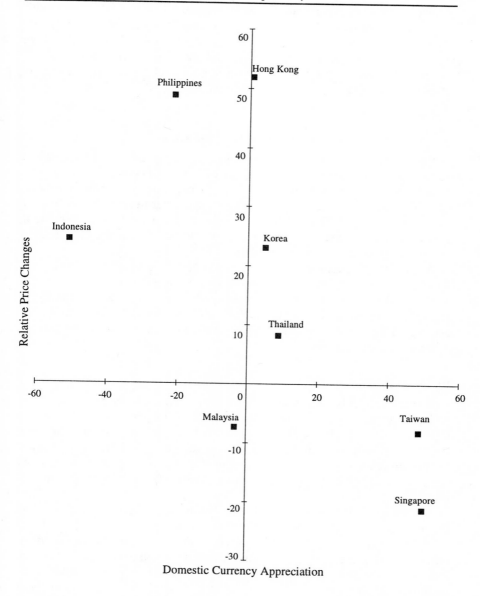

NOTE: Positive values indicate domestic currency appreciation relative to U.S. dollar or higher domestic CPI inflation relative to U.S. CPI inflation.

tion of its currency is entirely associated with a large rise in the price level (49 percent relative to the United States). While both Malaysia and Indonesia experienced real exchange rate depreciations since 1985, they were effected in quite different ways. Malaysia had a relatively trendless nominal exchange rate peg but slow price growth—7 percent less than the United States over the period. Indonesia's currency, by contrast, depreciated more than 51 percent in nominal terms, which, combined with a relative price level rise of 24 percent, led to a 27 percent real depreciation.

Explaining Low Inflation

We have argued above that exchange rate pegging has not worked as a mechanism to dampen inflation for many of East Asian countries. In general, those countries such as Taiwan and Singapore that allowed their currencies to appreciate in the face of capital inflows and other factors tended to have lower inflation rates. Thus exchange rate pegging has made it more difficult to maintain low rates of inflation than would have been the case if their exchange rates had been more flexible.

The question remains why East Asian countries generally had low inflation rates, particularly in comparison to other developing regions of the world. In the 1980s inflation in the region averaged 7 percent, close to the average for the industrial countries, but well below the average of nearly 30 percent for developing countries as a group, or the average of more than 50 percent for Latin America.

Inflation Bias[13]

Recent research suggests that an inflation bias will arise in economic policy if the perceived benefits exceed the costs. The perceived benefits from inflation will be higher if output growth is less than desired, or if political conditions raise the incentive to finance large budget deficits through inflationary policies. The costs of inflation will tend to be higher if an economy is highly open and high inflation leads to a loss of international competitiveness.

The perceived benefits from inflation in East Asia appear to be lower than in other regions. One reason is that the average growth of GNP per capita of over 5 percent from 1965 to 1990 in East Asia was more than twice that of other regions of the world (including the industrialized economies). Taiwan, Indonesia, Hong Kong, Singapore, and Korea are five of the top six countries in the world in terms of GDP per capita growth since 1965. Under these circumstances, there is less pressure to boost economic growth temporarily through a surprise inflation.

A second reason is that budget deficits in emerging Asian economies are by and large sustainable, or easily financed through conventional means. This implies less incentive to inflate in order to monetize public deficits than in countries with less sustainable fiscal deficits. For example, money creation as a percentage of GDP was always less than 4 percent in Malaysia, Thailand, and Korea between 1970 and 1989. In Argentina, Mexico, and Zaire—three economies with high average inflation rates over this period—money creation often exceeded 8 percent of GDP and at some points during the period exceeded 10 percent.

A number of factors have limited fiscal deficits in East Asia. In some cases the size of budget deficits is limited by law. For example, in Thailand deficits are limited to a small percentage of the year's total expenditure, and there is a cap on the percentage of the budget that can be spent servicing the foreign public debt. Budget authorities also must consult the central bank to assess the inflationary impact of budget deficits. In Indonesia, expenditures have been limited to the amount financed by domestic revenues and foreign aid since 1967.

Budget deficits also have been curbed by insulating the budget process from political pressure. For example, in Thailand and Indonesia, detailed budget formulation is primarily the responsibility of civil servants rather than politicians, and parliamentary rule restricts the legislature's ability to alter the budget. Some of the more successful Asian economies also have been able to avoid central bank subsidies to banks or large state enterprises. This type of financing often is not reflected in budget data, but it can be highly inflationary.

The inflationary impact of budget deficits has been limited even in those cases where the deficits are large. For example, Malaysia's very rapid growth and high rates of private saving allowed it to sustain large fiscal deficits (averaging 11 percent of GNP in the 1980s) without triggering inflation. Rapid growth and private saving increased the demand for money and domestic financial assets, thus raising the proportion of the deficit that could be financed by printing money without inflation, as well as the overall level of government borrowing that was willingly financed by domestic and foreign residents.

Turning to the costs of inflation, the dependence of emerging Asian economies on international trade implies that high inflation may generate relatively high economic costs if it results in real exchange rate appreciation and a corresponding loss of international trade competitiveness. Moreno (1994b) observes that emerging Asian economies are highly open—the ratio of exports plus imports to GNP ranges from a low of about 30 percent for the Philippines and Indonesia to a high of 260 percent for Singapore—and also that greater openness in these economies is associated with lower inflation—the Philippines and Indonesia have the highest rates of inflation, while Singapore has the lowest. Comparing the Asian and Latin American economies, he finds that the former are on average far more open and have less inflation than the latter. Using more formal statistical analysis for a large sample of countries for the period since 1973, Romer (1993) supports this conclusion by showing that openness (as measured by the ratio of imports to output) is significantly associated with lower inflation.

Precommitment Mechanisms

The above discussion argues that a smaller inflation bias helps explain why Asian countries have lower inflation rates. Nevertheless, to the extent that some inflation bias remains, policymakers will find it difficult to credibly precommit to noninflationary policies that maximize social welfare. The reason is that agents know that once price setting agreements are made in an economy, it will be in the central bank's best interest to inflate. Inflationary expectations will be set accordingly, and the inflation rate will be too high from the point of view of social welfare. It is therefore of interest to inquire whether, in addition to having a smaller inflation bias, Asian economies have adopted institutional mechanisms that allow credible commitments to non-inflationary policies. Such institutional mechanisms include (1) a credible commitment to a nominal policy rule, such as an exchange rate or monetary target; (2) an independent monetary authority with a conservative central bank governor; and (3) long-lived policymakers or governments which will be around to bear the long-run costs of inflation and not just its short-term benefits.

The extent to which East Asian economies use nominal targets to limit inflation varies. As demonstrated in the third section of this chapter, although these economies peg the exchange rate against the dollar to varying degrees, such pegs were not always conducive to stabilizing inflation. A number of Pacific Basin economies adopted monetary targets, and the massive efforts at sterilization reported above suggest that excessive growth in monetary aggregates is an important policy concern. Nevertheless, it is not clear that such monetary targets were explicitly used as a commitment device to limit inflation.[14]

It is often suggested that delegating monetary policy to a central banker who is particularly adverse to inflation, and insulating the central bank from political pressure, allow a credible longer-term policy commitment that can solve the inflation bias. This view is supported by statistical evidence that the legal and operational independence of the central bank is associated with low inflation rates among industrial economies (Cukierman, Webb and Neyapti 1992).

However, central bank independence does not help explain the low-inflation performance of East Asia. Moreno (1994b) observes that central banks in emerging Asian economies are not legally independent as a rule. Using Cukierman et al.'s measure (an index giving higher legal independence for long terms to central bank CEOs, independent instrument-setting authority, an explicit price-stability objective, and restrictions on central bank lending to the public sector), Moreno calculates an average independence index value for East Asian economies of about 3.0, slightly lower than the 3.3 average for all developing economies, and well below the values of 6.9 for Germany and 4.8 for the United States. However, average inflation in East Asia was much lower than the 29 percent rate for all developing countries. The contrast is even more striking when comparing East Asian economies to Latin America, where the independence index averaged 3.6 and inflation averaged 55 percent.[15]

It is also possible to avoid the inflation bias problem if policymakers value their reputations or are penalized heavily for deviating from a low-inflation policy. The stability and long-lived nature of most of the governments in East Asia means that reputation effects may be more important than in other parts of the world.

To make this argument concrete, suppose that the horizon is infinite and policymakers have a typical loss function where they value output gains and dislike inflation. Consider the case where the government starts by consistently following a noninflationary policy, but then is tempted to deviate and generate an inflation surprise. If an inflation surprise is generated, then the net gain is equal to the one-period gain less the present discounted value of losses in subsequent periods. The lower the discount rate, i.e. the more forward looking is the government, the lower is the present discounted net gain from an inflationary surprise and the more likely the government will continue with the precommitment policy.

Long-lived and more stable governments should ease the inflation bias problem by making longer-term policy commitments credible. Indeed, this is consistent with a body of evidence suggesting that political stability (e.g., few shifts in government) is associated with low inflation rates (Cukierman, Edwards, and Tabellini 1993; Motley 1997). But to what extent do emerging economies in Asia have relatively stable governments that can credibly commit to longer-term policies? Data from a study by Barro and Sala-i-Martin (1995) indicate that political instability, as measured by the frequency of political revolutions and assassinations, was relatively low in those East Asian countries with the best inflation performances—Malaysia, Singapore, Hong Kong, and Taiwan. In Indonesia, Thailand, Korea, and the Philippines, however, political instability was higher than the average of 97 countries in the study. On the other hand, work force instability, as measured by the frequency of strikes, was relatively low for all East Asian countries.

Conclusions

A pegged exchange rate is often seen as an effective device to limit inflation. Asian economies did peg to the U.S. dollar to varying degrees, but this probably does not explain their limited inflation. In the past decade, those economies that allowed their currencies to appreciate against the U.S. dollar experienced relatively less inflation than their neighbors in the region.

Asia's low inflation may be explained in part by the reduction in the inflation bias that resulted from rapid growth, limited budget deficits, and the importance of the traded goods sector. The use of nominal targets as a pre-commitment mechanism to control inflation was apparently limited. In a number of economies, pegging the exchange rate was not useful in limiting inflation, and while monetary targets were adopted, their role as a pre-commitment device is not entirely clear. Finally, political stability may have limited inflation by making longer-term policy commitments credible.

Appendix
Exchange Rate Regimes in Pacific
Basin Economies, 1980–1994

Indonesia. Since the link with the U.S. dollar was discontinued in January 1976, Bank Indonesia has set the middle rate of the rupiah in terms of the U.S. dollar, the intervention currency, by taking into account the behavior of a basket of currencies of Indonesia's main trading partners. In September 1989, the foreign exchange system was modified so that the exchange rate announced by Bank Indonesia applies only to certain transactions. For all other transactions, banks are free to set their own rates.

Korea. From January 1980 to March 1990, the won was linked to a multi-currency basket (consisting of a trade-weighted basket and a SDR basket), but other factors were also taken into account in setting the exchange rate. The Bank of Korea set a daily exchange rate of the won (Bank of Korea base rate) in terms of the U.S. dollar, the intervention currency. A market average rate system introduced on March 2, 1990, sets the won-U.S. dollar rate on the basis of the weighted average of interbank rates for won-U.S. dollar spot transactions of the previous day. During each business day, the Korean won-U.S. dollar exchange rate in the interbank market is allowed to fluctuate within fixed margins (plus or minus 1 percent in 1994) against the market average rate of the previous day. The won exchange rate against other currencies is determined by the rate at which these currencies trade against the U.S. dollar in the international market. Buying and selling rates offered to customers are set freely by foreign exchange banks.

Malaysia. The value of the ringgit is determined by supply and demand conditions in the foreign exchange market. Bank Negara Malaysia (the central bank) intervenes to maintain orderly market conditions and to avoid

excessive fluctuations in the value of the ringgit against a basket of currencies weighted in terms of Malaysia's major trading partners and the currencies of settlement.

Philippines. Prior to October 1984, the central bank intervened to keep
the peso exchange rate within a certain target. Since then, the value of the
peso has been determined freely in the foreign exchange market. However,
the central bank is a major participant in this market and intervenes when
necessary to maintain orderly conditions in the exchange market and to
support medium-term policy objectives.

Singapore. The Singapore dollar is permitted to float, and its exchange
rate is freely determined in the foreign exchange market. However, the
Monetary Authority of Singapore monitors the external value of the Singapore dollar against a trade-weighted basket of currencies. Historically,
Singaporean authorities have targeted the exchange rate (through intervention) to achieve a domestic inflation goal. Rates for other currencies are
available throughout the working day and are based on the currencies'
exchange rates against the U.S. dollar in international markets. Banks are free
to deal in all currencies, with no restrictions on amount, maturity, or type of
transaction.

Taiwan. A managed float was adopted in 1979, involving a daily exchange rate ceiling set by the central bank. The ceiling was abandoned in
March 1980, and reestablished in September 1982. Until 1989, the spot
central rate of the U.S. dollar against the New Taiwan dollar was set daily on
the basis of the weighted average of interbank transaction rates on the previous business day. Daily adjustment of the spot rate was not to exceed 2.25
percent of the central rate on the previous business day. In April 1989, the
limits on daily fluctuations of the interbank rate were rescinded, and a new
system of foreign exchange trading was established, based on bid-ask quota-
tions.

Thailand. The Thai baht was de facto pegged to the U.S. dollar from 1981
until 1984, when it was devalued. The baht was subsequently pegged to a
weighted basket of currencies of Thailand's major trading partners, but the
exchange rate can also be influenced by other considerations. The Exchange
Equalization Fund announces daily the buying and selling rates of the U.S.
dollar for transactions between itself and commercial banks. It also announces daily minimum buying and maximum selling rates that commercial
banks must observe when dealing with the public in various currencies. The
Exchange Equalization Fund intervenes to keep the relationship of the baht
to the basket of currencies within a margin and to maintain orderly conditions
in the exchange market.

SOURCES: IMF, *Exchange Arrangements and Exchange Restrictions* and
Working Paper version of Moreno (1994a).

Notes

Research assistance by Warren Chiang, Laura Haworth, and Thuan-Luyen Le is appreciated. The views presented in this paper are those of the authors alone and do not necessarily reflect those of the Federal Reserve Bank of San Francisco, the Board of Governors of the Federal Reserve System, or the University of California.

1. In this paper "East Asia" includes the more advanced newly industrialized economies (Korea, Hong Kong, Singapore, and Taiwan), as well as economies in Southeast Asia (Indonesia, Malaysia, the Philippines, and Thailand).

2. The Hong Kong dollar has been pegged at HK$7.80 to the U.S. dollar since 1983.

3. Analogously, much of the trend appreciation of the yen against the U.S. dollar in the past 30 years can be attributed to relatively greater productivity growth in Japan's tradable goods sector.

4. This section draws heavily on Glick and Moreno (1995).

5. Calvo, Leiderman, and Reinhart (1992) investigate capital inflows to ten Latin American countries. Calvo, Leiderman, and Reinhart (1993) compare inflows in these ten countries with those to eight Asian countries—the seven studied here, plus Sri Lanka. Schadler, Carkovic, Bennett, and Kahn (1993) analyze the capital inflow experiences of six developing countries, including one in the Pacific Basin —Thailand. Bercuson and Koenig (1993) examine capital flow episodes in Thailand, Malaysia, and Indonesia.

6. The data come from the IMF's *International Financial Statistics* or from national sources in the case of Taiwan. For further details about all data presented in this section, see Glick and Moreno (1995). Hong Kong is excluded from Figure 8.2 because of only partial availability of current account and capital account data.

7. Balance of payments accounting implies that the capital account surplus (i.e. net capital inflows) equals the current account deficit (i.e. the excess of domestic expenditures over income) *plus* the increase in official reserve assets.

8. Hong Kong had very large trade balance surpluses beginning in 1989, with reserve accumulation reaching 9 percent of GDP in that year.

9. Hong Kong also experienced capital inflow surges in 1987 and 1988, as speculators anticipated appreciation against the U.S. dollar. Hong Kong authorities ended the speculation by adopting a scheme that paid negative interest rates on foreign deposits. See Moreno (1990).

10. Frankel (1994) discusses how the success of sterilization depends on the nature of the shocks inducing capital inflows. Sterilization is likely to be more effective, he argues, at least in the short run, when shocks take the form of lower foreign interest rates, as in the case of East Asia, than when they take the form of increased domestic money demand, as in the case of inflation stabilization programs in Latin America.

11. Broad money is defined as the sum of "money" (currency and demand deposits held by the private sector) and "quasi-money" (time and savings deposits), both as measured by the IMF. It is equivalent to the M2 concept of money.

12. In Hong Kong's case, the determination of the general price level and real exchange rate is complicated by changes in the demand for nontraded goods and assets such as real estate arising from political and economic factors associated with its impending reunification with China.

13. This discussion draws on World Bank (1993) and Moreno (1994b).

14. One difficulty is that the objectives of monetary policy in East Asian economies are not limited exclusively to controlling inflation (with the possible exception of Singapore). Like many other central banks (including the Federal Reserve System), East Asian central banks must reconcile a mix of policy objectives, including growth, low inflation, and balance of payments stability.

15. More generally, these observations are consistent with Cukierman et al.'s (1992) failure to find a negative association between independence and inflation for the group of developing countries. The positive association seems only to hold among the group of industrialized countries.

References

Barro, Robert, and Xavier Sala-i-Martin. 1995. *Economic Growth.* New York: McGraw Hill.

Bercuson, Kenneth, and Linda Koenig. 1993. "The Recent Surge in Capital Inflows to Asia: Cause and Macroeconomic Effects." Occasional Paper No. 15. Kuala Lumpur: South East Asian Central Banks.

Calvo, Guillermo, Leonardo Leiderman, and Carmen Reinhart. 1993. "The Capital Inflows Problem: Concepts and Issues." IMF Paper on Policy Analysis and Assessment, PPAA No. 93/10. Washington, D.C.: International Monetary Fund.

————. 1992. "Capital Inflows and Real Exchange Rate Appreciation in Latin America: The Role of External Factors." *IMF Staff Papers* 40(1): 108–51.

Cukierman, Alex, Sebastian Edwards, and Guido Tabellini. 1993. "Seigniorage and Political Instability." *American Economic Review* 82(3): 537–55.

Cukierman, Alex, Steven B. Webb, and Bilin Neyapti. 1992. "Measuring the Independence of Central Banks and Its Effects on Policy Outcomes." *World Bank Economic Review* 6(3): 353–95.

Frankel, Jeffrey. 1994. "Sterilization of Money Inflows: Difficult (Calvo) or Easy (Reisen)?" IMF Working Paper No. WP/94/159. Washington: International Monetary Fund.

Frankel, Jeffrey A., and Shang-Jin Wei. 1994. "Yen Bloc or Dollar Bloc: Exchange Rate Policies of the East Asian Economies," in Takatoshi Ito and Anne Krueger, eds., *Macroeconomic Linkage: Savings, Exchange Rates, and Capital Flows.* Pp. 295–329. Chicago: University of Chicago Press. Previously issued as Working Paper No. PB93-01, Federal Reserve Bank of San Francisco, Center for Pacific Basin Monetary and Economic Studies.

Glick, Reuven, and Ramon Moreno. 1995. "Capital Flows and Monetary Policy in East Asia," in Hong Kong Monetary Authority, ed., *Monetary and Exchange Rate Management with International Capital Mobility: Experiences of Countries and Regions Along the Pacific Rim.* Pp. 14–48. Previously issued as Working Paper No. PB94-08. Federal Reserve Bank of San Francisco, Center for Pacific Basin Monetary and Economic Studies.

Moreno, Ramon. 1994a. "Exchange Rate Policy and Insulation from External Shocks: The Cases of Korea and Taiwan, 1970–1990," in Reuven Glick and Michael Hutchison, eds., *Exchange Rate Policy and Interdependence: Perspectives from the Pacific Basin.* Pp. 138–58. New York: Cambridge University

Press. Previously issued, with additional appendices, as Working Paper No. PB93-05. Federal Reserve Bank of San Francisco, Center for Pacific Basin Monetary and Economic Studies.

————. 1994b. "Explaining Asia's Low Inflation." Federal Reserve Bank of San Francisco, *Weekly Letter,* November 4.

————. 1990. "Monetary Lessons of Hong Kong." Federal Reserve Bank of San Francisco, *Weekly Letter*, September 7.

Motley, Brian. 1997. "Growth and Inflation: A Cross-Country Study." *Economic Inquiry*, forthcoming.

Romer, David. 1993. "Openness and Inflation." *Quarterly Journal of Economics* 108(4): 869–904.

Schadler, Susan, and Maria Carkovic, Adam Bennett, and Robert Kahn. 1993. *Recent Experiences with Surges in Capital Inflows*. IMF Occasional Paper No. 108. Washington, D.C.: International Monetary Fund.

World Bank. 1993. *The East Asian Miracle.* New York: Oxford University Press.

PART THREE

Issues for Exchange Rate Management

9

Intervention Strategy and Purchasing Power Parity

Richard J. Sweeney

Introduction

Liberalizing countries have experimented with a variety of exchange-rate regimes: managed floats with more or less intervention, soft pegs, hard pegs, crawling pegs, and currency boards. In all these regimes, policymakers must often adjust the nominal exchange rate. Under floating the government may intervene in the hope of affecting the exchange rate's course; under soft pegs governments often explicitly plan future peg changes, as with crawling pegs; hard pegs seldom result in no changes in exchange rates; and even currency boards are likely to face situations where there is strong pressure for changes in the peg (Sweeney 1996c). How frequently the government must act depends in part on the regime type. Under a managed float a government might intervene on a large majority of days; countries with hard or soft pegs may, though not necessarily will, have to intervene relatively infrequently; and with a currency board the frequency of intervention is determined by market behavior—light for many days, heavy for others.

Regardless of regime, virtually all liberalizing countries face the problems of when and how much to change nominal exchange rates and what guides to use in judging the timing and size of nominal exchange rate changes, as well as questions about the use of international reserves for sterilized intervention and the effectiveness of exchange-market intervention. These issues are not solely matters of theory but depend crucially on the answers to empirical questions.

In this chapter I focus on two of these questions. First, how effective is sterilized intervention—that is, intervention which is not allowed to affect the domestic money stock—in achieving exchange rate targets. Until recently there was very little evidence that sterilized intervention has any effect on exchange rates, but recent work supports the idea that intervention works. Second, how useful are exchange-rate targets based on Purchasing Power Parity (PPP) calculations. There is a great deal of disagreement over PPP's empirical usefulness in predicting exchange rate pressures and as a guide to the equilibrium long-run exchange rate. It is not clear to what extent PPP provides reliable information on the likely course of the real exchange rate and its long-run equilibrium level.

To answer these questions we need time-series data covering several decades, and these are not available for the new market economies. The questions being asked, however, are much the same for well-established market economies, for which one can get the necessary data, as for the liberalizing economies. Thus, I use data for developed market economies in the hope of answering some of the key empirical questions relevant for both new and well-established market economies.

Of course one must be careful about drawing conclusions based on evidence from a few developed economies with particular institutions and histories and over a limited period—in this case, 1973 to the present. Yet, it is questionable whether it would be wise for policymakers in liberalizing countries to ignore credible empirical results from other countries on these important policy questions. It will be years before the liberalizing countries generate time series of high-quality data lengthy enough to permit empirical analysis without use of developed country data. Further, should the evidence show that sterilized intervention can be effective in guiding the nominal exchange rate for developed countries with relatively thick, active and liquid foreign exchange markets, then it is likely that intervention would be even more effective in liberalizing economies with less developed financial markets.

The following section gives an overview of the policy issues discussed in this chapter and the conclusions drawn. There is strong evidence that intervention "works" in the sense of affecting exchange rates, though at the cost of changing exchange rate risk, sometimes in undesired ways. Further, PPP calculations show some ability to predict movements in the real exchange rate and may be useful in calculating its equilibrium long-run level, but the amount of error involved is still daunting. Calculations of PPP are only very rough and uncertain guides for exchange-market policies.

In the third section I discuss the effects of sterilized intervention in exchange markets. Intervention appears to have important effects on exchange rate appreciation through affecting appreciation's "beta" on the market. Beta is a measure of exchange-market risk that shows the association of the rate of appreciation with fluctuations in the rate of return on some overall market index (with beta often found as an OLS slope coefficient). It appears intervention raises the rate of appreciation by raising the beta risk of the currency; and this increase in risk can have undesirable side effects such as reducing inward direct foreign investment.

The fourth section evaluates the possibility of using purchasing power parity as a guide for exchange-market policies. Since the current period of managed floating began in mid-March 1973, many observers have reported that fluctuations in actual real exchange rates do not appear to tend to revert back to long-run equilibrium levels. More recent work suggests that even simple models of real-rate reversion to long-run equilibrium levels have some ability to explain actual movements; their explanatory ability is low, however. Thus, use of PPP calculations can reduce uncertainty about coming exchange-market pressures, say by 10 percent, but this still leaves a very large amount of uncertainty. Moreover, PPP calculations contain some information about the equilibrium long-term real exchange rate, but with a substantial amount of error.

I summarize the conclusions in the fifth and final section. Recent evidence supports the view that sterilized intervention has predictable effects on nominal exchange rates under managed floating, and that real exchange rates show tendencies toward mean reversion. Both views offer more support for the use of intervention to influence the economy's evolution than the common academic views that exchange rate changes are essentially random and that sterilized intervention has no or unpredictable effects. There remain important doubts, however, about the wisdom of practicing extensive exchange rate management through sterilized intervention.

Overview of Policy Issues

A government can peg its exchange rate for long periods if it owns (or can borrow) sufficient reserves for market intervention to support the peg, or if it imposes rigorous enough trade and capital controls. It can peg for an indefinite period if monetary and fiscal policies are geared towards maintaining the peg. Many governments are reluctant to commit their monetary and fiscal policies to this goal and rely on sterilized intervention to maintain the exchange rate parity. In the case of narrow-band hard pegs, the survival of the peg for a period, sometimes over several years, is evidence that sterilized intervention can work, at least a while.

Some observers argue that sterilized intervention has predictable effects on the behavior of market participants because it signals future monetary policy; Kaminsky and Lewis (1996) and Lewis (1995) find some evidence that Fed exchange-market intervention does signal its future policy intentions. Other observers argue that intervention may influence the exchange rate by changing the portfolio of assets available to the private sector, and thus the risk the private sector bears and the rate of return it demands for bearing this risk. These studies, however, typically make no distinction between the effects of intervention on nondiversifiable risk, which private asset holders have to bear, and effects on diversifiable risk, which do not affect private sector behavior because the changes in risk can be diversified away.[1]

Many observers argue that under managed floating, wide exchange rate bands, or softer pegs, sterilized intervention does not have exchange-rate effects beyond a few minutes or hours. In their view, unsterilized intervention works by contracting or expanding the money stock and has much the same effects as open-market operations. Dominguez and Frankel's (1993a) survey of previous empirical work on the effectiveness of sterilized intervention reports that these studies find no or at best minor evidence that intervention moves exchange rates. This evidence is also consistent with the idea that the effects of sterilized intervention are essentially unpredictable; that is, such intervention mainly adds more noise to the exchange market.

More recent evidence suggests that intervention does affect the nominal exchange rate. Dominguez and Frankel (1993a) present regression evidence that sterilized intervention is associated with exchange-rate changes. They point out, however, that their results are subject to simultaneous equations bias, the extent of which is unknown. Because of this bias it is not clear whether intervention is causing appreciation or appreciation is causing intervention; thus their results are inconclusive. Further, their approach does not tell us how much of the effect they found is due to changes in diversifiable risk and how much to changes in nondiversifiable risk. Dominguez and Frankel (1993b) report regression evidence that intervention affects exchange-market participants' expectations (as measured by survey data) through the portfolio channel. This study does not differentiate between effects on diversifiable and nondiversifiable risk either.

Sweeney (1996a, 1996b) and Sjöö and Sweeney (1996a, 1996b) present results from models designed to avoid the simultaneous equations bias problem that plagues Dominguez and Frankel (1993a). They use intervention lagged a day, so that they measure the association of intervention today with appreciation between today and tomorrow (Dominguez and Frankel 1993a use intervention today to explain appreciation from yesterday to today). Further, in their models intervention may affect appreciation's market beta. Because beta is a measure of nondiversifiable risk, their approach allows one to discriminate between the effects of intervention on nondiversifiable risk, which require changes in expected appreciation because of changes in risk, versus changes in diversifiable risk, which should not affect expected appreciation because the changes in risk can be diversified away. Their results are consistent with the view that sterilized intervention affects beta risk.

If this is so, a country under exchange-rate pressures can intervene to strengthen its currency. Intervention raises the exchange-rate risk of the country's currency, and thus raises the expected rate of appreciation that asset holders must be paid to induce them to hold assets denominated in the country's currency. In this sense, intervention works. It carries the cost, though, of raising the perceived risk and thus reducing the attractiveness of investments in that country which are affected by currency risk: an example would be foreign direct investment, where repatriated profits are subject to larger exchange-rate risk, with the increased risk nondiversifiable. Policymakers may well want to consider whether the gain in exchange rate stability from intervention is worth the cost of inducing higher exchange rate risk.

To be sure, caution is required in interpreting with these results. It is not clear whether intervention causes these detectable changes in risk or is simply correlated with them, possibly because both intervention and changes in risk are the result of other factors. Thus, the relationship between intervention, risk, and exchange rates may be subject to the Lucas critique; government attempts to exploit the relationship may change it, perhaps in unknown ways.

Those who believe that sterilized intervention is effective offer a varied list of possible intervention strategies.[2] Among the most popular strategies are those that make use of purchasing power parity (PPP). Purchasing power parity strategies generally, but not universally, assume that there exists an equilibrium long-run real exchange rate consistent with international economic fundamentals. In one strategy, when the current real exchange rate is more than a certain amount away from the long-run real rate, the government intervenes to change the nominal exchange rate enough to keep the real exchange rate within the government's target range. For example, if the nominal exchange rate is overvalued by, say, 25 percent or more relative to the long-run rate calculated from PPP, the government may intervene to reduce the currency's exchange rate and move the real rate closer to the long-run PPP value. Those who advocate such a strategy argue that over time the real exchange rate will move back to its equilibrium long-run level, and that intervention serves to hasten the return to equilibrium. Instead of allowing disequilibrium to continue, perhaps even prolonging it by intervention to support the overvalued real rate, the government intervenes on the side of exchange market pressures to reduce its currency's value.

Basing intervention strategies on calculated PPP rates is controversial. Some observers argue that the equilibrium real exchange rate may be a moving target that has no long-run value towards which it tends; using out-of-date PPP calculations may be worse than no management at all. One possibility is that the real rate has no tendency to return to any past level (or technically, has a unit root). In this case, it would be meaningless to calculate a long-run, "mean" PPP rate. Evidence that the real rate shows no reversion tendency is presented by Roll (1979), Pigott and Sweeney (1985a, 1985b), Adler and Lehman (1983), Huizinga (1987) and others. Another possibility is that the real exchange rate may have a long-run equilibrium value to which it tends to return, but that this value shifts from time to time, perhaps in unpredictable ways.[3]

More recent evidence (Abuaf and Jorion 1990, Jorion and Sweeney 1996) suggests that real exchange rates show a tendency to revert towards equilibrium long-run real rates. The evidence is stronger for European countries relative to the German mark as the base currency, but there is also evidence of reversion for the Group of Ten with the U.S. dollar as the base currency (Jorion and Sweeney 1996). Although it seems that real exchange rates tend to revert to an equilibrium value, there is evidence that this equilibrium value shifts over time—on some occasions in unpredictable ways that are hard to detect in real time—and for some countries it may have a time trend. This means that PPP calculations have to be updated for movements in the equilibrium real rate that will be hard to detect in the data. Further, the speed of adjustment (speed of reversion) seems to be imprecisely estimated and may be relatively slow. Jorion and Sweeney's (1996) estimates imply adjustment of the current to the equilibrium real rate of perhaps 2.5 percent per month (30 percent per year). If these relatively slow adjustment speeds are taken as simply sluggish adjustment of the real rate to its long-run equilibrium value, intervention that moves the nominal and real exchange rate may be beneficial in speeding up the adjustment process. Alternatively, one may adopt a more "real business cycle" view that the economy is in short-run equilibrium at all times, and that these sluggish movements in the real exchange rate represent an optimally slow adjustment of current equilibrium real rates to their constant long-run equilibrium. In this case intervention would be counterproductive. For example, a supply-side shock may require several years for full adjustment even if the economy is in moving equilibrium over this period. Thus, there is a problem of observational equivalence: the same evidence may be interpreted as a strong case for intervention or as a strong argument against intervention. Further, in an out-of-sample forecasting horse race between the mean-reversion model and a random walk with no drift, the mean-reversion model is superior, but by an unimpressive margin. For the Group of Ten with the U.S. dollar as the base currency, Jorion and Sweeney's (1996) model outperforms the naive forecast that the real rate next month will be what it is today, but only by about 10 percent. This suggests that new disturbances dominate mean reversion tendencies; substantial and prolonged intervention may be necessary to guide the real rate over time.

The Effects of Sterilized Intervention

For the current regime of generalized, managed floating that began in mid-March 1973, most studies find no or little evidence that sterilized intervention affects exchange rates.[4] Many studies use variants of the portfolio balance model; in this approach, if all governments sterilize their intervention, then intervention does not affect money stocks but does alter the currency composition of the international portfolio of government bonds in the public's hands. The country that buys foreign currency sterilizes this by selling its bonds, thus increasing the ratio of its bonds to those of foreign governments (with the foreign bonds often but not always denominated in foreign currencies). If the public views the various governments' debts as virtually perfect substitutes, intervention has no effect on financial asset prices, including exchange rates. Failure to find effects of debt on financial asset prices is then taken as implying government debts are virtually perfect substitutes and thus sterilized intervention has no effects. Other studies use signaling models. Sterilized intervention is treated as a useful predictor of coming changes in monetary and fiscal policies that affect economic fundamentals and thus future equilibrium exchange rates, with the current exchange rate moving to reflect these forecasted changes. Ghosh (1992) finds evidence of a statistically significant but economically quite small effect; Kaminsky and Lewis (1996) and Lewis (1995) find evidence that Fed intervention contains some information about coming monetary policy.[5] Many studies do not focus on intervention data, but use quarterly or monthly data on stocks of government debt outstanding. Until recently, intervention data were not publicly available, although the Fed now makes them available with a lag of over a year.[6]

More recently some observers have offered substantial evidence that sterilized intervention affects nominal exchange rates. Dominguez and Frankel (1993a), for example, regress U.S. dollar/German mark exchange rates on a variety of intervention variables, including Federal Reserve and Bundesbank exchange-market intervention, over several time periods. Though the importance of variables changes over estimation periods, they conclude that intervention has important, somewhat reliable effects on exchange rates. Table 9.1 reproduces some of their results. One of their regressions is

(1) $s_{t+1} - s_t = f_0 + f_1 NEWS_{t+1} + f_2 REPINT_{t+1} + f_3 SECINT_{t+1} + e_{t+1}$,

where s_t is the natural log of the dollar/mark spot exchange rate on day t; $NEWS_{t+1}$ is a (1, 0, -1) indicator variable for official exchange rate announcements (excluding interventions) on day $t + 1$; $REPINT_{t+1}$ is a (1, 0, -1) indicator variable for interventions that are reported in the newspapers; and $SECINT_{t+1}$ is a (1, 0, -1) indicator variable for interventions that are secret (not reported in the newspapers). In this regression, the change in the exchange rate from the close of day t to the close of day $t + 1$ is associated with the amount of intervention on day $t + 1$. Dominguez and Frankel's results, as

TABLE 9.1 Association of Intervention and Exchange-Rate Changes

Period	Plaza	Louvre	Full	Fed Only

$$s_{t+1} - s_t = f_0 + f_1\, NEWS_{t+1} + f_2\, REPINT_{t+1} + f_3\, SECINT_{t+1} + e_{t+1}$$

Parameter				
f_1	-0.693	-0.402	-0.588	-0.296
s.e.	0.091***	0.079***	0.062***	0.133**
f_2	0.180	0.306	0.239	0.285
s.e.	0.126	0.065***	0.066***	0.067***
f_3	-0.500	0.427	0.197	0.317
s.e.	0.351	0.143***	0.155	0.079***

NOTES:
s.e. is the standard error of the coefficient; s_t is the natural log of the dollar/mark spot exchange rate; $NEWS_{t+1}$ is a (1, 0, -1) dummy variable for official exchange rate announcements (excluding interventions); $REPINT_{t+1}$ is a (1, 0, -1) dummy variable for reported interventions; $SECINT_{t+1}$ is a (1, 0, -1) dummy variable for secret interventions. Periods: Plaza, January 1985–January 1987; Louvre, February 1987–December 1988; Full, January 1985-December 1988; Fed only, February 1987–December 1990, takes account only of Fed intervention, not foreign central bank intervention.
*, **, *** are significant at the 10, 5 and 1 percent levels.
SOURCE: Dominguez and Frankel (1993a).

they point out, are subject to simultaneous equations bias. In one interpretation, the intervention "causes" the exchange-rate change; in another interpretation, the intervention is in reaction to the exchange-rate change and does not affect the amount of the change; and the truth might be an average of these two views. They note that if intervention does affect exchange rates, one explanation for their results is that intervention affects risk. In their approach, however, it is not possible to discriminate between intervention effects on nondiversifiable (beta) risk versus diversifiable risk.

The predicted signs of the coefficients in Table 9.1 are all negative (given the way that Dominguez and Frankel define the variables), but the slopes on the intervention variables tend to be positive (one is negative but insignificant). They explicitly attribute this to simultaneous equations bias.

One way around simultaneous equations bias is to jointly estimate a reaction function that shows how appreciation from yesterday to today affects intervention today and a function showing how intervention affects appreciation. There are few variables that are available on a daily basis, however: only financial asset prices and some "sensitive" goods prices. For a reaction function, the observer is reduced to regressing intervention on a constant, lagged values of itself and current and lagged appreciation, as do Dominguez and Frankel. As an alternative, one may stick with single-equation methods, but take steps to mitigate simultaneous equations bias.

Sweeney (1996a) and Sjöö and Sweeney (1996a, 1996b) take the latter approach in their estimates of the association of intervention and exchange-rate appreciation by examining whether intervention by the close of day t affects the change in the exchange rate from the close of day t to the close of day $t + 1$. By doing this they lose information on contemporaneous associa-tion but mitigate simultaneous equations bias. Their results are consistent with the view that sterilized intervention is strongly associated with exchange-rate changes through intervention affecting systematic risk in the foreign exchange market, at least for the U.S. and possibly for Sweden; intervention may also be associated with non-systematic risk. Their results are much the same whether lagged values of exchange-rate changes are included or not; thus, it does not appear that intervention spuriously causes exchange-rate changes in the Granger-Sims sense.

Sweeney (1996a, 1996b) and Sjöö and Sweeney (1996a, 1996b) start with a standard market model of appreciation (net of the interest rate differential):

$$R_{t+1} = a + b\, R_{M,t+1} + \epsilon_{t+1}.$$

Because they are interested in exploring the beta-risk channel for intervention affecting appreciation, they augment the standard market model by making appreciation's market beta a function of Fed (or for Sweden, Riksbank) intervention. The market beta $b_t = b_0\, R_{M,t+1} + b_1\, IV_t$, where Fed intervention IV_t is measured alternatively as intervention; cumulative intervention; and as a $(1, 0, -1)$ indicator variable capturing whether intervention is positive, zero or negative on day t. Their base-case estimating equation is

(2) $\qquad R_{t+1} = a + b_0\, R_{M,t+1} + b_1\, (R_{M,t+1}\, IV_t) + \epsilon_{t+1},$

where (for the U.S.) R_{t+1} is the continuously compounded rate of appreciation of the foreign currency relative to the U.S. dollar from day t to day $t + 1$, plus the difference in the continuously compounded rates of return on foreign and U.S. dollar overnight deposits, as of day t; $R_{M,t}$ is the CRSP (Center for Research in Securities Prices) value-weighted rate of return on the market, including dividends, from day t to day $t + 1$ (results using other indices, including the Morgan Stanley World Market Index are comparable); IV_t is the Fed intervention variable, here cumulative Fed intervention around its sample mean, $CI_t - CI'$; and $(R_{M,t+1}\, IV_t)$ $[= R_{M,t+1}\, (CI_t - CI')]$ is the product of cumula-tive intervention by the end of day t and the market rate of return from day t to day $t + 1$. Some of the more striking results are found using cumulative intervention.[7]

Results for the United States

Table 9.2 shows results from Sweeney (1996a) for Federal Reserve intervention in the German mark (DM) and Japanese yen (yen) for the period 1985 to 1991. For both currencies, the estimated coefficient of the intervention-market interaction term $R_{M,t+1}$ $(CI_t - CI')$ is positive and significant at the 1 percent level, whether or not lagged appreciation is included. The interpretation is that Fed sales of German marks (yen) raise the expected appreciation of the U.S. dollar relative to the German mark (yen) by raising the beta risk of the dollar and hence its ex ante risk premium, equal to beta times $(ER_{M,t+1} - i_{USD,t})$ or to $(b_0 + b_1 CI_t)$ $(ER_{Mt+1} - i_{USD,t})$, though this may be association rather than intervention causing changes in beta. Thus, Fed intervention appears to be successful in raising expected appreciation of the dollar, but at the cost of raising the systematic risk of the U.S. dollar; that is, making the dollar more exposed to market movements and hence making dollar holding riskier.

This increased exposure of the U.S. dollar to beta risk also makes uncertain the ex post effects of intervention. An extra one million dollars of intervention changes actual appreciation by b_1 $(R_{Mt+1} - i_{USD,t})$. Though the ex ante market risk premium is positive, $(ER_{M,t+1} - i_{USD,t}) > 0$, the ex post risk premium can easily be positive, zero or negative, $(R_{M,t+1} - i_{USD,t}) >$ or < 0 as $R_{M,t+1} >$ or $< i_{USD,t}$. Consequently, intervention that increases expected appreciation of the dollar may have the effect of intensifying depreciation, and so be counterproductive. In the sample Sweeney (1996a) uses, the ex post risk premium $(R_{M,t+1} - i_{USD,t})$ is greater than zero somewhat over 54 percent of the days, and is thus negative on a bit less than 46 percent of days. The longer the Fed maintains its position, the higher is the probability that intervention will "work" in the desired direction, but for any time period over which the average value of the ex post risk premium is negative, Fed intervention is counterproductive on average; and there are many periods of several months over which the average ex post risk premium on the market is negative.

To summarize these results, the U.S. dollar's market beta relative to either the German mark or the yen seems to be positively associated with Fed cumulative intervention at any conventional significance level. The association of cumulative intervention with ex post appreciation is much less reliable because intervention is counterproductive whenever the ex post risk premium on the market, $R_{Mt+1} - i_{USD,t}$, is negative.

There is some evidence that cumulative intervention enters the augmented market model separately and not just through beta. For the whole period, Sweeney (1996a) reports that the estimated slope coefficient on cumulative intervention is significant at the 13 to 15 percent level for the yen, but highly insignificant for the German mark. Table 9.3 shows that for many calendar

TABLE 9.2 Association of Intervention and Net Exchange-Rate Appreciation Through Beta OLS Estimated Augmented Market Models of (Net) Appreciation, 1985–1991[a]

Variable	Coefficient	Std. Error[c]	T-stat.[c]	2-Tail Sig.
Model 1[b]				
DEM				
Intercept	0.0003717	0.0001755	2.1178986	0.0343**
Market	-0.0091692	0.0179612	-0.5105015	0.6098
Interact	1.129E-05	3.246E-06	3.4789837	0.0005***
JPY				
Intercept	0.0003361	0.0001566	2.1465909	0.0320**
Market	-0.0096363	0.0161301	-0.5974133	0.5503
Interact	2.111E-05	4.015E-06	5.2582725	0.0000***
Model 2[b]				
DEM				
Intercept	0.0003195	0.0001566	2.0396961	0.0415**
Market	-0.0095826	0.0161160	-0.5946027	0.5522
Interact	2.091E-05	4.012E-06	5.2124243	0.0000*
Appr. Lag	0.0569471	0.0236514	2.4077703	0.0162**
JPY				
Intercept	0.0003512	0.0001756	2.0001462	0.0456**
Market	-0.0093893	0.0179500	-0.5230829	0.6010
Interact	1.096E-05	3.246E-06	3.3773171	0.0007***
Appr. Lag	0.0528312	0.0237902	2.2207117	0.0265**

NOTES:

a. Definitions of variables. *Dependent variable*: the continuously compounded rate of appreciation of the foreign currency relative to the U.S. dollar from day t to day $t+1$, plus the difference in the continuously compounded rates of return on foreign and U.S. dollar overnight deposits, as of day t. *Market*: the CRSP value-weighted rate of return on the market, including dividends, from day t to day $t+1$. IV_t: the Fed intervention variable, here cumulative Fed intervention around it sample mean, $CI_t - CI'$. *Interact*: the product of cumulative intervention by the end of day t and the market rate of return from day t to day $t+1$. *Appr. Lag*: the lagged value of the dependent variable.

b. Models estimated: *Model 1*: $R_{t+1} = a + b_0 R_{M,t+1} + b_1 (R_{M,t+1} IV_t) + \varepsilon_{t+1}$. *Model 2*: $R_{t+1} = a + b_0 R_{M,t+1} + b_1 (R_{M,t+1} IV_t) + c R_t + \varepsilon_{t+1}$.

c. OLS standard errors are listed here and used to calculate the *t*-statistics listed. Sweeney (1995a) presents evidence that residuals are heteroscedastic. The *t*-statistics for intervention-market interaction terms for the period 1985–1991,

(continued)

TABLE 9.2 (continued)

calculated with both OLS and White heteroscedastic-consistent standard errors, fall
in the latter case, but no inference is changed; this is also true of comparisons based
on OLS and M-GARCH standard errors (see footnote c, Table 3, and Table 4 and
Appendix to Sweeney 1995a).
*, **, *** are significant at the 10, 5 and 1 percent levels.
SOURCE: Sweeney (1995a).

years the slope on cumulative intervention entered separately is not significant at conventional levels for either currency. (The year 1986 is omitted
because the Fed intervened in neither currency in that year.) The model is as
above (without lagged appreciation) except that cumulative intervention is
also included separately.

Table 9.3 shows test results across calendar years when only predetermined CI_t is included. Under the null that cumulative intervention does not
enter separately and assuming that t-values are asymptotically distributed
$N(0, 1)$,[8] the sum of calendar-year t-statistics on cumulative intervention,
divided by $6^{1/2}$, $\sum_{j=1}^{6} t_j/(6)^{1/2}$, is asymptotically distributed $N(0, 1)$. The sum of
the squares of the six years' t-statistics, $\sum_{j=1}^{6} (t_j)^2$, is asymptotically distributed
χ^2 with 6 degrees of freedom (10, 5 and 1 percent critical values are 10.6,
12.6 and 16.8). For the German mark $\sum_{j=1}^{6} t_j/(6)^{1/2}$ is 2.4459 and $\sum_{j=1}^{6}(t_j)^2$ is
17.3516; for the yen, 2.0683, and 6.0660.[9] From Table 9.3, t-statistics for
both currencies are unstable across years; more important, the slopes as well
as the t-values for cumulative intervention are unstable across years.

It is not clear whether intervention causes these detectable changes in risk
or is simply correlated with them, possibly because both intervention and risk
changes are the result of other factors. For example, during a period of
international tension in the Middle East the dollar's beta may rise as people
move funds to safe haven in the U.S. and hence become more exposed to
U.S. dollar risk, while the ups and downs of the crisis lead to more Fed
intervention.

An important caveat is that the association of intervention with appreciation, through either the systematic risk or non-systematic risk channel, is
unstable. Though the association of beta and cumulative intervention is
statistically reliable, because the ex post risk premium on the market is
unreliable as to sign, so the ex post association of intervention with appreciation is also unreliable. It is necessary to look across several years to find
evidence of the association of appreciation with cumulative intervention
through non-systematic risk; though there is evidence of association, the
estimated slope coefficients show substantial instability across years.

TABLE 9.3 Cumulative Intervention Enters Separately and Through Beta

Currency/Year	t-statistic	t^2
DEM		
1985	0.7031	0.4943
1987	-.6277	0.3940
1988	2.4749**	6.1251**
1989	2.5943***	6.7304***
1990	-.8514	0.7249
1991	1.6979*	2.8829*
$\sum_{j=1}^{6} t/(6)^{1/2}$	2.4459**	--
$\sum_{j=1}^{6} t^2$	--	17.3516***
JPY		
1985	0.7294	0.5320
1987	-0.0662	0.0044
1988	-0.2246	0.0285
1989	1.3048	1.7025
1990	1.2704	1.6139
1991	1.4708	2.1633
$\sum_{j=1}^{6} t/(6)^{1/2}$	2.0683**	--
$\sum_{j=1}^{6} t^2$	--	6.0666

NOTES:
a. The model is: $R_{t+1} = a + b_0 R_{M,t+1} + b_1 (R_{M,t+1} IV_t) + d_1 CI_t + \epsilon_{t+1}$. $\sum_{j=1}^{6} t/(6)^{1/2}$ is asymptotically distributed N(0, 1). $\sum_{j=1}^{6} t^2$ is asymptotically distributed Chi-square with 6 degrees of freedom; 10, 5 and 1 percent critical values are 10.6, 12.6 and 16.8; for individual years t^2 is distributed Chi-square with 1 degree of freedom, with critical values of 2.71, 3.84 and 6.63, giving the same inferences as the t-statistic.
*, **, *** Statistically significant at the 10, 5 and 1 percent levels.

Results for Sweden

Sjöö and Sweeney (1996a, 1996b) present results for Sweden, using daily intervention data over the years 1986–1990. During these years Sweden kept the krona pegged within a 3 percent band relative to a basket of foreign currencies including the U.S. dollar and the German mark. The Riksbank, the Swedish central bank, used both the U.S. dollar and German mark as intervention currencies; there are some indications that the large bulk of intervention was in U.S. dollars. This pegging-through-intervention strategy was an obvious success over this period in the sense that the peg was maintained. Of course this assessment takes no account of possible adverse policies, say monetary and fiscal policies, that this pegging strategy might have led to or facilitated.

Given that Riksbank intervention was successful in maintaining the peg, it might seem unnecessary to investigate the association of Riksbank intervention with krona appreciation. The Riksbank was not targeting the krona/ U.S. dollar rate, however, when it bought or sold U.S. dollars but was trying to maintain the krona's peg with the basket. In contrast, Fed intervention in the German mark or yen was often aimed at moving those currencies relative to the U.S. dollar, sometimes even with quantitative goals in mind. Further, even prejudging that the Riksbank's intervention affected the exchange rate in a predictable way, one might still wonder to what extend intervention acted through effects on beta risk rather than directly on the exchange rate.

Sjöö and Sweeney base their work on the augmented market model in (2) above. They investigate both the krona/dollar and krona/German mark net appreciation rates, because some intervention, even if only a relatively minor part, was in German marks. For the market index they use either the Stockholm stock market index or a U.S. index, with both indices measured in terms of krona. (That is, the U.S. index multiplied by the krona/dollar rate to express the index in krona. This is equivalent to reversing the sign of the appreciation variable and using the market indices in U.S. dollar terms.)

Results for the krona/dollar rate show a weaker association of Riksbank intervention with the market beta of krona/dollar net appreciation than found above for Fed intervention in the German mark and yen. Similarly, the evidence that Riksbank intervention affected nonsystematic risk is weaker and more unstable than that found for the U.S.

One interpretation is that Riksbank intervention has no predictable, detectable effect on the krona/dollar exchange rate; another is that effects are there in the data but are hard to detect and unreliable.

A naive view of the mechanism by which Riksbank intervention affects the exchange rate is that when the krona weakens relative to currencies in the basket other than the U.S. dollar, the Riksbank buys krona with dollars to strengthen the krona relative to the dollar and thereby offset the fall of the krona relative to the other currencies. Of course, the purchases of kronas and sales of dollars, even if sterilized by both central banks, are likely to affect the krona relative to other currencies if they affect the krona relative to the U.S. dollar. This might occur because the krona strengthens but no basket currency changes in reaction, with the krona then rising relative to all the basket currencies. This is possible if the main effect of Riksbank intervention is through signaling. Market participants may perceive that fundamentals have changed in such a way that the Swedish government must alter policies in order to maintain the basket peg over the longer term, with speculators putting downward pressure on the krona until they see signs that such policy changes will be forthcoming. Ongoing Riksbank intervention may serve as a signal of the government's commitment to polices that will preserve the peg. In this view the size of Riksbank intervention in the U.S. dollar, relative to the perceived need for policy changes, may be more important to speculators than any effect of the intervention on actual krona/dollar net appreciation.

This interpretation requires that the market must have a sense of the size of ongoing interventions. Riksbank intervention is secret in its details but relatively well known in its broad outlines. For example, the Riksbank announces in advance when it is going to pay off or refund foreign-denominated debt. Similarly, the market seems to know on which days Riksbank intervention is heavy, light or zero. (Approximately 60 percent of trading days see some intervention.)

The Differences in Fed and Riksbank Results

Because of the relative size of their populations, Sweden has substantially less economic and financial weight than the United States or Germany, even though their per capita wealth levels are roughly the same. This may partly explain why it is more difficult to detect an association of Riksbank intervention with net appreciation of the krona/dollar rate through either systematic or nonsystematic risk than it is to find an association between Fed intervention and either yen or German mark net appreciation relative to the U.S. dollar.

An alternative, perhaps complementary explanation is that the Fed and the Riksbank were pursuing fundamentally different exchange-rate strategies that may have different consequences for risk in augmented market models. The Fed intervened on approximately 10 percent of the days in the German mark or yen, its two intervention currencies, and then often intervened for several days in a row, whereas the Riksbank intervened in approximately 60 percent of all days. Often, but hardly always, Fed intervention was triggered by exchange-rate crises when one or both of the currencies had moved "too far, too fast," and at other times did not intervene. The Riksbank intervened frequently, not in response to crises by and large, but to maintain the basket peg on a day-to-day basis. The Fed was interested in two key bilateral rates; the Riksbank was interested in the value of the krona relative to a basket of currencies. The Fed had to have detectable effects on intervention currencies to be successful. The Riksbank did not have to have detectable effects on intervention currencies for success, but rather needed the basket rate to stay within the preannounced zone. The Riksbank could be successful on a day when it sold U.S. dollars for krona and still saw the dollar strengthen relative to the krona, provided the intervention was associated with a rise in other basket currencies that relieved pressure on the krona rate.

Based on the above discussion, one might assume that governments can effect exchange rates through sterilized intervention on average, although the results are likely to vary a good deal from one episode to another. This raises the issue of how governments might decide on intervention policies—one commonly suggested guide is purchasing power parity.

Purchasing Power Parity as a
Guide to Intervention Policy

Economists' views on the usefulness and applicability of PPP have varied sharply over time. In the aftermath of World War I, Cassells offered PPP as a rough approximation, useful for giving orders of magnitude, of the equilibrium exchange rate based on how national price levels had changed since the start of the war. Until the mid 1960s, economists largely viewed PPP as holding only approximately and only over the long run. Frequent and perhaps prolonged deviations from PPP were observed, and many articles presented estimates of long lags in adjustment to long-run PPP. Although some early models based on the monetary approach to the balance of payments assumed PPP holds exactly on a quarterly or monthly basis (Johnson 1972, Bilson 1978),[10] empirical work from the late 1970s through the mid 1980s suggested that it holds only in the very long run or not at all. In particular, authors such as Roll (1979), Pigott and Sweeney (1985a, 1985b), and Adler and Lehman (1983) reported results suggesting that the real (or PPP-adjusted) exchange rate contains a unit root (or more generally was not mean stationary). By the late 1980s and early to mid 1990s, authors reported test results rejecting the null of a unit root in real exchange rates (Abuaf and Jorion 1990, Jorion and Sweeney 1996). Even before these controversies, many observers (for example, Willett 1982) were skeptical about using PPP calculations as a guide for exchange rate policies. These drastic revisions in views, particularly about empirical relationships, intensified skepticism about using PPP as a guide for either government exchange-rate policymaking or private firms' international investment decisions.

Figure 9.1 shows the U.S.-German real exchange rate from April 1973 to December 1988 (before reunification). The data are normalized so the sample mean is 100. Many observers detect distinct cycles in the real exchange rate; they see it rising above and falling below its average, but tending to revert to this average—that is, showing mean reversion. Others argue that this pattern is to be expected if the real exchange rate shows no tendency to revert to a long-run level (technically, if the real exchange rate has a unit root, as for example in a random walk series). Since at least Roberts (1959), economists

Figure 9.1 U.S.-German Real Exchange Rate: April 1973 to December 1988

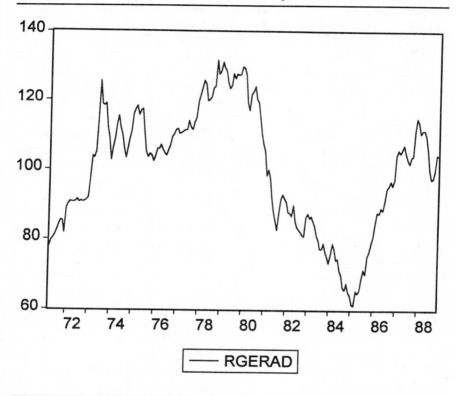

SOURCE: Author's calculation from IMF's *International Financial Statistics* data.

have known that the levels of such series contain ex post patterns that jump out to the eye but are wholly spurious.

The view that the real exchange rate shows mean reversion is the basis for graphs occasionally published in the *Wall Street Journal*. These plot a measure of the U.S. real exchange rate that fluctuates over time around a horizontal line that is supposed to show the long-run real rate. Many observers argue for using intervention to move the nominal exchange rate in order to reduce deviations in the real rate from its long-run value. For example, some target zone advocates propose intervention when the real rate moves more than a certain distance from the equilibrium long-run real exchange rate. Finding the "right" value of the real exchange rate, or the horizontal line, though, is full of uncertainty. (Some observers charge that governments use intervention to attempt to keep their real rates undervalued in order to promote exports as part of an export-led macroeconomic and development strategy, a charge leveled against Japan through the 1960s and 1970s.)

Figures 9.2 and 9.3 for April 1974–December 1982 and January 1983 to December 1988 illustrate one problem. The mean of the series in Figure 9.2 is 110. If this is taken as the long-run equilibrium rate,[11] the ability of this long-run rate to predict the behavior of the actual real rate over the coming period is quite slight, as shown by Figure 9.3 where the mean is 87. For most of the second period the rate is far from the first period's mean value. On the one hand, this might be taken as showing the need for intervention to move the rate to its equilibrium value. On the other, this might be taken as showing that the mean in Figure 9.3 is the appropriate estimate of the long-run real rate, and that intervention based on the previous period's mean would be counterproductive.

Figure 9.2 U.S.-German Real Exchange Rate: April 1974 to December 1982

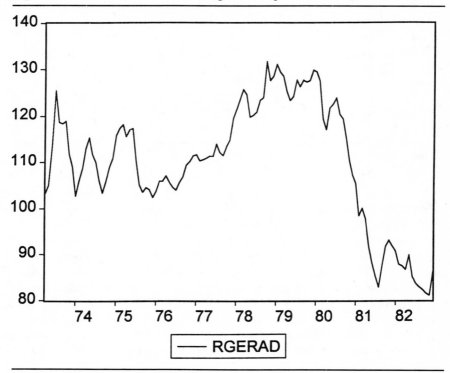

SOURCE: Author's calculation from IMF's *International Financial Statistics* data.

Figure 9.3 U.S.-German Real Exchange Rate: January 1983 to December 1988

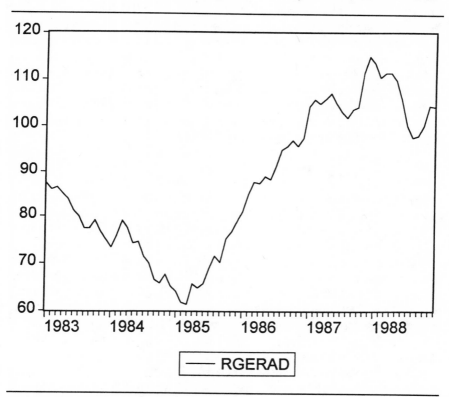

SOURCE: Author's calculation from IMF's *International Financial Statistics* data.

Because of the importance of whether the real rate shows mean reversion, and if so, to what long-run rate, observers have reported numerous tests for mean reversion in real rates. Unfortunately, the results are mixed, though there is now substantial evidence of mean reversion. Some authors who report results rejecting the null of no mean reversion in real exchange rates use annual data over long time periods (Abuaf and Jorion 1990, Diebold, Husted and Rush 1991, and Lothian 1991). This has the drawback of looking across periods of stunning economic change, causing some doubt about the stability of the statistical process generating real exchange rates. These papers look at one real exchange rate at a time. Studies looking at the current period of generalized managed floating, which began in March 1973, typically cannot reject the null of no mean reversion when testing a single real exchange rate on monthly data.

Jorion and Abuaf (1990) examine together the real exchange rates of the Group of Ten (G10)[12] countries relative to the U.S. dollar. They assume that the speed of adjustment of each real exchange rate to its long-run value is the same across countries. They report borderline rejection of the null of no mean reversion for this system in a model with stringent constraints.[13] In effect, they get more observations by their pooling, because real exchange rates are not perfectly correlated across countries.[14]

Jorion and Sweeney (1996) present perhaps the strongest evidence to date that real exchange rates show mean reversion over the current managed float period. They focus on the regression equation

$$(3) \qquad R_{i,t} = \alpha_i + \alpha_i{}'D + \beta_i R_{i,t-1} + \gamma_i t + u_{i,t},$$

where $R_{i,t}$ is the (natural log of the) real exchange rate for country i in period t, α_i an intercept, D a $(0, 1)$ dummy that shifts in the middle of the sample, $\alpha_i{}'$ a constant, with ($\alpha_i + \alpha_i{}'D$) an intercept that shifts once for all countries at the same time,[15] β_i a slope coefficient on the lagged dependent variable, $R_{i,t-1}$, γ_i a slope coefficient on a time counter, t, and $u_{i,t}$ a random shock to the real rate for country i in period t. They report results for Seemingly Unrelated Regressions (SUR) estimation where $\beta_i = \beta$ for all i, that is, the slope on the lagged dependent variable is restricted to be the same across countries. In their most restrictive model, they set $\alpha_i{}' = \gamma_i = 0$ for all i and test the null of $\beta = 1$ against the alternative of $\beta < 1$ (that is, test the null of no mean reversion against the alternative of mean reversion).

Their study examines systems of real exchange rates for the G10 countries with the U.S. dollar as the base currency, and also systems of seven European countries with the German mark as the base currency.[16] They note that during the current float, the dollar has fluctuated much more relative to the German mark than has the German mark on average relative to other European currencies, many of which were formally or informally members of the pegged exchange rate based European Monetary System (EMS) that started in 1979. Because unit-root tests have less power the more volatile the series, the results may be sharper for European currencies relative to the German mark.

Table 9.4 reports some of the regression results. In testing the null of no mean reversion for a system of real exchange rates with a common speed of adjustment, the data reject the null in the case where the null is taken as nonzero intercepts and $\beta = 1$, against the alternative that $\beta < 1$ (Model 2). The rejection is stronger for European countries relative to the German mark as the base currency, but there is also evidence of reversion for the Group of Ten with the U.S. dollar as the base currency (rejections at the 0.6 and 1.6 percent significance levels respectively).

TABLE 9.4 Mean Reversion in the Real Exchange Rate : $R_{i,t} = \alpha_i + \alpha_i' D + \beta_i R_{i,t-1} + \gamma_i t + u_{i,t}$

	G10 with U.S. dollar as base currency				European countries with DM as base currency			
	Model 2	Model 3	Model 4	Model 5	Model 2	Model 3	Model 4	Model 5
Parameters	$\alpha_i' = \gamma_i = 0$	$\alpha_i = 0$	$\gamma_i = 0$	Full model	$\alpha_i' = \gamma_i = 0$	$\alpha_i' = 0$	$\gamma_i = 0$	Full model
β	0.9749	0.9640	0.9667	0.9646	0.9674	0.9551	0.9584	0.9542
s(β)	0.0042	0.0051	0.0050	0.0053	0.0054	0.0067	0.0066	0.0069
τ	-6.03	-7.00	-6.70	-6.73	-6.01	-6.69	-6.34	-6.63
(p-value)	0.016*	0.219	0.144	0.586	0.006*	0.052	0.046*	0.170
Critical 10%	-5.34	-7.38	-6.54	-8.12	-4.56	-6.30	-5.94	-6.97
Critical 5%	-5.57	-7.65	-7.18	-8.43	-4.87	-6.70	-6.30	-7.31
Critical 1%	-6.21	-8.32	-7.83	-9.11	-5.48	-7.23	-7.07	-7.87

NOTES: * denotes asymptotic significance at the 5 percent level. The test statistic is defined as $\tau = (\beta - 1)/s(\beta)$. Empirical p-values and critical values obtained from simulations under the null. Data are period-ending exchange rates and consumer prices from *International Financial Statistics*, from July 1973-December 1993. The European countries are Belgium, France, Germany, Italy, the Netherlands, Sweden, Switzerland and the United Kingdom. The remaining G10 countries are Canada, Germany, Japan and the United States.

SOURCE: Jorion and Sweeney (1996).

Jorion and Sweeney (1996) report that the data also give some support to more complicated real exchange-rate dynamics (Models 3 through 5 in 9.4). Perron (1989) and Perron and Vogelsang (1992) provide evidence that there are shifts over time in the equilibrium values toward which real exchange rates tend to revert, on some occasions in unpredictable ways that are hard to detect statistically in real time. There may also be time trends in some real exchange rates. The results from Model 3 with time trends allowed but no mean shifts ($\alpha_i' = 0$, γ_i freely fitted), and from Model 4 with mean shifts but no time trends (α_i' freely fitted, $\gamma_i = 0$) lend support to these views for the European Group. For the case with the German mark as the base currency, in Models 3 and 4 the null of no mean reversion ($\beta = 1$) is rejected in favor of the alternative of mean reversion ($\beta < 1$) at the 5.2 and 4.6 significance levels.[17] For the European Group, none of the individual-country α_i' is significantly different from zero; these shifts may, however, be economically important and would be difficult to recognize in real time.[18] Thus, it appears that there is important evidence in favor of mean reversion, especially for the European group, but there is also evidence that long-run real exchange rates may be moving targets that shift over time and are quite difficult to estimate.

Further, the speed of adjustment seems to be imprecisely estimated. Though the data allow rejection of the null in some experiments that Jorion and Sweeney (1996) report, there is a substantial range of doubt about the actual value of the speed of adjustment. The implied estimated speed of adjustment is $(1 - \beta_i)$; in the absence of further shocks, the real rate adjusts as $R_t - R_{t-1} = \beta(R^* - R_{t-1})$. For the Group of Ten systems, the one significant β_i gives a speed of adjustment of 2.51 percent per month or 30.12 percent annually (= 2.51×12),[19] and a maximum across fitted models of 3.54 percent per month (42.48 percent annually). For the European systems, the significant estimated speeds of adjustment are 3.26, 4.49 and 4.16 percent per month (39.12, 53.88 and 49.92 annually), with a maximum estimated speed of 4.58 percent per month (54.96 annually). On the one hand, a speed of adjustment of approximately 4.5 percent per month or 54 percent annually for the European group (or 2.5 percent per month and 30 percent annually for the Group of Ten) implies the real exchange rate adjusts to eliminate one-half of the disequilibrium in one year (one and two-thirds years), to some observers impressively fast adjustment for macro variables. On the other hand, as Figure 9.1 illustrates, deviations of the real rate from its sample mean can be very large for (non-Canadian) currencies relative to the U.S. dollar, although such deviations for European currencies are substantially smaller relative to the German mark than the dollar (save for Sweden[20] and the U.K.).

Many observers believe that the nominal exchange rate shows no signs of mean reversion. This implies that the mean reversion detected in real exchange rates arises through adjustments in relative national price levels. Looked at this way, the speed of adjustment of the European Group may be surprising. It is widely thought that Western Europe's economies have substantial rigidities and are slow to adjust in terms of reductions in employment, labor force relocation and downward wage (and benefits) inflexibility. Evidence for this rigidity is often seen in the high and persistent levels of unemployment in Western Europe. An alternative interpretation is that labor market rigidities, coupled with price adjustments forced through international competition, are what lead to unemployment; output market price adjustment may be substantially greater than factor market adjustment.

There has been relatively little work on the economic determinants of the speed of macroeconomic price adjustment across countries. One influence is decision makers' expectations regarding macroeconomic policies. For instance, in the face of a shock requiring price cuts relative to foreign competitors' prices, it makes no sense to cut prices if the monetary authorities will produce a ratifying currency depreciation. But if the monetary authorities have credibly committed not to ratify any shocks by exchange rate changes, price adjustments may be much more likely. Hochreiter (Chapter 1 in this volume) discusses how a credible commitment to a strong peg to a neighbor's currency can cause substantial changes in domestic institutions to increase the adaptability of the economy to disturbances that cannot be met with exchange-rate changes. Austria and the Netherlands are often taken as examples of countries that have adapted to the requirements of a strong peg, in both cases to the German mark.

It might appear anomalous that European countries seem to adjust more quickly than the Group of Ten as a whole, because the Group of Ten includes the U.S. economy, which is thought to be substantially less rigid than European economies. Note that the estimated speeds of adjustment for the European group are higher than for the Group of Ten, but the amount of adjustment required is substantially smaller. Thus the proportion of disequilibrium made up each month is larger for the European group, but the absolute amount of adjustment done is likely larger for the Group of Ten because of the larger absolute amounts of disequilibrium. And it should be noted that differences in estimated speeds of adjustment may be due to estimation error.

Table 9.5 reports out-of-sample root-mean-square forecasting errors from Jorion and Sweeney (1996) measured as (continuously compounded) percent deviations of forecast from actual values of real exchange rates.[21] They arbitrarily split their sample in halves (similar to the experiment in Figures 9.2 and 9.3) and ask which of four models estimated in the first half works best out of sample: random walks, random walks with drifts fit individually, OLS fit individually, and SUR as described above with $\alpha_i' = \gamma_i = 0$. This is a strong standard, as Figures 9.2 and 9.3 show. Further, there is some evidence that α_i' and γ_i may be important, and no account is taken of this: if α_i' is important, random walks are likely to be superior, and if γ_i is important, random walks with drifts will tend to be superior.[22] For forecasting horizons

TABLE 9.5 Forecasting Mean Reversion in Real Exchange Rates (Root Mean Square Error, Equally Weighted Portfolio of Real Exchange Rates)

Horizon	1-month	3-month	6-month	12-month
G10				
Random Walk	3.06	5.65	8.38	12.31
Random Walk with trend	3.08	5.75	8.66	13.18
OLS model	3.23	6.09	8.76	11.07
SUR model	3.04*	5.55*	8.03*	11.06*
Random Walk - SUR	0.02	0.10	0.35	1.257
European Countries				
Random Walk	0.941	1.810	2.634	3.917
Random Walk with trend	0.955	1.880	2.821	4.425
OLS model	1.130	2.377	3.554	4.822
SUR model	0.939*	1.787*	2.551*	3.582*
Random Walk - SUR	0.002	0.023	0.085	0.235

NOTES: Source, Jorion and Sweeney (1995). Monthly data. Figures are root mean square errors (RMSEs) in continuously compounded percentage terms, measured as deviation of the real rate from its forecasted value. Models are estimated over July 1973–September 1983; RMSEs are calculated over the period October 1983–December 1993. The equally weighted portfolio is the simple average of 10 (7) log real exchange rates for the G10 (seven European countries).
* indicates lowest RMSE for the forecast horizon across the four forecasting models

of 1, 3, 6 and 12 months, and for an equally weighted portfolio of real rates, the SUR model outperforms the other three—but often just barely. In all but one case (Group of Ten, 12-month horizon) the random walk models give the second-best performance; at lengthening horizons, the superiority of the SUR forecasts is .02, .10, .35 and 1.25 for the Group of Ten relative to the U.S. dollar, and is .002, .023, .085, and .235 for the seven European countries relative to the German mark.

The relative closeness of the SUR and random walk forecast errors does not arise from the two forecasts being close, especially at the 6- and 12-month horizons and when the real rate differs substantially from the estimated long-run rate. The random walk forecast is that the real rate in any future month will be what it is today, and the SUR model predicts reversion from the current rate to the long-run rate estimated from first-period data. Random walk models go wrong by predicting no change when there are in fact substantial changes, the SUR model by predicting substantial reversion when in fact reversion is relatively small or the rate moves even farther from the long-run rate, as can happen in the face of new shocks.

The superiority of SUR over random walk forecasts is still in doubt of course. The out-of-sample forecasting period is only 10-plus years long and the margins of superiority at even the 12-month horizon are not overwhelming. Tentatively, it appears that there is little use for SUR forecasts at 1-month horizons; for 12-month horizons, SUR's superiority is more impressive, though a large amount of error remains. It is possible its superiority would increase as the forecasting horizon is lengthened to, say, 24 months. For private trade and investment purposes, the timing of short-term transactions appears insensitive to which forecasting model is used. For longer-term investments, the 12-month horizon results suggest that it is worthwhile paying attention to tendencies to mean reversion, while recognizing that these tendencies are easily swamped by new disturbances. For government intervention purposes, the importance of mean reversion tendencies at long horizons suggests that intervention this month will have effects that are discernible in the real exchange rate only after many months. Further, chance can easily obscure the effects of one bout of intervention, so that a government can only hope to see effects on average over many bouts evaluated in each case over relatively long time horizons.

Summary and Conclusions

Much conflict over PPP-based intervention strategies focuses on two empirical issues. First, is sterilized intervention predictably effective? Second, is there a long-run equilibrium real exchange rate towards which the actual real rate tends? Even if the answer to both questions is yes, further questions remain. What strategy should the government follow and how likely is it to do so? How likely is it to let political concerns lead to policies that generate disequilibrium rates? How exactly does intervention affect the nominal exchange rate? By affecting risk? Is the equilibrium real exchange rate constant in the long run? If not, how fast does the equilibrium rate evolve and how effective is intervention at pushing the real rate towards equilibrium by affecting the nominal exchange rate?

Recent evidence supports the view that sterilized intervention can affect nominal exchange rates under managed floating, and that real exchange rates show tendencies toward mean reversion. These views allow the possibility of successful exchange market intervention to influence the economy's evolution. It appears that intervention has effects on the nominal exchange rate that are at least partly predictable and may offer scope for moving the real rate in the desired direction. Purchasing power parity seems to have enough content about the long-run real exchange rate and its adjustment that PPP may serve as a useful guide for intervention. There remain important doubts, however, about the wisdom in practice of extensive exchange-rate management through sterilized intervention.

First, the association of intervention with risk, i.e., with expected exchange-rate movements seems to arise mainly through association of intervention with movements in currency betas. The association is statistically highly significant and in this sense reliable, because the direction of beta's influence on actual appreciation depends on the sign of the rate of return on the market in excess of the risk-free rate. Because this sign is highly uncertain (over the sample, only 54-plus percent of days had positive excess rates of return), the association of intervention with actual appreciation through beta is highly uncertain. Even assuming a causal relationship between intervention and beta, intervention will often have a counterproductive effect on actual appreciation. Given the inability of the Federal Reserve to predict the excess rate of return on the market, in almost 46 percent of days in the sample the effect of intervention would have been counterproductive. Further, though there is evidence that intervention has an important, direct association with actual appreciation outside the beta channel, this association appears to be quite unstable over time.

Second, though out-of-sample forecasting tests show that mean reversion models (estimated as in Jorion and Sweeney 1996) beat random walk models, the margin of superiority is small at short horizons and only becomes important at a 12-month horizon. Even over a year, the mean reversion model has large root mean square errors, not too much smaller than from random walk forecasting. Thus, intervention will often take a long time to have discernable effects, and will often appear to fail.

Third, even though a long-run equilibrium real exchange rate exists, deviations from it may represent temporary equilibria rather than disequilibrium. If so, intervention that moves the real rate towards its long-run value disequilibrates the system by forcing it to move at a faster than optimal rate to the long-run level. Further, there is some evidence that the equilibrium long-run real rate may contain time trends for some countries or may be subject to permanent shifts that are hard to detect in real time.

Fourth, many advocates of intervention view exchange-rate movements as frequently being the result of destabilizing speculation, or perhaps of insufficient stabilizing speculation. There is some evidence that exchange-rate movements for the Japanese yen and German mark relative to the U.S. dollar offer exploitable trading opportunities and are thus inefficient, but this is not necessarily support for some governments' views that speculation is an ongoing *serious* problem. Heavy intervention based on PPP signals would thus be a substantial bet on unsubstantiated views about the generally negative role of speculation, or at the least speculators' causal role in exchange-rate movements that trigger PPP-based intervention signals.

Notes

For helpful comments, thanks are due to Boo Sjöö, Clas Wihlborg, Thomas D. Willett and participants in the Conference on Exchange-Rate Policies in Transition Economies, Institute for Advanced Studies, Vienna. This is part of a series of papers on the real exchange rate's behavior and implications for public and private decision makers. Also included in this series are Jorion and Sweeney (1996), Siddique and Sweeney (1998a, 1998b). Much of this paper was written at the Göteborg School of Economics. Research grants from Georgetown University and the Georgetown Business School provided summer support

1. See, for example, Dominguez and Frankel (1993a) and Edison (1993) for surveys of the pre-1993 literature.

2. See for example Marston (1988) and Willett (1982) for critical surveys of exchange-rate management and targeting.

3. Or, technically, the real rate is not trend stationary because of discrete breaks in the level of time trend in the real rate process; on this see Frankel and Rose (1995), Froot and Rogoff (1995), Perron (1989), Perron and Vogelsang (1992), Jorion and Sweeney (1996), Taylor (1982).

4. See Dominguez and Frankel (1993a) and Edison (1993)for reviews of this literature.

5. It is well understood that a government may have asymmetric, superior information about its coming policies as compared to market participants. It is also possible that, aside from the government's own policies, it has superior information about economic fundamentals that it signals with its sterilized interventions.

6. In the related literature on whether government foreign-exchange intervention is profitable, researchers sometimes use data on changes in reserves rather than on intervention (Taylor 1982). Szakmary and Mathur (1997) use reserve changes to explain private profits from technical trading systems as arising from Fed losses on its intervention. Sjöö and Sweeney (1996b) discuss how reserve changes can be substantially and misleadingly different from intervention.

7. See Sweeney (1996a) for discussion of results from using intervention or the (1, 0, -1) indicator variable.

8. Sweeney (1996a) discusses the distributions of statistics, including the circumstances under which they are $N(0, 1)$.

9. Sweeney (1996a) also presents tests with multiple lags of CI_t, with the significance of the CI_t terms judged with t-tests on individual coefficients and with χ^2 tests of the restrictions either that $\sum_{j=1}^{N} d_j = 0$ or that all $d_j = 0$. Across calendar years, the results are much the same *mutatis mutandis* as for the tests in Table 9.3.

10. In other models using the monetary approach to the balance of payments, substantial deviations from long-run PPP may occur, for example, in Dornbusch's (1976) overshooting model.

11. In terms of the model in (3), but with $\alpha_i' = \gamma_i = 0$, the equilibrium long-run (log) real exchange rate for country i is $R^* = \hat{\alpha}_i /(1-\hat{\beta}_i)$, where the hats indicate estimated values. R^* is typically close to the sample mean R' when the model is fit with OLS over the sample $(1, T)$. Differences between the two depend on T and the values of R_T and R_1 (with the true values of R^* and R' equal if $R_T = R_1$), and on truncation error in calculating R', $\hat{\alpha}_i$ and $\hat{\beta}_i$.

12. In fact, they use the Group of Ten but with Norway in place of Sweden.

13. Tests of the null in a range of models are discussed below.

14. The results in Abuaf and Jorion (1990), as opposed to other results in the literature on single currencies during the current floating rate regime, arise from simultaneous estimation of the system, including off-diagonal variances, and restriction of the speed of adjustment to be the same across countries. Restricting the covariance matrix to be diagonal appears to have little effect on results.

15. All intercepts are arbitrarily assumed to shift at the mid-point of the time series, in order to avoid data mining arising from search for the "best" common shift point or shift point for each country individually.

16. One other paper has used the German mark as the base currency for European rates: Edison and Fisher (1991) analyze bilateral EMS real exchange rates, using univariate tests, but cannot find evidence against the null of no mean reversion.

17. Note that the null of no mean reversion ($\beta = 1$) cannot be rejected for the G10 countries. One interpretation is that this arises because there are not enough observations relative to the complexities of the model's fit.

18. If the alternative of mean reversion is taken to hold provisionally for the Group of Ten, in both models Japan is the country with either a significant intercept shift or time trend.

19. This is an approximation that ignores continuous compounding and the fact that the gap between the current and long-run real rate diminishes with adjustment.

20. Many of the European countries were in the European Monetary System or it predecessor snake arrangements for much of the sample period, but Sweden pursued different policies. In particular, in the mid 1980s to early 1990s, Sweden targeted a weighted average of its trading partners' currencies, with non-EMS countries having important weights.

21. For extensions of this approach, see Siddique and Sweeney (1998), Siddique, Akhtar, and Richard J. Sweeney (forthcoming).

22. With α_i' important, random walks approach the new R^* eventually, but SUR and OLS R^*s are constant over the forecast period; if γ_i is important, random walks with drift will tend to pick this up, though at the danger of estimation error, while the other models cannot pick this up. Even with $\alpha_i' = \gamma_i = 0$, it is likely that for some i, $\beta_i \neq \beta$. In this case, OLS may be superior to SUR, though at the cost of potentially greater estimation error.

References

Abuaf, Niso, and Philippe Jorion. 1990. "Purchasing Power Parity in the Long Run." *Journal of Finance*, March 1990: 157–74.

Adler, Michael, and Bruce Lehmann. 1983. "Deviations from Purchasing Power Parity in the Long Run." *Journal of Finance* 38(5): 1471–87.

Bilson, John F. O. 1978. "The Current Experience with Floating Exchange Rates: An Appraisal of the Monetary Approach." *American Economic Review*, May: 392–97.

Corrado, Charles J. and Dean Taylor. 1986. "The Cost of a Central Bank Leaning against a Random Walk." *Journal of International Money and Finance*, September: 303–14.

Diebold, Francis X., Steven Husted, and Mark Rush. 1991. "Real Exchange Rates under the Gold Standard," *Journal of Political Economy*, December: 1252–71.

Dominguez, Kathryn M., and Jeffrey A. Frankel. 1993a. *Does Intervention Work?* Washington, D.C.: Institute for International Economics.

———. 1993b. "Does Foreign-Exchange Intervention Matter? The Portfolio Effect." *American Economic Review* 83(5): 1356–69.

Dornbusch, Rudiger. 1976. "Expectations and Exchange Rate Dynamics." *Journal of Political Economy*, December: 1161–76.

Edison, Hali J. 1993. The Effectiveness of Central-Bank Intervention: A Survey of the Literature after 1982." Special Papers in International Economics No. 18. Princeton: Princeton University, Department of Economics, International Finance Section.

Edison, Hali J., and Eric Fisher. 1991. "A Long-run View of the European Monetary System." *Journal of International Money and Finance*, March: 53–70.

Frankel, Jeffrey A. 1982. "A Test of Perfect Substitutability in the Foreign Exchange Market." *Southern Economic Journal* 46(2): 406–16.

———. 1993. "In Search Of The Exchange Rate Premium: A Six-Currency Test Assuming Mean-Variance Optimization," in *On Exchange Rates*, edited by J. Frankel. Pp. 219–34. Cambridge, Mass.: MIT Press.

Frankel, Jeffrey, and Andrew K. Rose. 1995. "Empirical Research on Nominal Exchange Rates," in Gene Grossman and Kenneth Rogoff, *Handbook of International Economics,* vol. 3. Pp. 1689–1729. Amsterdam: Elsevier Science.

Froot, Kenneth A., and Kenneth Rogoff. 1995. "Perspectives on PPP and Long-Run Real Exchange Rates," in Gene Grossman and Kenneth Rogoff, *Handbook of International Economics,* vol. 3. Pp. 1648–88. Amsterdam: Elsevier Science.

Ghosh, Atish R. 1992. "Is It Signalling? Exchange Intervention and the Dollar-Deutsche Mark Rate." *Journal of International Economics*, May: 201–20.

Huizinga, John. 1987. "An Empirical Investigation of the Long-Run Behavior of Real Exchange Rates." Carnegie-Rochester Conference Series on Public Policy, June: 149–214.

Johnson, Harry G. 1972. "The Monetary Approach to Balance-of-Payments Theory." *Journal of Financial and Quantitative Analysis*, March: 1555-71

Jorion, Philippe, and Richard J. Sweeney 1996. "Mean Reversion in Real Exchange Rates: Evidence and Implications for Forecasting." *Journal of International Money and Finance* 15(4): 535–50.

Kaminsky, Gabriella, and Karen K. Lewis. 1996. "Does Foreign Exchange Intervention Signal Future Monetary Policy?" *Journal of Monetary Economics* 37(2): 285–312.

László, Halpern, and Charles Wyplosz. 1995. "Equilibrium Real Exchange Rates in Transition." CEPR Working Paper No. 1145. London: Centre for Economic Policy Research, April.

Lewis, Karen K. 1995. "Are Foreign Exchange Intervention and Monetary Policy Related, and Does It Really Matter?" *Journal of Business*, April: 185–214.

Lothian, James R. 1991. "A History of Yen Exchange Rates," in *Japanese Financial Market Research. Contributions to Economic Analysis*, No. 205 edited by William T. Ziemba, Warren Bailey, and Yasush Hamao. Pp. 267–87. New York: Elsevier Science.

Marston, Richard. 1988. "Exchange Rate Coordination," in Martin Feldstein, eds., *International Economic Cooperation*. Pp. 79–135. Chicago: University of Chicago Press.

Perron, Pierre. 1989. "The Great Crash, The Oil Price Shock, and the Unit Root Hypothesis." *Econometrica* 57(6): 1361–401.

Perron, Pierre, and Timothy J. Vogelsang. 1992. "Nonstationarity and Level Shifts with an Application to Purchasing Power Parity." *Journal of Business and Economic Statistics*, July: 301–20.

Pigott, Charles, and Richard J. Sweeney. 1985a. "Purchasing Power Parity and Exchange Rate Dynamics: Some Empirical Results," in Sven Arndt, Richard J. Sweeney and Thomas D. Willett, eds., *Exchange Rates, Trade, and the U.S. Economy*. Pp. 73–89. Cambridge: Ballinger.

———. 1985b. "Testing the Exchange Rate Implications of Two Popular Monetary Models," in Sven W Arndt, Richard J. Sweeney, Thomas D. Willett, *Exchange Rates, Trade, and the U.S. Economy*. Pp. 91–106. Washington, D.C.: American Enterprise Institute.

Roberts, Harry V. 1959. "Stock Market Patterns and Financial Analysis: Methodological Suggestions." *Journal of Finance* 14 (March): 1–10.

Roll, Richard. 1979. "Violations of Purchasing Power Parity and their Implications for Efficient International Commodity Markets," in Marshall Sarnat and Giorgio Szego, eds., *International Finance and Trade*. Pp. 133–76. Cambridge: Ballinger.

Siddique and Richard J. Sweeney, 1998a. "Forecasting Real Exchange Rates," *Journal of International Money and Finance*, forthcoming.

———. 1998b. "Adjustment Costs, the Real Exchange Rate and the EMU." Unpublished manuscript.

Sjöö, Boo, and Richard J. Sweeney. 1996a. "Central Bank Intervention Profits: The Evidence from Sweden." Georgetown University School of Business Working Paper, Washington, D.C.

———. 1996b. "The Profitability of Central Bank Intervention in Exchange Markets: The Evidence from Sweden." Georgetown University School of Business Working Paper, Washington, D.C.

Sweeney, Richard J. 1996a. "Does the Foreign-Exchange Market Beat the Fed?" Georgetown University School of Business Working Paper, Washington, D.C.

———. 1996b. "Mean Reversion in the Real Exchange Rate: Evidence from Equities Markets." Georgetown University School of Business Working Paper, Washington, D.C.

———. 1996c. "Exchange-Rate Crises in Emerging Market Economies: Are Currency Boards the Answer?" Chapter 12 in this volume.

Szakmary, Andrew, and Ike Mathur. 1997. "Central Bank Intervention and Trading Rule Profits in Foreign Exchange Markets." *Journal of International Money and Finance*, August: 513–35.

Taylor, Dean. 1982. "Official Intervention in the Foreign Exchange Market, or, Bet Against the Central Bank." *Journal of Political Economy*, April: 356–68.

Taylor, Mark P. 1995. "Exchange-Rate Behavior under Alternative Exchange-Rate Arrangements," in Peter B. Kenen, ed., *Understanding Interdependence: The Macroeconomics of the Open Economy*. Pp. 34–83. Princeton, N.J.: Princeton University Press.

Williamson, John. 1983. *The Exchange Rate System*. Washington D.C.: Institute for International Economics.

Willett, Thomas D. 1982. "The Causes and Effects of Exchange Rate Volatility," in Jacob S. Dreyer, Gottfired Haberler, and Thomas D. Willett, eds., *The International Monetary System: A Time of Turbulence*. Pp. 24–64. Washington, D.C.: American Enterprise Institute for Public Policy Research.

10

Trade and Payments in Eastern European Economic Reform

Sven W. Arndt

Introduction

What is the appropriate exchange rate regime for the emerging economies of Eastern Europe? Would a given regime suit all of them equally? Is there a regime that is as appropriate for the transition as for the long run? What are the relative merits of fixed and flexible rates in this context and what, if any, is the role of capital controls?[1]

These are some of the questions facing policymakers in Eastern Europe. Transforming an economy from a centrally planned to market-driven regime is in part an exercise in "getting prices right," and one of the more important prices is the real exchange rate. The real exchange rate fluctuates even when the nominal rate is fixed, because it is influenced by changes in aggregate economic conditions at home and abroad.

The real exchange rate may be viewed as the relative price between tradable and nontradable goods and services. As such it is particularly useful in understanding certain features of adjustment during economic transition. As Eastern Europe's economies are opened to world trade the tradables/non-tradables mix in national output is altered, a process in which the real exchange rate plays a key role. Moreover, as the economy becomes integrated into the global market, capital is reallocated from sectors and industries that were important in a closed, centrally planned economy to sectors and industries reflecting comparative advantage. Capital reallocation takes the form of depreciation and disinvestment in declining industries and investment and capital accumulation in expanding industries.

In the present context, restructuring is usefully viewed as a two-stage process. Stage one is characterized by an increase in investment outlays and in the demand for capital goods and construction services; stage two is described by the opening of new productive capacity. Thus the first stage is dominated by demand shocks, the second by supply shocks. Both types of shocks have implications for the real exchange rate and together may generate real exchange rate cycles. Determination of the real exchange rate in the second stage is complicated by the fact that national income will have grown and with it will come demand growth in both sectors. When the nominal exchange rate is fixed, cycles in the real rate are reflected by cycles in relative goods and factor prices.

These relationships are explored below. In the next section the analytical framework is developed. The third section considers the role of financial markets and capital, and the fourth section deals with adjustment in factor markets. The final section draws some conclusions.

The Analytical Framework

As noted above, reconstruction may be viewed as a multi-stage process: the initial phase is marked by investment and capital formation, while later phases witness the opening of new productive capacity and the expenditure consequences of national income growth. I examine the implications of this process in the context of a small, open, two-sector economy producing tradable and nontradable goods and services.

Tradables are goods and services which have readily available foreign substitutes so that their prices are essentially tied to prices abroad. The small economy is a price taker, so that for given foreign prices the home prices of tradables move with the nominal exchange rate. Nontradables, on the other hand, are goods and services without readily available foreign substitutes, so that their home currency prices are determined by the interaction between domestic demand and supply. In the context of Eastern European transition, important examples of nontradables are certain types of capital goods and a range of construction goods and services.

At any moment, the economy's stock of productive resources—capital and labor—is assumed to be given. In the short run, therefore, and assuming full resource utilization, expansion of one sector requires contraction of the other. In the tradition of the specific-factors model, capital is assumed to be sector-specific in the short run, so that output expansion in either sector occurs through additional labor inputs. Under conditions of full employment additional workers must be drawn away from the other sector; otherwise, additional workers may be drawn from the ranks of the unemployed. In either case, however, the presence of increasing costs assures that short-run sectoral supply curves are positively sloped. In the long run, capital accumulation is an important source of output expansion in either sector.

The real exchange rate, e, defined as the ratio of tradables prices (p_t) to nontradables prices (p_n), plays a key role in the sectoral allocation of resources and in the sectoral distribution of aggregate demand. This definition of the real rate is readily derived from its more conventional cousin, the nominal exchange rate, E (expressed as the price of foreign exchange in terms of the home currency), adjusted by the ratio of foreign (P^*) to home price levels (P), that is, $e = E \times P^*/P$. The domestic price index is defined as $P = \lambda p_n + (1-\lambda)p_t$, where λ represents the proportion of nontradables in the index. The foreign price level, P^*, is defined analogously. Substituting these definitions of P and P^* into the conventional definition of the real exchange rate and assuming that domestic and foreign tradables prices are linked by the law of one price, i.e., $p_t = E \times p_{t^*}$, yields the following:

$$e = E[\lambda^* p_{n^*} + (1-\lambda^*)p_{t^*}]/[\lambda p_n + (1-\lambda)Ep_{t^*}]$$

The real exchange rate, e, is thus equal to the nominal exchange rate, E, adjusted by foreign tradables prices and by foreign and domestic nontradables prices. Since the small country takes foreign prices as given, the real value of its currency rises with the nominal value and falls with the home price of nontradables. If the country fixes its nominal rate, movements in the real rate are driven by movements in nontradables prices. Real depreciation, represented by a rise in e, is accomplished by a decline in nontradables prices, while real appreciation, represented by a fall in e, is achieved by a rise in nontradables prices.

The basic structure of this economy is given in Figure 10.1.[2] The right panel shows home tradables demand and supply. Demand rises as the relative price of tradables falls. Supply rises as the real exchange rate, e, rises, that is, as tradables prices rise relative to those of nontradables. In the short run, capital is assumed to be fixed in each sector, making labor the only variable factor. Increases in output are achieved by increases in labor inputs. Additional labor needed in one sector comes either from the unemployment pool or from the other sector. The short-run tradables supply curve is upward sloping because combining more labor with a given quantity of capital reduces the productivity of labor and thus increases unit costs. In the long run, the sectoral stock of capital is increased by capital reallocation from the other sector and by the creation of new capital in the economy. A rise in a sector's capital stock shifts the sector supply curve out.

Nontradables demand and supply are depicted in the left-hand panel. Since the price measured on the vertical axis is the ratio of tradables to nontradables prices, the slopes of the nontradables demand and supply curves have the inverse of their "normal" shapes. Demand slopes upward, because an upward movement along the vertical axis represents a reduction in the

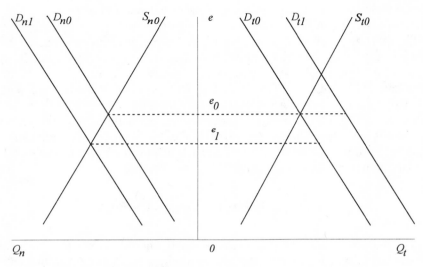

FIGURE 10.1 Nontradables and Tradables Demand and Supply

relative price of nontradables. Supply slopes downward, because a rise in the relative price of tradables reduces nontradables production.

Initial equilibrium is given by curves subscripted with 0. The equilibrium real exchange rate is the rate that clears the nontradables market. This follows from the assumption that nontradables have no readily available foreign substitutes or markets, so that in equilibrium domestic supply and demand must be equal. I assume for convenience that tradables supply and demand are initially also in balance.

Demand and Supply Shocks

An increase in investment demand for nontradables shifts demand to D_{n1}, reducing relative price to e_1. This is a real appreciation, which is needed in order to clear the nontradables market. Its effect on the current account, given by the gap between the tradables demand and supply curves in the right panel, is to produce a deficit.

The intuition here is that the increase in domestic production of non-tradables, which is the only way of satisfying the increase in domestic demand for nontradables, is achieved by a real appreciation which (1) causes mobile resources to be shifted from tradables to nontradables and (2) induces an inflow of tradables to cover the resultant shortfall of domestic tradables

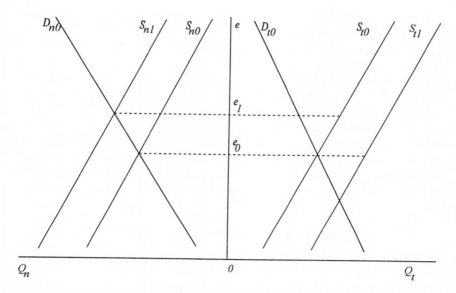

FIGURE 10.2 Supply-Side Shocks to Tradable and Nontradable Goods

output. Whether such a trade imbalance can in fact be sustained depends on the availability of capital inflows. That issue is discussed below.

An increase in investment demand for tradables, on the other hand, shifts demand in the right panel to D_{t1}. Under given assumptions, the real exchange rate is unaffected, but the current account deteriorates. This result reflects only the impact effect of the rise in investment; additional repercussions are taken up below.

Supply-side shocks are examined in Figure 10.2. A rise in nontradables supply shifts the S_n curve out in the left panel, producing a real depreciation, while an increase in tradables supply, shifting out the S_t curve in the right panel, generates a current account surplus without, however, directly affecting the real exchange rate.

Hence, shifts in nontradables demand and supply determine the real exchange rate, while shifts in tradables demand and supply alter the current account. If economic restructuring consists of a series of phases in which an investment boom is followed by an expansion of productive capacity, and if the boom involves nontradables to any extent, then the real exchange rate will first fall and then rise. The current account, on the other hand, will first deteriorate and then improve, regardless of which sector is affected by the investment program.

If the nominal exchange rate is fixed, then the foregoing movements in the real rate require accommodating movements in nontradables prices. When the real rate falls in the first stage, nontradables prices must rise; when it rises later, they must fall.

If the investment boom increases overall capacity in the transitioning economy, then GNP and national income will increase; and this increase will spill over into higher consumption outlays. Thus, a full cycle of reconstruction activity might consist of an initial stage during which demand increases in both the tradables and nontradables sectors as a result of the investment boom, followed by later stages in which supply curves in both sectors shift out as additional capacity comes online and demand in both sectors also expands as a result of the rise in national income.

Financial Markets and Capital Flows

Because of current account deterioration during the initial stage of reconstruction, it is immensely helpful if the transitioning program is supported by foreign resources. An import surplus places more goods and services at the disposal of consumers and producers than would otherwise be possible, easing the shock of transformation. However, if current account financing is not available, say because of the presence of capital controls and restrictions on convertibility, then the current account is constrained to zero, so that both the pace and the extent of economic reconstruction are constrained by domestic resources. Consequently, a rise in investment demand cannot then spill over into the foreign sector. Instead, any increase in reform-related demand for nontradable capital goods or construction services must be "accommodated" by reductions in nontradables demand elsewhere in the economy; that is, "crowding-out" occurs in the nontradables sector. As is well known, one way to crowd out low-priority uses is by means of higher domestic interest rates.

The effect of a rise in interest rates on nontradables demand is to shift the D_n curve inward, thereby tending to offset outward shifts of the curve that are the result of the initial rise in reconstruction investment demand for nontradable goods and services. Higher interest rates also reduce the demand for tradables, shifting demand inward and thereby helping to maintain balanced trade.

Convertibility and the Real Exchange Rate

In the absence of capital controls, capital inflows reduce or eliminate the need for crowding-out. Interest rates may still rise in order to attract foreign capital, but in the case of a small, price-taking country with fully open capital markets, domestic interest rates are closely tied to world rates. In this case, capital inflows finance imports of goods and services at the real exchange rate that clears the market for nontradables.

Policymakers in Eastern Europe express concerns about the possibility that capital inflows will "cause" the home currency to appreciate.[3] Such appreciations are viewed with alarm, because they are seen to make domestic exports less competitive and to encourage imports.

The foregoing analysis suggests, however, that appreciations of this kind are not only consistent with equilibrium during reconstruction, but desirable. They are supposed to reduce exports and bring in imports. It is not the capital inflow but the transformation program that is the primary "cause" of the real exchange rate change. To be sure, the capital inflow allows the exchange rate change to take place, but it is not the primary cause. It is a result of the transformation strategy. The required real exchange rate change is determined in the market for nontradable goods and services. Limiting capital inflows would squeeze the reconstruction program, constraining it to available domestic resources. In this context, therefore, a policy to limit capital inflows is a policy to restrain the transformation process.

Such restraint on reconstruction may very well be justified, especially if the transitioning economy shows signs of becoming overstressed. But the decision to control capital inflows should come as part of the transitioning strategy, rather than as an independent exercise in exchange rate policy.

Rather than a sign of competitive weakness and a signal of danger, therefore, this real appreciation serves to channel domestic resources into nontradables production, where they are needed. Without such redeployment, the domestic nontradables output needed for reconstruction will not be forthcoming and economic reforms will be impeded. As the relative price of nontradables rises and resources are pulled out of tradables production, the excess demand for tradables is accommodated by imports, which are available only if there are capital inflows to finance them.

The Current Account

The current account, which typically deteriorates in the initial phase, improves in subsequent phases of reconstruction, when new capacity becomes available and supply shifts out. Note that capacity expansion does not have to take place in tradables in order to generate current account improvements. An outward shift in tradables supply following an increase in capacity does, of course, improve the current account at a given real exchange rate (along the lines shown in Figure 10.2). But an outward shift of nontradables supply due to an increase in nontradables capacity also improves the current account by bringing about a real depreciation. In general, the second-phase effect of a given reform program on the current account depends on the

234 *Sven W. Arndt*

relative movements of both demand and supply in both sectors. The effect on the real exchange rate depends only on the relative movements of demand and supply in nontradables.

Improvements in the current account may be achieved without lavishing resources on tradables industries to the neglect of the rest of the economy. The importance of this insight is not always fully appreciated, particularly in view of the contemporary popularity of export-led or trade-led growth and development strategies. The foregoing analysis suggests that a judicious program of investment in the "domestic" (nontradables) economy will over time reduce the relative price of nontradables as supply shifts out relative to demand, bringing about real depreciation and current account improvement. Such real depreciations, moreover, are not signs of economic weakness, just as the appreciations discussed above were not.

Reconstruction programs designed to build up tradables industries will bring long-run improvements in the current account if outward shifts in tradables supply over time outpace outward shifts in tradables demand and if the relative movements of nontradables demand and supply do not produce excessive real appreciation. In each sector, demand shifts depend on long-run income elasticities.

It follows that reconstruction focused on tradables industries may lead to long-run current account improvement, but that improvement may be associated with real appreciation as well as depreciation. Appreciation is the more likely outcome, the more the reform program starves the nontradables sector of resources.

Choosing the Transition Regime

The details of the reconstruction regime thus matter.[4] A perennial favorite is export-led development or, in the present context, transformation based on expansion of the tradables sector. The stylized character of such a program is to channel the bulk of capital formation into the tradables sector.

In the first phase of such a program investment-based demands for tradables and nontradables both rise, the latter rising to the extent that nontradable capital goods and construction resources and services are needed during the process of investment in tradables capacity. During this phase the currency appreciates in real terms, while the current account deteriorates and capital inflows increase. When new capacity becomes available, the tradables supply curve shifts out. The tradables demand curve also shifts out as the growth-induced rise in aggregate income raises consumption outlays. The current account improves, so long as the supply shift dominates the demand shift.

As the rise in national income increases the demand for nontradables, demand in that sector shifts out, causing the currency to appreciate in real terms. That appreciation tends to reduce a current account surplus or to increase a deficit.

Hence, a reconstruction program that is strongly biased in favor of expansion of tradables industries, combined with relatively low income elasticities of demand for nontradables, is capable of generating a long-run pattern of real appreciation and current account improvement. But the current account and real exchange rate patterns that emerge can take on a variety of characteristics, depending on the bias of the reconstruction program and the relevant income- and price-elasticities in both sectors.

The long-term evolution of real exchange rates and trade balances in Eastern Europe's transitioning economies is, thus, closely tied to the specifics of the restructuring programs themselves.

Adjustment in Factor Markets

The real exchange rate fluctuates during reconstruction. When the nominal rate is fixed, adjustments in the real rate occur via movements in nontradables prices. With the nominal rate fixed, a real appreciation is brought about by rising nontradables prices and a real depreciation by falling nontradables prices. It is, however, not only nontradables prices, but factor prices that must adjust. Thus, a real depreciation that is brought about by a decline in nontradables prices will exert downward pressure on wages and capital rentals throughout the economy. In the short run, when capital is sector specific, the decline in nontradables prices is accompanied by a decline in capital rentals in that sector only. The downward pressure on capital rentals is confined to nontradables as long as sector specificity holds. Downward pressure on nominal wages, on the other hand, spreads through the economy even in the short run, because the labor market is assumed to be integrated across the two sectors.

The decline in nominal wages will typically fall short of the decline in the price of nontradables, so that the nontradables product wage, that is, the nominal wage deflated by the price of nontradables, rises. The real wage also rises, in view of the assumption of a fixed nominal exchange rate and of given foreign tradables prices, and assuming further that the typical worker consumes at least some nontradables.

Bringing about a reduction in nominal wages may be politically difficult, even when it is not accompanied by losses in workers' purchasing power. In that case, a system of flexible nominal rates is to be preferred, so that real depreciation may be achieved by means of the additional instrument of nominal exchange rate changes. Indeed, under flexible nominal exchange rates nontradables prices may even rise, provided that they rise less rapidly than the nominal exchange rate.

This may be an important consideration in several Eastern European countries which have yet to bring their inflation rates in line with those of their main trading partners. The expression for the real exchange rate given above suggests that under a fixed nominal exchange rate, when nontradables prices carry the entire burden of adjustment, those prices must rise less rapidly than nontradables prices abroad. That is a difficult policy recipe in several reforming countries. The fact that price discipline must be imposed on nontradables is especially important here, because nontradables include a variety of public and private goods and services which governments everywhere have found notoriously difficult to control. High-inflation countries may thus have no choice but to keep nominal exchange rates flexible.

Concluding Remarks

The implications for the real exchange rate and the current account of economic transformation in Eastern Europe have been examined in terms of a model focusing on investment and the sectoral allocation of capital. During the initial phases of such programs, when investment, manifest mainly through increased expenditures, dominates the transition, movements in the real exchange rate and in the current account reflect associated demand shocks in both tradables and nontradables sectors. In subsequent periods, when additional capacity comes online and when the growth of national income raises domestic consumption, changes in both the real exchange rate and the current account may reverse direction. The pattern is one of cycles in the real exchange rate and the current account during the course of the transformation program.

Developments in the part of the economy that is sheltered from the world market play a major role in determining the behavior of the real exchange rate and hence of the current account. Among the important components of this sector are certain types of capital goods and a variety of construction goods and services.

Under a broad range of reform conditions, initial real appreciation will be followed by real depreciation. In small open economies, which act as price takers in world goods and services markets, real depreciation is achieved by nominal depreciation or by a decline in nontradables prices. When foreign prices are given and the nominal exchange rate is fixed, the entire burden of real depreciation falls on nontradables prices and on factor prices. Nontradables prices and nominal wages and capital rentals must fall. If such reductions are difficult to implement politically, floating exchange rates may be preferable.

In Eastern Europe, where several countries have not been able to control domestic inflation, fixing nominal exchange rates means that domestic nontradables prices—including prices of a variety of public goods and services—must be made to rise less rapidly than similar prices abroad, whenever the pressures emanating from the restructuring program call for real currency depreciation. That may be a requirement that is beyond the reach of many governments.

The current account, too, is subject to cycles over the course of a restructuring program. The importance of current account deficits is that they provide access to foreign resources, thereby expanding the range of restructuring options. But current account deficits need capital inflows to finance them and hence touch on the question of convertibility.

Many policymakers in Eastern Europe have expressed concerns about the possibility that capital inflows may "cause" real appreciation. The foregoing analysis suggests that capital inflows cannot be a cause of appreciation: the cause is to be found in movements in nontradables demand and supply and those movements are governed by the details of the restructuring program. Capital inflows merely facilitate the implementation of a transformation program. Hence, policy decisions about capital controls and convertibility cannot be made independently of the restructuring strategy.

Notes

I am indebted to Richard Sweeney, Clas Wihlborg, Thomas Willett and participants of conferences at Georgetown University, at the University of Konstanz, and at the Institute for Advanced Studies in Vienna for valuable comments on earlier drafts.

1. For an overview, see Corbo, Coricelli, and Bossak (1991). See also Hochreiter and Backé (1992). See Hanke and Schuler (1992) and Bergsten and Williamson (1990) for discussions of currency convertibility. For a discussion of real exchange rate rules, see Adams and Gros (1986) and Montiel and Ostry (1992). For a critical analysis of choosing exchange rate regimes in developing countries, see Aghevli, Khan, and Montiel (1991).

2. See Arndt (1990) for an application of this approach. For a model of fiscal policy and capital accumulation, see Barry (1987).

3. See Bergsten and Williamson (1990), Hanke and Schuler (1992), and Montiel and Ostry (1992) for related discussions.

4. See Adams and Gros (1986), Aghevli, Khan, and Montiel (1991), and Hochreiter and Backé (1992) for related discussions.

References

Adams, Charles, and Daniel Gros. 1986. "The Consequences of Real Exchange Rate Rules for Inflation: Some Illustrative Examples." *IMF Staff Papers* 33 (September): 439–76.

Aghevli, Bijan B., Mohsin S. Khan, and Peter J. Montiel. 1991. *Exchange Rate Policy in Developing Countries: Some Analytical Issues.* IMF Occasional Paper No. 78. Washington, D.C.: International Monetary Fund, March.

Arndt, Sven W. 1990. "Industrial Structure, Competitiveness, and Trade." *The North American Review of Economics and Finance* 1 (Fall): 217–24.

Barry, Frank G. 1987. "Fiscal Policy in a Small Open Economy: An Integration of the Short-run, Heckscher-Ohlin and Capital Accumulation Models." *Journal of International Economics* 22 (February):103–21.

Bergsten, C. Fred, and John Williamson. 1990. "Currency Convertibility in Eastern Europe," in *Central Banking Issues in Emerging Market-Oriented Economies.* Pp. 35–49. Kansas City: Federal Reserve Bank of Kansas City.

Corbo, Vittorio, Fabrizio Coricelli and Jan Bossak, eds. 1991. *Reforming Central and Eastern European Economies: Initial Results and Challenges.* Washington, D.C.: The World Bank.

Hanke, Steve H., and Kurt Schuler. 1992. *Currency Convertibility: A Self-Help Blueprint for the Commonwealth of Independent States.* Foreign Policy Briefing No. 27. Washington, D.C.: Cato Institute, January 22.

Hochreiter, Eduard, and Peter Backé. 1992. "Policies for Stabilization and Adjustment in the Transition Period," in Christopher T. Saunders, ed., *Economics and Politics of Transition.* East-West European Economic Interaction Workshop Papers, Vol. 13.

Montiel, Peter J., and Jonathan D. Ostry. 1992. "Real Exchange Rate Targeting Under Capital Controls." *IMF Staff Papers* 39 (March): 58–78.

11

Real Exchange Rate Targeting in Economies in Transition and the Sterilization Problem: The Hungarian Experience

Pierre L. Siklos and István Ábel

Introduction

The economic liberalization of Central and Eastern Europe has provided countries in Western Europe and the rest of the industrialized world with an opportunity to develop new markets and to retain their competitive edge in world markets by gaining access to skilled and relatively low wage labor forces in the liberalizing economies. Hungary, especially, benefitted early on from the capital inflows, which are necessary to restructure the economy after the ravages of central planning, although Poland and the Czech Republic caught-up quickly.[1]

A significant share of the foreign direct investment portion of capital flows was generated by the various privatization programs initiated in the formerly centrally planned economies (henceforth referred to as the transitioning economies). Privatization has tended to progress in fits and starts, which perhaps helps to explain the different records of the transitioning economies in attracting capital flows from the industrialized world.[2]

Different types of exchange rate regimes were adopted by the transitioning economies at the outset of the transition from centrally planned to market economies (see Hallwood and MacDonald 1994, Table 18.1, for a convenient summary for most of the transitional economies). The choice of exchange rate regime affects, among other things, the macroeconomic consequences of large inflows of capital in the space of a relatively short time. In the transitioning economies it has typically resulted in real appreciation of the exchange rate. Given the need for these economies to become competitive in world markets rather quickly, in large part to minimize the severe economic costs of the transition, real appreciations are unwelcome since they tend to reduce external competitiveness. Capital inflows are nevertheless a vitally important source of funding for the transitioning economies as they seek to rebuild and recover from the severe economic distortions created by the combination of central planning and forced industrialization under the Soviet regime.[3]

Developments in the real exchange rate are also influenced by the ability of the central banks in these countries to sterilize capital flows. The ability to engage in sterilized interventions gives central banks some control over the growth of the domestic monetary base and, therefore, inflation. It also permits some control over the exchange rate and, as a result, influences real exchange rate developments. An assessment of the role of sterilization also helps us determine to what extent capital inflows affect the monetary base and, consequently, the ability of transitioning economies to control inflation.

This chapter considers the use of sterilization by the National Bank of Hungary. We focus on Hungary for a number of reasons. First, Hungary has experienced substantial capital flows (measured as a percentage of GDP) for a much longer period than have any of the other transitioning economies. Second, the available time series are not only relatively longer for Hungary but are available for a much wider spectrum of macroeconomic variables than in other transitioning economies. This allows the estimation of reaction functions for the National Bank of Hungary, thereby permitting us to evaluate the effectiveness of sterilization. Third, the IMF and other international organizations (e.g., the European Bank for Reconstruction and Development) have, at various times, expressed reservations about the direction of Hungary's macroeconomic policy. In light of the events in 1994 and 1995 in Mexico, it is also timely to broadly evaluate Hungary's actual policy stance.

The plan of the chapter is as follows. The next section provides an overview of exchange rate developments in Hungary and briefly contrasts these with the Polish and Czech approaches. The third section describes the sterilization option in transition economies and contrasts this with the experience in the Southern Cone. The fourth section outlines the specification and estimation of a reaction function for the National Bank of Hungary. Section five presents estimates of reaction functions for the National Bank of Hungary and provides a quantitative assessment of the extent to which inflows of foreign capital were allowed to affect the monetary base. We do not, however, specifically address the consequences of incomplete sterilization on investment, the government budget or foreign debt. The sixth section concludes.

Briefly, we find that sterilization did not take place until possibly the middle of 1994, that is, subsequent to the return of the former Communists to power. Thus, rather than implementing a looser monetary policy under the former Communists, the National Bank of Hungary began to demonstrate more firmly its independence from the government by tightening monetary policy after May 1994.

Exchange Rate Developments and Policies in Hungary: 1987–1995

It is difficult to date precisely the beginning of the transition process, especially for Hungary which has pursued a policy of gradual economic liberalization since at least the late 1960s. We chose 1987 as a reasonable starting point since that is when the National Bank of Hungary began to operate like a conventional central bank.[4]

Unlike Poland, which adopted a crawling peg following a brief experience with a pegged exchange rate (see, for example, Sachs 1993 and Kemme 1994), or the Czech Republic (and its predecessor Czechoslovakia) which adopted a fixed exchange rate (Hrnčíř and Klacek 1991), Hungary chose an adjustable peg exchange rate regime, which kept open the option to devalue when needed.[5] Moreover, since at least 1991, it has been the expressed policy of the National Bank of Hungary to target the real exchange rate. This is clearly stated by the National Bank of Hungary (1995b:144):

> Monetary policy intends to stabilize the exchange rate.... it means that the exchange rate policy must aim for the *stability of the real exchange rate* (italics in original).[6]

Curiously perhaps, the Act of the National Bank of Hungary (1990, as amended in 1994) gave the bank limited authority to change the forint exchange rate on its own account (most recently by a margin of +/- 5 percent) following consultations with the government.[7] In most countries the Treasury retains full authority to decide which exchange rate regime will be followed. At the beginning of 1995, the government, now controlled by the former Communists, signaled a major shift in its policies with the appointment of a new finance minister and the return of a former central bank governor (Hírmondó, 10 February 1995), both apparently committed to continued economic liberalization and inflation control (Hírmondó, 15 March 1995). In March 1995, the Governor of the National Bank of Hungary announced that, henceforth, Hungary would implement a crawling peg devaluation scheme (National Bank of Hungary 1995, and "Hungary Tries to Show it Means

Business," *The Financial Times*, 15 March 1995, p. 2). While foreign exchange transactions are fully convertible on the current account, Hungary has only very recently (1996) liberalized the capital account. Moreover, until April 1, 1995, enterprises could not hold their foreign exchange revenues, but had to sell them to the National Bank of Hungary within eight days of receipt.

Figure 11.1 plots the real exchange rate for the forint since 1987. The vertical bars indicate the months in which the National Bank of Hungary and/or the government devalued the currency (Table 11.4 in the Appendix provides the details of the devaluations). A few considerations have to be kept in mind when interpreting the data in Figure 11.1. First, while the

FIGURE 11.1 Real Exchange Rates in Hungary 1987–1994

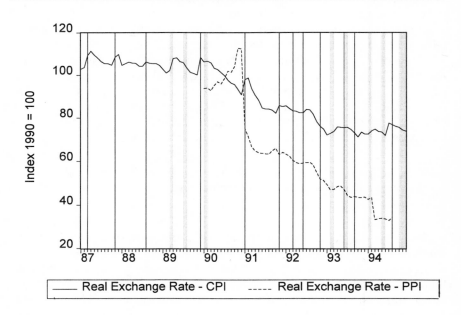

NOTE: The real exchange rate is evaluated as $e[P^{Ger}/P^{Hun}]$ where P^{Ger} and P^{Hun} are the consumer price indices for Germany and Hungary, respectively, and e is the nominal exchange rate (forint price of DM). The vertical bars indicate months during which a devaluation of the Hungarian forint took place.
SOURCE: National Bank of Hungary, *Monthly Reports* (various issues), and authors' calculations.

calculations are based on the exchange rate vis-à-vis the German mark (DM), the actual exchange rate was pegged to a basket of currencies whose composition was subject to revisions over time.[8] Second, and perhaps more importantly, the behavior of the real exchange rate is quite sensitive to whether calculations are based on the Consumer Price Index (CPI) or the Producer Price Index (PPI). As Sándor (1994) and Hochreiter (1995a) point out, there are a number of technical and practical difficulties in using the CPI measure of the real exchange rate for transitioning economies.[9]

The real exchange rate data in Figure 11.1 are defined in such a manner that a *fall* in the real exchange rate signals a real *appreciation*, and for Hungary the foreign price level used was the German CPI or PPI.[10] While Figure 11.1 reveals stabilization in the level of the CPI-based real exchange rate by, roughly, the beginning of 1993, the apparent downward trend (appreciation) in the PPI-based real exchange rate continued into 1994. Nor does there appear to be a relationship between the timing of devaluations and the behavior of any of the real exchange rate measures.[11] While the National Bank of Hungary is not explicit about which real exchange rate it targets, a reading of its annual and monthly reports suggests that the preferred price measure has changed over time.[12]

What are the major ingredients contributing to the real appreciation—a common phenomenon among the countries in transition—of the exchange rate over time? While it is difficult to establish a dominant causal role for inflows, we argue that, for Hungary at least, these inflows did significantly contribute to the magnitude of the real appreciations of the Hungarian currency. As noted above, foreign direct investment in Hungary has been relatively large. Countering or offsetting the impact of foreign direct investment (which includes privatization proceeds) on the exchange rate has been Hungary's relatively large foreign debt, payable in hard currencies.[13] Finally, the pent-up demand for consumer goods, durables and nondurables, has produced a growing deficit on the current account.[14]

Figure 11.2 shows the development of the monetary base and international reserves since 1987. International reserves (right-hand scale) are in billions of U.S. dollars while the monetary base (left-hand scale) data are in billions of forint. Following a sharp rise in reserves lasting until late 1992, international reserves became more stable beginning in 1993 and the monetary base followed suit, an indication perhaps that the degree of sterilization initiated by the National Bank of Hungary may have varied over time. Indeed, a crude measure of the scale of sterilization, namely the ratio of the change in international reserves (valued in forint) to the change in the monetary base suggests that sterilization was modest in 1991 and 1992, while for the 1993–94 (September) period there is an inverse relationship between changes in the two series.[15] Moreover, the figure suggests that a change in monetary policy

FIGURE 11.2 International Reserves and the Monetary Base: Hungary

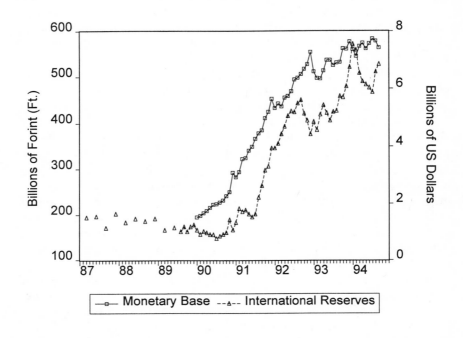

NOTE: The monetary base is calculated as currency in circulation plus mandatory reserves of commercial banks. International reserves are in billions of U.S. dollars and include gold (a very small fraction of the total).
SOURCES: National Bank of Hungary, *Monthly Reports* (various issues), *International Financial Statistics* (CD-ROM).

took place between 1993 and 1994. Thus, whereas the level of international reserves began once again to climb rapidly during the second half of 1993, growth in the monetary base was quite modest. By the end of 1993 international reserves fell sharply while the base level was stable. The seeming policy change is perhaps not surprising in view of the rise in the current account deficit, the rising inflation rate (both actual and expected) and budget deficits. Concerns were also expressed domestically, and especially in international circles, about the perceived direction of fiscal policy, especially in late 1993 and early 1994; these concerns were heightened by political events such as the reelection of the former Communists in May 1994 and disagreements over monetary policy between the finance minister and the central bank governor.[16]

The Sterilization Option in Transitioning Economies

For reasons that are well-known to students of Latin American economic history of the last two decades or so (see Rebelo and Végh 1995, and Calvo and Végh 1994), some form of exchange rate pegging has been the policy of choice for those economies that wished to disinflate quickly and credibly. The need to disinflate in the transitioning economies was prompted by a combination of at least two factors. First, there were worries about a monetary overhang, although this proved to be largely unfounded (Bruno 1992). Second, there was a need to rein in inflation following the immediate impact of price liberalization, which policymakers knew would result in very high short-term inflation rates.[17] Implementation of such policies was driven primarily by the need for a credible and clear signal about the government's intent to pursue policies resulting in lower and steadier inflation. This was believed to be an important ingredient in a successful transition to a market economy.[18] Countries which embarked on such a course experienced large capital inflows and consequently real appreciations.

Inflows of reserves can be sterilized via open market operations. In the transitioning economies, an additional weapon in controlling what would otherwise translate into domestic credit growth is the manipulation of reserve requirements for the banking sector. In Hungary, open market operations were used early in the transition. As shown in Figure 11.3, household sector holdings of government bonds increased rapidly. This is particularly evident in 1992, when reserves of foreign exchange also rose rapidly (see also Figure 11.2).[19] Reserve requirements, which were high (18 percent of deposits; see Kemme 1994 for details), were reduced to 14 percent in 1994 before being raised back to 18 percent in 1995 in a bid to restrain credit creation.[20] Of course, as the National Bank of Hungary (1995) has itself admitted, this policy can also lead to disintermediation. Nevertheless, reserve requirements represent an important tool of monetary policy in the transition economies where commercial banking is underdeveloped.[21] Finally, in 1993 the National Bank of Hungary provided forward repurchase transactions for short maturities (one to three months) at what became known as the repo rate. In 1994 the term was extended for up to one year with a daily limit of 8 billion forint (or 1 billion on a weekly basis). These were available only to commercial banks with assets of over 100 billion forint. In 1995 these repo facilities were severely cut back.[22]

Concerns have also been raised recently not only about the size of capital flows but also about their composition, especially in light of the differences between Latin American and Asian countries. Real exchange rates have appreciated more in Latin American than in Asian countries. Some observers suggest that whereas capital inflows to Latin America have been used to finance private consumption, or have stemmed from privatization, for the

FIGURE 11.3 Holding of Government Bonds and Notes by the Household Sector

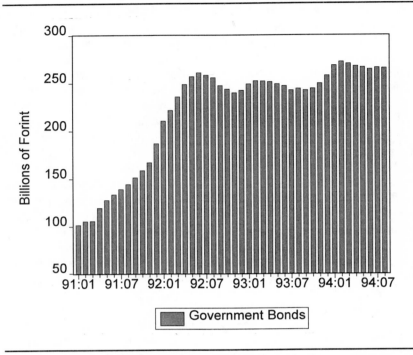

NOTE: Hungarian forint value at issue of government bonds and savings notes purchased by the household sector.
SOURCE: National Bank of Hungary, *Monthly Reports* (various issues).

most part capital inflows in Asia have been put to more productive uses (Bank for International Settlements 1995:113–14). Turning to the experience of Hungary, privatization proceeds have certainly been one component of inflows with the share of investment goods in exports, by 1993, comparing favorably to the entire OECD (Obláth 1995).[23] Table 11.1 presents data since 1988, broken into the major capital flow components. It is clearly seen that revenues from privatization represent but a small component of overall flows.

The consequences of the National Bank of Hungary's policies, and those of the government, are also clearly recognizable on inflation and the external debt situation. Both variables began to rise in 1993 and again during 1994, in contrast to improvements on both accounts during the early 1990s. These events may have pushed the former Communists to reverse their policies in early 1995 (see Table 11.1 for the debt/GDP ratio data).

TABLE 11.1 Capital Flows and External Debt in Hungary (millions of U.S. dollars unless otherwise stated)

	1988	*1989*	*1990*	*1991*	*1992*	*1993*	*1994*
Net Medium and Long-term Capital	568	1192	-31	1668	-894	3066	1161
Direct Investment Income (net)	14	187	311	1459	1471	2339	1146
Privatization Revenues *of which:*	NA	NA	10.6	419.5	947	889	92.9
% Hard Currency Sales	NA	NA	79.1	78.4	54.8	31.2	6.6
Net Short-Term Capital Flows	288	-44	-893	-617	5	459	960
Net Debt/GDP Ratio (%)	NA	NA	48.5	46.6	35.8	39	45.9
Debt Service/GDP Ratio (%)	NA	NA	12.6	12	11.4	11	12.6

SOURCE: National Bank of Hungary, *Monthly Reports,* April 1995, pp. 102–3, 105, and Hungarian Privatization and State Holding Company, *Privatization Monitor,* May 31, 1995, p. 6. Data refer to revenues generated by the State Property Agency. Original data in billions of Hungarian forint, converted into U.S. dollars at average annual exchange rates. NA means not applicable or available.

A Reaction Function for the National Bank of Hungary

Specification and Estimation

We follow a fairly conventional approach to the specification of a reaction function which has been used by many authors (e.g., see Cumby and Obstfeld 1983 and Obstfeld 1983).[24] The monetary authorities may attempt to sterilize the monetary effects of the balance of payments by changing their domestic assets according to the following:

$$(1) \qquad \Delta DA_t = Z_t - a(CA_t + K_t)$$

where DA represents domestic assets of the central bank, CA is the current account balance of payments and K equals net capital flows.[25] The coefficient a represents the degree of sterilization while Z is a vector of variables which are also thought to affect monetary policy (see below) and $CA + K$ is the balance of payments, that is, the net change in foreign assets held by the central bank (ΔFA, namely changes in international reserves; i.e., $CA + K \equiv \Delta FA$ from the balance of payments accounting identity). Obviously, when valued in domestic currency units one needs to adjust (1) to exclude valuation increases due to periodic devaluations. Another difficulty arises because of changes in reserve requirements. As noted earlier, changes in reserve requirements also represent a feature of monetary policy, and this is particularly true of transitioning economies (Kemme 1994). In what follows, we define the monetary base (the measure used to proxy central bank credit creation) in *adjusted terms*, namely corrected for the impact of changing reserve ratios over time. Since changes in the monetary base are then captured by a combination of changes in the adjusted base, and changes in the domestic and foreign assets of the central bank, Cumby and Obstfeld (1983) use an expression which links changes in the current level of the adjusted monetary base, ΔBA, to changes in the domestic and foreign assets of the central bank (ΔDA and ΔFA, respectively) and is written:

$$(2) \quad \Delta BA_t = \Delta FA_t + \Delta DA_t + \Delta BA_t^*$$

where ΔBA_t^* is the change in the monetary base due to a change in reserve requirements.[26] From (2) they derive an indicator of monetary policy (MP) written in functional form as follows:

$$(3) \quad \Delta MP_t = f(\Delta DA_t, \Delta BA_t^*)$$

Given the above expression, we now write a reaction function for the National Bank of Hungary in regression form:

$$(4) \quad \Delta MP_t = \alpha_0 + \alpha_1 \Delta FA_t + \alpha_2 \Delta y_t + \alpha_3 \Delta \epsilon_t + \alpha_4 DEF_t + \alpha_5 DEV_t + u_t$$

In equation (4), where FA represents the foreign assets of the central bank (proxied by international reserves), sterilization neutralizes the impact of inflows by offsetting effects on domestic credit. When $0 < \alpha_1 < 1$ sterilization is less than perfect, and nonexistent when the coefficient is zero. Finally, a positive value for α_1 indicates that internal monetary control or balance is being sacrificed for external balance, with the tradeoff toward external balance being greater, the higher is α_1.

The remaining variables in (4) capture other influences on monetary policy (i.e., the vector Z_t in equation 1). These include the rate of change in output (y), the rate of change in the real effective exchange rate (ϵ), government deficits (DEF), and a variable to capture irregular devaluations of the forint (DEV).[27] If the data are not seasonally adjusted, additional dummies to capture the impact of seasonality may also be added. The specification therefore permits us to identify the degree to which the relationship between reserves and the base is due to offsetting capital flows or whether it is the result of sterilized interventions by the National Bank of Hungary.

Since most of the right-hand-side variables in (4) are endogenous, estimation via Ordinary Least Square (OLS) may be inappropriate.[28] Two-stage least squares is used to estimate (3) with the intercept, lagged values of the endogenous variables (y, ϵ, DEF, MP), the (lagged) Hungarian-German interest rate differential, and the (lagged) gap between borrowing and lending rates as instruments.[29]

Clearly, capital flows, the Hungarian budget deficit[30] and, therefore, monetary policy are directly influenced by the interest rate differential relative to Germany. The gap between borrowing and lending rates at commercial banks in Hungary reflects a combination of factors which can significantly impinge on the behavior of the variables in (4). The gap is a function of the costs of obtaining liquidity from the National Bank of Hungary and/or foreign sources, as well as being a reflection of the perceived risks of commercial lending to the so-called enterprise sector, and an indicator of the potential for disintermediation. As such, a rise in the gap will signal a potential contraction in domestic credit to the enterprise sector if the gap is due to a rise in the lending rate relative to the borrowing rate. Similarly, a contraction in deposits following a reduction in the borrowing rate relative to the lending rate will result in a contraction of commercial loans since these are viewed as being riskier than holding government debt. Thus, while the gap will affect monetary policy, the direction of the effect is unclear.

Data

Monthly data from 1989 to the end of 1994 from the National Bank of Hungary's *Monthly Reports* were employed for the monetary, fiscal, and some of the exchange rate variables (i.e., DA, BA, ϵ, DEF, DEV). Data for industrial production, consumer and producer prices are from the International Monetary Fund's *International Financial Statistics* CD-ROM, as well as the National Bank of Hungary data source. All series, before differencing, are in domestic currency units (e.g., billions of forint) or in percent (e.g., interest rate and devaluation).

Ideally, one might have wished to rely on, say, a measure of the output gap instead of the rate of change in output. Given that economies in transition are undergoing radical changes in economic structure it would seem futile, or at least of limited value, to attempt to estimate anything resembling a potential output series at this stage. Output then is proxied by industrial production since the data are sampled at the monthly frequency.

Next, in order to identify the *short-run* impact of sterilization on monetary policy it is also important not to specify what might look like a long-run relation. In other words, we wish to avoid possibly estimating a spurious regression or one which is misspecified. All the relevant series are stationary in first differences (see Table 11.5 in the Appendix).

In addition to the definition of monetary policy in equations (2) and (3), changes in monetary policy are also proxied, as in other such studies, by the change in domestic credit; this is essentially the sum of credits to the government, enterprises (large and small) and household sectors.[31] These data are also from the National Bank of Hungary. Finally, the real exchange rate is measured in terms of German prices (i.e., $e[P^{Ger}/P^{Hun}]$, where e is the nominal exchange rate) and converted into an index by the IMF with a 1987 base year.

Estimation Results

As noted above, the existing literature gave relatively little thought to the statistical properties of the time series under consideration. Developments in time-series analysis over the past decade have altered the manner in which regressions such as (4) are estimated. Thus, the estimation of (4) can be misspecified if a long-run equilibrium relationship exists between the central variables of interest and this relation is not explicitly recognized in the estimated equation. The reason is that (4) is a *short-run* reaction function which omits a *long-run* equilibrium condition which might be present among *MP*, *FA*, y, and ϵ. As Engle and Granger (1987) have pointed out, there is an isomorphism between the long run—statistically represented by the condition of cointegration—and the short run represented by the addition in (4) of an error correction term, which shall be labeled *EC*.[32] Table 11.2 then presents results of several cointegration tests applied to the data. These tests represent the necessary, but not sufficient, conditions for the finding of a long-run statistical relationship among the series considered. It should also be kept in mind that the brevity of the sample should make one cautious about reading too much into the results. Nevertheless, such testing is an important step in the proper estimation of short-run relationships. The results in Table 11.2 are based on Johansen's test, one of several cointegration tests in existence. The principal drawback with some of the other tests is that they do not permit the uncovering of more than one cointegrating relationship between the time series examined. Thus, for example, it is quite plausible that separate long-run equilibrium relationships exist between, say, the monetary policy variable

TABLE 11.2 Cointegration Tests

Null Hypothesis[1]	Alternative Hypothesis	Test Statistic (λ_{max})[2]
Vector:[P, y, FA, ϵ - CPI based]		
$r = 0$	$r = 1$	28.59*
$r \leq 1$	$r = 2$	19.26
$r \leq 2$	$r = 3$	9.99
$r \leq 3$	$r = 4$	.25
Cointegrating Vector: [1, -1572, -1.383, -2230.8]		
Vector: [MP, y, FA, ϵ - PPI based]		
$r = 0$	$r = 1$	30.12*
$r \leq 1$	$r = 2$	19.34
$r \leq 2$	$r = 3$	12.64
$r \leq 3$	$r = 4$	2.04
Cointegrating Vector: [1, -3236.1, -3.23, -2025.2]		
Vector: [DC, y, FA, ϵ - CPI based]		
$r = 0$	$r = 1$	23.43
$r \leq 1$	$r = 2$	11.24
$r \leq 2$	$r = 3$	8.05
$r \leq 3$	$r = 4$	.03
Vector: [DC, y, FA, ϵ - PPI based]		
$r = 0$	$r = 1$	26.10
$r \leq 1$	$r = 2$	16.97
$r \leq 2$	$r = 3$	12.04

* signifies statistically significant at the 5% level. The test assumes that the series are trended in the levels.

[1] r represents the number of cointegrating vectors.

[2] λ_{max} is the maximal eigenvalue test.

MP and the central bank's foreign assets *FA* (as might be implied by Figure 11.2) and between ϵ and *Y*. In this particular case one would conclude that two cointegrating vectors exist (i.e., $r = 2$ in the notation of Table 11.2). Four cases were examined in Table 11.2, depending upon whether the real exchange rate (ϵ) is calculated on a CPI or PPI basis and whether domestic credit (*DC*) is used to proxy monetary policy (*MP*)(as in Obstfeld 1983).

The results clearly reveal that when *DC* is used to proxy *MP* there is no evidence of any long-run relationship between the variables (i.e., the null $r = 0$ cannot be rejected). By contrast, when *MP*, as defined in (2) is used, the tests reveal that a single vector or linear combination can characterize the relationship between the four variables considered.[33] The estimates of the co-integrating vectors are also given in Table 11.2. These suggest that higher industrial production—an indicator of business cycle expansion and thus signaling higher future inflation—implies a tighter monetary policy (i.e., *MP* falls), and the same is true when there is an appreciation of the real exchange rate (i.e., ϵ falls).[34] Indeed, the long-run coefficient on *FA* is not statistically different from -1 (under the null, the test statistic is distributed as a χ^2 with one degree of freedom with a test statistic of 0.97 (.33 significance level)), which would imply complete sterilization or the complete neutralization of capital flows in the long run. Similar cointegration test results are obtained when the real exchange rate is measured on a PPI basis, except that the sterilization coefficient is much larger (the null that $\alpha_1 = -1$ in the long-run is rejected; $\chi^2 (1) = 5.96$ (.02 significance level)) which would suggest an overreaction to capital inflows by the National Bank of Hungary.

We now turn to the estimation of short-run National Bank of Hungary reaction functions augmented, where needed, with the appropriate long-run restriction from the cointegration tests just discussed. These are given in Table 11.3. The estimates shown are based on the two-stage least squares technique with the list of instruments used provided in the notes to the table.[35] Regressions were generated according to whether the real exchange rate was measured using the CPI (columns labeled 1) or the PPI (columns labeled 2). Separate tests were also generated by including the error correction term for the full sample case only.[36] Moreover, because heteroskedasticity was found in most of the estimated models, all *t*-ratios are based on heteroskedasticity-consistent standard error estimates.[37]

The results in Table 11.3 are mixed. A substantial amount of sterilization appears to have taken place during 1993–94 if the PPI-based real exchange rate measure is used. When *DC* (domestic credit) is used to proxy the National Bank of Hungary's monetary policy, then sterilization is not apparent. Given the potential importance of events in 1994, due primarily to the return to power of the former Communists, we were also interested in determining whether our results could be sensitive to sample choice.[38] In most cases, the lack of sterilization is seen to be possibly a feature only of the subsample. This is an indication that the election of the former Communists signaled a somewhat tighter monetary policy, and not the looser monetary policy they advocated during the election campaign.[39] This interpretation is also consistent with our description (see Figure 11.2) of the relationship between international reserves and the monetary base. Assuming that a PPI-based real exchange rate and *MP* are the preferred indicators of policy, there is both evidence of sterilization—with a coefficient somewhat higher than those obtained for many, but not all, other countries (e.g., see Rivera-Batiz and

TABLE 11.3 National Bank of Hungary Reaction Functions: Two-Stage Least Squares

Dependent Variables	MP				DC			
	Samples							
	1991:01–1994:12		1991:01–1994:04		1991:01–1994:12		1991:01–1994:12	
Independent Variables	(1)	(2)	(1)	(2)	(1)	(2)	(1)	(2)
$\Delta F.A$	-.96(.90)	-.69(1.89)*	-.77(.49)	-.40(.98)	-.11(.08)	-.42(.78)	-.20(.81)	-.28(.99)
Δy	.94(.16)	1.91(.40)	3.30(.22)	2.88(.38)	-2.54(.34)	-1.05(.25)	-1.19(.42)	-.82(.27)
$\Delta \epsilon$	-3.06(.11)	-4.13(.71)	-1.45(.05)	-5.34(.76)	19.44(.50)	7.00(.66)	-1.78(.51)	-1.72(.46)
ΔDEF	-.001(.44)	-.001(.79)	-.007(.37)	-.002(1.47)+	.0003(.08)	-.001(.24)	.001(1.13)	.001(.96)
DEV	18.58(2.57)*	17.44(2.98)*	30.86(1.41)+	21.91(2.91)*	-4.45(.59)	-2.55(.47)	-.65(.29)	-2.05(.68)
JAN	31.41(.94)	29.87(1.04)	-8.97(.09)	14.82(.61)	15.00(.30)	8.16(.20)	10.99(.41)	16.39(.52)
DEC	57.01(1.02)*	54.96(2.41)*	75.91(.79)	63.07(2.16)*	71.09(1.09)	83.93(1.80)	62.27(1.73)*	77.30(1.73)*
Constant	8.40(.30)	.03(.002)	1.94(.04)	-9.50(.56)	28.89(1.09)	24.65(1.26)	12.34(2.43)*	12.50(2.04)*
R^2 adj.	.27	.24	.08	.08	.11	.21	.07	.09
S.E. Regr.	47.44	45.75	94.62	39.39	59.49	35.90	32.05	30.42
F (sig. lev.)	2.41(.04)*	4.12(.002)*	.56(.08)*	3.38(.01)	.84(.56)	1.77(.13)	2.91(.02)*	2.49(.04)*
EC_{t-1}	.24(.20)	-.06(.38)	-	-	NA	NA	NA	NA

NOTES: Estimates for a real exchange rate using the CPI in column (1); using the PPI in column (2). The list of instruments used is as follows: Δy_{t-1}, $\Delta (R^{hun} - R^{Ger})_{t-1}$, ΔGAP_{t-1}, $\Delta \epsilon_{t-1}$, $HDEV$, JAN, DEC, ΔMP_{t-1} (or ΔDC_{t-1}), and the constant. The t-ratios, in parentheses, are based on heteroskedasticity-consistent standard errors. Error correction term is omitted in final estimates shown but the coefficient is given for the appropriate cases shown based on the results in Table 11.2. JAN and DEC are seasonal dummies retained; others were omitted for parsimony and because they were found to be statistically insignificant.

Rivera-Batiz 1994:413)—and of a tightening of monetary policy during the second half of 1994. The results are also broadly consistent with the view that the National Bank of Hungary permitted real appreciations of the forint until recently, when stabilizing the real exchange rate became the dominant objective of monetary policy. This might also explain why sterilization in Hungary is a relatively recent phenomenon.

Turning to some of the other coefficients we find no significant reaction by the National Bank of Hungary to any of the fundamentals except devaluation which, in effect, captures the monetization of exchange rate devaluations and reflects the continued softness of the government's budget constraint during the period considered.[40] Finally, we see that the error correction terms are insignificant, which brings into question whether the long-run equilibrium relationship detected earlier actually holds.

Conclusions

We have considered the performance of Hungary's monetary policy during the early 1990s. During this period, Hungary experienced large capital inflows under its system of quasi-fixed exchange rates with limited capital mobility. Despite Hungary's large foreign indebtedness, these net inflows of capital were large enough to raise questions about the bank's actions in the face of such inflows. An attempt to sterilize inflows is akin to attempting to conduct an independent monetary policy even when exchange rates are fixed. Our results suggest that only during the second half of 1994 did the National Bank of Hungary successfully sterilize capital inflows in order to pursue its objective of targeting the real exchange rate of the forint. However, no sterilization effect could be detected when a subsample which excludes the period when the former Communists returned to power is considered, as well as when the real exchange rate is measured using consumer prices rather than producer prices or when domestic credit is used to proxy monetary policy actions. Nevertheless, other more descriptive and anecdotal evidence also suggests that a policy change took place sometime during mid 1994, when the National Bank of Hungary moderated monetary base growth via sterilization, in line with its more restrictive monetary policy and contrary to the wishes of the newly elected government. Despite the small sample size and other statistical problems raised in the paper, the reaction function estimates presented here are consistent with a policy change by the National Bank of Hungary around May 1994. The present era of restraint announced with much fanfare in early 1995 (see Siklos and Ábel 1995a) with the appointment of a new finance minister and the return of an old central bank governor, can actually be traced to many months before their appointment.

Appendix

TABLE 11.4 Schedule of Hungarian Forint Devaluation Rates: 1987–1994

Year	Date (day/month)	Size of Devaluation	Reference Basket (weighted average of several currencies)
1989	March 21	5	
	April 14	6	
	July 18	.5	
	July 25	.1	
	July 29	.1	
	August 1	.07	
	August 8	.53	
	August 15	.2	
	December 15	10	50% $US - 50% ECU [from 8/12]
1990	January 31	1	
	February 6	2	
	February 20	2	
1991	January 7	15	
	November 8	5.8	
1992	March 6	1.9	
	June 23	1.6	
	November 9	1.9	
1993	February 12	1.9	
	March 26	2.9	
	June 7	1.9	
	July 9	3	
	September 29	4.5	[from 2/8] 50% $US - 50% DM
1994	January 3	1	
	February 16	2.6	70% DM - 30% $US
	June 16	1.5	[from May] 70% ECU - 30% $US

SOURCE: National Bank of Hungary, *Monthly Reports* (various issues).

TABLE 11.5 Unit Root Tests: Sample 1991: 01– 1994:12

Series	Test Statistic	Lags
MP	-1.46	4
y	-3.03	1
FA	-2.31	2
ε-CPI based	-1.87	0
ε-PPI based	-3.46	5

NOTE: Test is the augmented Dickey-Fuller test with the number of lags reported selected by first estimating the test equation for 5 lags and then running the test with the final lag length found by choosing the longest statistically significant lag term in the AR correction portion of the test equation. All test equations include an intercept and a trend except for the ε-PPI basis which includes an intercept only (the results were highly sensitive to lag length and the inclusion of a trend term for this series alone).

Notes

The financial support of OTKA T018211 is gratefully acknowledged. Pierre Siklos is grateful to the Justus-Liebig Universität, Giessen, Germany, the International Monetary Fund, and the University of California, San Diego, where portions of this paper were written while he was on sabbatical leave. An earlier version was presented at the Association for Comparative Economic Studies Conference, San Francisco, January 5–7, 1996. Comments by Ronald McKinnon on a previous draft are appreciated.

1. Data on foreign direct investment is contained in the National Bank of Hungary's *Monthly Report* (various issues), the National Bank of Poland's *Information Bulletin* (various issues) and the Czech National Bank's *Financial Statistical Information* (various issues). Thus, for example, in 1992 the flow of foreign direct investment (in millions of U.S. dollars) into Hungary was $1337, $1210 for the Czech Republic and $830 for Poland. In the previous year, Hungary had attracted $1338 in foreign direct investment while the Czech Republic received only $200 and Poland $470.

2. It is inappropriate to go into details here but political considerations led to numerous delays in privatizing certain sectors of the Polish economy. The Czech government (as has the Polish government since) chose the approach of issuing coupons or shares widely distributed among the public. By contrast, Hungary has opted for the case-by-case approach. In Hungary, it is estimated that while 80 percent of foreign direct investment in 1990 was due to privatization, this percentage had fallen to around 50 percent in 1993.

3. A word of caution is in order here. According to Classens, Dooley and Warner (1995), "labels" such as long-term and short-term capital flows (or foreign direct investment for that matter) do not provide much information about the time series properties of these flows (i.e., volatility, persistence and predictability) in a sample of industrialized and emerging market economies.

4. This may be a slight exaggeration to the extent that the legislation enabling the National Bank of Hungary to carry out central banking functions came into effect somewhat later (1990). Nevertheless, in all aspects but the legal one, the National Bank of Hungary functioned as a central bank when two-tier banking was introduced in 1987. As Várhegyi (1995:17) points out, two years earlier the Hungarian government had begun preparations for the introduction of two-tier banking and in effect "simulated" the new system for one year before its formal introduction.

5. Bulgaria, by contrast, chose a fully flexible exchange rate regime. It is reasonable, of course, to ask why the transitioning economies chose exchange rate based monetary policies as opposed to monetary or interest-rate or price-level targeting. The immaturity of the financial systems in the transitioning economies and the inability to identify a stable money demand function are some of the reasons given. See Siklos and Ábel (1995b) for a discussion of monetary policy strategies in Hungary and the Czech Republic.

6. The seeming clarity of the policy goal stated here is contradicted by the National Bank of Hungary itself. For example, National Bank of Hungary (1995a:5) states: "The main goals of monetary policy in 1994—a current account deficit substantially lower than in the preceding year...." while not inconsistent with a policy of real exchange rate targeting need also not be congruent with such an objective. Obláth (1995) also suggests that the National Bank of Hungary's exchange rate policy gave mixed signals.

7. It has not always been the case that the decision to devalue was agreed to by the government. The June 10, 1994 devaluation, in particular, coming soon after the return of the former Communists in the May 1994 elections, was publicly opposed by the new government. In part to demonstrate its independence and its determination to target the real exchange rate, the National Bank of Hungary proceeded to announce the devaluation. Such devaluations were not taken lightly, as these created by law a non-interest bearing claim on the National Bank of Hungary. By 1994, these claims were gradually turned into interest-bearing state debt as a result of National Bank of Hungary initiatives with significant consequences for the state budget which was already experiencing a growing deficit by then.

8. Until December 8, 1991, the exchange rate was pegged to a basket of currencies, the contents weighed according to trading patterns in the preceding year. Between December 9, 1991, and August 1, 1993, the basket weights were 50 percent ECUs and 50 percent U.S. dollars. From August 2, 1993, to May 15, 1994, the basket was 50 percent U.S. dollars and 50 percent DM. Since May 16, 1994, the basket's composition was redefined as 70 percent ECUs and 30 percent U.S. dollars. A comparison with Bank for International Settlements (1995) data, which calculates real exchange rates using a basket of currencies for 21 industrial countries, reveals patterns almost identical to those shown in Figure 11.1.

9. Among the various reasons cited by Hochreiter (1995a) for transitioning economies in general and by Sándor (1994) for Hungary, in particular, are the following: the CPI includes services, usually a nontradable good whose prices behave rather differently from those for tradeable goods and the level and scope of price liberalization affects the CPI and PPI measures differently. Thus, the CPI may reflect more the impact of exchange rate movements on aggregate demand and inflation rather than the true state of competitiveness.

10. Other versions of the real exchange rate (e.g., IMF, Bank for International Settlements—see Hochreiter 1995b) reveal similar patterns.

11. Siklos and Ábel (1995a) also confirm this statistically.

12. For example, the March 1995 issue of the National Bank of Hungary's *Monthly Report* (page 18) uses the so-called domestic sales price index. Previous issues also report calculations based on the CPI and the PPI.

13. The National Bank of Hungary's (1995a) figures reveal that net debt as a percent of GDP was as follows (with years in parenthesis): 48.5 (1990), 46.6 (1991), 35.8 (1992), 39.0 (1993), and 45.9 (1994). Meanwhile, however, the import coverage ratio has improved substantially. The data are as follows: 2.3 (1990), 5.3 (1991), 5.2 (1992), 7.1 (1993), and 7.2 (1994). The latter indicator is expressed in months.

14. Starting from an average monthly surplus of $US 27 million in 1992, the current account balance went into deficit in 1993 (average monthly balance of $US 288.42 until September 1994). Data are from the National Bank of Hungary's *Monthly Report* (various issues).

15. The ratio calculation for 1993–94 omits an outlier for the month of June 1993. The high value for the ratio in 1991–92 (.98) means that attempts to control the monetary base were essentially nonexistent.

16. For fuller details see, among others, Mosolygó (1994), Csillik (1994), and the National Bank of Hungary (1995b).

17. Sahay and Végh (1995) develop a very appealing model, based on the cash-in-advance methodology, to show that inflation following the end of central planning in transitioning economies is a function of the choice of nominal anchors following price liberalization. In particular, they note the importance of wage policies in such countries relative to market economies, again a peculiar legacy of the era of central planning.

18. An important and unresolved question in this respect is, what is the appropriate level of inflation at which steady economic growth will be maximized? See "World Bank Discussion on Second-Generation Transition Issues," *Transitions* 6 (May/June 1995:1-6), Bruno and Easterly (1995), and Burdekin, Salamun and Willett (1995).

19. Ábel, Bonin and Siklos (1994) explain how, in a financial system with weak banks and a narrow set of financial instruments, government bonds which paid positive real ex post interest rates were especially attractive to the public.

20. Given inflation rates of 20 to 30 percent and nominal interest rates of 25 to 35 percent during the period in question, interest rates of 28 percent on forint reserves and 11 to 18 percent on foreign exchange rate reserves clearly implied a substantial opportunity cost to the banking sector.

21. The following data give the required reserves as a percent of nominal GDP in Hungary with the years in parenthesis: 4.7 percent (1991), 6.4 percent (1992), 4.8 percent (1993), 3.7 percent (1994). By way of comparison, these figures are higher than in all the EU countries with the exception of Greece and Italy. Data are from the Bank for International Settlements, *Economic Indicators for Eastern Europe*, the National Bank of Hungary's *Monthly Reports* (various issues), and the European Monetary Institute's *Annual Report 1994* (Table 15).

22. These repos proved especially popular in September 1993 when, for "technical reasons," repo rates were lower than the return on government Treasury bills.

This, of course, produced an excess demand (relative to the daily limits) for use of the repo facility. See Mosolygó (1994).

23. Moreover, savings rates in Hungary have been declining so that this does not appear to be a potential remedy (via the reduction in interest rates it would create) for Hungary, at least in the short-run.

24. Argy (1994:398–400) and Rivera-Batiz and Rivera-Batiz (1994:411–14) briefly survey the literature.

25. Equation (1) can also be related to a structural model of the type developed by, say, Obstfeld (1983).

26. For simplicity we have assumed that the *base* reserve ratio and the current reserve ratio are the same in (2). See Cumby and Obstfeld (1983:252). Clearly, for ΔBA^* to be different from zero there would have to be a change in the reserve ratio between time $t - 1$ and t.

27. This series takes on a positive value (i.e., the size of the devaluation in percent) in the month when a devaluation takes place and zero otherwise. In months when more than one devaluation took place we simply summed the devaluations for that month. We also tried a dummy variable which captures political instability in Hungary (see Siklos and Ábel 1995a). This variable proved to be statistically insignificant and was dropped from the final specification.

28. Frenkel (1983) points out that OLS estimates of (4) may be biased but that the direction of the bias in unknown.

29. A structural model might be more appropriate, but the short length of the sample justifies resort to single equation methods. Obstfeld (1983) uses nonlinear least squares (with a correction for serial correlation) although he also points out that a more "thorough" analysis requires the application of two-stage least squares (Obstfeld 1983:173, n. 17).

30. To the extent that it is monetized, a far more likely occurrence among transitional economics than in, say, industrialized economies.

31. When domestic credit proxies monetary policy, no adjustment could be made for the impact of changing reserve requirements due to data limitations.

32. For additional details on the relationship between cointegration and error correction, see Banerjee, Dolado, Gabraith and Hendry (1993), and Hendry (1995).

33. At a slightly more generous significance level there is evidence of two co-integrating vectors but subsequent testing (results not shown) rejects the presence of a second vector.

34. Note that *MP* and *FA* are measured in billions of forint.

35. We did experiment with the list of instruments such as trying longer lags but none of these attempts altered our conclusions.

36. The *EC* term was included in both the Ordinary Least Squares and 2SLS versions of the model with no impact on the conclusions.

37. Obstfeld (1983) and Cumby and Obstfeld (1983) also adjust for first-order serial correlation in their applications to German and Mexican data. In the present study, we also experimented with versions of (4) with an AR(1) correction factor estimated via maximum likelihood but found little impact on the coefficient estimates for sterilization. In any event, we did not find much support for serial correlation in the residuals. Finally, we also produced estimates using the Newey-West (1987) procedure with no impact on the conclusions.

38. Given the date of the election (May 1994) we were unable to perform a structural test for a "break" in the relationship.

39. We did try estimates of (4) with the addition of an electoral dummy variable, but this proved to be statistically insignificant. See also Siklos and Ábel (1995b) for the view that the events of the second half of 1994 were a reflection of the growing independence of the National Bank of Hungary vis-à-vis the government.

40. The statistical significance of the *DEC* variable may also be capturing fiscal influences as this is the year end when the deficit seems to experience a seasonally induced increase reflecting year-end spending of allocated budgets.

References

Ábel, István, John P. Bonin and Pierre L. Siklos. 1994. "Crippled Monetary Policies in Transforming Economies: Why Central Bank Independence Does Not Restore Control," in Pierre L. Siklos, ed., *Varieties of Monetary Reforms: Lessons and Experiences on the Road to Monetary Union.* Pp. 367–82. Boston: Kluwer Academic Press.

Argy, Victor. 1994. *International Macroeconomics.* London: Routledge.

Banerjee, Anindya, Juan Dolado, John W. Galbraith and David F. Hendry. 1993. *Co-integration, Error-Correction and the Econometric Analysis of Non-Stationary Data.* Oxford: Oxford University Press.

Bank for International Settlements. 1995. *65th Annual Report.* Basle, Switzerland.

Bruno, Michael. 1992. "Stabilization and Reform in Eastern Europe: Preliminary Evaluation." IMF Working Paper No. 92/3. Washington, D.C.: International Monetary Fund, May.

Bruno, Michael, and William Easterly. 1995. "Inflation Crises and Long-run Growth." Working paper. Washington, D.C.: The World Bank.

Burdekin, Richard C.K., Suyono Salamun and Thomas D. Willett. 1995. "The High Costs of Monetary Instability," in Thomas D. Willett, Richard C.K. Burdekin, Richard J. Sweeney and Clas Wihlborg, eds., *Establishing Monetary Stability in Emerging Market Economies.* Pp. 13–32. Boulder, Colo.: Westview Press.

Calvo, Guillermo, Ratna Sahay, and Carlos Végh. 1995. "Capital Flows in Central and Eastern Europe: Evidence and Policy Options." IMF Working Paper 95/57. Washington D.C.: International Monetary Fund, May.

Calvo, Guillermo, and Carlos Végh. 1994. "Inflation Stabilization and Nominal Anchors." *Contemporary Policy Issues* 12(2): 35–45.

Claessens, Stijn, Michael P. Dooley and Andrew Warner. 1995. "Portfolio Capital Flows: Hot or Cold?" *The World Bank Economic Review* 9(1): 152–74.

Csillik, Péter. 1994. "Az 1994. évi monetáris politika tapasztalatai" [The Experience of Monetary Policy in 1994]. *Bankszemle* 9/10: 9–18.

Cumby, Robert E., and Maurice Obstfeld. 1983. "Capital Mobility and the Scope for Sterilization: Mexico in the 1970s," in Pedro A. Armella, Rudiger Dornbusch and Maurice Obstfeld, eds., *Financial Policies and the World Capital Markets: The Problem of Latin American Countries.* Pp. 245–69. Chicago: University of Chicago Press.

Engle, Robert F., and Clive W.J. Granger. 1987. "Co-Integration and Error-Correction: Representation, Estimation and Testing." *Econometrica* 55(2): 251–76.

Frenkel, Jacob A. 1983. "Comment," in Pedro A. Armella, Rudiger Dornbusch and Maurice Obstfeld, eds., *Financial Policies and the World Capital Market: The Problem of Latin American Countries.* Pp. 269–76. Chicago: University of Chicago Press.

Hallwood, C. Paul, and Ronald MacDonald. 1994. *International Money and Finance*, 2nd ed. Oxford: Blackwell.

Hendry, David F. 1995. *Dynamic Econometrics.* Oxford: Oxford University Press.

Hochreiter, Eduard. 1995a. "Central Banking in Economies in Transition," in Thomas D. Willett, Richard C.K. Burdekin, Richard J. Sweeney and Clas Wihlborg, eds., *Establishing Monetary Stability in Emerging Market Economies.* Pp. 127–44. Boulder, Col.: Westview Press.

————. 1995b. "Necessary Conditions for a Successful Pursuit of a Hard Currency Strategy in an Economy in Transition." Chapter 1 in this volume.

Hrnčíř, Miroslav, and Jan Klacek. 1991. "Stabilization Policies and Currency Convertibility in Czechoslovakia." *European Economy*, special edition no. 2: 17–40.

Kemme, David. 1994. *The Reform of the System of Money, Banking and Credit in Central Europe.* Unpublished manuscript, Wichita State University.

Mosolygó, Zsuzsa. 1994. "Késés a monetáris politikában"[Delays in Monetary Policy], *Bankszemle*, May: 28–34.

National Bank of Hungary. 1995a. *Accounts for the Year 1994.* Budapest.

————. 1995b. "Excerpts from the 1994 Monetary and Credit Policy Guidelines." Budapest.

————. 1995c. Az 1995. *Évi Monetáris Politikai Irányelvek [The Guidelines for Monetary Policy in 1995].* Budapest.

Newey, Whitney, and Kenneth West. 1987. "A Simple Positive-Definite, Heteroscedasticity and Autocorrelation Consistent Covariance Matrix." *Econometrica* 55(3): 703–08.

Obláth, Gabor. 1995. "Exchange Rate Policy and Exchange Rate Regimes: A Comparison of Experiences in Hungary and Some of the Other Economies in Transition." Paper presented at the ACE Conference on the Macroeconomics of Recovery in East-Central Europe, Budapest, June 1995.

Obstfeld, Maurice. 1983. "Exchange Rates, Inflation, and the Sterilization Problem." *European Economic Review* 21(1-2): 161–89.

Rebelo, Sergio, and Carlos A. Végh. 1995. "Real Effects of Exchange Rate Based Stabilizations: An Analysis of Competing Theories," in Stanley Fischer and Oliver Blanchard, eds., *Macroeconomics Annual 1995.* Pp. 125–73. Cambridge, Mass: MIT Press.

Rivera-Batiz, Francisco L., and Luis A. Rivera-Batiz. 1994. *International Finance and Open Economy Macroeconomics*, 2nd ed. New York: MacMillan.

Sachs, Jeffrey. 1993. *Poland's Jump to the Market Economy.* Cambridge, Mass.: MIT Press.

Sándor, Gy. 1994. "Financial Liberalization in Central and Eastern Europe and Its Impact on the Exchange Rate," in John P. Bonin and István P. Székely, eds., *The Development and Reform of Financial Systems in Central and Eastern Europe.* Pp. 161–78. London: Edward Elgar.

Sahay, Ratna, and Carlos A. Végh. 1995. "Inflation and Stabilization in Transition Economies: A Comparison with Market Economies." IMF Working Paper No. 9 5/8. Washington, D.C.: International Monetary Fund, January.

Siklos, Pierre L., and István Ábel. 1995a. "Fiscal and Monetary Policies in the Transition: Searching for the Credit Crunch," in Thomas D. Willett, Richard C.K. Burdekin, Richard J. Sweeney and Clas Wihlborg, eds., *Establishing Monetary Stability in Emerging Market Economies*. Pp. 237–68. Boulder, Colo.: Westview Press.

———. 1997. "Monetary Policy Strategies in Transition: An Evaluation of the Hungarian and Czech Experiences," in Pál Gáspár, ed., *The Macroeconomics of Recovery in East-Central Europe*. Budapest: MTA.

Várhegyi, Éva. 1995. *Bankok Versenyben* [*Banks in Competition*]. Budapest: Pénzügykutató Rt.

PART FOUR

Currency Areas and Currency Boards

12

Exchange Rate Crises: Are Currency Boards the Answer for Emerging Market Economies?

Richard J. Sweeney

Introduction

The main argument for pegging the exchange rate, in my view, is that it may help impose monetary discipline on a country's government and reduce its scope for running monetary policies that result in home-country inflation crises. A currency board is likely the best pegging scheme for imposing discipline. A strong, independent central bank, devoted to the single goal of domestic price-level stability, may do an equally good job under managed floating; some might use the record of the Bundesbank to support this position.

The main argument against pegging is that the pegging country makes real exchange rate changes by deflation or inflation rather than by the simpler, quicker, more uniform and less costly means of a change in the nominal exchange rate.

Exchange rate adjustments can be usefully thought of in terms of Type I and Type II errors. An exchange rate authority may mistakenly change the peg when the better policy is to maintain it, or may maintain the peg when the better policy is to change it. So we should ask, does a currency board do a better job of minimizing the costs of these two types of mistakes than would other pegging mechanisms ? The currency board that restrains a government from bad policies in some cases restrains it from wise policies in other cases. A well-designed currency board, however, is less likely than other pegging regimes to persist in a nominal peg that leaves the real exchange rate significantly above or below its equilibrium value for prolonged periods.

Much discussion of currency boards focuses on how to design boards that make it very difficult for the board, other monetary authorities, or the government to alter the peg so as to enforce monetary discipline, yet also allow parity changes in appropriate circumstances. Historically, the record is not encouraging: until the 1980s and 1990s, no currency board has lasted very long nor has any of their pegged rates. Indeed, some say that "permanently fixed exchange rates" is an oxymoron. The fact that the country maintaining the peg must often take action to protect the peg's value means that there may come a day when the game appears not worth the candle, and the "permanent" peg is changed.

A currency board is one among many mechanisms for running a fixed exchange rate. The most fervent currency board advocates recognize that there are either formal, de jure escape hatchs that allow changes, or informal, de facto ways that allow changes (peg changes are historically accompanied or preceded by changes from a currency board to some other form of exchange rate management, usually a central bank). Most currency board advocates view the establishment of a nominal anchor as the board's main contribution. The rules that govern a currency board impose monetary and, perhaps to a lesser, indirect extent, fiscal discipline, and keep the country from inflating as much as it otherwise would. To the extent the currency board succeeds, it spares the country the costs of high and erratic inflation.[1] Further, establishing a (strong) currency board may help lend credibility to the government's commitment to fight inflation; a credible commitment to an anti-inflation policy reduces inflation more quickly, and at lower cost, than a commitment that proves itself only gradually and incurs the cost of output losses and excess unemployment. In addition, many currency board advocates envision the board as operating in the context of free-market international trade and no or relatively minor capital controls. By contributing to financial and monetary stability, the board helps the economy reap the benefits of international openness, benefits less available to countries with substantially less discipline. In evaluating the benefits of a currency board relative to other systems of exchange rate management, a board's main attraction is that it is better able to prevent levels of domestic inflation that ultimately require devaluation.

Analysis of the relative net benefits of a currency board versus other systems of exchange rate management depends crucially on how the board is supplemented by a "monetary agency."[2] This agency may provide emergency liquidity, hold international reserves for the country beyond the board's holdings, supervise domestic banks, adjust capital controls, and even run a type of monetary policy by making changes in required reserve ratios or through open-market operations where it buys and sells assets for its own liabilities.[3] However, the more a monetary agency is in a position to help the currency board's peg survive political and market challenges, the more the monetary agency is in a position to help generate the type of inflationary crisis that the currency board is supposed to help avoid.

There is no credible way for a current government to bind all future governments to maintain an exchange rate peg. Good design of a currency board requires explicit discussion of when and according to what criteria it will change its peg, a point not adequately discussed in the literature. Central banks have more discretion than currency boards for acquiring and using international reserves to fend off devaluations that would improve welfare. If pressures on a country's fixed exchange rate occur mainly from speculative bubbles and fads rather than changes in underlying economic fundamentals, a strong central bank is likely better able than a currency board to defend the exchange rate against speculative excesses.[4] Thus, an observer who believes that anti-inflation discipline is important, and that changes in the equilibrium real exchange rate mainly arise from changes in economic fundamentals rather than from bubbles or fads, is likely to find a well-designed currency board attractive relative to other pegging strategies.[5]

Currency Boards

A currency board is a combination of familiar elements. It is an exchange rate system in which the currency is pegged but with exchange rate adjustment mandated or allowed under conditions that are more or less, but never completely, spelled out (see Hanke et al. 1992 for their proposal on the stringent conditions under which an Estonian currency board would be allowed to change the pegged rate). It operates under a cash-stock supply rule; in strict, "orthodox" versions, the board buys and sells the reserve currency on demand at the pegged rate, with marginal changes backed 100 percent with reserves.[6] Under this rule, the strict currency board forgoes control of any of the monetary aggregates and interest rates; this is not the Milton Friedman x-percent rule, but it is a monetary rule.[7] The currency board's charter is a monetary constitution: it tells when and how the currency board may or must act and gives the board specified protections from influence by other governmental actors or by private actors.

A key difference between a currency board and a more usual peg is the cash-stock supply rule. Under Bretton Woods–type pegs, the central bank commits to maintain the peg but can run any type of discretionary or rule-based money stock or interest rate policy it likes. The central bank claims to run policies that will not necessitate either a devaluation or painful deflationary policies, but if it fails in this goal, it can devalue. The monetary discipline of a Bretton Woods–type peg is all prospective: the central bank better run

sound policies now or at some point in the future it will face the devalua-
tion/deflation choice. The currency board faces continuous discipline: it must
adjust the stock of its currency one-to-one to private decisions to buy or sell
its currency for the reserve currency, at least in strict currency board arrangements.[8]

Different types of monetary authorities may supplement a currency board.
On the one hand a monetary agency may regulate banks (and presumably
some other financial institutions) for prudential purposes, or may insure bank
deposits held by the private sector. On the other hand, an monetary agency
may create high-powered money. Some observers suggest establishing a
currency board with no outside monetary agency (Hanke, Jonung and Shuler
1992, Appendix I:54–56), though possibly with a government insurance
scheme for depositors (p. 60–62). The more powers a monetary agency has,
the more scope the government has to evade the monetary discipline that is
the key argument for a currency board. The fewer powers the monetary
agency has, the more likely it is that major shocks to the equilibrium real
exchange rate will cause major damage to the economy, or the collapse of the
currency board system, or a change in the peg.[9]

The key issue in evaluating the attractiveness of a currency board is the
extent to which pressures for exchange rate changes arise from changes in
economic fundamentals that require real exchange rate adjustment for equilibrium rather than from speculative bubbles or fads unrelated to equilibrium.
If pressures for exchange rate changes arise mainly from changes in fundamentals, a well-designed currency board might respond by changing the
nominal rate, though historical and proposed currency boards allow little or
no scope for this. If most pressures for exchange rate changes arise from
bubbles or fads, meaning a nominal rate change would be disequilibrating
relative to fundamentals, a central bank may be better prepared to defend the
nominal rate at lower costs than is a currency board. Speculative outflows
lead to one-to-one falls in the cash stock under a currency board, but a central
bank has the option of sterilizing these flows. To the extent that a cash-stock
fall under a currency board is not associated with an offsetting rise in cash's
velocity, there is downward pressure on domestic prices, perhaps with a real
contraction and a rise in unemployment.

A government may be able to escape some of the discipline of a currency
board. In ordinary times, a government can try to chisel on discipline by
getting the currency board or the monetary agency to help finance the fiscal
deficit or to stimulate aggregate demand through monetary expansion. Legal
restraints on the government's ability to chisel reduce its ability to carry out
actions that at least some observers find beneficial. For example, a monetary
agency, separate from the currency board, might issue liabilities that banks
have to hold as reserves, with the monetary agency also acting as a lender of
last resort. Reasonable people may disagree on whether a lender of last resort

is desirable; the point is that the more scope an monetary agency has for doing good on this margin, the more it has for doing harm on the discipline margin.

In extraordinary times, a government can abolish the currency board or alter the board's behavior, as part of government's general ability to alter the rules of the game. For example, at the start of World War II Britain froze the reserves that its colonies and Commonwealth countries had on deposit in London. Often statutory restrictions on government monetary and financial policies can be ignored or quickly revised; statutory limits on the size of the U.S. federal debt are frequently increased. Constitutional restrictions that cannot be quickly overturned can often be ignored. For example, amending the U.S. constitution can take a substantial amount of time, but in crises parts of the constitution can and have been ignored or reinterpreted. During the U.S. Civil War, the federal government suspended habeas corpus, a clearly unconstitutional step; the U.S. government interned Japanese citizens and American citizens of Japanese descent during World War II, an act likely to be ruled unconstitutional today.[10] Britain's unwritten constitution provides stringent restraints on government actions in some cases, though not for monetary policy; the Soviet Union's elaborate constitutional safeguards had virtually no effect on governmental lawlessness. The empirical evidence is mixed on the relation of statutory or constitutional guarantees of central bank independence relative to how independent the central bank is in practice. Burdekin and Willett (1995) argue that there is a reasonable correlation for industrialized countries, but not for developing countries.

Constitutionally mandated inflexibility can contribute to instability. For example, a blow to the payments system, say the collapse of one big bank in a system with only six banks, might be more likely to cause the system's collapse if it is known that the government will obey a constitutional mandate not to intervene.[11] In other circumstances, doubt about the government's commitment to constitutional or statutory mandates may cause a crisis; for example, if currency holders doubt the government's commitment to the peg, they may dump holdings of the local currency and also assets denominated in it.

There is no way to make a peg truly permanent.[12] Some might argue that a peg with no escape hatch is unwise and, in the end, not credible. Economic actors will recognize that promises of no peg change ever, no matter how solemn the promise or how strong the created institutional structure to enforce the promise, can and will be overridden in extremes and perhaps in cases that are not extreme. A currency board that is uncompromising in not ratifying any domestic inflationary pressures gains credibility each time it is tested by these pressures. A currency board that completely resists peg changes in response to changes in the underlying equilibrium real exchange rate gains a reputation for imposing substantial pain, creates domestic political opponents, and increases the likelihood of its being replaced with an exchange authority that is less able to refuse economically sensible peg changes; but is also very likely to be less able to resist politically motivated expansionary policies.

Why Countries Change Their Pegs

Countries which adopt a crawling peg accept exchange rate changes as an integral part of the regime. Others adopt a permanent peg, with some countries going to great lengths to maintain its parity, especially if adjustment of the peg is seen as undercutting the credibility of a package of price stability measures. For example, fear of a loss of anti-inflation credibility is one reason that France resisted revisions of European Monetary System (EMS) parities in the speculative crises of September 1992 and July through August 1993; the move to wide bands for the EMS on August 1, 1993, caused considerable loss of face for French politicians and monetary authorities.

A country changes its peg when political decision makers' expected costs of maintaining the peg exceed their expected benefits. The costs are of two types. First, a central bank that unsuccessfully resists a peg change suffers greater reserve losses[13] than if it had altered the peg sooner, and similarly suffers greater loss of face. The threat of reserve loss may make the bank change the peg sooner rather than later, or may induce the bank to hold out longer to try to avoid recognizing massive losses.[14] Second, the contractionary policies that central banks use to fight devaluation, particularly high interest rates, can disrupt financial markets and, if the fight is protracted, inflict substantial losses on the country in terms of real output losses. Where investors expect immanent devaluation, the costs are exacerbated by "speculative attacks" which force the bank to raise interest rates ever higher to maintain the peg. Developed countries with good reputations can in principle resist devaluation indefinitely; over a large range where there is no question of debt repudiation, they can borrow reserve currencies from lenders that offer a highly elastic supply. In this case, the government devalues not because it runs out of (gross or net) reserves, but because it views the fight as too costly on balance.

If there is a shock that requires a devaluation of the real exchange rate, the central bank can in principle ignore it, letting deflationary pressures reduce domestic wages and prices over whatever time is required. However, even with great flexibility in the economy, the time required to achieve the required devaluation can be substantial and the output and employment losses large. As Hochreiter and Winckler (1995) note, the degree of price/wage flexibility is endogenous. To the extent that adherence to a cash-stock supply rule makes a currency board's reliance on price and wage changes to adjust the real exchange rate more credible, the greater will be such flexibility under a currency board than under a central bank.[15]

Currency board advocates sometimes argue that a currency board reduces the likelihood of exchange rate crises relative to a peg, and on balance this is correct because of the currency board's focus on a single goal, the cash-stock supply rule, rather than multiple goals, as a central bank is likely to be given, either explicitly or implicitly. Sometimes the tone of the arguments in favor of a currency board suggests the board will not face exchange rate crises at all, or that the crises will be minor, of low cost and short lived. This is not so: the extent and severity of exchange rate crises depend at least in part on the credibility both of the currency board in adhering to a strict cash-stock supply rule and of politicians to the maintenance of the currency board, and neither is perfect nor can be.

A currency board can face pressures for a peg change, though its cost-benefit calculus will be different from a central bank's. Holders of assets denominated in the board's currency know that there is always a chance that the board will change the peg, with the probabilities varying with the size of the shock, the power of the currency board relative to the monetary agency and the government, the commitment of the board's decision makers to maintaining the parity, the willingness of politicians to press for a change, the severity of constitutional provisions against change, and the effectiveness of the prohibitions, etc.

In exchange rate crises, a currency board faces a huge discontinuity: holders of its currency might turn in (most or) all of it for the reserve currency; the economy then uses the reserve currency for transactions as the domestic currency falls into disuse. For a particular currency board, there is likely some stage in the demonetization of its currency at which it would prefer to devalue rather than let the domestic currency collapse. Currency holders know that demonetization, and devaluations to forestall this, are possibilities. For any individual, a run that leads to devaluation gives a profit, provided the devaluation is large and quick enough to offset the foregone domestic interest and the transactions costs of switching assets. If the run produces demonetization of the domestic currency, the individual who switches to the reserve currency is clearly better off than if he had continued to hold the domestic currency, though likely worse off than if the board had initially met the shock with a devaluation. If the run fails, the individual suffers the opportunity cost of holding the reserve currency rather than the more liquid domestic currency, the one-way option under pegged rates.

Commercial banks are another source of pressure on the currency board to devalue in the face of real exchange rate shocks. Commercial banks typically promise instant repurchase of their demand deposits with domestic currency. The depositor who believes the board is close to devaluation or collapse will want to convert (some or all) of his domestic deposits denominated in local currency to deposits denominated in the reserve currency or to cash holdings of the reserve currency. Further, a substantial portion of the holdings denominated in reserve currency will be held abroad because of the likelihood that the exchange rate crisis will precipitate a banking system crisis. Because the domestic banks do not have 100 percent reserve backing of deposits, in a true crisis they will be unable to fulfill their instant repurchase guarantee. The financial system might fall apart or might stagger on with deposits denominated in the domestic currency selling at a discount relative to domestic currency—a split-rate situation that is, in effect, a devaluation. The potential for financial disarray puts pressure on a currency board to devalue to achieve a new equilibrium exchange rate.

Exchange Rate Crises

Exchange rate adjustments often result from crises. The monetary agency's powers and scope are important determinates of the currency board's ability to weather crises.

Consider five types of crises (the taxonomy is incomplete) and how a currency board system handles them. First, a government's policies can create an economic crisis, particularly if it is running excessively expansionary policies that generate inflationary pressures in excess of those in the reserve currency country. The principle argument in favor of a currency board—discipline—is precisely that a currency board helps prevent this situation from arising. A powerful, active monetary agency can, however, undercut the board's discipline; to prevent self-inflicted inflationary crises, a nonexistent or weak monetary agency (one limited to, say, prudential regulation) is desirable. Even if there is no monetary agency, a government can create an inflation/debt crisis by excessive spending financed by domestic and international borrowing. *Mutatis mutandis*, the same considerations apply to a central bank that has the same degree of strictness as the currency board.

Second, world securities markets might crash as, for example, in October 1987 or in the October 1989 mini-crash. Many countries' central banks expanded their stocks of high-powered money to provide liquidity to markets as investors fled from equities and corporate bonds and to high-quality assets such as U.S. T-bills and T-bonds. A currency board is ill-equipped to handle this type of crisis. At a time when it need to increase liquidity by expanding the domestic supply of money, a currency board is likely to have domestic currency presented for conversion to the reserve currency, as international investors who fled to U.S. government securities did in the 1987 and 1989 crises. This flight reduces the stock of domestic currency as well as that part of the country's international reserves that the currency board holds. In turn, domestic banks are less willing to provide liquid assets, and depositors are more interested in holding the reserve currency directly (or liabilities of the reserve-currency country).[16]

A domestic monetary agency parallel to the currency board might expand liquidity, as measured by the domestic money stock, through open market operations. There may well be a flight from domestic assets to reserve-currency assets. The monetary agency can preserve the exchange rate by selling reserve currency obtained from selling its own liquid holdings denominated in the reserve currency or by borrowing reserve-currency assets, either commercially from foreign banks or from the reserve-currency central bank. A small country with only a brief track record and low international holdings will likely find it difficult to preserve the exchange rate parity; a monetary agency that has the holdings and power to preserve the parity is likely also to have the power to undercut currency board discipline over monetary and fiscal policy.

Disturbances to Equilibrium Real Exchange Rates

Third, the currency to which the board pegs may come under pressure from output market disturbances in the reserve-currency country. An example is the pressure on the European Exchange Rate Mechanism (ERM) after German reunification to either revalue the German mark or devalue the other ERM currencies relative to the German mark.

My interpretation of the September 1992 and July–August 1993 crises in the European Monetary System is that they arose in substantial part from the reunification of Germany.[17] German aggregate demand rose substantially more than German aggregate supply. This increase caused upward pressure on German interest rates (with some observers arguing that the increase in interest rates was exacerbated by German reluctance to use taxes rather than bond issuance to finance the increased spending[18]); in addition, the Bundesbank put upward pressure on interest rates to combat the increased inflation arising from reunification. With narrow exchange rate bands, interest rates in ERM countries had to rise along with German rates. This rise in interest rates led, ceteris paribus, to a fall in aggregate demand in these countries. In one line of analysis, the rise in interest rates reduced the market value of assets in place relative to their replacement costs and so, ceteris paribus, reduced expenditures on new plant and equipment. In net present value terms, the rise in interest rates increased the discount rate and reduced projects' net present value. These countries' prices had to fall to raise aggregate demand to its previous level; in net present value terms, the cost of the investment had to fall to make net present value positive. One way to accomplish this price-cost change was revaluation of the German mark or devaluations of the other ERM currencies. Many of these countries, particularly

France, opposed any parity changes.[19] The only remaining route for changing real exchange rates within ERM was for the group's non-German members to run inflation rates lower than Germany's for however long it took to reduce the real exchange rate to a new equilibrium level. Before the July 1993 crisis, commentators pointed out that France's inflation was lower than Germany's and sometimes argued that pressure on the franc was thus misguided. These views missed the point: there would be pressure on the franc until France had inflation rates lower than Germany's for a sufficient period to reduce the French real exchange rate to the appropriate new equilibrium level.

A country pegged to the German mark through a currency board would face the same kind of deflationary/recessionary pressure that the U.K. faced before it allowed the pound to depreciate in September 1992, or France faced before the ERM abandoned its narrow bands in August 1993. France was able to hold out against realignment in part because its central bank was free to do many things closed to an orthodox currency board. For example, the Banque de France borrowed German marks that it then used to intervene to keep the franc within its narrow parity band. Recent evidence supports the view that sterilized intervention affects nominal exchange rates;[20] thus, the Banque de France's strategy can be interpreted as at least partially sterilized intervention that kept the French money stock from falling as it would have under unsterilized intervention.[21] The result of this strategy was a smaller fall in aggregate demand for French output, less unemployment, and more gradual adjustment. A currency board would be unable to sterilize the effect of capital outflows on the domestic money stock. Rather it would have to rely on monetary contraction and hence recessionary pressure on output to reduce domestic prices and wages to accomplish a change in the real exchange rate.[22] A currency board that successfully maintained its peg would thus lead to a quicker adjustment of prices than a central bank that pursued the more gradualist policies used by the Banque de France;[23] a currency board unsuccessful in maintaining its peg would have to adjust the peg sooner than the Banque de France did. My view is that France was misguided to stick to its parity.[24] Someone thinking France was correct is, at least marginally, nudged to favor an monetary agency with substantial powers.

Fourth, a large real shock to the currency-board country can destroy the parity. As an example, consider Estonia and suppose that Russia makes threats, moves forces to the border, and perhaps occupies several border posts (the example could be in terms of Lithuania and its currency board). Estonia's German mark peg likely could not survive in free markets. Many crises last a few days and are then resolved one way or another: in this example, Russia might occupy Estonia; Estonia might defuse the crisis with political concessions, for example, regarding rights of ethnic Russians in Estonia;

U.N. Security Council actions might cause Russia to back down; Russia might declare that the whole situation was a misunderstanding and withdraw. A quick resolution that leaves Estonia free and its economy unhampered might allow a quick return to the previous level of the peg. A prolonged though low-level crisis would require a depreciation of Estonia's real exchange rate with Germany. If the pegged rate were maintained, real exchange rate depreciation would require price and wage cuts in Estonia that might be achieved only over a substantial, painful period. A rich and insulated enough monetary agency might be able to maintain the peg through a protracted deflation. But one must ask, why would this be good for the country?

Under the current regime of managed floating, real exchange rates have shown substantial variability. An index of the U.S./German real exchange rate, normalized to average 100, varied from a low of 60 to a high of over 130 during the 1980s.[25] As is well known, much of the change in the real exchange rate can be attributed, in at least in an accounting sense, to variations in the nominal exchange rate. It is not, of course, clear how much of this real exchange rate variability was excessive relative to equilibrium real rates (perhaps arising from excessive nominal exchange rate variability) and how much arose from shifts in equilibrium real rates. But suppose that as much as half of variations arose from equilibrating changes in real rates. Then the equilibrium U.S./German real exchange rate fluctuated by perhaps 40 percent (from say 80 to 115). In the absence of nominal exchange rate changes, the absolute value of the sum of the percentage changes in U.S. and German prices would have to be approximately 40 percent, a huge change. Germany's prices and wages appear to be substantially less flexible than the U.S.'s, and the U.S.'s appear to be less flexible now than before the First World War and in the interwar period. It is useful to recall that even during the Great Depression, it took about three years— from the Depression's start in late 1929 to its nadir in early 1933—for U.S. prices and wages to fall by approximately one-third.

Establishing a rigorous currency board that pegs to the German mark then makes most sense if (1) most of the variations in the U.S./German real exchange rate in the 1980s were due to excessive nominal exchange rate volatility (that could be cured by pegging the rate);[26] (2) the pegging country has substantially less variability of its equilibrium real exchange rate relative to Germany than does the U.S.; and (3) the pegging country has substantial price and wage flexibility.

Judging real exchange rate volatility by looking at cases with the U.S. as the base country can easily overstate the problems faced by an emerging market economy considering a currency board that pegs to the German mark. It is conventional to view the United States and the European Union as competing blocks with large changes in the equilibrium real exchange rate between the blocks as compared to changes in equilibrium real rates within Europe. There is much to this view. For example, compare the percentage changes in Belgium's real exchange rate relative to the U.S. dollar and its real rate relative to the German mark. Over the two decades 1973 through 1993, the standard deviation relative to the U.S. dollar is 3.53 percent per month, relative to the German mark 0.87 percent per month (Jorion and Sweeney 1996).

The disequilibrium in real exchange rates may still be large even among the European Union's members. As one indication, the day the U.K. left the ERM in September 1992, the pound fell approximately 10 percent relative to the German mark and the other ERM currencies that remained (in effect) pegged to German mark—a 10 percent real depreciation of the pound. Over the next several months, France complained that this gave the U.K. an unfair competitive trade advantage.

Bubbles and Fads

Fifth, speculative bubbles or fads might put pressure on the exchange rate. As opposed to managed floating, pegged rate systems may have an advantage in fighting exchange rate bubbles and fads[27] by not letting them get started—it may be that speculators have to see the bubble/fad in action for the bubble to become self-feeding.[28]

A currency board fights fads and bubbles in exchange rates by not letting its exchange rate change as speculation drains domestic currency from system—this is unsterilized intervention. A central bank pegged-rate system can use owned or borrowed reserves to sterilize intervention. For a given amount of speculative capital flight, a central bank causes less pain for the domestic economy than does a currency board. Given the output-employment pain a country is willing to endure to break a bubble, a central bank system is lower cost and more effective than a currency board. It is a question whether the pain that speculators see the currency board endure causes flight to be smaller than under a central bank system; a tough currency board may be able to break a run that a central bank cannot break if the central bank cannot endure the pain that a currency board can. Price-wage flexibility can reduce the real output-employment costs a currency board has to endure (though these are not the only costs involved; instability in financial markets can have substantial costs).

Adopting a currency board might endogenously increase the pain that a country is willing to endure, because of the higher costs of changing arrangements, and thus a currency board might be better able to resist peg changes than a central bank. In this case, adoption of the currency board is a forecast of the country's increased willingness to face a crunch, perhaps without the government fully understanding this implication of adopting a currency board. Alternatively, adoption of a currency board might be a signal that the country understands and is willing to endure pain; in this case, the causation runs from willingness to the currency board as a signal. Thus, adoption of a currency board system raises the issue of causation versus correlation; a country less willing to bear pain than are countries with successful currency boards will find its currency board less credible and less successful.

If bubbles/fads are important, frequent or dominant problems, a central bank seems to be the better pegging system. But this view ignores the possibility that fads and bubbles are partly endogenous and will be less likely to arise under a currency board than a central bank system: a country with a history of poor central bank performance may find fewer and less severe fads and bubbles by going to a currency board.

Alternatively, output market shocks requiring real exchange rate adjustments may be important, frequent or dominant problems. By the same reasoning, a central bank that can and does refrain from changing the nominal exchange rate to adjust the real rate causes extra pain for the economy. A conventional currency board is designed to hold out even longer and thus causes more pain, though this view ignores the fact that wages and prices may become more flexible when an economy has a currency board. A currency board that is designed to or that will tacitly give up and adjust the rate may be less costly than a conventional currency board or even than a central bank.

The problem is how to accommodate real exchange rate changes. If most pressure for exchange rate changes comes from changes in the equilibrium real rate, nearly automatic nominal rate changes would be beneficial. This could occur under a currency board designed for this purpose, and indeed costs may be lower in this case than under a central bank.

Suppose a country has a serious discipline problem but pressures for real rate changes tend strongly to be equilibrating. In this case, it would be desirable for the currency board to strongly resist government pressure, but to give in relatively easily to exchange-market pressure. If the government has few discipline problems, and applies little pressure for monetary ratification, if there are few and small changes in equilibrium real exchange rates, and if there are major problems of bubbles or fads, then an independent central bank devoted to pegging the exchange rate may well work better than a currency board supplemented only by a weak monetary agency.

Frequently, observers believe they see circumstances that make the choice between a currency board and a central bank hard. When discipline is a major problem, and bubbles and fads are important and/or frequent, it is desirable to have the strength of a currency board to resist government pressure, and the strength of a powerful central bank to resist speculative pressure.

The Example of Estonia[29]

A country with a currency board can face major changes in its trade-weighted real exchange rate. Take the case of Estonia as an example. A report in late 1991 urged that Estonia establish a currency board based on the Swedish krona. In a book that grew from the report, Hanke, Jonung and Shuler (1992) argue the advantages of pegging to the krona:

> The purpose of the currency board system is... to promote more credibility than a domestic central bank could achieve .... [T]he krona itself is linked to the currencies of the European Monetary System, of which the most important is the German mark. Sweden is in fact eager to become a full member of the European Monetary System .... After the "irrevocable" fixing of exchange rates among members of the European Monetary System that is scheduled to occur late in this decade, the Swedish central bank will become a type of currency board, as will the German central bank.

At the time of the report, the krona was pegged to a basket of trade-weighted currencies (weights based on the previous year's trade, except for the U.S. dollar which had twice its weight). In 1992, Sweden switched to a peg based on a basket of EMS currencies only, weighted according to their weights in the ECU. This re-weighting caused an effective devaluation of the krona (and many observers thought the devaluation was at least one of the attractions of shifting to the ECU basket when Sweden did); any currency pegged to the krona would have been devalued also. In the speculative crisis of September 1992, the Riksbank staved off a run against the krona and held its peg to the EMS currencies. But the depreciation-devaluation of some EMS currencies (the U.K. floated, Italy and Spain devalued) meant that the Swedish real exchange rate rose against the European Union as a whole, and particularly against the U.K.; this revaluation was at a time when Sweden was already in a severe recession. In November 1992, the Riksbank quietly surrendered and devalued the krona. Had the Estonian kroon been pegged to the krona, it would have had to follow all of these ups and downs in Swedish policies and performance.

Instead, the Estonians pegged to the German mark in June 1992, at a rate of eight German mark to the kroon. The kroon was then subject to pressures on the German mark. In 1992 and 1993 these included the currency crisis of September 1992, where the kroon appreciated relative to the average EU exchange rate, and the July–August 1993 crisis, where the ERM's narrow bands were abandoned (save for the special relationship of the guilder to the German mark); and the kroon once again appreciated against the average EU exchange rate. Hanke, Jonung and Shuler's optimism regarding the irrevocable pegging of European rates is now subject to much more doubt than it was before September 1992.

Sweden and Finland are likely to be Estonia's major trading partners and its major sources of inward foreign direct investment (figures from mid 1993 showed each representing more than 30 percent of Estonia's inward foreign direct investment). These factors make a case for Estonia to peg to the Swedish krona or Finnish markka (or, perhaps, to a weighted average of the two). Experience since 1992 shows that pegging to either would have led to trouble. Both Sweden and Finland faced serious economic trouble; their inflexible economies were forced to make major transitions. Even if one of these countries ran an exchange rate policy that was ex post optimal (by whatever standard the observer chooses), it is not clear that Estonia would have been wise to accept all the costs of another economy's restructuring.

Estonia instead bought other troubles. It appreciated relative to the other EU currencies along with the German mark. The initial German mark-kroon rate was set to undervalue the kroon to allow for catch-up inflation in the prices of nontraded goods, but not to compensate for the September 1992 and July–August 1993 crises.

It may be that Estonia can weather this possible overvaluation caused by pegging to the German mark relatively easily: Estonia's economic policy-makers are aware that the Estonian economy faces conditions that require substantial flexibility. To counter overvaluation of the real exchange rate, Estonian prices must be lower than otherwise. Accomplishing this may well be easier than in Sweden, Finland, Germany or indeed most of Western Europe. Nevertheless, the ease with which Britain changed its nominal and hence real exchange rate by 10 percent in one day makes it look needlessly costly to reduce the real exchange rate through relative deflation (though the fact that trade is a larger share of GDP in Estonia than in the U.K. may mean Estonia would reap fewer benefits from a devaluation than did the U.K.). Further, the costs of relative deflation look particularly bad when the deflation is relative to Germany, a country with generally low inflation.

Conclusions

A currency board has the main advantage of imposing anti-inflation discipline. It generally does a better job of imposing this discipline than a central bank under pegging, because the board follows a strict currency-stock supply rule: it buys and sells the reserve currency in unlimited amounts for its own currency. No currency board can credibly pledge it will exist forever. No currency board can credibly pledge that it (or a successor institution) will never change its peg; instead, every currency board has implicit or explicit conditions under which it will or can change the peg. Governments can supplement the currency board by a monetary agency that can strengthen the board's ability to resist pressure for a parity change by its sales and purchases of international reserves, but only at the cost of making it easier for the government to avoid the board's anti-inflation discipline. On discipline grounds, an orthodox currency board supplemented by only a weak monetary agency is desirable. On grounds of resisting disequilibrating exchange rate pressures, a strong monetary agency is desirable. If the observer believes that a substantial share of pressures for exchange rate changes arise from exchange market bubbles or fads rather than from changes in fundamentals that imply a changed equilibrium exchange rate, the case for a strong monetary agency is strengthened: the strong monetary agency is able to resist changes in the nominal exchange rate that would cause disequilibrating changes in the real rate. If the observer believes that the pressures arise mainly from shifts in equilibrium real rates and the economy adjusts prices, wages and resource allocation only sluggishly, the case for a weak monetary agency is strengthened; the monetary agency and the board will then have relatively little power to avoid nominal exchange rate changes that serve to re-equilibrate the real exchange rate.

Notes

For helpful comments, thanks are due to Eduard Hochreiter, Clas G. Wihlborg and Thomas D. Willett, to participants in an International Monetary Fund Discussion Center presentation, a Western Economics Association session, and the Georgetown Business School Workshop on Emerging Market Economies. Summer research support from Georgetown University and the Georgetown School of Business and partial summer research assistance from the Georgetown Center on Business-Government Relations are gratefully acknowledged. Part of this paper was written at the Göteburg School of Economics, Sweden.

1. High inflation is often associated with variable inflation and also fluctuations in real growth rates. See, for example, Logue and Willett (1976), Logue and Sweeney (1981) and Burdekin et al. (1995).

2. This conceptual distinction between a currency board and a parallel monetary authority is owed to Osband and Villanueva (1992).

3. The Lithuanian currency board described in this volume has done all of these. Although this board cannot by law buy or sell government securities, it carries out open-market operations in its own liabilities.

4. Observers note that a credible currency board is likely to discourage such exchange rate pressures from arising by reducing the likelihood of exchange rate realignment. The same deterrent effect also arises from a central bank that is credibly and single-mindedly devoted to price level stability. Other observers argue that speculative pressures are less likely to arise under fixed exchange rates; this view is more problematical. Surely the timings of speculative pressures are different for fixed and flexible rates. Under flexible rates, the exchange rate is likely to move each day, and the exchange rate authority—in practice the central bank in most countries—may have to intervene quite frequently; between 1986 and 1990 the Swedish

central bank intervened on approximately 60 percent of days. Under a fixed-rate system, there are often long patches with little speculative activity, but punctuated with crises. These crises are more frequent and perhaps involve more speculation per crisis if the exchange rate authority, currency board, or central bank is recognized to have overly expansionary policies or to be unable to restrain other governmental actors from such policies; but this gets back to the merits of a strong currency board versus a strong central bank devoted to price-level stability.

5. Countries that meet criteria for a fixed-rate regime in the optimum currency area literature are the best candidates for a currency board. Among the conditions that make a country a better candidate for fixed rates, the literature cites being small and open, having a large share of its trade with the country to which it pegs, and having symmetric shocks with the other country.

6. As Osband and Villanueva (1992) and Schwartz (1993) point out, some currency boards have reserves in excess of the value of their outstanding cash; further, a board may have variations on the 100 percent marginal backing principle. The observer must decide how far a board may be from the orthodox model before the arrangement does not merit the name of currency board. Alternatively, any actual currency board can be viewed as a pure currency board supplemented by a monetary authority, as discussed below.

Some observers distinguish between an orthodox currency board that pegs "once-and-for-all" to a given currency and less orthodox currency boards that, for example, may allow for a crawling peg (Osband and Villanueva 1992). For further discussion of currency boards, see Eichengreen (1993, 1994), papers in Liviatan (1993), and Williamson (1995).

7. In a blurb on the cover of Hanke, Jonung and Shuler (1992), Friedman says, "A currency board such as that proposed ... is an excellent system for a country in Estonia's position."

8. Some less strict currency boards can be thought of as running policies analogous to the gold standard, where international reserves served as an overall, long-term constraint on the amount of money issue but in the short and intermediate runs there was a good deal of room for sterilization.

9. Historically, currency boards have had no or only very limited formal, de jure powers to change the peg. Of course, the currency board can be abolished, the establishing statute or constitutional provision can be changed, or the government can force a peg change without regard for legalities. As noted above, in this case the institutional form of the exchange rate authority is likely to change to some kind of central bank. Nothing prevents the government from continuing to call the exchange rate authority a currency board. In the case under discussion, the nominal peg change in response to a shock to the real exchange rate may enhance the credibility of an ongoing currency board; if a currency board changes the peg in response to home-made inflationary pressures, the currency board surely loses much of the credibility it has left after the domestic inflation pressures have occurred.

10. Congress passed an act in the 1980s to apologize to those interned and to pay them modest compensation over time.

11. Sweden has six large commercial banks (and several large savings banks). When a number of these banks were in danger of going under, starting in 1992, the

government bailed them out. There was no constitutional mandate for doing so, and a number of observers argued against these bailouts.

Though Swedish government intervention may have reduced short-term instability, or its probability, the intervention might have been unnecessary and might in the longer run be counterproductive by leading to less dependence on market forces than otherwise.

Canada has six large banks. Pattison (1992) argues that there is negligible danger to the Canadian payments system because these banks have the flexibility to act quickly to preserve the system.

12. Of course different pegging regimes and countries have different, often very different, expectations for how long the peg will endure.

13. If the country rebuilds its reserves to the pre-crisis level, then a rough measure of the central bank's losses is the amount of reserves it must reacquire times the new, higher exchange rate (in home country terms) less the previous rate. Central banks are loathe to report losses on their exchange market intervention (Sweeney 1996; Sjöö and Sweeney 1996a, 1996b).

14. Corporations adopt various strategies to avoid having to announce poor earnings (Baber et al. 1991).

15. Increases in the extent to which a central bank focuses on maintaining a peg or to which a currency board follows a strict one-to-one cash-stock supply rule may reduce the real economy's flexibility. Political pressure groups may succeed in making it more difficult for firms to reduce current employment and in increasing government programs to reduce unemployment. Predictions that a currency board will induce greater real-sector flexibility are implicitly based on the view that domestic actors take the existence of the currency board as exogenous, but it is not. For economic actors the relative net benefits of adopting greater flexibility versus taking action to revise the terms of the exchange rate authority will differ across countries. The correct view is that a currency board will stimulate flexibility in some cases, inflexibility and political pressures in others, with the difference depending in part on the country's political and economic institutional structure.

16. A country that joins a currency union with the reserve currency country, instead of creating a currency board that pegs to the same currency, relies on the reserve currency country to inject liquidity; presumably the reserve currency country has appropriate incentives to stabilize the unified economy. Under a currency board the problem is a differential change in demand for liquidity between holders of assets denominated in the reserve currency versus assets denominated in the board's currency.

17. See Sweeney (1994) for an elaboration of this view.

18. That is, some observers argue that bond/deficit financing of the increased spending was more inflationary than if taxation were used.

19. I am grateful to Eduard Hochreiter for discussion on this point.

20. See Dominguez and Frankel (1993a, 1993b), Sweeney (1996), and Sjöö and Sweeney (1996a, 1996b).

21. Alternatively, French interest rates rose less than otherwise.

22. Estonia was in a fortunate position with its new currency board (which went into effect in June 1992). Estonian authorities explicitly recognized that nontradables

prices would rise to catch up with tradables prices that were now pegged to German tradables prices. Deflationary pressures from the peg to the German mark could be met in substantial part simply by lower inflation in nontradables prices, not cuts in these prices and associated wages.

23. As footnote 15 above discusses, existence of a strict currency board may induce political pressures that change institutions in ways that reduce flexibility of prices, wages and resource allocation.

24. Some observers agree that fundamentals required a real exchange rate change but argue that French opposition to ERM realignment was sensible in that French policymakers were trying to preserve hard-won credibility gains. In terms of Types I and II errors, this can be thought of as sticking to a peg when it would be better to change it, or making a Type II error; the government establishes credibility about not making Type I errors by holding to the peg when the probability looks high that it is making a Type II error. It might be better to establish a credible record of resisting peg changes when the probability of a Type I error looks high, but altering the peg when the probability of a Type II error looks high. A major problem is that a government might talk itself into assessments of probabilities of Types I and II errors that differ substantially from market assessments.

25. As discussed below, calculating the real exchange rate relative to the U.S. dollar can result in substantially larger volatility than calculating the real rate relative to some other major currency.

26. If pegging the rate led only to the same real-rate fluctuations as under floating, but through price-level changes, pegging would not help very much. Of course, prices and wages are not flexible enough in any economy for observed real exchange rates to fluctuate to the same extent under a peg as under floating. Under a pegged rate regime, exchange rate pressures are manifested in higher unemployment and lower output. If pegging requires capital controls and other distorting or discriminatory policies, such as were used under the Bretton Woods system, the stability gained in the real rate might be more than offset by the costs on these other policies.

27. The analysis here makes no important distinction between bubbles and fads. The currency board that restrains a government from bad policies in some cases restrains it from wise policies in other cases. A well-designed currency board, however, is less likely than other pegging regimes to persist in a nominal peg that leaves the real exchange rate importantly different from equilibrium values. As price rises, investors might believe there will be further price rises, setting off a bubble. Thus, an episode thought of as a fad might be a bubble with a particular start, whereas bubbles in general might arise from a variety of causes.

28. The same sort of mechanism may allow a central bank to pursue excessively expansionary policy for a time. Speculative runs that force equilibrating change in the exchange rate may rely on one speculator seeing others making a run. A central bank may not face a run until many investors have some confidence that an important fraction of other investors believe a run would succeed.

29. After drafts of this section were written, I came across Anna Schwartz's (1993) somewhat similar views. Lanjouw (1996) gives an interesting discussion of the course of the Estonian real exchange rate.

References

Baber, William, Patricia Fairfield and James Haggard. 1991. "The Effect of Concern about Reported Income on Discretionary Spending Decisions: The Case of Research and Development." *Accounting Review* 66(4): 818–29.

Burdekin, Richard C. K., and Thomas D. Willett. 1995. "Designing Central Bank Arrangements to Promote Monetary Stability," in Thomas D. Willett, Richard Burdekin, Richard Sweeney, and Clas Wihlborg, eds., *Establishing Monetary Stability in Emerging Market Economies*. Pp. 115–26. Boulder, Colo.: Westview Press.

Burdekin, Richard C. K., Syuono Salamon, and Thomas D. Willett. 1995. "The High Cost of Monetary Instability," in Thomas D. Willett, Richard Burdekin, Richard Sweeney, and Clas Wihlborg, eds., *Establishing Monetary Stability in Emerging Market Economies*. Pp. 13–32. Boulder, Colo.: Westview Press.

Dominguez, Kathryn, and Jeffrey Frankel. 1993a. *Does Foreign Exchange Intervention Work?* Washington, D.C.: Institute for International Economics.

———. 1993b. "Does Foreign Exchange Intervention Matter? The Portfolio Effect." *American Economic Review* 83(5): 1356–69.

Eichengreen, Barry. 1994. *International Monetary Arrangements for the 21st Century*. Washington, D.C.: Brookings Institution.

———. 1993. "European Monetary Unification." *Journal of Economic Literature* 31(3): 1321–57.

Frankel, Jeffrey, and Kathryn Dominguez. 1993. "A Foreign Exchange Intervention: An Empirical Assessment," in Jeffrey Frankel, ed., *On Exchange Rates*. Pp. 327–45. Cambridge: MIT Press.

Hanke, Steve, Lars Jonung, and Kurt Shuler. 1993. *Russian Currency and Finance. A Currency Board Approach to Reform*. London: Routledge.

———.1992. *Monetary Reform for a Free Estonia: A Currency Board Solution*. Stockholm: SNS Forlag.

Hanke, Steve, and Kurt Shuler. 1993. "Currency Boards and Currency Convertibility." *Cato Journal* 12 (3): 687–705.

Hetzel, Robert. 1993. "Currency Boards: Their Past, Present and Possible Future Role. A Comment." *Carnegie-Rochester Conference Series on Public Policy* 39 (December): 189–93.

Hochreiter, Eduard, and George Winckler. 1995. "The Advantages of Tying Austria's Hands: The Success of the Hard Currency Strategy." *European Journal of Political Economy* 11(1): 83–111.

Lanjouw, Ger. 1996. "Fixed Exchange Rates in Transition Economies." University of Groningen Working Paper, Groningen.

Liviatan, Nissan, ed. 1993. *Proceedings of a Conference on Currency Substitution and Currency Boards*. Washington, D.C.: World Bank..

Logue, Dennis E., and Richard J. Sweeney. 1981. "Inflation and Real Growth: Some Empirical Results." *Journal of Money, Credit and Banking* 13(4): 497–501.

Logue, Dennis E., and Thomas D. Willett. 1976. "A Note on the Relation Between the Rate and Predictability of Inflation." *Economica*, May: 151–58.

Meltzer, Allan. 1993. "The Benefits and Costs of Currency Boards." *Cato Journal* 12(3): 707–10.

Osband, Kent, and Delano Villanueva. 1993. "Independent Currency Authorities: An Analytic Primer." *IMF Staff Papers* 40(1): 202–16.

Pattison, John C. 1992. "The ECB: A Bank or a Monetary Policy Rule? Discussion," in Matthew B. Canzoneri, Vittorio Grilli, and Paul Masson, eds., *Establishing a Central Bank: Issues in Europe and Lessons from the U.S.* Cambridge: Cambridge University Press.

Schwartz, Anna. 1993. "Currency Boards: Their Past, Present, and Possible Future Role." *Carnegie-Rochester Conference Series on Public Policy* 39 (December): 147–87.

Sjöö, Boo, and Richard J. Sweeney. 1996a. "Central Bank Intervention Profits: Evidence from Sweden." Working paper, Georgetown School of Business, Washington, D.C.

———. 1996b. "Foreign Exchange Intervention: New Methods and Results on the Profitability of Central Bank Intervention." Working paper, Georgetown School of Business, Washington, D.C.

Sweeney, Richard J. 1996. "Does the Foreign Exchange Market Beat the Fed?" Washington, D.C.: Georgetown School of Business, working paper.

Sweeney, Richard J. 1994. "Ten Days That Shook the EC," in Berhanu Abegaz, Patricia Dillon, David H. Feldman and Paul F. Whiteley, eds., *The Challenge of European Integration: Internal and External Problems of Trade and Money.* Pp. 237–52. Boulder, Colo.: Westview Press.

Williamson, John. 1995. *What Role for Currency Boards?* Washington, D.C.: Institute for International Economics.

13

The Estonian Currency Board

Märten Ross

Introduction

Estonia was the first country to leave the former ruble zone after regaining independence in 1991. Since then, the Estonian exchange rate policy has been to peg the Estonian kroon to the German mark at eight kroon to the mark. Estonia uses a currency board-like arrangement to enhance the credibility of the peg, successfully enough that the peg is perceived as credible in the medium, and even in the long term.

The initial objective of the currency board arrangement was to establish a stable monetary environment quickly. The introduction of external price stability was, and is, viewed as an intermediate target for achieving this general objective. Still, in transitional economies where structural price realignments are occurring, the connection between external and internal stability is so tenuous it will be years before we have enough observations to empirically model the relationship.

Assuming high capital mobility and free movement of funds, a country that adopts a fixed exchange rate virtually gives up the option of pursuing discretionary monetary policy. Thus, by fixing the kroon to a stable currency, Estonia was able to immediately introduce a stable monetary environment.

A currency board has three main features: first, narrow money is fully covered by gold and (in the Estonian case overwhelmingly) by foreign currency reserves; second, the exchange rate is fixed in the long term; and third, the monetary authority commits itself to exchange domestic currency for foreign currency, and vice versa, without any restrictions. Thus, a currency board arrangement could be considered as an instrument for the implementation of a credibly fixed exchange rate with high capital mobility. Under the currency board arrangement the money supply is completely endogenous.

It depends solely on the economic system's ability to generate a trade surplus and to attract net foreign investment. Therefore, there is a built-in self-regulating mechanism in a currency board that determines the money supply via the balance of payments. The credible functioning of a currency board requires an independent monetary authority that is in a position to resist political pressure.

If the monetary authority is a central bank, as in Estonia, the currency board arrangement does not in principle prevent the central bank from fulfilling other traditional central bank functions, e.g. to provide refinancing facilities for the banking sector or even to carry out fiscal lending. The currency board system sets very strict limits on these kinds of activities, however. Every extended credit has to be accompanied by an increase of currency board cover to maintain the foreign reserve backing of a note issue by sufficient reserves in excess of the required minimum cover. Furthermore, a currency board-type arrangement essentially eliminates active money market liquidity management by the central bank.

In the next section I describe the legal framework designed to create a credible pegged exchange rate. In the third section, the role of convertibility is discussed. I then discuss the functioning of the Estonian exchange rate system and its resilience in the fourth section. The concluding comments follow.

Legal Basis of Estonian Monetary Policy

Estonia implemented the arrangements of a currency board simultaneously with the introduction of a national currency. These principles constitute the basis for the entire Estonian monetary system. Simultaneously, a high degree of convertibility of the currency was introduced.

Four fundamental laws form the legal basis for Estonian monetary policy: the Currency Law, the Law of the Republic of Estonia on Security for the Estonian Kroon, the Law on the Central Bank, and the Foreign Currency Law. The first three laws are discussed in this section, while the Foreign Currency Law is interpreted in the next section.

The Currency Law of the Republic of Estonia and the Law of the Republic of Estonia on Security for the Estonian Kroon were passed by the Supreme Council on May 20, 1992. The currency law establishes that (1) the monetary unit of the Republic of Estonia is the Estonian kroon, (2) the Bank of Estonia has the sole right to issue kroons, and (3) the kroon is the sole legal tender in Estonia, and legal persons and individuals located in Estonia have no right to use any other tender in domestic transactions.[1]

The currency board arrangement was implemented by the Law on Security for the Estonian Kroon. It states that (1) the initial issue of the kroon was fully secured by Estonia's gold and convertible foreign exchange reserves, (2) the exchange rate of the kroon will be determined by the Bank of Estonia with respect to the German mark and the Bank of Estonia has no right to devalue the kroon, (3) the Bank of Estonia guarantees unconditional current account convertibility of the kroon, and (4) the Bank of Estonia can change the amount of kroons in circulation only if there is a corresponding change in its gold and foreign exchange reserves.

The exact exchange rate to the mark was set by the Monetary Reform Committee, which was established to carry out the reforms. Its decrees are comparable to a law passed by the Parliament. Thus, a future change in the exchange rate will require parliamentary approval.

The position of the Bank of Estonia in the Estonian monetary system is determined by the Law on the Central Bank, passed by the Parliament on May 18, 1993. According to that law, the main responsibilities of the Bank of Estonia regarding the conduct of monetary policy are as follows. It has to (1) manage currency circulation and maintain the stability of the national currency, and (2) carry out Estonian monetary and banking policy. Moreover, the Bank of Estonia is responsible for carrying out an independent monetary, credit and banking policy, and the Estonian government may not make important economic policy decisions without considering the opinion and advice of the Bank of Estonia.

The description given of the central bank's responsibilities implies that the Bank of Estonia is solely responsible for the implementation and conduct of monetary policy in Estonia. Furthermore, this policy should be conducted with the stability of the national currency as the primary objective. The law does not explicitly refer to both internal and external stability, and it does not repeat the limitations placed on the central bank's activities by the Law on Security described above.

Although the medium- and long-term goal—price stability—is unconditional, situations may arise during the transition when temporary preference has to be given to either price or exchange rate stability. In such a situation the central bank is to give priority to exchange rate stability. Thus, the exchange rate is the intermediate and operational target of monetary policy. In the long run, however, the price stability goal is generally consistent with a fixed exchange rate to the German mark.

The central bank law provides the Bank of Estonia with a high degree of independence. The bank is independent of all governmental agencies, it reports only to the Parliament, and it is subordinated neither to the government nor to any other institution of executive power. The Bank of Estonia is not responsible for the state's financial obligations and vice versa. Moreover, it is prohibited from lending to the government in order to avoid political pressures from the government on the conduct of monetary policy.

The independence of the Estonian central bank is strengthened further by provisions of the law governing the nomination and accountability of the bank's management. The chairman of the board is nominated by the president of the republic, while the chairman nominates the rest of the board. All board members are appointed by the Parliament[2] for a period of five years.[3] The president of the Bank of Estonia is nominated by the chairman of the board and appointed by the president of the republic. The chairman and members of the board, as well as the governor, can be dismissed only if found guilty of a crime by a court of law.

Current and Capital Account Convertibility

A currency board arrangement provides the authorities with a viable opportunity to liberalize capital flows without threatening the stability of the monetary system. Substantial convertibility is also essential for the automatic regulatory mechanism of the currency board to function properly.

From the early days of the monetary reform period a relatively liberal regime for currency convertibility was an important aspect of the monetary system in Estonia. General regulations for currency convertibility were set in the Law on Security for the Estonian Kroon and in the Foreign Currency Law.[4]

The kroon was made fully convertible for current account transactions when it was introduced, and no restrictions on capital account convertibility for non-residents were imposed.

Regulations concerning capital account transactions for Estonian residents, on the other hand, were in effect until the beginning of 1994. These regulations were fairly liberal, however. The only prohibition for individuals (until 1993) was on the opening of foreign exchange accounts and deposits with Estonian commercial banks. Other transactions, such as depositing funds abroad or carrying out any other kind of cross-border transactions, were not subject to any limitations.

Only residential non-banking enterprises were actually restricted in any of their capital account transactions. Initially, these legal limitations included a prohibition on depositing longer term funds abroad. Permission was required to open transaction accounts abroad and to engage in cross-border lending activities. Mandatory repatriation requirements for earnings abroad were imposed. The time limit for repatriation was two months.[5]

These permission procedures were established for information gathering purposes and, in practice, no serious limitations were set on carrying out these transactions. Actual convertibility of the currency was therefore broad.

With increasing public confidence in the national currency, a gradual liberalization of the remaining restrictions took place throughout 1992 and 1993, and the abolition of all restrictions on the convertibility of the Estonian kroon became reality in May 1994, with the nullification of the Foreign Currency Law.

Functioning of the Estonian Monetary System

As noted, a fixed exchange rate regime, and even more so a currency board setup, does not provide nor require much maneuvering room for the monetary authority. Furthermore, Estonian legislation sets very strict limits on the operations of the central bank, although it does not prohibit the Bank of Estonia from carrying out the operations of a "full-fledged" central bank.

The balance sheet of the central bank can be thought of as divided into two parts: that of an issue department and that of a banking department. The former represents the currency board, i.e., the foreign reserves that are necessary to cover the whole monetary base. The latter balance sheet has entries for all other assets. All traditional central banking activities must be performed within the limits of the foreign assets on the balance sheet of the banking department. It has to be emphasized, however, that for the time being there is no such formal structure either on the balance sheet or in the organizational chart of the Bank of Estonia.

The currency board arrangement itself leaves the Bank of Estonia with a very limited set of instruments to pursue a so-called independent monetary policy. The use of a fixed exchange rate as a nominal anchor, and the one-to-one relationship between changes in the domestic currency and changes in reserves, offset in the medium and even in the short term the impact of any steps taken by a policy-independent central bank to influence the money supply. The Bank of Estonia does not participate actively in the interbank money market and it does not initiate daily open-market operations. Naturally, the bank frequently intervenes in the market by buying or selling foreign exchange through its standby facility on the foreign exchange market.

The currency board setup and the fixed exchange rate regime imply that there is no particular need for the Bank of Estonia to operate additional, purely monetary policy instruments. Daily liquidity management of the financial system is solely in the hands of commercial banks. Commercial banks convert their foreign exchange reserves to kroon as the demand conditions in the market require and vice versa. Domestic money market interest rates are determined fully by the market itself. They must follow their counterparts in the German money market to a great extent, as a result of the fixed exchange rate. Thus, the money supply is predominantly demand determined, as it should be under a fixed exchange rate regime. There is no scope for government mismanagement of monetary policy instruments for political reasons.

At the same time, however, a smoothly and efficiently functioning financial system is vital for the currency board system to succeed. Therefore, the central bank has continued to find ways to provide the financial system with instruments and tools that could foster the credibility and efficiency of the mechanism. Still, it is often difficult to separate purely monetary instruments from those aimed at supporting prudent management of banking institutions.[6]

Estonian commercial banks must hold mandatory reserves in non-remunerated accounts with the central bank or partly in cash. Since the beginning of 1993 the level of mandatory reserves has been 10 percent for all deposits and most other liabilities. This requirement's main function is to provide buffer reserves for the settlement system in order to guarantee regular daily payments, i.e, within the time frame when banks' foreign assets cannot be returned to the domestic money market. Required reserve levels have to be met on a monthly average basis, and banks not meeting the average level are charged a penalty interest rate that is well over the ordinary market interest rate level. Moreover, the reduction of reserves below 20 percent of the requirement also incurs a penalty.

The Estonian banking system does not as yet have an operating deposit insurance scheme. Therefore, the maintenance of relatively high liquidity reserves is considered vital to confront the possibility of a panicky reaction by depositors.

Ordinary central bank refinancing facilities are almost nonexistent in the Estonian banking system, because the currency board arrangement imposes strict limits on the lending capacity of the central bank. Its lending capacity is determined by the amount of reserves held in excess of domestic liabilities. Thus, the commercial banks have to solve their liquidity problems in the money market, and there exists virtually no domestic "automatic" discount window from which additional liquidity can flow into the system without commercial banks' initiating foreign exchange buying and selling transactions.

Emergency liquidity for commercial banks from the central bank can be provided only under special agreements and exceptional circumstances. Such agreements were entered into during the banking crisis at the beginning of 1993 in order to allow time for negotiations between banks and the government.

Major emphasis is put on the rapidly developing interbank money market. That segment of the money market is important for the credibility of the currency board arrangement, as a liquid, efficient interbank market is required for the risk premium to be minimized. The interest rates in this most liquid segment of the market are very close to German interest rates. Liberalized mark-kroon operations provide banks with an easy opportunity to use German money markets when there is excess liquidity, and German mark deposits can be used as reserve assets.

However, the domestic interbank money market provides only short-term domestic financing possibilities for the banks and will probably continue to play only an assisting role in banks' general liquidity management. The overwhelming majority of such transactions are overnight lending activities.

The Estonian government has not issued any treasury bills because the budget has been kept in balance and additional financing has been obtained easily from external sources, mainly in the form of direct loans from international organizations. The government issued long-term paper with a 10 percent coupon rate with a maturity of six to ten years at the beginning of 1993 to help resolve the banking crisis mentioned above. The outstanding amount of these instruments is moderate, equaling only 300 million kroon.[7]

Since May 1993, the Bank of Estonia has auctioned very limited amounts of its CDs (Certificates of Deposit) with a maturity of 28 days. The rationale behind this issue was that the lack of a low-risk instrument hampered the development of the money market. In no way are the CDs meant to be used as an active monetary policy instrument.

Conclusions

By 1997, the Estonian currency board arrangement had been in operation for five years without any exchange rate realignments taking place. Many observers in the early 1990s were pessimistic about the future of the arrangements because of the rapid price increases in Estonia. It was thought that the initial undervaluation of the kroon would not be sufficient to maintain competitiveness. The pessimists have been proven wrong, however, and the kroon peg has achieved substantial credibility.[8]

Credibility has been achieved even though the Estonian currency board arrangement is not an orthodox one,[9] where the foreign exchange reserves correspond exactly to the amount of domestic currency and commercial banks cannot hold reserves in a central bank.[10] Under the Estonian arrangement there are ways for the central bank to legally influence the money supply. For example, the central bank is able to conduct open market operations and thereby evade the automatic restrictions of a currency board. The Estonian central bank has not behaved this way, however. Rather, its actions during the banking crisis and notes issues have contributed to the maintenance and enhancement of its credibility.

Notes

1. This law is stronger than a legal tender law that simply establishes that the legal tender cannot be refused for payment. As stated, the law establishes that transactions in other currencies do not have legal protection.

2. The president is automatically a member of the board from the moment of his or her appointment. The membership terminates upon resignation.

3. It should be noted that a new Parliament is elected every four years.

4. Both laws were passed by the Parliament on May 20, 1992.

5. The Bank of Estonia had the right to prolong that period for each economic agent separately.

6. The Bank of Estonia is also responsible for supervising the banking system.

7. As a comparison, the Lithuanian government has issued several series of treasury bills as noted in Chapter 14.

8. See empirical evidence in Chapter 6 by Dubauskas, Wihlborg and Willett.

9. Dubauskas distinguishes between orthodox and other types of currency board arrangements in Chapter 14.

10. See Chapter 14 by Dubauskas for a discussion of currency boards with different degrees of strictness on the money supply process.

14

The Lithuanian Currency Board

Gediminas Dubauskas

Introduction

Following independence Lithuania adopted a flexible exchange rate (beginning October 1, 1992), but switched to a fixed exchange rate pegged to the U.S. dollar in a currency board arrangement on April 1, 1994. The purpose of exchange rate pegging was to create an anti-inflationary mechanism, and the currency board arrangement was designed to increase the credibility of the litas, the Lithuanian currency.

In this chapter the operation of the Lithuanian currency board system is discussed and evaluated. Of particular interest is whether the currency board system has contributed to the credibility of the exchange rate peg and Lithuania's monetary policy. In an orthodox currency board system the board issues banknotes and coins in domestic currency, which can be exchanged on demand at a fixed exchange rate into a foreign "reserve currency." The orthodox currency board does not even accept deposits from commercial banks. To guarantee the convertibility of the notes and coins, it links the issue of domestic currency to inflows of foreign exchange from a selected reserve currency country. The notes and coins issued by the currency board are therefore backed 100 percent by a reserve that is converted via the fixed exchange rate and guarantees full convertibility. The reserve currency country should therefore be highly stable in monetary terms to provide a nominal anchor for the domestic currency (Hofman and Sell 1993).

A slightly less orthodox form of currency board accepts commercial bank deposits when banks exchange their foreign currency holdings for the domestic currency. These deposits are then considered reserves of the commercial banks. I call this system a *strict* currency board arrangement. It is strict in the sense that changes in the monetary base, including notes, coins, and commercial bank deposits in the central bank, are directly tied to changes in foreign exchange reserves. Other currency board arrangements are less strict because changes in the monetary base need not match changes in foreign exchange reserves exactly.[1]

One important objective of a currency board arrangement is to provide credibility for an anti-inflationary policy with respect to controlling the growth of domestic currency. Credibility can be evaluated based on three criteria that, according to Hofmann and Sell (1993), must be fulfilled to achieve the confidence of economic agents. These three criteria are "transparency," "competence," and "creditor protection."

Transparency implies that monetary policy objectives are clearly defined, observable and achievable by well-defined policy instruments. For example, the Lithuanian litas is pegged to the U.S. dollar rather than to the SDR or another basket of currencies, because pegging to one currency that is continuously traded and priced in markets contributes to transparency.

Competence is the ability of the monetary authority to follow the institutional rules. Competence depends, for example, on the relative power of the government and the monetary authority to determine monetary policy. It also depends on factors such as the size of foreign exchange reserves relative to the magnitude of autonomous changes in these reserves during adjustment processes.

The third criterion of *creditor protection* refers to the ability of individuals and firms holding litas to abandon the currency if there are fears that its value may be eroded. Convertibility into the reserve currency and sufficiency of reserves contribute to creditor protection and enhance credibility.

Introduction of the Lithuanian Currency Board

On March 17, 1994, the Lithuanian parliament adopted a quasi-currency board arrangement almost identical to the Estonian model.[2] Steve Hanke, author of several currency board proposals and advisor to the Lithuanian government, had proposed an orthodox currency board, implying that the central bank should be disbanded and a currency board alone should back the currency. Minimum reserve requirements and the lender-of-last-resort functions of a central bank would have been ruled out under such an arrangement. Furthermore, Hanke suggested that a majority on the board should be non-Lithuanians, and perhaps the board's headquarters should be moved to a foreign country. The political infeasibility of such an extreme solution is obvious.

The Hanke proposal was strongly supported by the IMF (International Monetary Fund 1993) and the Lithuanian prime minister (*The Baltic Independent* 1994), but strongly opposed by the Bank of Lithuania, the commercial banks and some industrialists. The law of March 17 is weaker than Hanke's proposal and similar to the Estonian law in that it creates a "strict" currency board. Nevertheless, the minister of the economy resigned in protest when the law was adopted.

With the implementation of the currency board on April 1, 1994, the Lithuanian government, in consultation with the Lithuanian central bank, pegged the litas to the U.S. dollar at the rate of four litas to one dollar. This was a compromise between the IMF's proposal that had recommended a rate around 3.8 to the dollar and industrial groups that had favored a higher rate of 4.2 to the dollar (*The Baltic Independent*, April 1, 1994).

The Lithuanian arrangement is only a partial currency board, "if it is a currency board at all," according to the Bank of Lithuania's vice-chairman, Jonas Niaura.[3] Its many targets and instruments are those of a central bank. Technicalities of the law, including rules for borrowing reserves and commercial bank reserve requirements, were under discussion until early 1996. Nevertheless, so far the central bank has been operating like a strict currency board. Domestic currency and commercial bank deposits at the Bank of Lithuania are backed fully by U.S. dollars and gold reserves. Access to foreign exchange for litas is available to all at the fixed rate of four litas to a dollar. Domestic assets cannot be used to back the litas liabilities of the central bank. Therefore, any government deficit must be financed by borrowing from the private sector or commercial banks. The government can also borrow abroad, but it cannot borrow from the central bank. By law, the Bank of Lithuania cannot purchase government securities. The seigniorage revenues earned by the currency board are divided between the central bank and the government. With respect to the central bank's role as lender of last resort, it is allowed to provide loans to the banking system in emergencies, but only up to the limit of its excess foreign exchange reserves.[4] (It is not clear what would be considered "excess" reserves because of the currency board's requirement that it increase the monetary base proportionally to reserves growth. The current surplus is due to the initial currency board settlement when loans from the IMF were allocated to the central bank's reserves.) The accumulated revenues and other sources of the central bank's own capital are available for emergencies.[5] The Bank of Lithuania does not have a discount window for commercial banks.

In the next section we look carefully at institutional arrangements in order to evaluate the credibility of the anti-inflationary objective in more detail.

The Law on Credibility

The law on credibility is shown in the Appendix. Careful study of this law shows that there are possibilities for the central bank to change the exchange rate and the money supply contrary to the rules of a strict currency board. Thus, the credibility of the system will depend on the central bank's behavior in the initial stages.

One important aspect of the law of March 17, 1994, was the power to change the exchange rate. According to article 3, the government, in consultation with the central bank, had this power. There was concern that this would not provide sufficient credibility. An amendment was accepted in the fall of 1994 where the power to change the exchange rate lies with the central bank in consultation with the government. A "double key" system where exchange rate changes would require the approval of both the government and the central bank could possibly enhance credibility further.[6]

According to the law of the Bank of Lithuania, the Lithuanian Bank is strongly independent; in fact it was even before the currency board's introduction. The chairperson of the bank is appointed for a term of five years by the Seimas (Parliament) of the Republic of Lithuania upon the recommendation of the president of the republic. The intention is that the government should not have much direct influence on central bank decisions. This situation could enhance the credibility of monetary policy, but it is known that leaders of the bank were against the introduction of the currency board: they did not find the possible loss of traditional monetary policy tools an attractive option.

Another important issue for credibility is the central bank's ability to conduct open market operations influencing the money supply. From article 2 of the "Law on the Credibility of Litas," open market operations cannot be conducted with assets issued by the government. During discussions about "how pure is the currency board?" with Lithuanian bank officials, they confirmed that open market operations are not allowed. The bank is able to issue its own securities, however, and use these to conduct open market operations (see article 2 of the law in the Appendix). Furthermore, room for monetary expansionism is provided by the excess of foreign exchange reserves relative to the litas monetary base the board possessed when it began operation. Last, but not least, monetary expansion is possible if foreign exchange reserves are increased by means of central bank or government borrowing abroad.

Currently, the Bank of Lithuania has double balance sheets; one is for the pure currency board and the other for the excess foreign exchange reserves. (This is similar to the Estonian arrangments.) The excess foreign exchange reserves could be used to expand lending to commercial banks, undermining the credibility of the litas peg relative to a "strict" currency board.

Under the currency board arrangement, the government should finance its debt by issuing securities to the private sector, especially to commercial banks. The government sector has issued debt this way so far; a first auction of government securities was held on July 19, 1994. The issue of government treasury bills is increasing over time. The demand for securities may be insufficient if the government runs budget deficits, requiring it to issue more and more treasury bills. In 1994, the Lithuanian bank held 19 auctions of government securities, selling securities worth 563.3 million litas (nominal value). During the second quarter of 1995, the bank organized 19 auctions of short-term government bonds, selling securities amounting to 608 million litas. In the third quarter of 1995, the bank organized 18 auctions of short-term government bonds, during which it sold securities amounting to 723.2 million litas. By mid 1996, commercial banks had purchased more than 50 percent of the total amount of Treasury bills auctioned.

An important aspect of the central bank's credibility with respect to monetary policy is its ability and willingness to act as a lender of last resort for commercial banks facing liquidity problems. If foreign exchange and gold reserves exceed the monetary base, then the bank can issue promissory notes to commercial banks, expanding their liquidity (see article 2 of the "Law on the Credibility of the Litas"). So far, there has not been any issue of promissory notes, "because of uncertainty in the regulations for this kind of financial means."[7] The bank can provide a limited amount of credit (up to 20 million litas worth) to commercial banks that have liquidity problems according to an amendment to the law on credibility accepted in June 1995. "Twelve of the twenty-eight commercial banks in Lithuania have a serious problem with their solvency," according to the chairman of the Bank of Lithuania, "but savings deposited in the bankrupt banks formed only 3 percent from all deposits in Lithuanian commercial banks."[8] This was before the commercial bank crisis at the end of December 1995.

According to the Lithuanian bank authorities, they would exercise rescue operations mainly for large banks, since a large bankruptcy could have a negative impact on all Lithuanian financial markets.[9] When the two largest private commercial banks in Lithuania went bankrupt at the end of 1995, the central bank did not act as lender of last resort. However, the central bank and the government did recapitalize state-owned banks to avoid a similar crisis in mid 1996.

The Bank of Lithuania can change commercial banks' reserve requirements while maintaining the monetary base unchanged. A strict currency board, but not an orthodox board, has this monetary policy tool available.

Commercial banks' fractional reserves must be kept at the central bank. Initially, the Bank of Lithuania had a 10 percent reserve requirement, but since July 1993 it is 12 percent. At the end of 1994, the central bank allowed the commercial banks to buy governmental treasury bills with their own reserves at the central bank.[10] These short-term treasury bills were considered part of the commercial banks' reserves. In this way, the central bank solved a problem of insufficient demand for government securities caused by a portfolio shift in favor of U.S. dollars.

According to the *Bulletin of the Bank of Lithuania* (1995, vol. 1) the increased demand for U.S. dollars took place because of discussions in the mass media about a possible devaluation of the litas. By allowing treasury bills to be counted as bank reserves, the central bank "sterilized" the effect of capital outflows contrary to the intentions of a strict currency board.

The arrangements designed to create credibility for the litas are similar to those of the Estonian currency board. The main formal difference is that the Lithuanian central bank, Lietuvos Bankas, can change the litas' exchange rate only in consultation with the Lithuanian government, while in Estonia the fixed exchange rate can be changed only by a decision of the parliament. The weaker Lithuanian rule lessens the credibility of the currency board. Lithuanian citizens do not put much trust in either the parliament or the government.

Currency board arrangements have several drawbacks. First, the foreign exchange reserves held at foreign banks are nonproductive funds in terms of the domestic economy. Second, loans to the government from different international institutions are partly used to increase Lithuanian foreign currency reserves; the government pays high interest rates for these loans while its own reserves are held in foreign banks at lower annual interest rates.

There is a debate about the use of interest earned on reserves held abroad. The Lithuanian bank uses interest profits for reserve expansion. Seventy percent of profits go to form the reserve capital of the bank, and the remaining profit is be paid to budget of the republic. Many political groups are convinced that more of these profits should be used by the government. This type of debate over whether to strengthen the currency or expand spending represents a threat to the currency board arrangements.

Rumors inside Lithuania about the possible devaluation of the litas have damaged the fragile credibility of the litas. Government and central bank officials have tried to discredit these rumors. "Devaluation of litas is not being considered by the government, or by the central bank, and the issue will not be raised," said the bank chairman Jonas Niaura in February 1995, after a period of reserve losses. According to the law on the credibility of the litas, the bank is not responsible for the inflation rate. Therefore, its activities are quite simple. "If Lithuania continues to carry out an economic policy in which the litas will never have to be devalued, it will be an honor for the country, not the Bank of Lithuania," the chief banker said (*The Baltic Observer* 1995).

Dr. Niaura has also mentioned that in practice there are very high costs to maintaining the currency board. Markets for international trade in goods and financial assets are not well developed in the small Baltic states, and they are very sensitive to external economical shocks. Predominantly, these shocks come from their biggest trading partner, Russia. More recently the growing strength of the dollar in the spring of 1997 can be considered an external shock, since the lita is pegged to the U.S. dollar.

The resulting appreciation of the litas against the German mark put additional pressure on the Lithuanian currency board, because of losses of domestic exporters. The continued current account deficit can be explained in part by local producers' uncompetiveness against cheap imports in the period of transition.

Conclusions

The main objective of adopting a currency board arrangement by the Central Bank of Lithuania was to increase the credibility of the domestic currency, the litas, and to keep inflation under control. The government has to finance any deficit by borrowing from the private sector or commercial banks, but cannot borrow from the Bank of Lithuania. Therefore, the government issues debt to the private sector. Similar currency board arrangements helped establish currency credibility and stability in Estonia. The period after the reforms in Lithuania, and even in Estonia, is likely still too short to draw definitive conclusions.

Deposit and loan interest rates in Lithuania for different currencies are important signals of the outlook for the economy and the credibility of the currency. After less than a year under the currency board arrangements, confidence in the litas had increased substantially, as shown by lower interest rates and a smaller gap between rates for litas and foreign convertible currencies in Lithuania. (See Chapter 6 by Dubauskas, Wihlborg and Willett.) Under a successful currency board, the domestic interest rates should converge toward those of the reserve country, the United States.

The inflation rate (CPI) in Lithuania during the transition has been and still is much higher than in the U.S. The inflation can be partially explained by the initial undervaluation of the exchange rate, the productivity bias favoring the traded goods sector and the high inherited inflation rate that has a momentum of its own, the distortion of prices for goods and services in the market inherited from a centrally planned economy, and the lack of competition that allows the exercise of monopoly pricing in some fields. It is clear from interest rate developments, however, that inflation has been falling and expectations about future inflation have also been dampened under the currency board arrangement. Although this process had begun before the currency board arrangement was initiated, progress has continued under its operation.

In 1997, the Lithuanian currency board system came under political pressure in spite of its apparent success in improving the credibility of the currency. The source of this pressure was the appreciating dollar which caused the litas to appreciate relative to the currencies of Lithuania's major trading partners in Europe.

It is possible that pegging the litas to the German mark, as the Estonian kroon is, would make it easier to maintain credibility, because the long-term variation in Lithuania's real exchange rate would likely decrease. However, while alternatives to the current currency board arrangements may have economic merit, it is difficult to publicly consider them without undermining the credibility of the current arrangements. This is one of the disadvantages of fixed exchange rate regimes.

Appendix
Law of the Republic of Lithuania No. 1-407
on the Credibility of the Litas
March 17, 1994, Vilnius

Article 1. Guaranteeing the Credibility of the Litas

The litas put into circulation by the Bank of Lithuania are fully covered by the gold and foreign exchange reserves of the Bank of Lithuania.

Article 2. The Amount of Litas in Circulation

The Bank of Lithuania shall guarantee that the total amount of litas put into circulation does not exceed the gold reserves (at market prices) and foreign exchange reserves (according to the official exchange rate of the litas) of the Bank of Lithuania at any time.

The total amount of the litas put into circulation shall consist of:

1. bank notes and coins in circulation;
2. the sum of the balances of nominal accounts of other banks and holders of litas accounts kept with the Bank of Lithuania; and
3. the sum of the securities and promissory notes of the Bank of Lithuania in litas.

Foreign exchange reserves shall consist of:

1. bank notes and coins of convertible currency held by the Bank of Lithuania;
2. the amount of convertible currency held by the Bank of Lithuania in correspondent accounts in foreign banks and the International Monetary Fund; and
3. promissory notes, certificates of deposit, bonds, and other debt securities payable in convertible currency, which are held by the

Bank of Lithuania. The Bank of Lithuania may change the total amount of the litas in circulation only by changing gold and foreign exchange reserves respectively.

Article 3. The Official Exchange Rate of the Litas

The official exchange rate of the litas shall be established against the currency chosen as the anchor currency. The official exchange rate of the litas and the anchor currency shall be established or changed by the Government of the Republic of Lithuania upon co-ordination with the Bank of Lithuania.

Article 4. The Exchange of the Litas

The Bank of Lithuania shall guarantee to the extent of its gold holdings and foreign exchange reserves free exchange of the litas specified in paragraph 2 of article 2 into the anchor currency according to the official exchange rate of the litas, as well as free exchange of the anchor currency into the litas within the territory of the Republic of Lithuania. Other foreign currencies shall be exchanged into litas and litas shall be exchanged into other foreign currencies according to the market exchange rate. Maximum amounts of charges for exchange operations shall be established by the Bank of Lithuania for all banks. Commercial banks shall be liable under law for the violation of the procedure of exchange operations.

Article 5. Information on the Litas

The Bank of Lithuania shall publish information on the total amount of litas in circulation, gold holdings, and foreign exchange reserves in the "Valstybes zinios" [Government Records] at least once a month.

Article 6. Entry into Force

This law shall become effective as of April 1, 1994.

Article 7. Validity of the Law of the Bank of Lithuania and the Statute of the Bank of Lithuania

The Law of the Bank of Lithuania and the Statute of the Bank of Lithuania shall be valid until the adoption of a new law of the Bank of Lithuania and to the extent it complies with the provisions of this law.

I promulgate this law adopted by the Seimas of the Republic of Lithuania.

President of the Republic of Lithuania

Resolution No. 213 of the Republic of Lithuania on Establishment of the Official Exchange Rate of the Litas and the Anchor Currency March 30, 1994, Vilnius

Subject to article 3 of the Law on the Credibility of the Litas the Government of the Republic of Lithuania upon co-ordination with the Bank of Lithuania hereby resolves:

1. to establish that the U.S. dollar shall be the anchor currency,
2. to establish that the official exchange rate of the litas shall be four litas against one U.S. dollar.

Prime Minister
Adolfas Slezevicius

Minister of Finance
Eduardas Vilkelis

October 12, 1994

Law of the Republic of Lithuania No. 1-603 On the Amendment to Article 4 of the Law of the Republic of Lithuania Currency

Second paragraph of article 4 of the Law of the Republic of Lithuania on currency was amended to read as follows:

"The Bank of Lithuania shall establish the anchor currency and the official litas exchange rate following the procedure set by the Law on the Credibility of the Litas."

Notes

1. Also see Chapter 12 by Sweeney in this volume.
2. The appendix contains excepts from the relevant laws for Lithuania. Chapter 13 by Ross in this volume describes how the Estonian currency board has functioned.
3. Based on interview with Jonas Niaura.
4. During all of 1994, the net issue was 577.8 million litas.
5. See Osborne and Villanueva (1995) for a general discussion of the lender-of-last-resort role of currency boards. For general analysis of currency boards, see also Bennett (1993, 1994), Hanke (1993), and Williamson (1995).
6. See Willett (1995).

7. From an interview with Jonas Niaura, then deputy chairperson of the Bank of Lithuania.

8. *Litas*, No. 62, August 1995.

9. There are few such banks. The three main ones are jointly owned by the state (51 percent of shares) and private investors. These are the Savings Bank of Lithuania, the Agricultural Bank, and the Commercial State Bank.

10. Economic review "Vartai" in *Lietuvos Rytas* [Lithuanian Morning] 1994.

11. Out of a total of 28 commercial banks, 12 went bankrupt during 1994 and 1995.

References

Baltic Independent, various issues.

Baltic Observer. February 1995. 1993–95. Various issues.

Bennett, Adam G. G. 1994. *Currency Boards: Issues and Experiences*. IMF Paper on Policy Analysis and Assessment. Washington, D.C.: International Monetary Fund, September.

———. 1993. "The Operation of the Estonian Currency Board." *IMF Staff Papers* 40(2): 451–70.

Garber, Peter, and Lars Svensson. 1994. "Properties of Monetary Regimes: Fixed vs. Flexible Exchange Rates." Preliminary draft for the *Handbook of International Economics*, forthcoming.

Hanke, Steven, H. Lars Jonung, and Kurt Schuller. 1993. *Russian Currency and Finance*. London: Routledge.

———. 1993. "Currency Boards and Currency Convertibility." *Cato Journal*, Winter 12(3): 687–705.

Hansson, Ardo. 1993. *The Estonian Kroon: Experiences of the First Year*. Report of a conference "The Economics of New Currencies" organized by the Centre for Economic Policy Research, London.

Hansson, Ardo, and Jeffrey Sachs. 1994. "Monetary Institutions and Credible Stabilization: A Comparison of Experience in the Baltics." Paper presented at conference on "Central Banks in Eastern Europe and the Newly Independent States," Budapest.

International Monetary Fund. 1993. *Economic Review: Lithuania*. Washington D.C.: International Monetary Fund.

Litas [Lithuanian periodical of economics and business]. No. 62, August 1995.

———. 1994–95. Various issues.

Meliss, C.L., and M. Cornelius. 1993. "New Currencies in the Former Soviet Union: A Recipe for Hyperinflation or the Path to Price Stability?" Bank of England Working Paper Series No. 26: 49–63.

Lithuania Today 1994. [weekly periodical of politics and economics]. "Future of the Litas." January/ February: 3–6.

———. 1994. March: 2–4.

Willett, Thomas D. 1995. "Guidelines for Constructing Monetary Constitutions," in Thomas D. Willett, Richard C.K. Burdekin, Richard J. Sweeney, and Clas Wihlborg, eds., *Establishing Monetary Stability in Emerging Market Economies*. Pp. 103–14. Boulder, Colo.: Westview Press.

Willett, Thomas D., and Fahim Al-Marhubi. 1994. "Currency Policies for Inflation Control in the Formerly Centrally Planned Economies." *The World Economy*, November: 795–815.
Williamson, John. 1995. *What Role for Currency Boards?* Washington D.C.: Institute for International Economics.

Statistical sources:
Bulletin of the Bank of Lithuania (Lietuvos Banko Biuletenis). 1993. Vol. 1–4.
_____. 1994. Vol. 1–4.
_____. 1995. Vol. 1–4.
Monetary Review Bank of Latvia. 1994. Vol. 1–4.
_____. 1995. Vol. 1–3.
Eesti Pank Quarterly Review. 1993. 1994. 1995.

PART FIVE

Experiences from the Emerging Market Economies

15

The Czech Case: Fixed Exchange Rates Through Stages of Transition

Miroslav Hrnčíř

Introduction

In 1990 the government of the former Czechoslovakia pegged the Czech-oslovakian koruna to a currency basket. A policy of nominal exchange rate stability was adopted to anchor the stabilization process following sweeping price and foreign exchange liberalization at the beginning of January 1991. However, no binding commitment was publicly made to maintain the fixed exchange rate regime and the given exchange rate level, neither indefinitely nor for any pre-announced period. The koruna was pegged to a basket of currencies within a rather narrow band of ±0.5 percent and maintained in the Czech Republic (following the split of Czechoslovakia into the Czech and Slovak Republics and the dissolution its common currency) through February 1996, i.e., for 62 consecutive months. Such exchange rate stability is exceptional for a transition economy and even in comparison with some OECD member countries. On February 27, 1996, the exchange rate band was widened to ±7.5 percent, although the central parity was left untouched.

Although rumors of a move to a more flexible exchange rate arrangement had been in the air for some time, the markets were caught by surprise both by the extent of the band widening and the timing of its announcement, given that parliamentary elections were scheduled for the end of May 1996.

In the spring of 1997 the central bank moved further towards a more flexible exchange rate arrangement. As of May 26, the Board of the Czech National Bank stopped pegging the koruna to a basket of currencies and allowed the currency to float. However, the Bank also declared its readiness to intervene in the market to smooth out excessive volatility at whatever level the exchange rate might be. The Bank's readiness to act has been demonstrated by its occasional resort to stabilizing intervention. In practice, the Czech Republic has maintained a managed floating exchange rate regime since May 1997.

The departure from a pegged regime was effected in the face of turbulent currency markets and, in particular, of repeated speculative attacks against the koruna. Beginning in 1995, high current account deficits developed that diminished the credibility of the koruna's peg. In 1996 the current account deficit reached an unsustainable level of 8.2 percent of GDP and continued to climb in the first quarter of 1997. More bad news came from an unexpected slowdown in the Czech economy's performance and from the increasing gap between budgetary revenues and expenditures. Moreover, the half-hearted policy measures adopted by the government in April 1997 to correct these evolving imbalances left investors unsatisfied and skeptical.

The sensitivity of the situation was further aggravated by deepening political instability. Although political stability had been one of the country's major assets in previous years, now the very survival of the governing coalition came under question.

The combination of macroeconomic and political weaknesses was perceived by investors and observers as increasingly resembling the situation in emerging market economies elsewhere, such as some of the ASEAN countries—particularly Thailand, which eventually suffered a currency crisis. Despite important differences between the Czech situation and events in those countries and its distance from those countries, the Czech currency's problems were to some extent due to contagion effects. The outcome was that the koruna depreciated around 10 percent from the previous central parity following the shift to a floating exchange rate regime.

Unlike the former Czechoslovakia, most of the emerging market economies of Central and Eastern Europe, including Slovenia, Bulgaria, Russia and almost all other countries in the Commonwealth of Independent States[1] resorted to a managed float, i.e., to a flexible type of exchange rate regime, at the beginning of their political and economic changes. Some of the others eventually found it necessary to depart from an initially fixed exchange rate. Among these were Poland and Hungary, as described elsewhere in this volume. Contrary to the trend towards more flexible arrangements, Estonia in 1992 and Lithuania in 1994 moved in the opposite direction, introducing currency board systems.

Evaluating exchange rate arrangements in the emerging market economies of Central and Eastern Europe with the benefit of hindsight, the following conclusions seem to follow.

1.   Exchange rate regimes have developed in a wide variety of ways across individual transition economies, from currency board systems to various options of managed float.

2.   Over the course of time the trend toward more flexible exchange rates has clearly prevailed with few exceptions.
3.   Although the available evidence on the comparative merits of exchange rate regimes in transition economies is as yet inconclusive, those countries which pegged early in their transtion (such as Poland, the Czech and Slovak Republics, Hungary and Estonia) seemed to have fared relatively better in their stabilization efforts and macroeconomic recovery.[2]

A fairly high degree of consensus seems to exist on the comparative advantages and drawbacks of exchange rate regime options as well as on the factors which may affect their choice. Those factors are, in particular:

1.   structural factors, i.e., the ability to adjust to shocks by means of relative price and wage adjustment and/or factor mobility;
2.   the type and frequency of shocks, whether real or monetary, endogenous or exogenous; and
3.   macroeconomic conditions, policy objectives and priorities of the given country.

This consensus notwithstanding, experience shows a wide diversity of exchange rate regimes across countries which would be expected to have similar exchange rate arrangements, according to standard criteria.[3]

Does this imply that an evaluation of the advantages and disadvantages of alternative exchange rate regimes must be inconclusive, as some authors seem to suggest?[4] This question has special relevance for the emerging market economies in Eastern Europe.

Conditions in the former centrally planned economies diverged considerably from the stylized setting of developed market economies, especially at the start of the transition. While they shared some constraints and goals in common with developing countries in macroeconomic dimensions, especially in the challenges of stabilization, liberalization and deregulation, the institutions of a market economy were underdeveloped or lacking. In the course of the transition, profound systemic and institutional changes had to materialize in only a few years. As a result, the environment for exchange rate policy and its role was changing relatively quickly in the early years of the transition. This is a specific feature distinguishing countries in transition from other countries in the world economy. At issue is how intensively and in what ways those macroeconomic, institutional and systemic changes affected exchange rate arrangements in the countries of Central and Eastern Europe relative to the factors envisaged by the standard theory. Can we identify how the separate transition stages affect the choice of exchange rate regime, its successive adjustments, and its role in exchange rate policy?

I advance the hypothesis that the exchange rate arrangements and developments in the transition economies interacted with extensive institutional and systemic adjustments. Accordingly, to assess the rationale of a given exchange rate regime for a specific country, and its relative costs and benefits, not only the country-specific, but also stage-specific conditions must be accounted for.

This chapter discusses and examines this type of causality in the case of the Czech Republic. In the next section I use the concept of financial openness as the organizing framework of the discussion and distinguish four development stages (model situations). In the third section the initial transition stage is examined. In the fourth section the stage of greater financial openness is analyzed. Conclusions follow in the final section.

Stages of Transition

Reflecting the institutional and systemic trends and making use of the concept of financial openness[5] as an organizing criterion, I devise a four-stage scheme to study exchange rate developments in the transitioning economies.

Stage One: Financially Closed Economy

In the pre-transition period of the former centrally planned economies exchange rates, though nominally existing, were in reality only exchange rate coefficients. They were derived from calculated data and did not reflect developments in domestic price ratios. Tightly regulated, they lacked the properties of an proper exchange rate and failed to reflect the market value of the given currency. As a consequence, a set of black market, shadow exchange rates developed, usually widely diverging from the official rates.[6] Trade, capital and foreign exchange flows were subject to administrative controls, both inward and outward, and the domestic currency was nonconvertible.

Stage Two: Rudimentary Financial Openness— The First Transition Stage

Compared to the previous stage, the principal change in the exchange rate sphere was the shift from exchange rate coefficients to an exchange rate proper. Price, trade and foreign exchange liberalization occurred, and a limited degree of financial openness was achieved.

Liberalization was generally confined to current account items, while capital flows were of limited importance and consisted mostly of long-term official capital.

Stage Three: Financial Openness in Transition

The liberalization process was extended to capital account flows. Currency convertibility, similar to that in developed market economies, was achieved quite rapidly in many transitioning countries. Private capital flows surged, supported by the further development of domestic financial markets and financial intermediation.

Stage Four: Financially Open Economy Meeting the Criteria of the European Monetary Integration Projects

Entry into this stage implies that the transition process has been successfully accomplished. Financial institutions, including the legal and regulatory framework, have reached a sufficient level of maturity for the country to be eligible for participation in the European monetary integration process.

In the suggested four-stage scheme, the transition itself takes place in the second and third phases. The first and last stages respectively, reflect pre-transitional and post-transitional conditions. The last stage has not yet been achieved in the transitioning economies. Although there are no clear-cut dividing lines between these stages in reality, and their distinguishing features may overlap, passing from one stage to another reflects a qualitative increase in the financial openness of the given transition economy.

Apart from the institutional and systemic changes, the macroeconomic development of the transition economies also went through very divergent stages. As seen in Table 15.1 covering the CEFTA countries, the deep and protracted "transition" recession of the first years turned into economic recovery and robust growth in recent years.

In a parallel way, the disinflation process advanced from the initial price-level jump following implementation of the liberalization package to the challenge of how to cope with relatively moderate, but stubborn inflation levels (see Table 15.2). The interaction between changes in the macroeco-

TABLE 15.1 GDP Growth in CEFTA Countries (Percentage Changes Relative to Preceding Year)

	1990	1991	1992	1993	1994	1995	1996
Czech Republic	-1.1	-14.2	-6.4	-0.9	2.6	5.9	4.1
Hungary	-3.5	-11.9	-3.0	-0.6	2.9	1.5	1.0
Poland	-11.6	-7.0	2.6	3.8	5.2	7.0	6.1
Slovak Republic	-2.5	-14.5	-6.5	-3.7	4.9	6.8	6.9
Slovenia	-4.7	-8.1	-5.4	2.8	5.3	4.1	3.1

DATA: National Statistics

TABLE 15.2 Consumer Price Inflation in CEFTA Countries (Percentage Changes Relative to Preceding Year)

	1990	1991	1992	1993	1994	1995	1996
Czech Republic	9.9	56.7	11.1	20.8	10.0	9.1	8.8
Hungary	28.9	35.0	23.0	22.5	18.8	28.2	23.6
Poland	585.8	70.3	43.0	35.3	32.2	27.8	19.9
Slovak Republic	10.6	61.2	10.0	23.2	13.4	9.9	5.8
Slovenia	549.7	117.7	201.3	32.3	19.8	12.6	9.7

DATA: National Statistics

nomic and institutional settings played, therefore, a key role in the formation of individual transition stages.

Both from an analytical and policymaking point of view the "turning points" leading to the next transition stage are particularly interesting. The Czech economy moved from the first to the second stage in early 1991, implementing a package of sweeping liberalization and stabilization measures. Maturing from the second to the third stage became the primary policy challenge in the mid 1990s.

Exchange Rate Arrangements in a Rudimentary
Stage of Financial Openness

Are Fixed or Flexible Exchange Rate Regimes
Better for the Start of Transition?

In the early stages of transition, conditions for a clean float typically are not fulfilled. In particular, thin currency markets, underdeveloped institutions, and the predominance of short-term arbitrage flows could be a source of high volatility, leading to the risk of substantial misalignment. Instability in a key price—the exchange rate—could possibly undermine the main aim of the program of currency convertibility to "import" rational price ratios and to discipline domestic agents.

Some exchange rate flexibility is called for, however, for a number reasons.

1. There was substantial uncertainty about the level of a reasonably competitive exchange rate.
2. The transition process itself promised a turbulent economic future, at least in the short run, due to extensive liberalization, adjustment and restructuring in the domestic economy. Under these conditions a persistent disparity in fundamentals compared to partner coun-

tries—in particular, a higher level of inflation—seemed inevitable for several years.

3. The emerging market economies of Central and Eastern Europe lacked the prerequisites for a sustainable fixed exchange rate regime. They lacked, in particular, a satisfactory level of international reserves and funds to defend a fixed exchange rate, well-functioning factor markets, including financial markets, and a reputation of monetary stability.

Many observers, such as Willett et al. (1992) and Schmieding (1991) argue on these grounds in favor of some form of exchange rate flexibility in the emerging market economies. Williamson (1991) points to the cases of currency overvaluation experienced in a number of Latin American countries in the 1970s and early 1980s as examples of mismanagement in transition economies with fixed rates.

Exchange rate flexibility should allow macroeconomic policies to be formulated without worrying about the competitive level of the exchange rate. This option looked attractive to emerging market economies as it promised a way to avoid potential foreign-exchange constraints. The fixed exchange rate option hardly seemed sustainable or credible.

Nevertheless, compelling arguments were presented in favor of a fixed exchange rate regime. First, a fixed exchange rate regime and nominal exchange rate stability could be a major instrument of macroeconomic stabilization in an economy undergoing a sweeping liberalization. The exchange rate could take the role of a key nominal anchor.

Second, a fixed exchange rate could provide a benchmark for the extensive price adjustment initiated by price and foreign exchange liberalization. Exchange rate fluctuations, on the other hand, could obscure price signals and distort expectations.[7]

Third, a fixed exchange rate regime could have a disciplining effect on economic agents, including government authorities and trade unions. After decades of arbitrary and non-transparent exchange rate ratios in the centrally planned economy framework, the disciplining impact of the fixed exchange rate "norm" could contribute to the re-orientation of behavior patterns.

These arguments were the cornerstones of the "nominal anchor approach" to exchange rate policy. This approach was advocated strongly in the IMF-sponsored stabilization programs launched in the former Yugoslavia in 1989, in Poland in 1990 and in the former Czechoslovakia in 1991. The parallel between these economies and destabilized countries elsewhere where the IMF's prescriptions had been tested in the 1970s and 1980s seemed self-evident. Nominal exchange rate stability was a major instrument of macroeconomic stabilization, anchoring both the current flows and expectations.[8]

The stance of the IMF was a major factor behind the fixed exchange rate regime in the Polish and Czechoslovak cases. Slovenia and Bulgaria, on the other hand, opted for managed floating primarily because of their lack of foreign exchange reserves.

Estonia and Lithuania, two of the newly independent republics of the former USSR, chose a currency board solution. Being very small economies and lacking the institutions and experience for monetary management, they looked upon the currency board as a feasible way to accomplish radical disinflation. (These countries are discussed in Chapters 6, 13 and 14 of this volume.)

The examples of these countries suggest that country-specific priorities and constraints generally determined the exchange rate regime implemented at the start of transition. Capital flows did not impose a serious constraint on the choice of exchange rate arrangements at this stage. As might be expected, most transition economies adopted exchange rate arrangements somewhere between the polar cases, i.e., in between "irrevocably" fixed and freely floating rates. To satisfy the competing requirements of stability and competitiveness, exchange rate policies as a rule resorted to compromise solutions. The arrangements included adjustable pegs, crawling pegs and various forms of managed floating. Given that extreme solutions seemed unattractive for most transition economies, the longevity of the currency board experiments of Estonia and Lithuania surprised many.

The Exchange Rate Level in the Initial Period of Transition

The official exchange rate of the Czechoslovak koruna has been tied to a currency basket since the early 1980s. Accordingly, when the authorities of the former Czechoslovakia opted for a fixed exchange rate regime in 1990, pegging the Czechoslovak koruna to a currency basket within a rather narrow band of ±0.5 percent, this seemed a small change from the previous system. However, the peg became operational and binding only after the departure from the rigid centrally planned economy framework.

In setting the peg the monetary authorities were confronted with the problem of selecting a suitable "entry" exchange rate level. The issue was twofold: to find the equilibrium level for 1990, and to determine how far to deviate initially from this level to secure exchange rate stability over, at least, a certain "desirable" period, given the expected persistent disparity in fundamentals, particularly continued inflation.

The standard definition of an equilibrium exchange rate says that this rate ensures the simultaneous attainment of internal and external balance (Williamson 1991). Though relatively clear-cut in theory, the concept of balance is much less straightforward in practice. External equilibrium is considered to be in place when the current account and sustainable capital flows are in balance. However, the identification of persistent capital flows is not unambiguous, and their level may vary over time. Internal equilibrium must be conceived as a medium-term concept independent of cyclical fluctuations.

When the Czechoslovak authorities had to choose an exchange rate level at the start of the transition, the very concept of an equilibrium rate was alien to former central planners. The assessment of macroeconomic variables and dimensions was, at this time, subject to a wide margin of error.[9] Moreover, policymakers had to consider arguments that called for a sizable initial undervaluation of the exchange rate. The decision had been made to introduce "internal" currency convertibility and to implement a sweeping liberalization of foreign trade at the very start of transition. As a consequence, an undervalued exchange rate seemed desirable; currency convertibility, however limited, would otherwise hardly be sustainable with a fixed exchange rate.

Additional policy constraints strengthened the case for undervaluation.

1. The level of foreign exchange reserves was too low to provide a desirable cushion for possible fluctuations in liberalized foreign exchange flows.
2. The abrupt collapse of Comecon institutions and markets made it necessary to re-orient the bulk of existing trade.
3. A persistent real exchange rate appreciation could occur as a result of inflation.

Policymakers faced a trade-off: a larger undervaluation would increase the chances of survival of the new exchange rate arrangements, but would strengthen inflationary cost-push pressures and mitigate the disciplining function of the exchange rate. The degree of uncertainty and the lack of consensus as to the proper entry level of the exchange rate were reflected in a rather wide dispersion of values suggested for the "initial" exchange rate level in 1990. Suggestions ranged from 16 Czechoslovak koruna per U.S. dollar, close to the existing "commercial rate," to 35–38 koruna, near the illegal parallel and "shadow" market rates.

The resolution of the authorities was to err, if necessary, by excessive undervaluation. Accordingly, the rate that was decided upon—28 Czechoslovak koruna per U.S. dollar—was closer to the existing parallel market rates than to the median value of the discussed corridor (see Figure 15.1). The implied depreciation amounted to 95 percent, as can be seen in Table 15.3. That radical change in exchange rate level was not implemented all at once but over the course of four follow-up realignments in 1990.

The official figures for the depreciations provide a distorted picture of the true size of the depreciations. One reason is that the exchange rate changes were announced relative to the "commercial rate" that was applied in the rigidly regulated framework of the centrally planned economy. That rate

Figure 15.1 Official Exchange Rate, Purchasing Power Parity and Parallel Market Rates of CZK (Koruna per USD)

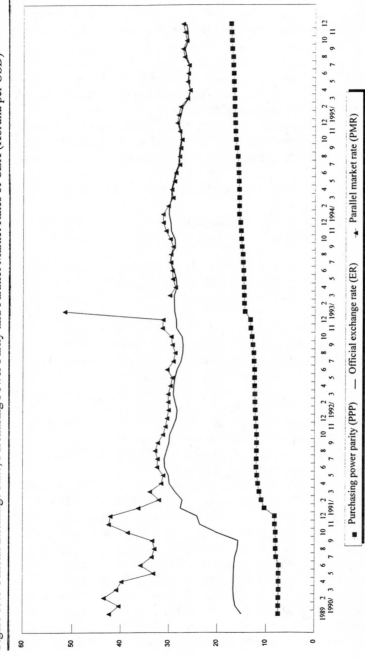

DATA: *Financial Statistical Information, Monthly Statistics of the Czech Republic*, Czech National Bank; *Main Economic Indicators*, OCED, August 1994.

TABLE 15.3 Realignments of the Czechoslovak Koruna in 1990

Date	New Rate per USD	Percentage Change
January 2	14.62	2.10
January 8	17.00	16.30
October 15	24.00	55.20
December 28	28.00	15.90

* The first devaluation of January 2, 1990, was made with respect to the "commercial rate," i.e., to the exchange rate coefficient then applied, which amounted to 14.31 koruna per U.S. dollar at the end of 1989.
DATA: *Financial Statistical Information*, Czech National Bank.

could not provide a relevant benchmark for the assessment of the "real" extent of the implemented exchange rate depreciation, since, as noted above, it was merely a coefficient.

The first three "devaluations" were introduced in an environment of almost entirely regulated prices. Only the last, on December 28, 1990, was a component of a liberalization and deregulation package, including domestic prices, foreign trade and foreign exchange liberalization.

The large 55 percent realignment on October 15, 1990, was not planned for that date. It was resorted to in distress, under the pressure of the deteriorating liquidity of domestic banks and of continued depletion of reserves due to capital flight and dramatically increasing imports in the latter half of 1990. Those trends resulted from widespread expectations of devaluation, fueled by public discussion of the forthcoming massive currency devaluation to be included in the liberalization and stabilization policy package. Thus, even in this rudimentary stage of financial openness, financial flows could influence the timing of exchange rate changes.

Policymakers were not unanimous with regard to the extent of a desirable devaluation. One dividing line existed between the members of the federal and the Czech governments. Their diverging views were related to different approaches to the pace of liberalization of external transactions.

According to one approach, priority ought to be given to domestic liberalization while the external regulations would be dismantled only later and step by step. The alternative approach that was eventually implemented implied a sweeping liberalization on both domestic and external fronts simultaneously. Those advocating a speedier approach to convertibility advocated a larger initial depreciation.

The large devaluation undoubtedly contributed to a higher than expected price level jump in the first months of 1991. Some 35 to 40 percent of the increase in the price level in that period was estimated to be due to the depreciation of the currency. It could therefore be argued that the process of price adjustment materialized at a higher price level than necessary. The favorable side of the developments was, however, that this initial jump in inflation subsided in three months without further repercussions.

Another aspect of the depreciation is that it widened the already existing wedge between the current exchange rate and the purchasing power parity rate (see Figure 15.1). The scope of the hoped for disciplinary impact of a fixed exchange rate was thus diminished or, possibly, its materialization was postponed. As a result, the environment for domestic enterprises became "softer," especially with regard to exports and competition from imports.

The above mentioned drawbacks of the depreciation overshooting were mostly confined to the short run. Benefits may also be claimed in the medium run. Specifically, the initial undervaluation of the exchange rate formed an exchange rate "cushion." This cushion contributed to the nominal exchange rate stability and to the positive inflation record of the Czech Republic compared to other emerging market economies of Central and Eastern Europe.[10] The nominal exchange rate would be maintained unchanged for five years despite a persistent real exchange rate appreciation and without any additional costs to defend it by specific policy measures. The overshooting also provided an extended time span for the equilibrating real exchange rate appreciation to materialize, once productivity and income started to grow in the later stages of transition.

A Fixed Exchange Rate Regime with Financial Openness

The Nominal Exchange Rate

Extensive adjustment and persistent real exchange rate appreciations in the transition economies made a degree of exchange rate flexibility desirable in many countries and usually inevitable once financial markets were opened to international influences. The distinguishing feature of the Czech developments has been their capability to sustain nominal exchange rate stability despite external shocks and a real rate appreciation as large as, even exceeding, appreciation in other emerging market economies.

From the start of the transition in 1990 until May 1997, the Czech koruna (Czechoslovak koruna until the split of the currency of the former Czechoslovakia in early 1993) was pegged to a basket of currencies, although the basket's composition was changed occasionally in the early stages of transition (see Table 15.4).

Most amendments to the basket's composition were motivated by "technical" considerations. There was no deliberate intention to make the peg either harder or softer: the changes were the product of a search for an optimum

Table 15.4 Currency Basket of the Czechoslovak and the Czech Koruna

	USD	DM	ATS	GBP	FRF	CHFR
June 1, 1981	45.83	29.78	10.65	9.06	4.6	n.a.
January 1, 1989	32.88	40.93	12.32	n.a	4.82	9.05
December 28, 1990	31.34	45.52	12.35	4.24	n.a.	6.55
January 2, 1992	49.07	36.15	8.07	n.a.	2.92	3.79
May 3, 1993	35.00	65.00	n.a.	n.a.	n.a.	n.a.

DATA: *Financial Statistical Information*, Czech National Bank

peg given the changed importance of individual major currencies in trade and payments flows. In the case of the last amendment, introduced in May 1993, the number of basket currencies was reduced from five to just two, the German mark and the U.S. dollar. The intention was to make the basket more transparent and to save on transaction costs.

During the period from 1991 to February 1996, nominal exchange rate developments of the Czech koruna (and the Czechoslovak koruna) reflected only the shifts in the cross-rates of the basket currencies. When the trends of the German mark and the U.S. dollar diverged, the basket arrangement contributed to a stabilization in the corresponding bilateral Czech koruna's ratios.

The dominant share of the German mark (65 percent) in the basket since 1993 implied that the nominal exchange rate of the koruna to some extent shadowed mark developments. Accordingly, the appreciating trend of the German mark in 1994 and 1995 resulted in a corresponding minor appreciation of the nominal effective exchange rate of the Czech koruna as well.[11] On the other hand, the weakening of the German mark relative to the U.S. dollar which developed in the first half of 1996 worked in the reverse direction.[12]

In February 1996, after five years in which the exchange rate was confined within a narrow band of only ±0.5%, the Czech koruna was freed to fluctuate within a wider band of ±7.5 percent. Consequently, for the first time in the course of transition the exchange rate level reflected changes in the market's assessment of economic conditions.

After the widening of the band, the impact of fluctuations in the cross-rates was combined with the more extensive autonomous fluctuations of the Czech koruna with respect to the central parity (i.e. with respect to the basket). Figure 15.2 demonstrates those fluctuations (the index value) together with developments in the bilateral Czech koruna/dollar and Czech koruna/mark rates.

Figure 15.2 Exchange Rates of the Czech Koruna 1995–1996

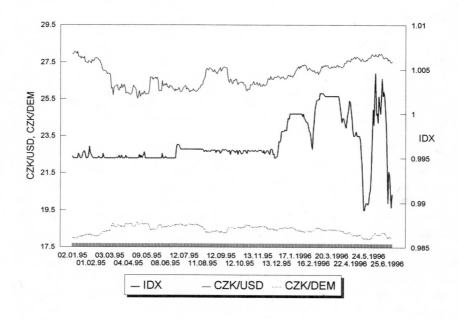

DATA: Czech National Bank.
NOTE: IDX identifies the deviation of the CZK exchange rate from the central parity (with respect to the basket = 1).

The Real Exchange Rate

The data on exchange rate developments in transition economies reveal a tendency to persistent real appreciation in the course of the transition. The rates of real appreciation differ across countries, however. These differences are due to the diverging developments in both components of real rates, i.e., in nominal exchange rates and in domestic price and cost levels vis-à-vis partner countries.

Three stages can be distinguished in the Czech developments since the start of transition. First, in 1990 the domestic CPI price level increased by only 9.9 percent (see Table 15.2). The depreciation amounted cumulatively to 95 percent. Second, during the period 1991 to 1995, on the other hand, nominal exchange rate stability with respect to the basket was maintained despite much faster domestic price level increases relative to partner countries. A persistent real exchange rate appreciation developed. Third, the resort to a wider band of ±7.5 percent in late February 1996 made more extensive fluctuations of the nominal exchange rate possible. Thus, nominal exchange rate movements started to play a role in real exchange rate changes. While episodes of nominal depreciation partially corrected for the disparity between domestic and external price level developments, this disparity further increased during periods of nominal appreciation.

The real exchange rate appreciation of the koruna has been rather high in the transition period examined here, i.e., since 1990 to mid-1997. As measured by either the CPI or PPI, the koruna's real appreciation peaked in the first months of 1997. From the base period of January 1990, cumulative real appreciation was 41.8 percent (CPI) and 36.5 percent (PPI) by February 1997. The nominal depreciation of the koruna since then—largely as a result of the induced exit from the pegged rate regime—diminished the level of real appreciation. By June 1997, the level of depreciation amounted to 27.5 percent (CPI) and 22.1 percent (PPI) from January 1990 (see Figure 15.3). Although the gap between the CPI and PPI measures has been gradually widening, their trends have continued to run roughly parallel. Accordingly, it makes little difference whether we study the process of real appreciation in terms of consumer prices or producer prices.

The cumulative real exchange rate appreciation of the Czech koruna is the largest among the countries of Central and Eastern Europe. Table 15.5 shows exchange rate appreciation based on trade-weighted indexes for five CEFTA countries over the period 1993 to the second quarter of 1997. The large real appreciation of the koruna developed in spite of a relatively favorable inflation record. The Czech economy was the first among the emerging market economies of Central and Eastern Europe to reach and sustain single-digit CPI inflation (see Table 15.2 for inflation rates in the CEFTA countries). However, although inflation was lower than in other transition countries, the nominal exchange rate of the koruna remained fixed for much longer.

Real exchange rate developments, not nominal, determine a country's competitiveness and its current account balances. The conventional wisdom views a real appreciation as a deterioration of international competitiveness with a resulting negative effect on growth and employment. Along this line of reasoning, the data on the Czech koruna's real exchange rate developments signaled an alarming loss of competitiveness and the risk of an increasingly overvalued currency, resembling developments in a number of countries whose delayed adjustments resulted in the failure of fixed exchange rate regimes and currency crises.[13] However, a priori parallels may be misleading. To assess the impact of real exchange rate appreciation and its consequences in the case of the Czech economy, the specific features of transition must be accounted for.

Figure 15.3 Effective Exchange Rates of Czech Koruna (.65 DM + .35 USD per CZK, January 1990 = 100)

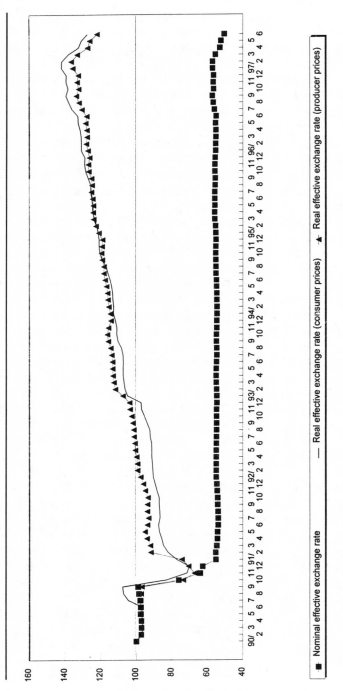

■ Nominal effective exchange rate   — Real effective exchange rate (consumer prices)   ▲ Real effective exchange rate (producer prices)

DATA: *Financial Statistical Information*, Czech National Bank; *Monthly Statistics of the Czech Republic*, Czech Statistical Office; *Main Economic Indicators*, OECD.

Table 15.5 Real Effective Exchange Rates of CEFTA Countries Currencies

CPI Based

	1993	1994	1995	1996	1997:I	1997:II
Czech Rep.	122.3	130.4	136.4	147.4	158.8	150.2
Hungary	110.5	109.7	104.6	107.6	115.0	116.1
Poland	107.6	108.0	114.9	125.5	128.9	132.4
Slovak Rep.	118.9	123.6	129.5	134.8	141.5	144.3
Slovenia	100.7	101.8	110.9	106.9	107.4	109.0

PPI based

	1993	1994	1995	1996	1997:I	1997:II
Czech Rep.	117.9	122.0	125.4	132.6	142.0	133.8
Hungary	105.9	100.6	96.0	98.9	109.0	108.5
Poland	107.4	103.1	107.4	111.4	109.4	108.0
Slovak Rep.	116.7	119.1	123.4	128.6	134.9	136.2
Slovenia	95.5	97.2	105.0	100.4	100.8	103.9

NOTE: Trade weighted indexes vis-à-vis 21 industrial countries, 1992 = 100.
DATA: Economic indicators for Eastern Europe, BIS, Basle.

The 1990 "entry" depreciation of the Czech koruna was eroded by the end of 1993. This does not necessarily imply that the exchange rate has been increasingly overvalued since. One reason is that the initial base period's level (January 1990) was possibly not an equilibrium rate. Another possibility is that the equilibrium rate has changed over the transition years.

As discussed above, the exchange rate adjustments of 1990 were calculated relative to the "commercial rate" inherited from the centrally planned economy. This rate was not a proper exchange rate, but a calculated coefficient, and accordingly was likely to diverge substantially from the equilibrium market level.

The possibility that the equilibrium real exchange rate has changed is particularly interesting. The PPP doctrine assumes a tendency in the movements of the nominal exchange rate to offset changes in the ratio of national price levels. The real exchange rate as a currency-adjusted ratio of national price levels ought, therefore, to be constant in the long run. A number of empirical studies suggest that in the case of the developed market economies, the PPP doctrine more or less holds in the long run. The observed deviations from the PPP benchmark reflect the temporary gains or losses in the country's external competitiveness. In the case of transition economies, there is in fact as yet no "long run," and the validity of PPP as a benchmark can be questioned. Specifically, the large systemic and external shocks and abrupt shifts in productivity and in income levels taking place within a relatively short time are not consistent with PPP theory relying on stable relative prices. Abrupt changes in the real dimensions of the economy, discontinuities and shocks may have shifted the equilibrium real exchange rate. A study of the contribution of real developments with associated relative price changes to "equilibrium" real exchange rate changes remains to be done.

To assess the impact of real exchange rate appreciation and its consequences for the competitiveness of an economy in transition, the specific features of the transition process must be accounted for. In the case of the Czech economy several arguments support the idea that some real appreciation was warranted: the initial level of the real exchange rate was strongly undervalued and, prior to the opening of the economy, the prices of nontradables were artificially low and productivity growth in the tradables sector significantly outpaced that in the nontradables sector. However, growing current account deficits and some other indicators suggested that the degree of real appreciation might become excessive, eroding the cost competitiveness of exporting and import-competing industries. A study assessing the character of the real appreciation, the role of individual factors—in particular the contribution of real developments and the associated relative price changes to "equilibrium" real exchange rate changes—remains to be done.

Conclusions: Is an Exchange Rate Peg Sustainable and Desirable in an Economy in Transition?

The experience of the emerging market economies of Central and Eastern Europe suggests there has been a tendency toward more flexible exchange rate regimes as the transition to a market economy advances. This certainly has been the case for the Czech Republic. Although the koruna remained rigidly pegged to a basket of currencies for a relatively long period, the substantial widening of the exchange rate band in February 1996 and especially the move to a managed floating late May 1997 represent a shift to a flexible type of regime. Such shifts from pegged exchange rate regimes to various more flexible options are a general phenomenon in emerging market economies world-wide, particularly in recent years. This leads to the question, are pegged rates no longer either sustainable or desirable given the conditions of economies in transition and for emerging market economies in general?

Pegged exchange rates have considerable potential merit for emerging market economies, in particular through the stabilizing and disciplining impact of an exchange rate anchor. Nominal exchange rate stability may, however, become a liability should the exchange rate's level substantially deviate from the underlying fundamentals. The adoption of a pegged rate regime implies that exchange rate changes are, in principle, given up as an instrument to restoring a country's external balance and competitiveness. Instead, the burden of adjustment rests with domestic variables, especially with wage rates, and success depends on their flexibility.

Theoretical arguments and the experience of exchange rate pegs in emerging market economies suggest there is a role for the exchange rate as a nominal anchor in two types of situations (compare Corden 1991). The first is in conditions of high inflation when the country is ready to disinflate. In this case the use of the exchange rate as a nominal anchor can only be temporary; in principle it should be confined to a short period of radical disinflation. The second is when countries already have a favorable price stability record and have earned credibility for their anti-inflationary policy stance. In this case there may be a role for a sustained nominal exchange rate anchor.

Given the character and magnitude of the adjustment required, Begg (1996) concludes that for countries in transition "The original anchor is unlikely to survive intact as transition continues...Where countries begin with an exchange rate peg, the issue may not be whether it should be abandoned but at what stage and with what it should be replaced" (p. 57).

The Czech experience with pegged exchange rates points to two different developments in the course of the transition that affected its benefits and costs. In the first transition stage the koruna peg was not seriously tested and it was not necessary for the central bank to defend it. This was due to two specific features of the existing environment: first, the "entry" undervaluation of the koruna made it possible for persistent real appreciation to occur without undermining competitiveness or generating an imbalance in the external accounts; second, unlike the trade sphere which underwent a sweeping liberalization, Czech financial markets had reached only a rudimentary stage of financial openness. Domestic financial markets and the financial infrastructure were only in their infancy by international standards; the koruna remained a nonconvertible currency and capital flows were subject to extensive regulation. As a result, domestic variables continued to be relatively unaffected by external financial flows, and the implied interest rate differential had only a marginal impact on capital flows.

Given this situation, monetary policy could focus on the requirements of domestic stabilization and disinflation, without being constrained by its impact on capital flows or the current account. Thus, the rudimentary stage of financial openness and transition-specific factors made a fixed exchange rate regime consistent with an autonomous monetary policy. Monetary targeting, while addressing the requirements of disinflation, worked at the same time towards nominal exchange rate stability, i.e., towards a slower flattening of the exchange rate "cushion" created through the koruna's initial undervaluation.

The institutional environment and the underlying conditions affecting the sustainability of a fixed exchange rate regime radically changed in the later stages of transition. For instance, Czech financial markets have continued to develop and are now strongly influenced by developments in foreign financial markets. The continued real appreciation of the koruna has largely eroded the earlier undervaluation of the currency. This implies that the peg could exert an increasingly binding effect on cost and price developments in the open sectors of the economy. At the same time, however, external competitiveness and current account developments have become more strongly affected by real exchange rate changes.

Moreover, although open to external influences, some of the inherent properties of an economy in transition have persisted, in particular large inflation and interest rate differentials vis-à-vis the basket currency countries. Domestic financial markets and institutions are not yet "mature," and the banking sector is burdened with bad loans.

Given these features, the growing financial openness of the Czech economy proved to be increasingly inconsistent with the existing fixed exchange rate regime. The room for monetary policy autonomy turned out to be severely constrained and, at the same time, the pressures arising from massive capital flows and from their volatility became an increasingly important destabilizing factor. The resulting policy response was a substantial widening of the exchange rate band in February 1996. This shift loosened the abovementioned constraints and enhanced the autonomy of monetary policy, providing more room for maneuver.

However useful such a regime change was, it was not a panacea. One consequence of the increased financial openness was that the exchange rate could not deviate long from "equilibrium" rates as assessed by financial market participants. The shift to a wider band alone could not substitute for the proper policy mix.

Like all transition economies, the Czech Republic has gone through a long period of real appreciation. An important question is whether this appreciation has reached the point where the Czech economy is losing competitiveness or whether the appreciation is a reflection of "equilibrium" real exchange rate changes caused by relative price and productivity developments. The long period of fixity of the Czech currency—achieved without really trying—led to the belief that real exchange rate changes would not erode competitiveness. This belief was reinforced when the currency was allowed to float within a wide band in February 1996 and the exchange rate continued to fluctuate close to the central parity, later moving to the strong side of the band.

However, the path of the nominal exchange rate reflected for some time primarily the impact of capital flows motivated by lucrative interest rate differentials. At the same time, the current account deficit was increasing, reaching the unsustainable ratio of 8.2 percent of GDP in 1996. The positive productivity differential linked to the process of catching up was not high enough to correct for the inflation differential and, consequently, the Czech fundamentals became increasingly misaligned, given the existing pegged rate. As a result, the koruna became vulnerable to the changing perceptions of market participants. In May 1997, it became target of speculative attacks, leading to the abandonment of the pegged regime and a depreciation of the koruna in the range of 10 percent with respect to the previous central parity.

Notes

This research has been supported by the European Commission's Phare/ACE Programme 1994 under contract number 94-0772-R entitled "Governance and Economic Performance in Eastern Europe." The views expressed in this chapter are those of the author and do not necessarily reflect the position of the Czech National Bank. The author wishes to thank Clas Wihlborg for his valuable comments and help in revising the text.

1. The Commonwealth of Independent States is the institutional framework linking the majority of republics of the former USSR.

2. This conclusion is broadly in line with the findings of some other studies which have pointed out the relative advantages of fixed rates in fostering macroeconomic stabilization. Among the studies covering exchange rate regimes in central and eastern Europe, see Fischer, Sahay and Végh (1997). Nevertheless, the arguments may be turned around: the more favorable inflation and stabilization records made it possible to maintain fixed rates. Whichever the implied causality may be, the feedback effects are relevant.

3. Austria and Switzerland, for example, are small open economies, closely integrated in real terms with their neighbor Germany, and subject to similar external factors. Although a similar degree of price stability and of macroeconomic performance was achieved in the past, their exchange rate regimes remained persistently entirely different.

4. "Which is better, a fixed exchange rate or a flexible one? No question in economics has been debated more fiercely or more inconclusively. The reason is that neither system is without its flaws, and nobody has been able to quantify the trade-off" (Krugman 1995:17).

5. This concept reflects the conditions in which residents acquire assets and liabilities in foreign currencies and non-residents operate in the given country's financial markets. Accordingly, the degree of financial openness reflects the ease for both inward and outward transactions, as well as for domestic transactions in foreign currencies.

6. In the case of former Czechoslovakia, the diversity of exchange rate ratios was as follows at the end of 1989, i.e., just before the start of the transition:

- official exchange rate of koruna: 7.20 per $US
- so-called commercial rate of koruna: 14.30 per $US
- parallel market rates fell in the range of 40–45 koruna per $US

It should be noted, however, that both exchange rate extremes were of only marginal relevance. The official rate was maintained unchanged during the entire postwar period (since the currency reform of 1953) despite its growing overvaluation and was of almost no real importance. Such rigidity was possible only due to administrative regulation. Parallel market rates, i.e., unofficial koruna rates quoted by some foreign banks, were heavily biased as they reflected only a very narrow and specific market segment.

7. The argument followed Friedman's (1976) logic about extracting information on relative prices in conditions of volatile inflation. "The broadcast about relative prices is, as it were, being jammed by the noise coming from the inflation broadcast" (p. 20).

8. However, the programs for some other countries in transition which started later opted for more flexible exchange rate arrangements.

9. The extent of potential error in assessing macroeconomic developments in the first transition year is demonstrated by a comparison of the predicted and actual magnitudes for 1991. For instance, a current account surplus of US$ .3 billion was achieved instead of the envisioned deficit of US$ 2.5 billion, estimated by both the government and the IMF, and the government predicted a drop of 5 to 6 percent in GDP but the actual fall was almost 15 percent, three times greater than expected. Obviously, the opposite deviations in the financial and real spheres were related; the deeper fall in GDP was "counterbalanced" by the more favorable current account result.

10. The Bank for International Settlements's *Annual Report* (1993) claimed "the Czech and Slovak Republics maintained remarkable macroeconomic stability last year...To a large extent this stability must be ascribed to the fixed exchange rate policy, which contained inflationary pressures despite a relaxation of macroeconomic policies" (pp. 39–40).

11. The effective exchange rate of the koruna appreciated in nominal terms by 1 percent between January 1994 and December 1995, from 54.6 in January 1994 to 55.7 in December 1995 (January 1990 = 100). See Hrnčíř (1995). Compared to the initial stage of transition, the December 1995 level implied a nominal appreciation of .5 percent from January 1991.

12. By mid 1996 the Czech koruna had depreciated by about 5 percent against the U.S. dollar, but gained about 2 percent against the German mark compared to the beginning of the year.

13. In the 1980s, several countries in Latin Amercia were hit by such failures, among them Chile. Learning from this experience, Chile made a competitive exchange rate and and export-oriented development its policy priorities, and it has become one of Latin America's success stories in the 1990s.

References

Begg, David K.H. 1996. "Monetary Policy in Central and Eastern Europe: Lessons After Half a Decade of Transition." IMF Working Paper No. 108, Washington D.C.: International Monetary Fund.

Bank for International Settlements. 1993. *63rd Annual Report*. Basle, June.

Corden, W. Max. 1991. "Exchange Rate Policy in Developing Countries," in Jaime de Melo and Andre Sapir, eds., *Trade Theory and Economic Reform: North, South, and East: Essays in Honor of Bela Balassa.* Pp. 224–45.Oxford and Cambridge, Mass.: Blackwell.

Fischer, Stanley, Ratna Sahay, Carlos A. Végh. 1997. "Stabilization and Growth in Transition Economies: The Early Experience," in S. Zechini, ed., *Lessons from the Economic Transition.* Paris: OECD.

Friedman, Milton. 1976. "Inflation and Unemployment: The New Dimension of Politics." The 1976 Alfred Nobel Memorial Lecture, Stockholm, December.

Hrnčíř, Miroslav. 1995. "Exchange Rate Regimes in the Stages of Transition." Conference Paper, Prague 1995.

Krugman, Paul. 1995. "Monetary Virtue Leads Two-Peso Tussle." *Financial Times*, June 13, p. 17

Schmieding, Holger. 1991. "Lending Stability to Europe's Emerging Market Economies." Kiel Working Paper No. 481.

Willett, Thomas D., Fahim Al-Marhubi, Rihad Dahil. 1992. "Currency Policies for Eastern Europe and the Commonwealth Countries." Conference Paper, July.

Williamson, John. 1991. "Advice on the Choice of an Exchange Rate Policy," in Emil-Maria Claassen, ed., *Exchange Rate Policies in Developing and Post-Socialist Countries.*" 395–403. San Francisco: ICS Press.

———. 1994. "The Management of Capital Inflows." International Finance Corporation, Conference Paper, December.

16

Exchange Rate Policy in Hungary Between 1989 and Mid 1995

Pál Gáspár

Introduction

Exchange rate policies play a crucial role in the transition from centrally planned to market economies. The choice of exchange rate regime simultaneously influences the costs and outcomes of stabilization policies and the speed, sequencing and sustainability of trade and financial sector liberalization and other important structural changes.

Unfortunately, economists do not agree on what are the most appropriate exchange rate policies for a transition economy. Theoretical considerations and lessons learned from exchange rate policies in the industrial economies and the stabilization programs of developing countries in the 1980s have produced advice ranging from the adoption of permanently fixed exchange rates via the establishment of a currency board to the use of fully flexible exchange rates. There are good arguments for each case.

Most of the transition economies initially experienced either high repressed or open inflation where exchange rate changes strongly influenced the evolution of nominal variables. Under these conditions a fixed exchange rate could be an aid to disinflation by acting as a nominal anchor in a stabilization program. Proponents of this view point to the relatively rapid stabilization of high inflation in Argentina after 1991 or in Israel in the 1980s following the adoption of pegged exchange rates.

Flexible exchange rates, however, eliminate the need to determine the exchange rate's equilibrium value at the start of the stabilization program. In transition economies the factors affecting the equilibrium value change rapidly in the face of structural and financial reforms, and the values of currencies to which the currency might be pegged also vary. Consequently, fixed exchange rates may rapidly become misaligned. Flexible exchange rates correct disequilibrium situations without requiring a parity revaluation that could have sizable credibility costs.

The majority of liberalizing Eastern European countries initially chose some type of fixed exchange rate, either a currency board (Estonia) or some weaker form of pegged rate (Poland, the former Czechoslovakia). A few countries established flexible exchange rate regimes (Slovenia, Bulgaria and Latvia).

In contrast, at the beginning of its economic transition Hungary adopted an adjustable peg. Under central planning exchange rates had become overvalued, so almost all the transition economies had to sharply devalue their currencies early on. The initial depreciation of the exchange rate was followed by the establishment of a fixed or floating exchange rate regime. In Hungary, which adopted an adjustable pegged exchange rate, the exchange rate adjustment was smoother and the dynamics of exchange rate changes also differed.

This chapter analyzes Hungary's exchange rate policy. It discusses why an adjustable peg regime was chosen, examines the factors explaining the exchange rate regime's development, and analyzes its macroeconomic effects. During the time the adjustable peg was in place, the objectives of exchange rate policy frequently shifted between increasing external competitiveness to improve the current account and mitigating the inflationary pressures stemming from price liberalization, structural reforms, and undisciplined macroeconomic policies. The major shifts in exchange rate policy and their characteristic features are discussed below.

The last section draws some conclusions regarding the use of exchange rate policy in transitional economies. More specifically, I discuss the changes in macroeconomic policies required for Hungary to successfully stabilize under the "forward-looking" crawling peg regime adopted in March 1995.

The Choice of the Adjustable Peg Regime

Hungary had balance of payments difficulties during most of the 1980s stemming from high debt service and weak trade performance. Between 1987 and 1989 Hungary eliminated a substantial number of price controls and import restrictions.[1] Import growth stemming from import liberalization and the declining competitiveness of Hungarian exports in the light of substantial price increases led to pressing balance of payments difficulties. An exchange rate policy of stepwise devaluation was implemented to improve the trade balance and the competitiveness of the trade sector. Consequently, the exchange rate did not become as overvalued in Hungary as in other Eastern

Bloc economies, and no significant initial adjustment was required to establish a unified market exchange rate.

Thus, compared to its Eastern Bloc neighbors Hungary had a relatively open economy and a less severely overvalued exchange rate when it began the transition to a market economy. The policy of steep devaluation followed by exchange rate fixing adopted by many of the other transition economies was viewed as inappropriate to Hungary's situation. Hungary's policymakers recognized that new rounds of import and price liberalization would lead to high inflation and exchange rate depreciation. But since the growth of domestic prices and wages was viewed as sensitive to exchange rate changes, it was thought that significant devaluation of the forint had to be avoided because the temporary gains in competitiveness would be rapidly neutralized by compensating wage growth.

Because further liberalization of prices and imports was foreseen, the adoption of a fixed exchange rate did not seem advisable either. It was clear at the beginning of the transition that the liberalization of the economy would be accompanied—even with credible and sustainable macroeconomic policies—by price increases due to changes in relative price structures and supply- and demand-side disturbances. Given the expectation of future price realignments, a fixed exchange rate regime did not appear to be sustainable over the longer term. Moreover, it was thought exchange rate changes were only weakly correlated with inflationary expectations. If this were so, an anchor based on a fixed exchange rate would do little to alter expectations.

The use of flexible exchange rates was rejected because Hungary lacked the sophisticated financial markets and institutions needed for efficient functioning of foreign exchange markets. There was no interbank foreign currency market, the use of export revenues was restricted by the government, and spot and forward markets did not exist. Although the Hungarian government planned to eventually move towards a more flexible exchange rate system, it initially assumed that institutional constraints would prevent the smooth functioning of a foreign exchange market. Moreover, the adoption of flexible exchange rates would have required greater convertibility of the forint, the establishment of which might have necessitated a larger devaluation than seemed desirable in light of growing inflation.

The monetary authorities also feared the exchange rate volatility that flexible exchange rates might introduce. Hungary had relatively liberal regulations regarding capital inflows and domestic capital markets were very thin, so the possibility of destabilizing speculative capital flows was seen as high. As the experiences of developing countries have shown, this could have created macroeconomic problems. Moreover, the difference between the speed of adjustment in financial markets and in real markets was thought to be much larger in Hungary than in the developing countries, so policymakers feared the problems would be even worse in Hungary.

Thus Hungary's initial stabilization program was not based on an exchange rate anchor; rather the growth of the nominal money supply played that role.[2] Monetary policy had been restrictive since 1988 and money-supply growth was moderate. Besides, compared to other transitioning economies the link between nominal variables and exchange rate changes seemed to be less direct in Hungary because of the lack of formal or informal wage or price indexation and the significant dollarization of the economy.

Evolution of Exchange Rate Policy

Under an adjustable peg regime the two factors that most determine the frequency and magnitude of exchange rate adjustments are the trade balance and inflation rate. Because the evolution of the trade balance depends partly on changes in the real exchange rate, and the value of the real exchange rate depends on inflation, exchange rate policy has different outcomes depending on its effect on the real exchange rate.

In Hungary the often conflicting goals of inflation control and external balance were given different weights between 1989 and 1995. As a result, exchange rate policy varied substantially. The evolution of Hungary's exchange rate policy can be described according to its emphasis on the external balance or inflation and the associated real exchange rate developments. Over a period of six years exchange rate policy falls into five distinguishable periods, the first four falling under the adjustable peg regime and the last during the collapse of the adjustable peg and the switch to a crawling peg:

1. the pre-transition period of strong nominal devaluations and real exchange rate depreciation against a basket of currencies between 1988 and mid 1990;
2. a period of relaxed domestic macroeconomic policies and neutral real exchange rate developments between mid 1990 and the end of 1991;
3. a period of irregular small devaluations remaining below the inflation differentials between Hungary and its major trading partners, leading to real exchange rate appreciation between 1992 and mid 1993;
4. a period of irregular but more frequent devaluations leading to the real exchange rate depreciating at an increasing rate from mid 1993 to the end of 1994; and
5. the collapse of the adjustable peg regime and its replacement by a "forward-looking" crawling peg regime in March 1995.

The Period of Pre-Transition Adjustments (1988 to Mid 1990)

The primary goal of economic policy in the late 1980s was to reduce the macroeconomic imbalances following the period of unsustainable economic growth between 1985 and 1987 and price and import liberalization after 1988. At this stage, exchange rate policy was directed at improving the trade balance and regulating the increase of imports after the relaxation of trade restrictions.[3]

Since fiscal policy was passive, the options for stabilization policy were restricted; therefore stabilization was based on restrictive monetary policy, wage controls, and exchange rate adjustments. The use of exchange rate policy was important. Under the program of import liberalization Hungary had abolished quantitative restrictions on imports, but did not introduce tariffs to replace them.[4] This left the authorities with no tool but devaluation to regulate the increase in import demand. Unease about rising imports coupled with problems servicing foreign debt led the government to under-take devaluations that resulted in significant real devaluation of the currency. Large devaluations were connected with rounds of price and import liberal-ization, while smaller devaluations were aimed at improving the competitive-ness of exports and reducing the trade deficit.[5] By leading to a decline in real wages and incomes, devaluation reduced domestic demand and so improved the trade balance.

Thus, exchange rate adjustments played an important role both in reducing the growth of import demand and in improving the competitiveness of the trade sector. The primary concern of exchange rate policy was the trade balance, and less emphasis was attached to reducing gradually accelerating inflation.

What were the results of this exchange rate policy? The real devaluation significantly increased the price competitiveness of Hungarian exports and improved the trade balance. Devaluation reduced the demand for imports and helped to sustain trade liberalization without strong resistance from pressure groups. It also reduced the spread between market and official exchange rates, thus weakening currency substitution, and gave room for later exchange rate appreciation to restrain price increases related to liberalization measures.

The exchange rate policy also produced some unfavorable results. Be-cause the devaluations were tied to announcements of new rounds of import and price liberalization, they were easily predicted by market participants, leading to adverse expectations, surges in import demand and delays in exports. When the devaluations then occurred, they justified these expecta-tions, resulting in a vicious circle between exchange rate adjustment and inflation.

Relaxing Macroeconomic Policies and Nominal Exchange Stability (Mid 1990 to 1991)

After the first period of real devaluation, exchange rate policy took a more neutral stance with respect to real exchange rate developments. This shift is apparent in changes in the frequency and magnitude of devaluations shown in Table 16.1. Whereas in 1989 the forint was devalued nine times, there were only five devaluations in 1991 and 1992. Compared to earlier exchange rate adjustments these devaluations were small, in the range of 1 to 3 percent, with the exception of a 15 percent devaluation in January 1991, which was related to the last round of price and import liberalization.[6] Moreover, starting in mid 1990, exchange rate adjustments became more dispersed—the intention was to reduce their impact on expectations and underlying inflation.

The main reason for the shift in exchange rate policy was that it became more important to restrain the inflationary consequences of simultaneous subsidy reduction and price liberalization; and exchange rate policy was directed more towards this goal. The government assumed that price liberalization would have a strong impact on inflation even if its macroeconomic policies remained firmly anti-inflationary and credible. Other factors besides liberalization—for instance the growing fiscal deficit and the relaxing of monetary and income policies—also forced the central bank to use exchange rate policy as an anti-inflationary device.

TABLE 16.1 Exchange Rate Adjustments, 1989–1994

Dates	Devaluation[a]	Dates	Devaluation
1989		*1992*	
March 21	5.00	March 16	1.90
April 14	6.00	June 23	1.60
July 18	0.50	November 9	1.90
July 25	0.10	*1993*	
July 9	0.10	February 12	1.90
August 1	0.07	March 26	2.90
August 8	0.53	June 7	1.90
August 15	0.20	July 9	3.00
December 15	10.00	September 29	4.50
1990		*1994*	
January 31	1.00	January 3	1.00
February 6	2.00	February 16	2.60
February 20	2.00	May 12	1.00
1991		June 10	1.20
January 7	15.00	August 25	8.00
November 8	5.80	October 11	1.10

[a]Rate of forint devaluation against the basket of currencies.
SOURCE: National Bank of Hungary *Monthly Report,* No. 12, 1994.

From 1987 to 1990 monetary policy was rather restrictive, but starting in 1990 it was relaxed (see Table 16.2). This change was due to the negative consequences of restrictive monetary policy on the output performance and financing of the enterprise sector in the late 1980s. Tight money had produced a credit crunch, and one way for firms to cope with the lack of monetary financing was not to pay their bills. This was reflected in the growth of inter-enterprise payment arrears and outstanding payments of the enterprise sector to the banking system. The easing of monetary policy was intended to slow this process. Another reason for the shift in monetary policy was the collapse of domestic incomes and demand after 1990, leading to a decline in imports. Consequently it was thought monetary policy did not have to be as restrictive as before, since income and domestic demand fell without further restrictions. As monetary policy was loosened, policymakers thought that exchange rate adjustments had to be moderated to avoid creating cost-push inflation during a period of rapid price liberalization.

The greater emphasis in exchange rate policy on inflation control was also related to shifts in the competitiveness of the trade sector after the collapse of the CMEA.[7] With the simultaneous collapse of the CMEA and domestic demand, the monetary authorities assumed that exports would be driven more by non-price factors and that the exchange rate's influence on export performance would be smaller.

These developments meant that production would have to switch from the nontradables to the tradables sector and from the relatively closed former CMEA markets towards those in developed countries. Moreover, it was thought that easier access to imports used in production and the inflow of foreign direct investment might stimulate the competitiveness of Hungarian exporters; therefore the competitiveness of the tradables sector and the trade balance might improve without further significant exchange rate adjustments.

TABLE 16.2 The Development of Monetary Variables (percentage change over the previous year)

	1989	1990	1991	1992	1993	1994
Domestic Credit Supply	16.2	11.1	7.4	10.4	18.4	19.7
Money Supply	14.0	28.7	28.7	27.4	18.1	13.7
Inflation Rate	17.0	28.9	35.0	23.0	22.5	18.8
Change in Nominal GDP	21.0	21.2	11.3	21.6	18.7	21.2
Money Supply in GDP	41.5	44.0	50.9	53.4	54.2	n.a

SOURCE: National Bank of Hungary, 1995.

This shift in goals led to greater nominal exchange rate stability and the real exchange rate remained basically neutral throughout 1991, as shown in Table 16.3. But the real exchange rate concealed significant swings in other variables. The neutral real exchange rate was the simultaneous product of nominal exchange rate adjustment and growing inflation.[8]

At first glance the outcome of the shift in exchange rate policy appeared successful as both the inflation and trade balance targets were met. After the initial jump associated with price liberalization, the inflation rate declined relatively rapidly.[9] Simultaneously an increasing gap emerged between the consumer and producer price indices (see Table 16.4). The exchange rate policy contributed to this gap: with liberalized imports the modest exchange rate adjustments held down producer price increases while consumer prices were growing due to the impact of other factors.[10] The increasing gap between the consumer and the producer price indices later had a significant impact on the evolution of the real exchange rate, as discussed below.

The trade policy goal was also met as exports rapidly increased and a modest trade surplus was achieved. The non-price factors forcing domestic producers to convert their production from the nontradables towards the tradables sector seemed to work as policymakers had assumed.

Notwithstanding these positive changes, two concerns could be raised regarding the exchange rate policy. First, the inflation and trade balance developments were influenced more by exogenous factors than by exchange rate policy. Second, the growth of exports was not based on increasing competitiveness, and therefore its sustainability was questionable. Finally, the exchange rate policy could not meet inflation and external balance targets simultaneously in the longer term: one would have to be sacrificed. This became even more clear since new inflationary pressures were building as fiscal and monetary policies became more expansive.

TABLE 16.3 Changes in the Average Nominal and Real Exchange Rates Between 1988 and 1993 (changes against the average of the previous year)

	1988	1989	1990	1991	1992	1993	1994
Nominal Change against the Basket	8.6	12.0	16.1	16.3	8.4	18.2	24.5
Real Exchange Rate Index of the Forint Using PPI Index as Deflator	107.6	100.6	98.7	89.2	100.1	102.9	111.0

SOURCE: National Bank of Hungary *Monthly Report,* No. 11, 1994.

TABLE 16.4   Change in Price Indices Between 1988 and 1994 (previous year's index = 100)

Year	Consumer Prices	Industrial Producer Prices	Domestic Sales Prices of Industry	Export Sales Prices
1988	115.5	104.7	104.1	106.0
1989	116.9	115.4	1113.4	118.2
1990	128.8	122.0	124.2	112.4
1991	135.0	132.6	131.9	130.2
1992	122.9	112.3	109.7	116.0
1993	122.5	110.8	110.7	112.3
1994	118.8	111.3	110.2	n.a

SOURCE: National Bank of Hungary, 1995

Period of Strong Real Exchange Appreciation (1992 to Mid 1993)

When Hungarian policymakers realized the inflationary character of their macroeconomic policies, there was a new shift in the primary goal of the exchange rate policy. From mid 1992, for the following year and a half, a policy of stable nominal and appreciating real exchange rates was pursued using small, unexpected and irregular devaluations. In 1992 and the first half of 1993, the nominal exchange rate was devalued on six occasions, between 1.5 and 2.9 percent each time.

The primary goal of exchange rate policy was now the reduction of inflation. At the beginning of the transition period, stabilization policy was money based, with money supply growth playing the role of nominal anchor. This changed as monetary policy became first neutral and then slightly expansive from 1992 to 1993. This shift is explained by three factors.

First, although inflation was falling, the output costs of disinflation were high and the prospects for economic recovery weak. This led the central bank to change tack. Jettisoning its firm anti-inflationary stance, the bank tried to speed the recovery from the post-stabilization recession by reducing interest rates to stimulate domestic demand and private sector capital formation.

Second, notwithstanding the legal independence of the central bank, it was under increasing pressure from the Treasury to reduce the debt-service costs associated with the growth of the fiscal deficit and high nominal interest rates. Lower interest rates were achieved partly by increasing money supply growth rates and partly through an agreement between the National Bank, the Ministry of Finance and the commercial banks to reduce nominal interest rates in a coordinated way.

Finally, both foreign direct investment and unrequited transfers grew resulting in significant foreign currency inflows. These flows increased the money supply because they were not sterilized; the National Bank feared the impact sterilization might have on interest rates.

The loosening of monetary policy contributed to an acceleration of inflation after mid 1992. More inflationary pressure came from further increases in the fiscal deficit, which reached 6 to 7 percent of GDP in 1992 and 1993, and from output constraints in agriculture and the resulting increases in agricultural prices.

Since the money supply no longer acted as an explicit anchor, exchange rate policy had to replace monetary policy as an anti-inflationary tool. The situation was exacerbated by the increasingly negative impact price increases exerted on the fiscal balance. Inflation eroded revenues due to the Olivera-Tanzi effect,[11] while expenditures—particularly debt service due to high nominal interest rates—were increasing.[12]

Finally, the shift in the goals of exchange rate policy was related to the inflow of foreign capital. Although policymakers perceived the need for stable exchange rates to reduce the risks to foreign investors, the inflow of foreign capital itself contributed to the growth of underlying inflation by increasing the money supply and domestic demand, and the shift in exchange rate policy was partly in order to offset this impact.

Nominal exchange rate stability coupled with growing inflation led to real exchange rate appreciation. Estimates of the size of the appreciation differ depending on which deflator is used, but it was about 10 percent using the producer price index and around 18 percent using consumer prices.

Accompanying this was a sharp reversal in the trade balance. As shown in Table 16.5, the earlier surplus was replaced by a slight deficit of $48 million in 1992, followed by a sharp decrease in exports and a huge trade

TABLE 16.5 Hungary's Balance of Payments Between 1988 and 1994 (in $US million)

	1989	1990	1991	1992	1993	1994
Trade Balance	537	348	189	-48	-3623	-3853
Current Account	-1437	127	267	324	-3455	-3500
Gross Debt	20390	21270	22658	21438	24560	28100
Net Debt	14900	15938	14554	13276	16927	23100
Currency Reserves	1725	1166	4017	4381	6736	6027
Debt-Service Ratio	38.5	43.2	32.0	31.9	38.1	n.a.

SOURCE: National Bank of Hungary, 1994.

deficit of $3.5 billion in 1993. But the decline in exports and worsening of the trade balance was not caused by exchange rate policy alone: it was partly due to supply side and institutional problems.[13] The deterioration of the trade balance was even greater than the decline in exports because import demand was rising due to growing domestic consumption and a slight increase in investment.

Exchange Rate Policy in Recovery (Mid 1993 to 1994)

The stance of exchange rate policy changed again after mid 1993, reflecting concern with macroeconomic developments. In 1993, and even more in 1994, the Hungarian economy presented a confusing macroeconomic picture. Beginning in the last quarter of 1993, the economy seemed to have put the initial transition recession and the post-stabilization stagnation behind it. Real GDP growth resumed after four years of contraction, increasing by 2.5 percent in 1994. The recovery was accompanied by a significant increase in investment and productivity, while consumption increased due to increasing real wages and incomes.

Unfortunately, the recovery was accompanied by increasing macroeconomic imbalances. The most pressing were the growth of the fiscal deficit and public debt. The deficit reached 7.5 percent of GDP in 1994 and public debt was over 90 percent of GDP. Net foreign debt also increased by about $10 billion between 1992 and 1994; its growth was related to the increasing current account deficit, itself partly caused by the rise in foreign indebtedness of the enterprise sector and of the central government.[14] The reduction of inflation achieved in 1992 was reversed, and consumer price inflation remained at a relatively high level of around 20 percent.

As the trade deficit soared and its long-term financing became doubtful, exchange rate policy once again focused on improving the trade balance. This could be achieved by a shift from maintaining a stable nominal exchange rate to maintaining a stable real exchange rate. Devaluations were undertaken to bridge the differences between domestic inflation and inflation in major trading partners. Exchange rate adjustments were based more on the higher consumer price index than the lower producer price index, speeding up the rate of devaluation and even causing a real depreciation.

The forint was devalued more frequently than in the years 1990 through 1992. Whereas the forint was devalued five times in 1991 and 1992, it was devalued nine times between mid 1993 and the end of 1994. Interspersed with the small, frequent devaluations were a couple of larger adjustments. The first, in September 1993, devalued the forint by 4.5 percent and the second, in August 1994, by 8 percent. While it was realized these devaluations would increase inflation and inflationary expectations, these concerns were overridden by two major problems.

First, the trade balance did not improve following the small devaluations, so policymakers assumed larger adjustments were required. However, export growth was only weakly dependent on exchange rate devaluation because other factors constrained it more. Furthermore, the growing import demand could not be reduced much by devaluation in the absence of credible and consistent macroeconomic polices. Thus the effectiveness of these exchange rate adjustments was questionable. The major problem was that these devaluations were not accompanied by restrictive macroeconomic policies. They fueled inflation while their possible positive impact on the trade sector was rapidly eroded by the increase of domestic wages and incomes.

Second, larger devaluations reflected the increasing impact of speculation against the forint. Speculation in the foreign exchange market was strong before the September 1993 devaluation, but—after a temporary decline—it became extremely strong in 1994, fueled by the inconsistency between the actual exchange rate policy and that implied by macroeconomic policies. Furthermore, this was an election year, so uncertainty about a possible change of the government and future macroeconomic policy increased. The news of worsening trade and fiscal deficits and a further increase of inflation resulted in renewed speculation against the forint. Because the foreign exchange market for the forint was thin, relatively small changes in demand and supply conditions could create strong speculative pressures against which the intervention of the National Bank was insufficient.

The National Bank tried to reduce adverse speculation and stave off devaluation by increasing the prime interest rate.[15] This drove up Hungarian interest rates in general and the interest expenditures of the central government. The National Bank finally had to devalue the currency when demand for forint assets could not be increased any further with interest rate adjustments. These exchange rate devaluations justified past speculation and therefore speculation increased.

The shifts in exchange rate policy are reflected in changes in exchange rate indices. Nominal devaluation reached 18 percent in 1993 and 24.5 percent in 1994 resulting in a real exchange rate depreciation of approximately 2 percent in 1993 and 11 percent in 1994, as measured by the producer price index. This development is a clear reversal of the situation prevailing in 1992 and the first half of 1993, but the intended macroeconomic results were not achieved.

The trade balance continued to worsen in 1994, reaching a $3.9 billion deficit. But unlike 1993, when the primary reason was the decline of exports, in 1994 exports and imports grew by 20 and 16 percent in dollar terms. Exchange rate adjustment can only partly explain the increase of exports; the growth of international demand was more responsible for its increase. The devaluations failed to reduce import demand, which grew rapidly due to the increase of investment and consumption.

The worsening trade balance was accompanied by an acceleration of inflation. Although other factors—such as the adjustment of certain administered prices—also contributed to inflation, the real devaluation of the domestic currency played a significant role. Devaluation was especially inflationary because domestic incomes grew at a rate far exceeding the growth of productivity, which partly justified price increases. At the same time, the fiscal deficit remained high without any signs of correction.

The macroeconomic problems were left uncorrected in the first quarter of 1995, leading to the collapse of the adjustable peg regime. The trade and fiscal deficits reached unsustainable levels and financing requirements were far above acceptable levels. Price increases accelerated and currency substitution increased, while savings in the national currency declined. The Mexican crisis in early 1995 only strengthened concern over the twin deficits. The soundness of macroeconomic policies and the continued availability of foreign financing were questioned. At the same time privatization was temporary halted and political uncertainties increased following the resignation of the minister of finance.

All these problems resulted in a run against the forint, and the foreign exchange market could no longer be calmed by small (1 to 2 percent) adjustments. Thus speculation and macroeconomic imbalances finally led to the replacement of the adjustable peg regime by a crawling peg.

The Shift to a Crawling Peg Regime (March 1995)

The worsening domestic and external imbalances required the implementation of a strong stabilization policy. In March 1995 new policies were introduced aimed at reducing the fiscal deficit from 9 percent of GDP to 6 percent and the current account deficit from $3.9 billion to $2.5 billion. The fiscal deficit was to be corrected by expenditure cuts and increased revenues from a new import surcharge and a reduction in tax evasion. To improve the trade balance, a 9 percent devaluation and the introduction of an 8 percent import surcharge were announced.

This new devaluation of the forint, the third in 1995 following two small corrections in January and February, signaled the abandonment of the adjustable peg regime. Since 1994 speculation against the forint had been a major factor behind exchange rate adjustment. This had led to high interest rates, as the central bank sought to defend the currency, and capital flight, reflecting expectations of further devaluation. By March the adjustable peg was simply no longer sustainable because it had fully lost its credibility.

At this point a crawling peg regime was instituted. The March devaluation was accompanied by the announcement of future exchange rate adjustments. A 1.9 percent monthly devaluation of the forint in the second quarter of 1995 was to be followed by monthly devaluations of 1.3 percent for the rest of the year. The devaluations were planned against the basket of currencies that the forint had been pegged to and were to be implemented daily. The aim was to produce a nominal devaluation of approximately 28 percent for the year, implying a sizable real exchange rate depreciation.

The purpose of a declining rate of devaluation was to reduce inflationary expectations by putting stronger pressure on price increases in the tradables sector. In addition, since real exchange rate developments would be more predictable, it was expected that investment in the tradables sector would increase. Finally, by preannouncing the size of future devaluations, it was hoped that the volatility of interest rates might be reduced and that the stabilizing impact of the new exchange rate regime would also result in lower interest rates.

The use of a crawling peg was not without recognized dangers. First, it was questionable how successful this exchange rate regime would be in improving the trade balance. Microeconomic studies revealed that the most significant impediments to Hungarian exports were the lack of credit and export guarantees and outdated infrastructure. Until these factors were corrected and as long as the import content of exports remained high, the impact of a real exchange rate depreciation remained doubtful.

Second, the shift to a crawling peg would—at least temporarily—increase the already slightly growing inflation rate. The experience of economies applying the crawling peg (for example, Poland) suggested that this regime might produce cost-push inflation.

Third, the shift from an adjustable peg to a crawling peg would not necessarily solve the problem of speculation against the forint. As long as the announced devaluations were consistent with expected inflation the credibility of the exchange rate policy might be maintained. This depended on the success of the anti-inflationary policy in reducing inflation below the preannounced rate of devaluation.

The initial results of the shift to a crawling peg regime were quite favorable. The new exchange rate regime was rapidly regarded as credible by market participants and remained so in the first six months of its operation. Speculative attacks on the forint ceased. Although domestic interest rates remained above the levels predicted by international returns plus the announced currency depreciation, the difference declined markedly. The credibility of the exchange rate policy was enhanced by the planned shift in July 1995 to a lower monthly rate of devaluation of 1.3 percent a month. It is thought that the monthly devaluation rate will be further reduced in 1996 to 1.2 percent per month.

The relative stability of exchange rate developments contributed to the improving macroeconomic performance. The introduction of the crawling peg and the steep devaluation of the currency produced a sizable real exchange depreciation that supported the rapid recovery of exports and a sharp improvement in the balance of payments. The competitiveness of the tradables sector was also enhanced by a 10 percent decrease in real wages.

The decreases in trade and current account deficits were accompanied by a decline in the fiscal deficit from 9 percent of GDP in 1994 to 4 percent in 1995 due to high revenues from privatization and an increase in revenues from the tradables sector. However, inflation accelerated, reaching 29 percent per annum.

Conclusions

Special features of the Hungarian economy influenced the design of its exchange rate policy. It was unique among the economies in transition in adopting an adjustable peg regime at the outset of the transition period. The lessons to be drawn from the Hungarian experience may be summarized as follows.

1. It might be beneficial for a transition economy to adopt an adjustable peg system if monetary discipline is not very strong and future changes in both the external balance and inflation are highly likely. In this situation the equilibrium real exchange rate will be rapidly changing, and this will require frequent adjustment of the nominal rate. A credible adjustable peg regime may reduce the costs to the trade balance of using exchange rate policy to pursue inflation goals, and vice versa.
2. To maintain the adjustable peg regime, domestic macroeconomic policies must be consistent with low inflation and a favorable balance of payments. High and persistent budget deficits and a monetary policy inconsistent with exchange rate goals undermine the credibility and sustainability of any type of pegged exchange rate regime. Strong speculation emerges easily, possibly leading to a run on the currency that destabilizes the exchange rate regime.
3. Although the adjustable peg regime allows some scope to pursue simultaneously trade balance improvement and inflation reduction, exchange rate and macroeconomic policies should be determined by which of these goals has priority. Both consistency and credibility problems arise if first one and then the other goal is pursued or if exchange rate policy tries to meet both goals at once.
4. It is important to consider the exogenous factors and the external shocks affecting the evolution of the exchange rate. As transition economies become increasingly open, the importance of external shocks also grows and these may strongly affect both exchange rate developments and exchange rate policy.

Thus, the long-term success of Hungary's crawling peg regime hinges on two crucial factors. First, it depends on the success of incomes policies. Can real wages be kept under control in order to reduce pressure on domestic inflation? Second, macroeconomic policies must focus on controlling inflation. One thing this will require is that the Hungarian government carry out long-postponed fiscal adjustments and reduce its public sector borrowing requirements. Successful fiscal adjustment is the critical test for the credibility of macroeconomic policies and the crawling peg regime.

Notes

1. Due to the reforms of the 1980s, about 40 percent of both prices and imports had been liberalized by 1988.

2. The stabilization programs in other transition economies generally used the exchange rate as the basic anchor, supplemented by strict incomes policies.

3. In comparison with many developing countries, trade liberalization in Hungary was rapid and radical, but compared to other transition economies (such as the former Czechoslovakia or Poland) it was gradual.

4. While the speed of import liberalization was relatively slow, its impact on domestic production, prices, and wage changes was substantial and rapid.

5. In this period the national currency was devalued against a basket of currencies representing the currency composition of foreign trade in the previous year. After December 1991, the composition of the basket changed to the U.S. dollar and the ECU, equally weighted.

6. By the end of 1991 more than 90 percent of prices and imports were liberalized.

7. Council for Mutual Economic Assistance—this was a trading system consisting roughly of the Soviet Union and its satellites.

8. The change in the dynamics of inflation was due to price liberalization, the shift in the stance of monetary policy, and the emergence of a significant fiscal deficit reaching 5 percent of GDP.

9. Price increases reached their highest monthly level in June 1991 when the CPI index grew by 35.6 percent per annum. After that the CPI inflation rate started to decline, approaching 20 percent in mid 1992.

10. Besides the exchange rate policy, this gap was also related to the increase in the share of the service sector in the national economy and to the increasing role of indirect taxes that had differential impacts on the growth of producer and consumer prices. The differences in the changes in the consumer and producer price indices were also related to the opening of the economy, as the producer price index reflected the growth of prices in the tradables sector restrained by import competition while the consumer price index was more determined by price changes in the nontradables sector.

11. According to the Olivera-Tanzi effect, real tax revenues decline with growing inflation due to collection lags.

12. The share of interest expenditures among all expenditures of the central government increased from 13 percent in 1991 to 30 percent in 1994.

13. The supply side problems arose from the drop in agricultural production, which had formerly accounted for 25 percent of exports. The institutional aspect of the export decline is related to the adoption of tough bankruptcy procedures, leading to the liquidation of thousands of state-owned and private enterprises. It is estimated that the enterprises in bankruptcy produced 30 percent of Hungarian exports in 1992 and 1993. The liquidation of these unviable firms led to decreasing exports.

14. The latter reflected the excess of public sector borrowing requirements over the amount of available household savings, while the former was the result of the strong crowding-out effect of the fiscal deficit.

15. The prime rate reached 25 and 28 percent when forecast inflation was around 20 percent.

17

Poland's Exchange Rate Policy in the 1990s

Tadeusz Kowalski and Renata Stawarska

Introduction

In this chapter we examine the role of exchange rate policy in the Polish economic transformation from 1989 to 1996. The analysis emphasizes the impact of exchange rate policy on real exchange rates, and their impact on foreign trade and on currency reserves. The relationships between monetary and exchange rate policies are also examined.

Through 1989 exchange rate policy was largely passive, but beginning in 1990 the exchange rate became the nominal anchor of a new stabilization package. Within a few years internal and external developments made it impossible to keep the nominal exchange rate fixed. Attempts to reconcile the conflicting goals of internal stability and balance of payments equilibrium led to the adoption of a more flexible preannounced crawling peg regime—in effect, the adoption of a real exchange rate anchor. This step increased the transparency of and created more stable conditions for decision making. In 1995 large capital inflows and a rapid increase in the level of currency reserves forced the monetary authorities to liberalize currency regulations and introduce a wider crawling band for the exchange rate.

Poland Before Stabilization

The primary symptoms of internal disequilibrium before 1989 were shortages of goods and services. These shortages resulted from price controls leading to an insufficient supply (producer's market), lack of competition from abroad, expansive macroeconomic policy and real wage growth, and overexpansion of the money stock. Together these developments led to a monetary overhang reflecting the existing disproportions.[1]

Inflation in Poland accelerated in 1987 and 1988 as a result of substantial rises in officially controlled prices and compensating increases in wages, along with soft financing of the economy. In 1987 inflation ran at an annual rate of 25 percent; in 1988 it climbed as high as 85 percent. Expansionary macroeconomic policy in 1988 and 1989 brought increases in real wages (42.2 percent higher in June 1989 than in June 1987) and a growing monetary overhang resulting from the simultaneous policy of expansion and price controls accompanied by shortages.[2] (Nominal demand could not be met by "official" supply and a black market emerged in response to this.) The budget deficit in 1989 reached 4.3 percent of GNP (Wernik 1992). The result was galloping inflation in the summer of 1989, increasing to 50 percent per month. The Solidarity government of Tadeusz Mazowiecki faced not only the problem of introducing radical systemic changes but also constraining hyperinflation.

Some of Poland's troubles were the fault of poor policies in previous decades. In the 1970s Poland experienced a considerable inflow of foreign loans. These were supposed to be repaid following the structural, pro-export transformation of the economy; however, in the absence of reforms and systemic transformation, those credits were largely allocated for consumption. In the short run the high consumption this allowed strengthened the government's position, but the policy resulted in a huge foreign debt, the servicing of which was a serious burden on the state budget. Above $40 billion of the present debt consists of state-guaranteed loans (the Paris Club) and approximately $13 billion in loans granted by private banks (the London Club).[3] Foreign trade was conducted with "areas" that were differentiated in terms of the currency: the transfer ruble in "area I," the U.S. dollar and other hard currencies in "area II." With strict control by the state it was possible to maintain external balance, but greater liberalization of foreign trade led to a deficit in hard currency trade in 1989 (see Table 17.1).

Trade liberalization in 1990 and economic transformation led to profound changes in the geographical structure of foreign trade. The introduction of U.S. dollar settlements together with the collapse of the Soviet economy (limiting its ability to export) caused a surplus in Poland's trade with the former Soviet Union which could not be cleared.[4] Moreover, existing barter agreements expired in 1990, leading to a drastic decline in trade.

Economic reforms created a role for the exchange rate in determining export competitiveness. The basic goal of the so-called submarginal exchange rate was to ensure the profitability of exports, which would balance the value of the "indispensable" imports. Its value was adjusted on the basis of foreign trade volume. In practice such an exchange rate ensured the profitability of only a part of exports. Further aims were to prevent the rise of domestic

TABLE 17.1 Poland's Exports and Imports: Settlements in Rubles and U.S. Dollars

	1987	1988	1989
$US Settlement (millions)			
Exports	7.072	8.297	8.446
Imports	7.005	8.351	9.161
Transfer Ruble Settlement (millions)			
Exports	10.950	11.938	2.217
Imports	10.935	10.819	10.106

SOURCE: Statistical Yearbooks (*Roczniki Statystyczne)* 1988, 1989, 1990 of the Central Statistical Office.

prices by holding down the price of imports and to push forward positive transformations in the structure and profitability of exports and production.

The overvalued official exchange rate combined with the lack of convertibility required export subsidies and import charges to achieve the desired trade balance. Due to payment difficulties (servicing the foreign debt required a growing trade surplus), the rate of exchange was "strengthened" by introducing export tax breaks and a system of retained hard currency allowances for exporters. This system of subsides and taxes made it possible to maintain the overvalued exchange rate of the Polish zloty, but it was both complicated and arbitrary and made the real profitability of foreign trade difficult to assess.

The initial situation before the introduction of the stabilization program is illustrated in Table 17.2. Lack of proper public finance discipline is reflected by the budget deficit to GNP ratio and by the rate of inflation. "Dollarization" (currency substitution) resulting from the inconvertibility of the currency is illustrated by the ratio of the official to the black market exchange rate.

The Stabilization Program of 1990

Deep macroeconomic disequilibria combined with favorable political conditions prompted the government of Tadeusz Mazowiecki to undertake radical economic reforms in 1990. In the short run, macroeconomic stabilization was oriented mainly towards reducing inflation. In the long run, it was recognized that it was necessary to change the structure of the economy to ensure economic competitiveness and growth.

In the autumn of 1989, Minister of Finance Balcerowicz and his team of experts designed a program of macroeconomic stabilization mainly based on the monetary approach. The program also used a fixed nominal exchange rate as the nominal anchor for the level of domestic prices, and fiscal adjustment was one of the mainstays of the stabilization policy. It was thought that

TABLE 17.2 Main Economic Indicators in Poland

Inflation (CPI)	351%
Rate of Production Growth	0% (averaged 1.4% in the 1980s)
Rate of Unemployment	0%
Balance of Trade Deficit	$US 1.8 billion
Foreign Debt (end of 1989)	$US 40.6 billion
Foreign Currency Reserves (end of 1989)	$US 3.0 billion
Black Market Exchange Rate as Compared to the Official Rate[a]	400% (average for 1989)
Budget Deficit	4.3 % of GNP

[a] Differential was 15% before introduction of the program.
SOURCE: *Statistical Yearbook* (*Roczniki Statystyczne*) of the Central Statistical Office and National Bank of Poland (Narodowy Bank Polski) data

achievement of a balanced fiscal budget stifles inflation only over a longer period (usually one year) and consolidates noninflationary economic processes (Wilczynski 1994; Gotz-Kozierkiewicz 1991a).[5]

Preparation and implementation of the stabilization program were accompanied by discussion of the timing of reforms (such as the opening of the economy, convertibility of the currency, etc.), the sequence of changes, and the speed of their implementation. Advocates of the gradual approach viewed convertibility as an obstacle to the process of transformation, putting restrictions on reform policy and hindering the pace of changes.[6] Advocates of shock therapy viewed the implementation of currency convertibility as an important part of the transformation process, arguing that it created a foundation for efficient domestic prices and for exposing the economy to international competition. Currency convertibility was also seen as adding credibility to the program of international stabilization (Szeguraj 1993).

The 1990 Stabilization Package

Qualitative Policy

The introduction of internal convertibility on January 1, 1990, meant that residents could buy, deposit in domestic banks and sell any amount of foreign currency. At the same time there was a ban on transactions in the zloty between residents and nonresidents, a requirement to resell foreign currency revenue obtained through exporting goods and services, and a ban on the invoicing of Poland's foreign trade transactions in the zloty (Pietrzak 1993).

The internal convertibility of the zloty was a main element of Balcerowicz's plan. The introduction of convertibility was economically and psychologically significant. It helped to establish a uniform rate for all types of transactions and to eliminate the black market for foreign currency. It restored, after a period of 50 years, the role of the exchange rate in resource allocation. The government set the exchange rate to promote internal over external equilibrium (stimulating exports to achieve export-led growth).

The introduction of internal convertibility required changes in hard currency reserves. Because the currency reserves held by the National Bank of Poland (Narodowy Bank Polski) were perceived as insufficient, the Bank for International Settlements in Basel granted a loan of $US 215 million in 1989 as a reserve supplement. The IMF also provided a $US 1 billion stabilization fund on the Polish government's request; this loan was guaranteed by the Ministry of Finance and validated by specific requirements regulating eligibility for various forms of financial assistance such as grants, low-interest loans and access to lines of credit.[7] The most noteworthy elements of this stabilization package included:

1. Price liberalization: limits were set on the number of centrally controlled prices. Liberalization would bring prices up to the market-clearing level.
2. Deregulation of foreign trade ending the state's foreign trade monopoly. The lack of domestic competition was to be offset by foreign competition to import price structures. Tax breaks, Export Development Fund grants and preferential loans ceased.
3. Other qualitative elements included the transformation of the institutional and organizational structure of the system. This included the privatization of state enterprises and institutional reforms to remodel banking, financial institutions and a new tax system along the lines of those operating in countries with market economies.

Quantitative Policy

The quantitative measures used two "nominal anchors": a fixed nominal exchange rate, and a tax on wage-bill increases. Money stock controls (e.g., ceilings on loans) and a positive real interest rate, designed to boost confidence in the zloty and increase savings, were introduced. The fiscal goal was to balance the budget by reducing state subsidies and eliminating corporate tax breaks. The main "nominal anchor" in the stabilization program, however, was the fixed nominal exchange rate.[8]

A fundamental issue was the choice of the level of the exchange rate, which was to remain unchanged for an extended period of time, even in the face of steadily rising prices. Experts proposed rates ranging from 5000 to 28000 zloty/$US. The large discrepancy signaled the extent of uncertainty present, the problems faced in controlling monetary processes and the methodological difficulties involved in forecasting in a hyperinflating economy.[9]

Foreign experts spoke in favor of linking the zloty to the U.S. dollar as a symbol of economic openness and the advantages of a convertible currency.[10] Some authors recalled the 1948 German reform, raising the possibility of eliminating the monetary overhang by exchanging money at rates dependent on different forms of investment. Other questions were whether the exchange rate should be determined by the market and made uniform for the current and capital accounts.

The initial exchange rate adopted by the National Bank of Poland was aimed at curbing inflation. The National Bank had to be prepared to cope with speculators and the export lobby's attempts to force devaluation. The following factors were taken into account when deciding upon the foreign exchange rate's initial level:[11]

1. the share in the total volume of foreign exchange transactions carried out in hard currencies held by the parallel market;
2. the inflation rate projected for January 1990 in the wake of price liberalization, a shift in exchange rates and the introduction of a new system for determining wages; and
3. the need to maintain adequate levels of reserves.

The final decision set the exchange rate at 9500 zloty/$US, devaluing the currency by 46.2 percent. The decision anticipated an increase in the 1990 money supply and aimed at depreciating the real value of the money stock held by economic agents. Later opinion saw the devaluation as excessive. Overdevaluation limits income in the short run and slows down long-term output production. Lack of proper valuation of the fixed assets in the balance sheets of enterprises together with insufficient depreciation allowances (due to inflation) led to an actual decrease of their capital (Kalicki 1990). Initially, at the beginning of 1990, the extent of devaluation drove "corrective" inflation to a higher level. With time, the fixed exchange rate became a stabilizing factor performing the role of a nominal anchor.

Fixed Exchange Rate Phase
Choice of Goals and Priorities
The principles of the 1990 economic policy and the outline for the following years were published in "The Government's Memorandum on Economic Policy." The main elements of the exchange rate policy:

1. introduced a unified currency market for legal persons;
2. committed the government to maintaining the zloty's rate from January 1st through the end of March;

3. permitted a decrease of foreign currency reserves of $US 290 million;
4. maintained a parallel market (for natural persons) where it was assumed that a deviation of this rate from the official rate by 10 percent would trigger central bank intervention (by both quantitative and intermediate instruments) in order to diminish that divergence; and
5. removed most foreign trade restrictions and introduced uniform tariffs.[12]

The principles of exchange rate policy outlined above were confirmed in the Parliamentary resolution concerning monetary policy for 1990. That document specified the goals of monetary policy as overcoming hyper-inflation, introducing a convertible zloty, and gradually stabilizing its purchasing power. Moreover the "exchange rate was to be set at a level guaranteeing a balance of demand for foreign currency with the supply thereof," and determination of its level was assigned to the President of the National Bank of Poland.[13] There was great uncertainty concerning the actual levels of the main macroeconomic variables at the time of the stabilization program's implementation. There was also uncertainty concerning the demand for money, especially taking into account the share of hard currencies in house-holds' overall deposits and the delay between implementation of the stabilization package and its total effect.[14] The memorandum assumed that a current account balance in hard currencies could be reached only in 1993. In reality, the accumulated trade balance showed a surplus of $US 2,064 million in 1990, and the level of official reserves increased from about $US 3 billion in January to $US 5 billion in December 1990 (see Figure 17.1). A large devalu-ation was reinforced by restrictive fiscal policy that squeezed aggregate domestic demand.

The choice of exchange rate level in January 1990 and its maintenance until May 1991 is controversial (see Gotz-Kozierkiewicz 1991b and Kolodko 1992). Many believe that the initial devaluation was excessive and aggravated corrective inflation.[15] Inflation (CPI) in the first four months of the program was 78.6 percent, 23.9 percent, 4.7 percent and 8.1 percent per month respec-tively, surpassing previous assumptions. High inflation combined with the fixed nominal exchange rate resulted in a real appreciation of the zloty (see Figure 17.2).

Estimation of the amount of overvaluation depends on the choice of the base period and reference rate. Fixing the zloty/$US exchange rate resulted in bilateral exchange rate fluctuations relative to other hard currencies in which Polish foreign trade was transacted. The restrictive monetary and fiscal policy led to a considerable decline in domestic aggregate demand and had a strong pro-export effect despite the real appreciation of the exchange rate from the second quarter of 1990 onwards (see Figures 17.2 and 17.3).

FIGURE 17.1 Official Reserves, December 1989–June 1996 (in million $US)

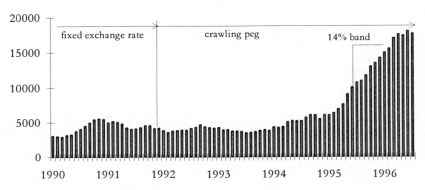

SOURCE: National Bank of Poland Information Bulletin

Changes in the Commodity and Geographical Structure of Polish Foreign Trade

Trends in exports and imports illustrate the fall in domestic aggregate demand. Exchange rate policy undoubtedly played an important role in this development.[16] For many firms exports were an important source of liquidity. The share in total exports of the metallurgy industry rose to 16 percent in 1991. Other industries such as timber-paper, foodstuffs and minerals also marked significant increases in export shares. However, attention must also be drawn to the decrease in exports of the electromechanical industry whose exports (mainly to CEEC) had constituted over 40 percent of all exports in 1985. The decrease in exports by this industry resulted from geographical changes in the pattern of Polish foreign trade (see Figure 17.4). Participation of the private sector in foreign trade increased considerably, from 5 percent (exports) and 14 percent (imports) in 1990 to 38 percent and 54 percent respectively in 1992. As trade with Central and Eastern European countries (including the former Soviet Union) diminished, there was a significant increase in the importance of trade with the European Union.[17]

From 1990 through 1991, the trend in imports shifted down as a result of substitution effects following price liberalization and due to the impact of more restrictive fiscal and monetary policy. This resulted in a large trade surplus in the first three quarters of 1990, totaling as much as $US 2,729 million. The surplus was accompanied by a growth in official reserves from February to October 1990. The exchange rate became significantly overvalued in mid 1990, however, and from November 1990 for the following seven months there was a trade deficit and a successive decrease in the profitability of Polish exports.

359

Figure 17.2 Trade Weighted Real Effective Exchange Rate of the Zloty (December 1991 = 1.0)

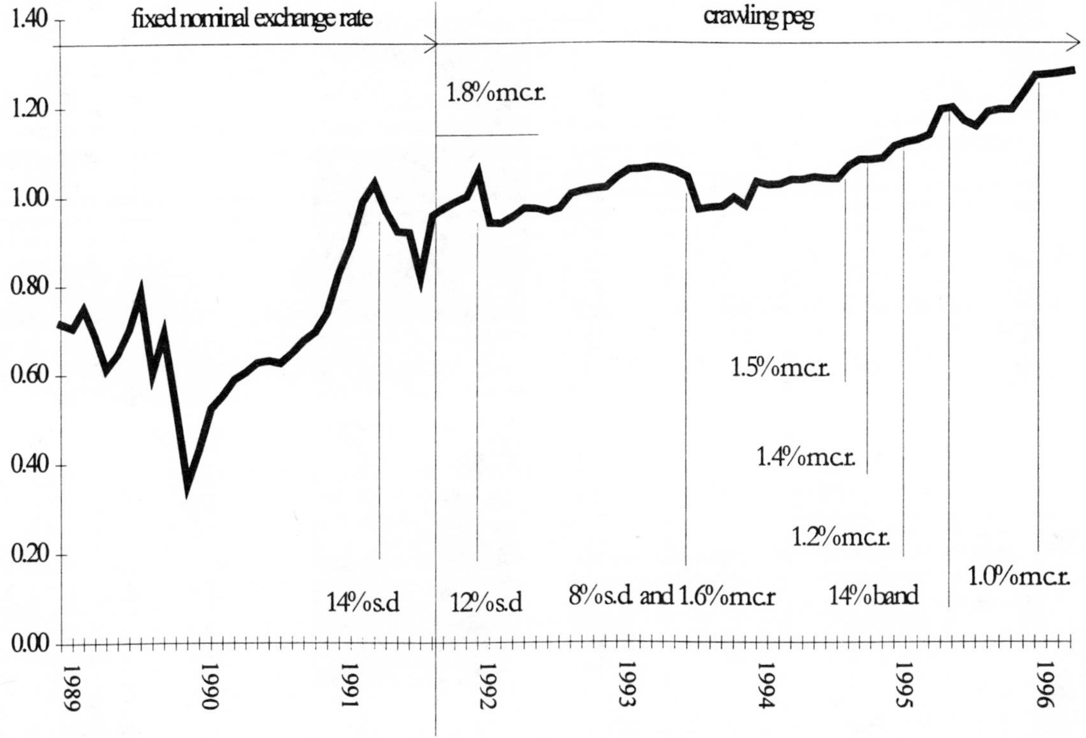

SOURCE: L. Jasinski.

FIGURE 17.3 The Monthly Trade Balance in Goods and Services, January 1990–
June 1996 (in million $US)

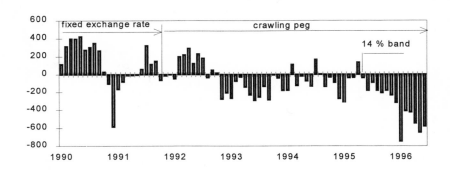

SOURCE: National Bank of Poland Information Bulletin

FIGURE 17.4 Geographical Structure of Polish Exports, 1989–1995 (percent
shares)

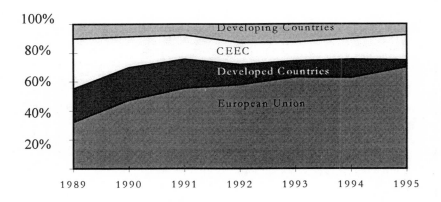

SOURCE: Central Statistical Office data.

The decision to devalue the zloty by 14 percent in May 1991 was triggered
by unfavorable developments in foreign trade, including a sharp increase in
imported consumption goods and decreasing foreign currency reserves.
Moreover, regulations fixing the exchange rate were also changed to reduce
the negative effects on trade produced by the exchange rate being pegged
solely to the U.S. dollar. After May 1991, the rate of exchange was based on

a basket of currencies weighted to reflect their shares in Polish foreign trade invoicing.[18] The main currency was still the U.S. dollar, which represented 45 percent of the basket, the other currencies being the German mark (35 percent), pound sterling (10 percent), French franc (5 percent) and the Swiss franc (5 percent). The effects of the devaluation on foreign trade were minor and brief. After only two months the zloty's effective exchange rate began to increase again and quickly regained its predevaluation value. The peg was maintained until mid-October 1991.

Policy on Tariffs

Under the fixed exchange rate regime, tariff policy was an important element in external economic relations. The general task of the stabilization program was to create the conditions necessary for the establishment of a competitive market system. As a result of this, the openness of the Polish economy (ratio of the value of imports to GDP) increased from 12.6 percent in 1991 to over 20 percent in the years 1992 to 1994. In order to stimulate competition and decrease inflationary pressure, domestic market protection was lowered considerably.[19] This step was also a reaction to the decrease in imports which resulted from the sharp devaluation in January 1990. From March to August 1990, customs duties on 80 percent of goods were suspended. During the first months of 1990, the exchange rate was the main instrument of market protection. After the devaluation of the zloty in mid 1991, tariff policy was revised and tariffs and duties were increased due to the deterioration in the balance of trade, the budget deficit and increasing pressure from producers. Some provisions were introduced (in accordance with GATT) that protected the domestic market from "excessive" imports. As a result, and in spite of the inefficient collection of customs duties, protection of the domestic market grew (Marczewski 1992). In the Polish stabilization program tariff policy acted as a shock absorber, offsetting the effects produced by the initial undervaluation of the exchange rate. Such a role was bound to lead to some instability of foreign trade regulations.

Monetary Policy

Control of the money stock was a crucial instrument. The combination of exchange rate movements and monetary control can lead to a comparatively high degree of variability in money creation that is strongly dependent on foreign trade and capital inflows. Under dollarization the money supply is vulnerable to changes in the exchange rate and the volume of trade in foreign currencies at bureaux de change. This factor defined the mutual relationship between Poland's exchange rate policy and the instruments of monetary policy, especially where one of the government's policy goals was to reverse the dollarization of the Polish economy. Apart from their anti-inflationary effect, positive real interest rates served this purpose, especially for long-term zloty deposits. This purpose was also served by a fall (in domestic terms) of the yield on hard currency deposits. The parallel market exchange rate during this period (January 1990 to December 1991) was very close to the official zloty rate. The average percentage deviation was 1.1 percent in 1990 (the maximum deviation was 2.8 percent in May 1990 and in August the rates were equal). In 1991 the average deviation between the rates was 1.7 percent, the greatest discrepancy occurring in December (5 percent).

Real zloty interest rates tended to be positive. This was seen as combating the dollarization of the economy and inflation; in fact, it fueled recession as well. A surplus in the balance of trade during the first three quarters of 1990 was a fundamental source of money creation. The National Bank of Poland decided to reduce the banks' capability to create money, and in August it raised the hitherto uniform required reserves rate of 15 percent to 27 percent on demand deposits and to 17 percent on savings deposits. The National Bank of Poland also introduced a mandatory 7 percent reserve rate on time deposits. When high liquidity continued, the National Bank raised required reserves again, so that in December 1990 they were 30 percent on demand and savings deposits, and 10 percent on time deposits. These rates were maintained until September 1991 when the rate on savings deposits was lowered to 25 percent.[20] The high liquidity of banks also prompted the Bank to issue its own bills. These bills, quite apart from credit limits, served as instruments to regulate banking sector liquidity.

In May the National Bank's bills were replaced by Treasury bills. The T-bills were the most significant monetary instrument introduced to finance the budget deficit in 1991.[21] In the third quarter of 1990 the National Bank lowered the rates of refinancing and rediscount credits. This move was triggered by a fall in inflation, pressure from the industrial sector and the opinions of some economists who thought that high interest rates were a major cause of inflation. The reduction in the central bank's interest rates triggered a reduction in the commercial banks' lending and deposit rates. Such an easing in monetary policy proved premature, however, and higher inflation made the National Bank increase interest rates again.

In 1991, the level of reserves fell, in contrast to 1990 (see Figure 17.1). This development, along with a negative balance of trade in goods and services, lasted for seven months (November 1990 to June 1991) and prompted the devaluation of May 1991 (see Figure 17.3). The devaluation reversed the balance of trade; in 1991 the surplus totaled $US 287 million. However, in October 1991 a decreasing level of reserves and pressure from exporters led the National Bank to abandon the fixed exchange rate regime and replace it with a preannounced crawling peg system.

Preannounced Crawling Peg Phase

Premises for the Change in Exchange Rate Regime

In October 1991 Poland introduced a preannounced crawling peg (1.8 percent per month relative to a basket of currencies). Abandonment of the fixed exchange rate was caused by the overvaluation of the zloty in relation to the basket, which reduced the competitiveness of Polish exports. Particularly threatened were consumer goods producers; the overvalued zloty caused high growth in consumer imports. Changing the exchange rate system was in part an attempt to reduce the uncertainty that accompanies a fixed exchange rate when there are large inflation differentials between trading partners. The crawling peg increased the predictability of real exchange rate values, creating more stable conditions for decision making.

The adoption of a crawling peg did not mean abandoning the basic principles of Poland's monetary and exchange rate policy.[22] Despite personnel changes in key posts in the government and at the National Bank of Poland, a coherent, restrictive monetary policy linked with the exchange rate was maintained, even though recession, growing unemployment and social tensions increased the unpopularity of successive governments and of the very idea of a market economy.[23]

The Crawling Peg and Foreign Trade

Implementation of the preannounced crawling peg reduced the rate of real appreciation of the Polish zloty.[24] Additional step devaluations (by 12 percent in February 1992 and 8 percent in August 1993) made the real effective exchange rate index much more stable (see Figure 17.2). Due to the new exchange rate mechanism and the continued monetary policy, the first ten months of 1992 (with the exception of January and August) showed a surplus in the trade balance (see Figure 17.3) amounting to $US 824 million for the year. Real GNP growth (2.6 percent) was initiated in 1992, and consolidated in 1993 and 1994 when the real rate of GNP growth reached 4 percent and 5 percent respectively.

The years 1989 to 1991 saw substantial changes in the geographical and commodity structure of Polish foreign trade. Under the crawling peg regime both trade patterns stabilized. In 1993–1994, the European Union countries' share in Poland's imports and exports exceeded 60 percent; trade with the countries of Central and Eastern Europe and with the former Soviet Union stabilized (see Figure 17.4). Lack of significant continued change in the commodity structure of trade reflected the exhaustion of the existing basic factors of export growth. The growth of aggregate demand in Poland, the insufficient competitiveness of Polish exports and a slowdown in the economies of Poland's main trading partners were responsible for a shift in the trade balance: the official foreign trade account went into deficit before the end of 1992 and remained there throughout 1993 and 1994 (see Figure 17.3). By August 1993 the worsening trade deficit and falling currency reserves led the National Bank, in spite of the relative stability of the real exchange rate, to devalue the zloty an additional 8 percent and to lower the rate of depreciation from 1.8 percent to 1.6 percent per month.[25] This measure reduced the growth of the trade deficit and together with flourishing, unrecorded trade along the border zones led to an increase in currency reserves (see Figure 17.1).

Monetary Policy and the Preannounced Crawling Peg

In the crawling peg phase of the stabilization program, the chief goal of monetary policy, supported by the National Bank's interest rate policy, was still to combat persistent inflation. During 1992 and 1993, the largest deviation in the average free market exchange rate from the average official exchange rate did not exceed 1.6 percent, whereas in 1992 and 1993 the average variance amounted to 0.7 percent and 0.8 percent.

Budget deficits characterized the years following 1990. Under restrictive monetary policy, public sector borrowing crowded out the private sector. Both in 1992 and 1993, the real money supply for the nonbudgetary sector decreased. The public sector debt in this period, however, increased considerably. Money creation was strongly influenced by the need to finance the budget deficit, movements of short-term capital and the trade balance. In 1992 export earnings were the main source of additional money supply for the corporate sector.[26] In November 1992, in anticipation of devaluation and expected restrictions in customs and fiscal policies, imports started to grow rapidly. This trend in imports persisted throughout 1993, but the 8 percent devaluation in August and the change in the monthly depreciation rate gradually slowed the increase in the trade balance deficit.

Growing aggregate demand along with a mild tendency for real appreciation of the zloty were the main reasons for the trade balance deficit in 1993. Despite the trade deficit, official reserves started to grow in mid 1993. This resulted mainly from movements of short-term capital (the purchase of currencies coming from the developing cross-border trade).[27] In February 1993, the National Bank slightly lowered the interest rate. Commercial banks also adjusted their deposit and lending rates. This contributed to the strengthening of the economic recovery and triggered adjustments that set the grounds for economic growth.

Starting in late 1993, the main problem for monetary policy was continuing inflation, overliquidity of the banking sector and the fast-growing official reserves of the National Bank. In 1994, exports of goods and services rose by more than 23 percent whereas imports increased by 11 percent. Despite that, recorded trade remained in deficit (of over $US 770 million). Meanwhile, the official reserves of the National Bank went up. This increase was caused mainly by massive purchases of foreign currencies flowing into the country as a result of a positive cross-border trade balance and from foreign direct investment amounting to $US 1.3 billion in 1994. The growing accumulation of currency reserves combined with a relatively low monetization of the economy became the primary factor influencing money supply.

Growing Foreign Currency Reserves and a Wider Crawling Band

In early 1995 gross currency reserves accumulated at a much increased pace (see Figure 17.1). In the first quarter of the year, reserves grew by $US 1.5 billion, fueled chiefly by a positive balance of cross-border trade. During that time, the level of currency reserves was also affected by foreign direct investment and adjustments in household portfolios involving gradual currency substitution, i.e., a departure from keeping savings in foreign currencies (cf. Table 17.3). Under the preannounced crawling peg system, the inflationary pressure and the specific source of currency influx left the National Bank with little room for maneuver (Durjasz and Kokoszczynski 1995).[28] In the banking sector, overliquidity was initially sterilized by reverse repurchase agreements and later also by outright sell operations (Slawinski and Osinski 1995). In addition, the National Bank increased its spread in currency transactions with banks from 1 percent to 4 percent and gradually lowered the monthly rate of devaluation (November 1994, February 1995), which in effect resulted in further real appreciation of the zloty. Such actions, taken in the face of a massive influx of foreign currencies (coupled with an inflow of speculative capital since the second quarter of the year) and the resulting overliquidity in the banking sector, proved insufficient (see Figure 17.5). Therefore, serious consideration was given to additional measures. In order to reduce the rate of increase in official reserves, the National Bank of Poland considered allowing exporters to open foreign currency accounts and lowering the import tax.

Expectations of an exchange rate mechanism correction aimed at increasing its flexibility and the resulting expectations of zloty appreciation prompted an inflow of speculative capital, originally invested in eight-week and thirteen-week Treasury bills (Slawinski and Osinski 1995).[29] With their high interest rate, Treasury bills guaranteed a relatively high rate of return in addition to the benefits investors earned on the expected exchange rate difference (appreciation of the zloty).[30] Thus the existing sources of foreign currency influx were reinforced and a new source emerged. Expectations of apprecia-

TABLE 17.3 Share of Foreign Currency Deposits in Households' Total Deposits and the Share of Foreign Currency Deposits of Non-Financial Sector in Total Money Supply (end of year, in percent)

	1990	1991	1992	1993	1994	1995	1996[a]
Households' Foreign Exchange Deposits/Total Household Deposits	58.0	38.5	44.7	48.7	48.6	34.9	28.7
Foreign Currency Deposits of Non-financial Sector/ Total Money Supply	31.3	23.0	24.8	28.8	28.5	20.4	18.8

[a]First quarter, 1996
SOURCE: Author's calculation based on National Bank of Poland Information Bulletins.

tion also affected the currency structure of household savings with foreign currencies being gradually substituted for the zloty (see Table 17.3).

In May 1995, the National Bank introduced a new exchange rate system. The parity rate was determined by the Bank in the same way as before, i.e., a preannounced monthly crawl of 1.2 percent against a basket of currencies,[31] but the exchange rate on the interbank exchange market was to fluctuate within a band of ±7 percent around the parity (central) rate. At the end of each working day, the National Bank set a fixing rate for the German mark and the U.S. dollar based on current supply and demand conditions in the interbank currency market. The fixing rate is used for statistical and accounting purposes. These measures led to appreciation of the zloty (cf. Figure 17.2), but failed to stop the rapid increase in reserves.[32] In May 1995, the National Bank of Poland reintroduced the Bank notes and used them in open market transactions designed to sterilize the overliquidity of the banking sector (see Figure 17.5).[33] Another step taken by the National Bank, dictated by falling inflation rates, was to cut interest rates.[34] On December 22, 1995, the National Bank revalued the central parity dollar rate by 6 percent in order to adjust this rate to the prevailing fixing rate. Since then, the average deviation has been between -2.5 percent to -1.5 percent rather than the previously observed -5 percent. In December 1995, exporters were no longer required to resell foreign currencies they acquired to the central bank and could deposit them in foreign currency accounts. Liberalization also affected current account transactions, and Poland officially accepted the obligations of Article VIII of the IMF's Articles of Agreement (Durjasz and Kokoszczynski 1995).

FIGURE 17.5 Zloty Securities Sales to Banks under Reverse Repurchase Agreements: Value of Bids Accepted, January 1995–June 1996 ($US millions)

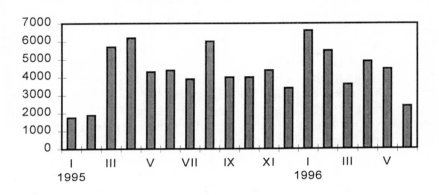

SOURCE: National Bank of Poland.
NOTE: The $US equivalent of zloty transactions was calculated using the daily average of the official rate during the month (since May 16, 1995, the fixing rate.

Expectations of further appreciation ran high through practically all of 1995. The main source of the increase in reserves was the continued positive balance of cross-border trade, which reached $US 6 billion. In addition, 1995 proved to be a record year for foreign direct investment, with $US 2.5 billion flowing in. The National Bank's possible responses were limited. Any readjustment of the interest rate would affect only a minor part of the increase in reserves. Such readjustments were also effectively blocked by continuing inflation and by the government's anti-inflation policies. The real appreciation of the zloty (about 14 percent) and a real increase in GDP of 7 percent contributed to a 40 percent rise in imports in 1995. However, despite the zloty's real appreciation, Poland's official exports of goods and services also rose by as much as 33 percent to reach nearly $US 23 billion that year.

In late 1995 and early 1996, the inflow of speculative short-term capital into the T-bill market gradually declined in response to the decreasing return on T-bills, uncertainty caused by the 14 percent exchange rate band and a drop in expectations of appreciation. Starting in the fourth quarter of 1995, the recorded trade deficit in the official trade in goods and services soared rapidly (in the first half of 1996 the deficit was about $US 3.3 billion, more than seven times the level of 1995—see Figure 17.3).[35] As a result, official gross reserves stabilized while the deviation of the fixing rate from the central rate decreased substantially.[36]

Since 1995, the interbank currency market has gained significance. The trend was caused by an increased inflow of foreign currencies and by the liberalization of relations between foreign currency banks and the National Bank. Average daily turnover exceeded $US 400–500 million (Slawinski and Osinski 1996). In foreign currency/zloty transactions, the U.S. dollar was the unchallenged currency of choice (approximately 70 percent of transactions) followed by the German mark. The average dealer transaction involved about $US 1–5 million while a transaction of $US 10 million was sufficient to change the market exchange rate (Rzeszutek 1995). Data illustrating the situation on the interbank currency market is presented in Table 17.4. As can be seen from the figures presented there, the interbank market is growing at a steady pace. As the volume of transactions grows, the market becomes less sensitive to short-term speculative movements of capital. A large and more liquid market will also provide favorable conditions for the development of currency options and futures. Equally notable is the rising share of banks with a foreign capital stake in the turnover of the interbank currency market.

In January 1996, in line with the monetary policy program for that year, the operational targets of monetary policy were changed. The new target was reserve supplies (liquid reserves of banks and notes and coin in circulation), replacing the previous interest rate target. It is also notable that July 1, 1995, marked the beginning of the process of T-bill dematerialization. This measure will have a strong positive impact on the development and functioning of the money market and also on the conduct of open market operations by the National Bank (Slawinski 1995). The dematerialization of T-bills will increase the technical options for official intervention in the interbank money market. It will become very important in the face of growing integration of the zloty and foreign exchange markets. The increase in the liquidity and thickness of these markets and of the stock market is one of the most important conditions for the sustainable growth of the Polish economy.

TABLE 17.4 Interbank Foreign Exchange Market in Poland in 1995

	Q1	Q2	Q3	Q4
Average Daily Turnover	366	432	487	508
Percent Share in Turnover				
Foreign Banks	23.6	30.5	25.5	34.3
Domestic Banks	76.4	69.5	74.5	65.7

SOURCE: Slawinski and Osinski (1996:25)

Conclusions

The stabilization program was a success. In assessing the Polish exchange rate policy, one should take into account the uncertainty and unique conditions faced in the start-up phase of the stabilization program.

The Polish government's main goal was combating inflation. Both monetary and exchange rate policies were used towards that goal. The large initial devaluation and the restrictiveness of other stabilization policy instruments promoted export growth and, contrary to earlier assumptions, led to a high foreign trade surplus due to squeezed domestic demand. The implementation of the stabilization program differed considerably from the predicted scenario. From the psychological point of view, internal currency convertibility, the export surplus and equilibrium in the goods market were visible symptoms of progress. It was probably for these reasons that, despite the growing real appreciation of the zloty in 1990 and 1991, the initial exchange rate was maintained for as long as 16 months.

In the first phase of the preannounced crawling peg regime, the zloty was depreciated monthly at a rate lower than the rate of domestic inflation, which slowed its rate of appreciation. The clarity of this mechanism helped economic agents to adjust gradually to new market conditions and facilitated microeconomic restructuring. The officially recorded trade deficit at that time was caused mainly by economic growth initiated as early as 1992.

Reducing inflation to single digits is a challenging task. Polish inflation is not of the cost-push variety and is reinforced by structural rigidities; therefore, exchange rate policy cannot be the main instrument used to combat it. Success requires action at all levels: sound fiscal policy, privatization, full introduction of free market mechanisms, and support for foreign investment. The fact that the Polish economy is increasingly more open to imports (in 1995 imports equaled 24.6 percent of GDP) makes it more vulnerable to external business cycles and shocks.

Large inflows of foreign currency expanded the money supply in 1995. The implementation of a wider exchange rate band (±7 percent) within the system of a preannounced crawling peg added flexibility and increased the government's room for maneuver in macroeconomic policymaking. The new, more flexible system allows market conditions to co-determine the exchange rate of the Polish zloty. Yet, with a wider band, the exchange rate no longer plays the role of an anti-inflation anchor. The rate of crawl cannot affect in a desirable way nominal variables (inflation) and real variables (the real exchange rate) at the same time. Real appreciation of the Polish currency had some negative impact on export profitability and the country's competitiveness, especially since the second half of 1995. This decline in competitiveness was reflected by a deepening official foreign trade deficit. A precise appraisal of the extent of appreciation and its impact on the country's competitiveness is difficult since the Polish currency was highly undervalued in the pre-stabilization period. It should be noted, however, that since 1990 there has been a sharp rise in productivity levels in both tradable and nontradable sectors.

Introduction of a stronger link between the zloty and the ECU would help better reflect the current geographic structure of Poland's foreign trade—about 70 percent of turnover is generated by transactions with the European Union. Despite improvements in market access resulting from the Europe Agreement, Polish exports are still subject to nontariff barriers and contingent protection.

Poland has expressed its willingness to join the European Union. Full membership will require sustainable monetary and fiscal policies oriented at meeting all the convergence criteria of the Maastricht Treaty. The experience of member states of the European Union indicates, however, that in order to stabilize the exchange rate of the zloty it will be necessary to proceed with caution, considering existing structural incompatibilities and the limitations of available instruments of economic policy.

Notes

The authors want to thank Clas Wihlborg, Richard Sweeney and Thomas Willett for suggestions and comments which helped to improve this article. All remaining deficiencies are our sole responsibility. Tadeusz Kowalski gratefully acknowledges support from the PHARE/ACE Program (ACE 94-0685R "Coping with Financial Reform in EMEs: Analytical Tools, Policy Implementation and the Case Studies of Estonia and Poland)."

1. In 1989 attempts by the Rakowski government to accelerate economic reforms without changing the political system resulted in the withdrawal of subsidies and introduction of market economy rules into the food sector. This led to hyperinflation and increased economic chaos. See *Ekonomista* (1990: 523).

2. The growth in real wages is estimated using the official GNP deflator; the real level of inflation under shortages, currency substitution (in 1989 84.2 percent of households' deposits were held in foreign currencies), and the black market exchange rate (for imports) was undoubtedly higher.

3. Agreements concluded with the Paris Club and the London Club make it possible to write off nearly half of the Polish foreign debt. Servicing the remaining debt might be a serious burden for the economy. The agreements introduced stability that favors the inflow of foreign direct investment. See Morgan Stanley (1994).

4. The problem of the ruble balance (expressed in transfer rubles) was combined with unsettled questions of global payments and liabilities between Poland and the former USSR. In 1985 above 50 percent of Polish foreign trade was carried out with the Soviet Union and COMECON countries.

5. According to other authors the program was based on "orthodox" elements (monetary and fiscal contractions) and "non-orthodox" elements in the form of nominal "anchors." See Calvo and Coricelli (1992).

6. The price Poland has paid for implementing convertibility in the early stages of reform is increased unemployment. "Gradualists" maintain that this fact confirms the validity of their approach. An often-quoted case is that of Western European countries which deferred the introduction of convertibility until the end of the 1950s and initially instituted only internal convertibility after the Second World War.

7. As stated in the initial declarations, each of the 12 donor-states confirmed in a separate agreement the amount to be contributed to the stabilization fund and approved the rules to be followed in accounting for the financial resources used.

8. The Polish program can be classified as a heterodox approach based on the exchange rate.

9. Cf. Solarz (1990). At the beginning many observers believed the extent of devaluation was insufficient and that it would not be possible to maintain a fixed rate for the planned period of three months.

10. Views expressed by Jeffrey Sachs, among others.

11. The January 1st devaluation was preceded by preparatory devaluations during the last quarter of 1989.

12. Special duties were temporarily introduced on imports such as alcohol, tobacco, and household electronics.

13. The Council of Ministers set the regulations for fixing the exchange rate. An obligation that "payments in foreign currencies should be made immediately to the country and resold at foreign exchange banks" was introduced.

14. At the end of 1989 the share of hard currencies in households' total deposits was above 80 percent.

15. The following examples of price rises in January 1990 testify to the scale of changes in officially set prices introduced within the stabilization program: electricity rose by 200 percent, transportation fares by 200 percent, coal for private consumers by 600 percent.

16. Devaluation of the zloty was accompanied by a serious deterioration in Poland's terms of trade. In 1990 the index fell to 83.7 from 116.6 in 1989 and 102.7 in 1988.

17. From 1991 all Polish foreign trade was carried out in hard currencies.

18. The zloty rate of exchange in relation to other currencies in the basket fluctuated together with the changes of these currencies in relation to the U.S. dollar. Bilateral rates were published five times a week by the National Bank of Poland.

19. The degree of protection might be measured as the ratio of the value of customs duties collected to the value of imports; by the end of 1990 it was about 5 percent. See Marczewski (1992).

20. Further changes in the required reserve ratios took place in April 1992. Rates of 25 percent for savings deposits and 30 percent for demand deposits were replaced by a uniform rate of 25 percent.

21. Moderate budget deficits seem to be a persistent feature of the Polish economy. The growing public debt has, to a certain degree, limited the government's options with regard to fiscal and monetary policy. See Stawarska (1994).

22. It meant the adoption of a real exchange rate anchor, which is more appropriate in a situation of high inflation differentials. See Fry and Nutti (1992).

23. Certain changes (including language and emphasis) can be seen in the goals and intermediate targets for 1994 formulated by the coalition government (Demo-

cratic Left Alliance and Polish Peasant Party). The direction and the main instruments of policy have not changed significantly.

24. Since 1992 the exchange rate on the interbank market in transactions between banks and non-bank firms could deviate by ± 2 percent from the official rate. The spread between the buy/sell rate of the National Bank was only 1 percent.

25. It is worth noting that the 8 percent devaluation of August was three times lower than that urged by some industrial organizations.

26. Growing credit risk led commercial banks to tighten criteria in assessing loan applications. As a result, the availability of credit was reduced.

27. Trade unrecorded in official statistics (mainly along the borders with Germany, the Czech Republic and the Slovak Republic) and massive purchases of consumer goods by citizens of the former Soviet Union, especially since 1994, contributed to the growth of foreign currency reserves.

28. The Ministry of Finance proposed to lower the National Bank's interest rates. The Bank rightly argued that such a move would contribute to increasing inflationary pressures. One proposed solution was to temporarily introduce a tax on T-bill purchases by foreign entities. In the end, this solution was not adopted.

29. The influx of speculative capital was also encouraged by an optimistic evaluation of the Polish economy in 1995 by Moody's and Standard and Poor's investment rating services. In April 1996, Standard and Poor's raised the rating of Poland's long-term foreign-currency denominated debt from BB to BBB-minus and assigned an A minus rating to long-term debt denominated in zlotys.

30. The Ministry of Finance allowed foreign investors to purchase T-bills and T-bonds as early as 1993. During the first months of 1995, foreigners bought approximately $US 0.5 billion worth of T-bills which accounted for approximately 8 percent of the market. According to the National Bank's estimates, during all of 1995, nonresidents invested about $US 800 million (net) in the primary and secondary T-bill markets. This amount accounted for 9 percent of the increase in gross official reserves (Kowalski 1995; National Bank of Poland 1996).

31. The National Bank intervened at approximately 5 percent thus preventing excessive appreciation of the zloty. The shallow foreign exchange market made it possible to avoid a massive intervention with transactions of approximately $US 30–50 million allowing the National Bank to effectively manage the market. Data about the extent of the National Bank's interventions in the market are not published in the Bank's *NBP Bulletin*. For more information on the subject, see Slawinski and Osinski (1996) and Rzeszutek (1995).

32. Assessment of the extent of appreciation depends on the price indices used; cf. Durjasz and Kokoszczynski (1995).

33. In 1994, average monthly absorption under reverse repurchase agreements was about $US 2.2 billion. In that year maximum absorption reached $US 3.3 billion in November and a minimum of $US 0.9 billion in April. Source: *NBP Monthly Bulletin*.

34. On May 29, the annual lombard credit rate was lowered from 34 percent to 30 percent while the rediscount credit rate was reduced from 31 percent to 27 percent.

35. According to the National Bank of Poland, purchases of foreign currencies from cross-border trade amounted to more than $US 3.4 billion in the same period.

36. In June 1996, the average deviation of the fixing rate from the parity rate was only 1.8 percent.

References

Calvo, Guillermo, and Fabrizio Coricelli. 1992. "Stabilizing a Previously Centrally Planned Economy—Poland 1990." *Economic Policy*, April: 175–227.
Durjasz, Pawel, and Ryszard Kokoszczynski. 1995. "From Fixed to Flexible Exchange Rate Regime: The Case of Poland 1989–1995." Mimeo, Narodowy Bank Polski (National Bank of Poland).
Ekonomista. 1991. "Ocena sytuacji spoleczno-gospodarczej kraju oraz stanu realizacji reformy systemowej w Polsce." 4(6): 523–31.
Fry, Maxwell J., and Domenico M. Nuti. 1992. "Monetary and Exchange Rate Policies During Eastern Europe's Transition: Some Lessons from Further East." *Oxford Review of Economic Policy* 8(1): 27–43.
Gotz-Kozierkiewicz, Danuta. 1991a. "Polityka walutowa w programie stabilizacji 1990 roku." *Ekonomista* 4(1): 11–31.
_____. 1991b. "Polityka kursowa a inflacja i recesja." *Ekonomista* 4(6): 458–87.
Kalicki, Krzysztof. 1990. "Wplyw stanu rownowagi pienieznej na poziom kursu walutowego. Empiryczna analiza przypadku Polski." *Bank i Kredyt* 21(7–9): 13–19.
Kolodko, Grzegorz. 1992. "Stabilizacja, recesja i wzrost w gospodarce post-socjalistycznej." *Ekonomista* 5(6): 603–31.
Kowalski, Tadeusz. 1995. "Dylematy i doswiadczenia polityki kursu walutowego w okresie transformacji. Przypadek Polski," in B. Winiarski and K. Wilk, eds., *Procesy transformacji w krajach postkomunistcznych; ocena, kierunki dalszych dzialan.* Pp. 35–42. Wroclaw: Wydawnictwo Akademii Ekonomicznej.
Marczewski, Krzysztof. 1992. "Wspolpraca gospodarcza z zagranica w okresie transformacji," in Leszek Zienkowski, ed., *Gospodarka polska w latach 1990–1992. Doswiadczenia i wnioski.* Pp. 115–32. Warszawa: Zaklad Badan Statystyczno-Ekonomicznych Glownego Urzedu Statystycznego i Polskiej Akademii Nauk.
Morgan Stanley. 1994. "Investment, Research—UK and Europe—Poland and Slovakia: That's the Way to Do It." March 21.
Narodowy Bank Polski (National Bank of Poland). 1996. *Raport o inflacji*, kwiecien. Warszawa.
Pietrzak, Edmund. 1993. "Czynniki wprowadzenia wymienialnosci zlotego oraz budowy rynku walutowego w Polsce." *Bank i Kredyt* 24(3): 13–18.
Rzeszutek, Ewa. 1995. "Kurs rynkowy zlotego—uwarunkowania ekonomiczne i instytucjonalne." *Bank i Kredyt* 26(6): 92–102.
Slawinski, Andrzej. 1995. "Operacje otwartego rynku - II kwartal 1995." *Analizy.* Pp. 42–49. Fundacja Edukacji i Badan Bankowych 7.
Slawinski, Andrzej, and Jacek Osinski. 1996. "Rynek pieniezny '95." *Materialy i Studia*, no. 58. Narodowy Bank Polski, Departament Analiz i Badan.
Solarz, Jan K. 1990. "Rola NBP w ksztaltowaniu kursu walutowego." *Bank i Kredyt* 21(7–9): 59–64.
Stawarska, Renata. 1994. "Poland—EC—Europe Agreement. Dilemmas of Polish Transition," in *Poland and European Communities*. Proceedings of the Confer-

ence "European Days" at the Poznań University of Economics held in Poznań on April 21–23, 1993. Pp. 109–17. Poznań University of Economics.

Szeguraj, I. 1993. "The Issues of Currency Convertibility in Eastern Europe, 1991 and Economic Reform in Eastern Europe." *IMF Survey*, February 8.

Wernik, Andrzej. 1992. "Równowaga budzetowa w latach 1990–1992," in Leszek Zienkowski, ed., *Gospodarka polska w latach 1990–1992. Doswiadczenia i wnioski*. Pp. 31–44. Warszawa: Zaklad Badan Statystyczno-Ekonomicznych Glownego Urzedu Statystycznego i Polskiej Akademii Nauk.

Wilczynski, Waclaw. 1994. "Transformacja gospodarki polskiej po pieciu latach 1989–1994." *Ruch Prawniczy, Ekonomiczny i Socjologiczny* 56(3): 63–77.

18

An Evaluation of Optimal Currency Areas for the Commonwealth of Independent States

King Banaian and Eugenue Zhukov

Introduction

Fifteen new countries were formed from the former republics of the Soviet Union. Each has its own leaders with their own ideas about economic policy, their own plans for the speed and scope of privatization, and their own ideas about reshaping the industrial base inherited from the central planners in Moscow. Initially, these countries did not plan to create their own currencies; rather they continued to rely on the Soviet ruble.[1]

The ruble zone had a single issuer of currency: the Central Bank of Russia. Any of the other central banks in the zone, however, could issue credits to banks and several issued credits directly to state-owned enterprises as well. These credits could be converted to cash rubles by the republic's central bank requesting additional credits from the Central Bank of Russia. Rapid credit expansion led to inflation, which was exported from the country originating the extra credits to others in the zone. The Russians had to choose between accepting this inflation or dissolving the ruble zone.

Optimal currency area theory would lead a researcher to approach this choice based on objective economic factors, such as the symmetry of shocks to the economies in the zone, labor and capital mobility, wage flexibility, etc. We argue that these factors played little role in Russia's decision to dissolve the zone in July 1993. Russia balanced its desire to maintain control over the former territories of the Soviet Union with the concern of appearing too hegemonic, and concluded that the benefits of control were too small. We also show, however, that optimum currency area theory can help explain the decisions of the former members of the Soviet Union about exchange rate policies once the dissolution of the ruble zone had occurred.

Genberg (1994) argues that the collapse of the ruble zone in November 1993 probably did lead to a last burst of inflation in the remaining member countries. Several did not have the institutional structures and reforms necessary to support an independent currency yet in place. Still, most of the countries forced from the zone have fared well in the medium term. Armenia and Georgia suffered very serious output declines in 1994, due in part to the economic turmoil after dissolution of the ruble zone, but have partially recovered from their output decline. In contrast, the Kyrgyz Republic, which left the ruble zone in 1993, before the Russian renunciation of the Soviet ruble, appears to have suffered more.

In this chapter we discuss the characteristics of the countries in the Commonwealth of Independent States in terms of the criteria delineated by the optimal currency areas approach. As discussed by Willett and Wihlborg in Chapter 3 of this volume, the core idea of this approach is that there is no exchange rate regime that is economically efficient for all countries and at all times. The relative costs and benefits of flexible versus fixed exchange rates vary across countries depending on their degree of openness, size, factor mobility, policy preferences, structure of economy and other characteristics. These factors may lead to different preferences for average inflation rates across countries. While these factors are important, we rely more on the "new" optimum currency areas approach which relies on a public finance explanation for differing preferences of inflation in the former Soviet republics. In particular, differences in preferences for the speed of reforms has played a substantial role in the choice of exchange rate regimes in these countries.

Economic Arguments for the Commonwealth of Independent States as an Optimum Currency Area

The optimum currency area literature has focused on four broad criteria for determining the proper scope of a currency area: the openness of the economies of the proposed area, their degree of wage and price flexibility and factor mobility, the degree of diversification of an economy's output, and the nature of shocks that the economies usually experience. The first three criteria are more in line with the traditional optimum currency area approach. The new approach places greater emphasis on the last.[2]

The first three criteria give conflicting answers to the question of whether the Commonwealth of Independent States is an optimum currency area.[3] The criteria are overlapping, so that there is no unique decision; two researchers looking at the same data can arrive at different conclusions. Moreover, the formation of currency areas can cause changes in the economic structure, that are typically not captured in economic models. Tavlas (1994) argues that if countries which specialize in producing a small number of goods join a currency area, they will diversify and become candidates for a fixed exchange rates. The choice of an exchange rate regime interacts with fiscal policy as well in a complex way. Particularly in economies in transition, these structural changes will over time affect the choice of an optimal exchange rate regime. Conclusions drawn from individual optimum currency area criteria should be viewed as a whole rather than separately, since the conclusions are interconnected.

Patterns of Trade

The economies of former Soviet republics have been closely integrated and very closely linked to the Russian economy. At the same time openness vis-à-vis the rest of the world was negligible for most of republics except for Russia at the outset of the transition. The degree of openness varies across republics. As can be seen in Table 18.1, in Belarus exports exceed 50 percent of its GNP, while in Russia the share of exports in GDP is only 20 percent. There is a high degree of openness among the Commonwealth countries, especially between Russia and other republics, but not nearly as much openness with countries outside the Commonwealth. For all of the Commonwealth states except Russia and Ukraine, inter-republic trade accounted for at least 85 percent of all trade in 1991. Unfortunately, comparable data for the period after the introduction of the new currencies are not available; we would expect that trade with non-Commonwealth states has expanded since 1993.

The initial level of commodity market integration may have been high enough to argue that the Commonwealth countries would benefit from a fixed exchange rate arrangement. But this integration was based on political arrangements, not economic fundamentals, and created substantial distortions. Most studies of likely future trade patterns among the Commonwealth countries predict that it is likely that by the end of the transition inter-republic trade volumes will decrease to 60 to 30 percent of their 1987 peak level. Fischer (1993:247) states that if the republics were to resort to bilateral balancing, the volume of trade would settle at 44 percent of its 1988 value. Fischer argues that this large shock could be mitigated by a form of payments union. Vavilov and Viugin (1993) use a gravity model to predict possible future trade patterns among the Commonwealth states.[4] Inter-republic trade volumes early in the economic transition are by their estimation implausibly large, when predicted by models of trade flows between market economies. If trade in the Commonwealth of Independent States approaches these predictions, the case for fixed exchange rates will lessen.

TABLE 18.1 International Trade in the Former Soviet States

	Total Trade as a Percentage of GDP	Intraregional Trade as a Percentage of Total Trade
Commonwealth of Independent States (1991)[a]		
Armenia	54.9	89.1
Azerbaijan	42.0	85.6
Belarus	51.4	85.8
Estonia	63.9	85.1
Georgia	44.3	86.5
Kazakstan	33.9	86.3
Kyrgyzstan	45.2	86.9
Latvia	54.6	86.7
Lithuania	54.9	86.8
Moldova	53.1	87.8
Tajikistan	41.6	86.3
Turkmenstan	39.3	89.1
Ukraine	34.1	79.0
Uzbekistan	39.5	85.8
Russia	22.3	57.8
European Community (1990)[b]		
Belgium	74.2	60.0
Denmark	32.7	41.7
Germany	29.8	48.2
Greece	26.8	49.4
Spain	19.8	45.3
France	23.3	55.6
Ireland	59.9	64.9
Italy	20.4	47.5
Netherlands	54.4	62.9
Portugal	42.1	58.4
United Kingdom	26.0	41.2

SOURCE: [a] International Monetary Fund, *Economic Review: The Economy of the Former USSR in 1991.* Washington, D.C., 1992. [b] International Monetary Fund.

The Soviet Union contained an abundance of raw materials, but many of these were used by central planners in large, inefficient factories built to produce substitutes for Western goods. When the Soviet Union fell, these manufacturers found themselves unable to compete in world markets. Raw material producers, in contrast, were largely able to sell their output to the

West at world prices (Tarr 1992). Republics such as Russia, Kazakstan and Turkmenstan that possessed these resources benefited, while those that ran the old Soviet factories lost.

If a country exports a wide variety of goods, then the effects of any shock to the whole economy will be less than the effect on output in individual industries. Thus, a diversified economy has less need to retain exchange rate flexibility to smooth the effects of shocks. Countries exporting a narrow range of goods are more likely to face demand shocks for their exports. Thus they would benefit from flexible exchange rates, which would help to mitigate these shocks. Using this criterion, the situation differs among the republics. The Slavonic republics have more or less diversified production and exports, while the republics of Central Asia and Kazakstan produce and export mainly raw materials and agriculture products. Hence the latter would be more likely to benefit from flexible exchange rates on these criteria. Gros (1993) has also argued that due to the similarity of their geography and their economic structure, the Baltic states will in the long run have trade patterns much like those of Finland, which conducts nearly half of its trade with the European Union. Any country on the periphery of the European Community tends to find the Community its largest trading partner.

Another criterion is geographic diversification of exports. Countries with a low geographic diversification would benefit by pegging their currency to that of their biggest trading partner. Most of the Commonwealth states' trade has been conducted with Russia, so the Russian ruble would be the best candidate for pegging to, if not for its instability.

One of the arguments for preserving the ruble area was that a common currency promotes trade through elimination of uncertainty connected with exchange rate fluctuations. However, it can be argued that in the case of the ruble area, it was the preservation of the ruble as a common currency that exacerbated problems for inter-republic trade. Countries that inflated faster attempted to dispose of their excess rubles by buying goods from other republics. To stem this flood of rubles many republics, particularly Russia, established export restrictions. If flexible exchange rate arrangements were in place, there would have been no need for export restrictions. Indeed, after the break up of the ruble zone Russia began to liberalize its trade restrictions. In May 1994 Yeltsin signed a decree that virtually eliminated all export quotas and licenses. The Central Asian republics, as well, formed customs unions after the introduction of their own currencies.

Wages and Price Flexibility and Factor Mobility

Adoption of a fixed exchange rate regime removes a potential mechanism for correcting disequilibrium wages and hence reducing unemployment. The removal of a trade deficit through market forces requires that the nominal expenditures of the countries in deficit decline relative to those of their trading partners. Where wages and prices are sticky, this fall in nominal income results in unemployment and lost output. In such circumstances exchange rate changes can help reduce the unemployment costs of the adjustment process.

The Soviet economy exhibited little wage flexibility. Union legislation regulated all salaries through a special set of rules that scaled salary by the industry, years of experience, location and special coefficients to compensate for different labor conditions. Although wage levels differed across the Soviet republics, it cannot be attributed to wage flexibility. For example, average income in Central Asia was 80 percent of the average for the whole USSR, but labor productivity was only slightly higher than 50 percent of the Soviet average.

Another labor market difficulty that can be partially compensated by flexible exchange rates is low labor mobility. If there is little mobility, wage disparities between trading partners will tend to persist. Goldberg, Ickes and Ryterman (1994) argue that low labor mobility is not a problem, since wages in the Commonwealth states can adjust on a regional basis without the movement of labor, and so wage rigidity can not be used as an argument for independent currencies. In their opinion flexibility of real wages is achieved through the difference in inflation rates between states, even though nominal rates do not adjust. But this difference could produce a real wage adjustment in the wrong direction. For example, if a country ran a trade deficit, its money supply would decrease, and if nominal wages are fixed, then real wages would rise rather than fall to decrease adjustment costs.

Measuring labor mobility is not easy, since it is influenced not only by wage differences but also by immigration restrictions, language and cultural differences, social benefits, etc. If mobility was determined only by economic factors, then the degree of labor mobility could be measured by the dispersion of unemployment rates, as proposed by Eichengreen (1991). Perfect labor mobility would imply that unemployment rates within the currency area would converge to a rate determined by structural factors.[5]

Labor mobility under the old Soviet system was limited by the requirements of residence registration that limited movement into the most popular cities. Moreover, until the end of the 1960s, a special set of regulations controlled the movement of the rural population into urban areas. Housing was administered by the state. Since the break up of the Soviet Union, labor has moved from the republics to Russia, though generally not for economic reasons. Civil wars in Tajikistan, Georgia and Nagorno-Karabakh induced large refugee flows to the cities of Russia. The presence of new borders can only decrease the degree of labor mobility within the Commonwealth.

Patterns of Shocks and Reform Strategies

Different patterns of shocks may call for different policy responses in terms of the degree of exchange rate flexibility. Pegged rates are usually more attractive for countries which experience many domestic shocks, allowing them to spread these disturbances abroad. On the other hand, countries that are subject to foreign shocks should usually favor a flexible regime because of its insulating properties.

The price liberalization carried out by Russia in January 1992 demonstrates the difficulties members of a currency zone face when subjected to a foreign monetary shock. Russia's liberalization came as a surprise for most of the republics, which were not consulted about it. Fearing spillover effects, most of the republics had to implement price reforms of their own since they all, with the exception of the Baltic countries, were using the ruble. If the republics had possessed their own currencies, they need not have followed Russia's example at that particular time. As it was, countries were compelled to choose a different speed of reform than they may have preferred on political or economic grounds.

Thus, constraints imposed by membership in a currency area on monetary and fiscal policy can be very costly. Even if the rates and scope of reform were uniform across all the former Soviet republics, it would still be difficult to coordinate monetary policies because cooperation requires the ability to make credible commitments. This would be difficult for countries with a high degree of openness, continued dependence on outside supplies, and trade partners facing uncertainty in production.

A second aspect of shocks relevant to optimum currency analysis is whether shocks are symmetric or asymmetric. If two or more countries face symmetric shocks, then flexible exchange rates would lose their insulating characteristics and would not be an effective policy instrument. One might think that similar industrial structures would result in symmetry of real shocks and vise versa. It is often argued that the Commonwealth republics do tend to experience the same pattern of shocks.[6]

De Grauwe (1991) argues that since most of the trade in western Europe is intra-industry trade, demand shocks will affect countries in the European Union symmetrically. This cannot be said about the former Soviet republics. The paradigm of the central planning system was the specialization of labor. The result was a highly monopolized economic structure, in which each republic was the dominant producer of a particular commodity. In this situation the likelihood of asymmetric shocks is higher and so, therefore, is the need for exchange rate flexibility. Although the source of shocks might be the same, we believe their effects would be different across the Commonwealth countries, these differences being caused by dissimilarities in the structure of Commonwealth economies, their levels of economic development, natural resources endowments, and demographics. Whereas per capita GDP in the European republics of the Commonwealth before the Soviet Union's disintegration was 1.7 to 1.9 times Central Asian levels, that figure is expected to grow to 2.8 to 3.0 times.

Demographic situations in the Commonwealth states also differ substantially. Whereas the European republics have experienced declines in population, Kazakstan and especially the Central Asian countries have experienced high population growth rates. This has serious implications for labor markets. Unemployment pressures in Central Asia have been building since the 1980s, exacerbated by the mistakes of the central planning system. Gosplan promoted capital-intensive industries in the region, while it is more suited to labor-intensive industries. Although this has no direct implications for exchange rate regime choice, one can argue that the Central Asian countries would need more wage and price flexibility before fixing their exchange rates.

A third aspect is whether these shocks are permanent or temporary. Temporary shocks can be cushioned through financing and do not require changes in exchange rates, while permanent shocks do require adjustments and are likely to also cause a shift in the equilibrium real exchange rate. We would argue that many of the shocks the Commonwealth states will be facing—large relative price adjustments and the loss of external financing—are permanent.[7]

Public Finance Considerations

Another avenue of study in the newer approaches to optimal currency areas turns on the issue of optimal seigniorage gains for each country in the proposed area. Recent inflation theory has emphasized the public finance aspects of inflation policy. Money creation generates revenues, which can then be used to finance additional government spending. Within a single country, the rate of inflation that is optimal equates the marginal cost of inflation (in terms of the welfare loss from reduced holdings of real balances) with the marginal cost of raising an additional amount of revenue through seigniorage.[8]

In terms of optimal currency area theory, research from a seigniorage viewpoint has been done by Canzoneri and Rogers (1990) and Casella (1992). Canzoneri and Rogers argue that by forming a currency area, the member countries open up the possibility of distorting fiscal decisions on spending for public goods. Casella's work shows that agreements between member countries of unequal size will be unsustainable unless the smaller countries are given a greater-than-proportional amount of influence in the governing monetary authority over the zone. The Central Asian states have experienced chronic fiscal problems and relied on implicit and explicit subsidies from the union government. Those subsidies made up as much as half the budgets of these republics in their first years of independence. Casella (1992), Krugman (1992), and Miller (1993) demonstrate clearly that there should be only one bank of issue in a currency area. When there is more than one, the smaller country has incentives to issue currency in excess of the agreed amount, since it will bear a smaller proportion of any losses from the resultant inflation. It can export part of the inflation to other members of the zone.

Would optimal inflation rates for these countries be roughly the same? Banaian (1995) discusses the factors involved in calculating an optimal inflation rate from a public finance perspective, and provides some estimates of these rates for several economies in transition. Revenue-maximizing and optimal rates of inflation are a function of the interest (or expected inflation) elasticity of money demand, the income tax rate, the velocity of the money supply, and the costs of taxation on other bases. For countries to wish to form a currency zone, either these factors must be roughly similar, or they must differ in such a way that the various factors will cancel out. In the case of the Commonwealth states, these factors would argue for a fairly high optimal inflation rate.[9] If there are uncertainty costs of inflation, however, the optimal rate would fall. Moreover, while one could argue that the degree of financial sophistication in each republic is roughly similar, their abilities to raise revenues from other sources are much different. Arbetmann and Kugler (1995) calculate the amount of tax revenue as a share of national output that each of these republics can be expected to raise. They argue that those countries with large mining and export sectors have lower costs of raising revenue, and thus can raise more. Countries with large agricultural sectors, on the other hand, typically raise less revenue. Thus the Central Asian countries, in particular Turkmenstan, Uzbekistan and Kazakstan, should be expected to run lower tax rates and have more efficient tax systems. Raising tax revenues in countries with relatively small mineral and export sectors, such as Ukraine or Lithuania, will be much harder.

We show in Table 18.2 a summary of these factors for several of the Commonwealth republics for 1992. The oil-producing countries Azerbaijan and Turkmenstan have fairly high tax revenue/GDP ratios. Turkmenstan raises about 70 percent of its revenues from an excise tax on natural gas revenues. Georgia, at the low end, has been fraught with civil war, while Kyrgyzstan and Armenia are relatively resource poor. Combined with the variation in velocity figures, we find that these countries have optimal inflation rates that vary by 40 to 50 percent around their means. A sharp divergence of optimal and revenue-maximizing inflation rates would make these countries unsuitable for a currency zone.

TABLE 18.2 Factors in Optimal Inflation: Commonwealth of Independent States, 1992

Country	GDP (bil. Rb)	Tax/ GDP	Velocity	Actual Inflation	Rev. Max. Inflation	Optimal Inflation	Def/ GDP
Armenia	90	17%	2.97	900%	59%	7%	-22
Azerbaijan	197	24%	2.07	533%	59%	11%	-3.6
Georgia	134	11%	1.72	1005%	61%	13%	-20
Kazakstan	1213	19%	2.85	799%	59%	8%	-7.2
Kyrgyzstan	137	11%	2.9	1487%	60%	8%	-13.5
Moldova	215	18%	2.59	1276%	60%	9%	-25.7
Turkmenstan	306	36%	2.89	1799%	56%	7%	+14.7
Russia	15000	12%	2.48	1314%	61%	10%	-7.5

NOTES: Calculations based on an interest elasticity of demand for money of -1.5, and a marginal cost of taxation of 0.5. Uses uncertainty cost of .1% GDP per 1% of inflation. Without uncertainty costs, the revenue-maximizing rate of inflation would be 66.7%, and the optimal rate would be 22.2%.

Institutional Arrangements and
Political Barriers to a Ruble Zone

John Williamson (1993) makes a distinction between a ruble *zone* and the ruble *area*. In a ruble zone, the member countries would use the ruble as common currency. In a ruble area, arrangements would be similar to the sterling area, under which countries have independent currencies but continue to use rubles for settlements between themselves. A currency zone can be set up by a cooperative agreement. Monetary policy would be handled by some supranational institution. An arrangement was negotiated among the Commonwealth states to establish a Banking Union, a fully cooperative system based on the U.S. Federal Reserve. But in the end, strikingly similar to difficulties in forming the European Union, the attempt failed due to a dispute over how many votes each country should receive when it came to setting monetary policy. Since then several other attempts have been undertaken to coordinate monetary policies. So far, all of them have proved unsuccessful.[10] Since 1994, no further serious attempts have been made towards a currency union, and it seems unlikely to occur in the near future. Since it is likely that the members of any cooperative monetary union would be hit by different shocks, competitive pressures would be expected to undermine cooperation and encourage the adoption of independent monetary policies.

Were such a zone to be created in the Commonwealth of Independent States, Russia would hold dominant economic and political power. In order to make this arrangement attractive to Russia, it would have to be given asymmetric power within the zone. Such an arrangement would mean the other states having to accept Russian interest rates and inflation and agreeing on credit policy with the Central Bank of Russia. But as Casella (1992) argues, some net inducement would have to be offered the other republics to gain their approval of an arrangement under which they would give up seigniorage revenues. This could take the form of an arrangement whereby the other republics are offered improved terms for energy and fiscal transfers from Russia.

Russian foreign policy towards its neighbors also looms large in these discussions. Although Russia was clearly the dominant partner in all discussions, it has been careful to respect the sovereignty of the other states. Russian insistence on stringent conditions for cash and credit rubles from the outset could have been interpreted as an attempt to reassert the Soviet Union. But as long as the other republics' central banks could create cash and credit rubles, inflation would always be exported towards Russia. When the Russians faced high inflation in their own country, they chose to assert their dominance in the ruble zone, and in so doing splintered it apart. Despite clamor from both ends of the Russian political spectrum for re-union of the USSR, foreign policy concerns have overall led to quiescence on an asymmetric currency union.

Asymmetric unions may not be in the best interest of the other republics either. Such unions can exacerbate the domestic business cycle in peripheral countries. For example, assume that only a peripheral country is hit by a negative terms-of-trade shock and a corresponding contraction in real income. Its monetary supply should be allowed to expand, but as a participant in a currency area, the country can not do this on its own. Unless there is a developed policy of financial transfers to depressed regions, membership in a monetary union will tend to lead to more volatile business cycles.

Rather than a currency zone, Williamson (1993) advocates instead the creation of a payments union to promote trade between Commonwealth states. This could easily operate as a ruble area in the sense discussed above. There are potential problems that can arise from this, however. If the union is provided sizable credits from external sources, intense bargaining over the amounts and terms of credit and disruptive operation of the clearing mechanism may arise. Second, a union can encourage trade among its members at the expense of trade outside the area, thereby enabling these countries to delay taking those measures which would make their currencies convertible. This problem is particularly acute in the case of the transition economies.

Those Commonwealth countries that have pegged their exchange rate have chosen a Western currency as a credibility-enhancing anchor. The Russian ruble would have seemed a natural target for many of these countries. But for several reasons, pegging to the ruble has not occurred. The high inflation in Russia was one obvious reason. In addition, the several leadership crises of the first Yeltsin administration may have made other Commonwealth countries wary of pegging to the ruble. The pace of reforms has been uneven aside from the many crises. And the ruble itself has been subject to speculative attack. For example, in the summer of 1993 Russian central bank intervention kept the exchange rate fixed to the dollar for three months, in spite of an average monthly inflation rate of 20 percent. The Central Bank of Russia also managed to earn more than $1 billion through foreign currency interventions during this period. However, in the fall of the same year it lost approximately the same sum as a result of further intervention which failed to hold the ruble steady. This has led some writers, such as Sachs (1996), to advocate a crawling pegged exchange rate, which has been adopted formally in Russia (known as the "corridor") and informally in Armenia. However, as Westbrook and Willett argue in Chapter 4, this approach has not had an impressive record over the longer term.

Conclusions

The countries within the Commonwealth of Independent States choose divergent monetary policies, speeds of adjustment and reform paths. As Conway (1995:57) argues, "monetary union requires fiscal coordination and fiscal restraint." Some republics, like the Baltics, have chosen to adopt firm monetary policies. Their currencies significantly appreciated against the ruble. Other republics were less successful. In most of these cases, the repeated attempts of Russia to seek coordination (and eventually submersion) of fiscal and monetary policies were rebuffed by countries wary of possible attempts to reestablish the Soviet Union. As a result, a diverse set of exchange rate regimes have emerged.

Judging from optimum currency area criteria this result is predictable. Small, open countries, like the Baltics, will likely fix their currencies, while a large country like Russia is most likely to continue its crawling peg policy. Countries interested in a fast pace of reforms will peg to Western currencies to demonstrate a commitment to price stability. The slower pace and the uncertainty involved in the direction of reforms in Russia have made the ruble less attractive as a reserve currency. Although it is unlikely that a new ruble zone unifying all Commonwealth countries will emerge soon, it is quite possible that some smaller groups of republics will create some sort of currency blocs.

An emerging tendency is the coordination of monetary policies between the Central Asian republics and Kazakstan. These countries share common borders and have historical ties. The best example is the simultaneous introduction of national currencies by Kazakstan and Uzbekistan in November 1993, which built upon the lessons learned from the Kyrgyz experience. Kazakstan, Uzbekistan and Kyrgyzstan later formed a trade area effective from February 1994. In contrast, save for Kazakstan, none of the Central Asian states have exports nor imports with Russia in excess of 10 percent of their GDP.

Kyrgyzstan exports largely manufactured goods (including substantial amounts of textiles) that require inputs from Russia and other Commonwealth countries. After introducing the som, it has had difficulty making payments within the Commonwealth and output has fallen. Uzbekistan and Kazakstan conduct about 5 percent of their total trade with each other (approximately $500 million in 1993). Both governments have expressed the hope that they could substitute another $400 million in trade with each other for trade outside the zone. With roughly similar economic structures, including substantial energy reserves, Kazakstan and Uzbekistan have some potential for forming a currency link.

Russia's largest trading partners in the Commonwealth are Ukraine and Belarus. The agreement between Russia and the latter country is justified at least on openness grounds, and some monetary or payments union with Ukraine could be economically desirable. Politically, however, Ukraine is unlikely to join such a union. Shortly after the passage of its constitution, Ukraine introduced its permanent currency, the hryvnia, in September 1996. This breaks any linkage to the ruble (the temporary currency was initially introduced as a supplement to the Soviet ruble.) Since 1994 there have been repeated attempts by Belarus to enter a new monetary union with Russia. Early proposals would have given the Belarussian central bank authority to issue Russian rubles. In the final version the sole right to issue rubles would have remained with the Russian central bank. In return Belarussian citizens would be permitted to exchange some of their currency for rubles at a highly overvalued exchange rate. This was opposed as too costly by reformers in Russia. Having witnessed the cost of German unification, Russia's desire for this union lessened. Opposition in Belarus existed as well (though much has been suppressed by President Lukashenko).

Elsewhere, the prospects for other currency blocs are weaker. Moldova has stabilized its own currency but remains committed to a flexible exchange rate. Ethnic considerations are likely to block any tie between the Transcaucasian republics (Armenia, Azerbaijan and Georgia). Azerbaijan may be a candidate for joining the Central Asian bloc, given its similar ethnicity and industrial structure, but internal conflicts have kept it from developing that link so far.

In summary, the costs of a ruble zone spanning the entire Commonwealth of Independent States were too large. The breakup of the zone was first initiated by republics that wished to move faster towards a market economy (the Baltics, and to a lesser extent the Kyrgyz Republic). Then Russia seemed to decide that the costs of monetary union were not worth the benefits, and repudiated the Soviet ruble. Unable to make a new agreement with Russia, the remaining countries, except Tajikstan, created their own currencies within six months.

One should not underestimate the importance of an independent currency as a national symbol that drives political decisions. Exchange rate regimes, after all, are not made in central banks but by legislatures and executives. Given the history of the area, political considerations reinforce economic ones to make it difficult to imagine the Commonwealth of Independent States embracing the Russian ruble in an EMU-style zone.

Notes

A previous version of this paper was presented at the Western Economics Association annual meeting, Vancouver, BC, Canada, June 30–July 3, 1994. This paper sprang from discussions with Professor Tom Willett, whom we both thank for the impetus to put these thoughts to paper and his guidance since then. We also thank Dmitry Panasevich for research assistance.

1. We use the phrase *Soviet ruble* to refer to the pre-1993 currency and to the Russian ruble up to the time that Russia ceased to honor its Soviet predecessor. *Russian ruble* refers to the current legal tender of the Russian Federation.

2. See Tavlas (1993).

3. The Commonwealth consists of Armenia, Azerbaijan, Belarus, Georgia, Kazakstan, the Kyrgyz Republic, Moldova, Russia, Tajikstan, Turkmenstan, Ukraine, Uzbekistan and the Baltic states of Estonia, Lativia and Lithuania.

4. The model predicts trade volumes among countries as a positive function of GDP, a negative function of distance between countries, and also depends on resource endowment, common borders, and membership in the same trade organization (such as the Common Market).

5. Existing official data on unemployment in the former Soviet Union greatly understate the true levels of unemployment. In Ukraine, for example, surveys in *Ukrainian Economic Trends* show that the average Ukrainian only works 16 days per month, although the reported unemployment rate is 0.4–0.6 percent of the labor force.

6. This type of argument was behind the IMF's recommendations in 1992 aimed at the preservation of a ruble zone encompassing most of the Commonwealth countries. See Conway (1995) and Sachs (1996).

7. A fourth aspect is whether shocks are nominal or real. Nominal exchange rate changes are likely to be more effective in insulating the domestic economy from foreign monetary shocks than from real shocks, as argued by Willett and Wihlborg in Chapter 3 of this volume.

8. For an argument that this rate ignores important uncertainty costs, and references to more recent literature, see Banaian, McClure and Willett (1994) and Banaian (1995). For evidence that these uncertainty costs can be quite large, see Burdekin et al. (1995).

9. For instance, assume a money demand function of $m/y = a \times \exp\{-\text{ß}i\}$, where m is money, y is output, i is the nominal interest rate, and a and are ß parameters (the latter being the interest semi-elasticity of demand). If ß = 1 and the marginal cost of taxation were 0.5 per unit of revenue raised, the revenue-maximizing inflation rate would be 100 percent, and the optimal rate would be 33.3 percent. Note that the tax rate and velocity are not factors when there are no uncertainty costs.

10. Winckler (1993) describes the situation in the ruble zone using a game theory "prisoner dilemma": Although a cooperative solution would be beneficial to all the former Soviet states, mutual mistrust and information problems make them behave in an uncooperative way.

References

Arbetmann, Marina, and Jacek Kugler. 1995. "The Politics of Inflation: An Empirical Assessment of Emerging Market Economies," in Thomas D. Willett, Richard C. K. Burdekin, Richard J. Sweeney, and Clas Wihlborg, eds., *Establishing Monetary Stability in Emerging Market Economies*. Pp. 81–102. Boulder, Colo.: Westview Press.

Banaian, King. 1995. "Inflation and Optimal Seigniorage in the CIS and Eastern Europe," in Thomas D. Willett, Richard C. K. Burdekin, Richard J. Sweeney, and Clas Wihlborg, eds., *Establishing Monetary Stability in Emerging Market Economies*. Pp. 63–80. Boulder, Colo.: Westview Press.

Banaian, King, James H. McClure, Thomas D. Willett. 1994. "The Inflation Tax Is Likely to Be Inefficient at Any Level." *Kredit und Kapital* 27(1): 30–42.

Banaian, King, and Eugenue Zhukov. "The Collapse of the Ruble Zone: 1991–93," in Thomas D. Willett, Richard C. K. Burdekin, Richard J. Sweeney, and Clas Wihlborg, eds., *Establishing Monetary Stability in Emerging Market Economies*. Pp. 209–30. Boulder, Colo.: Westview Press.

De Grauwe, Paul. *The Economics of Monetary Integration*. Oxford: Oxford University Press, 1992.

Eichengreen, Barry. 1990. "Currency Union: One Money for Europe? Lessons from the U.S. Currency Union." *Economic Policy* 10 (April): 117–87.

Fischer, Stanley. 1982. "Seigniorage and the Case for a National Money." *Journal of Political Economy* 90(2): 295–313.

Frenkel, Jacob, and Morris Goldstein. 1991. "Monetary Policy in an Emerging European Economic and Monetary Union." *IMF Staff Papers* 38 (June): 356–73.

Frenkel, Jacob, Morris Goldstein, and Paul Masson. 1991. "Characteristics of a Successful Exchange Rate System." IMF Occasional Papers No. 82. Washington, D.C.: International Monetary Fund.

Genberg, Hans. 1994. "Monetary Reform in Transition Economies." Paper presented at the conference *Exchange Rate Policies in Transition Economies*, Vienna, June.

Goldberg, Linda, Barry Ickes, Randi Ryterman. 1994. "Departures from the Ruble Zone: The Implications of Adopting Independent Currencies." *World Economy* 17(3): 293–322.

Goldstein, Morris, Peter Isard, Paul Masson and Mark Taylor. 1992. "Policy Issues in the Evolving International Monetary System." IMF Occasional Papers No. 96. Washington D.C., International Monetary Fund, June

Gros, Daniel. 1993. "Costs and Benefits of Economic and Monetary Union: An Application to the Former Soviet Union," in Paul Masson and Mark Taylor, eds., *Policy Issues in the Operation of Currency Areas.* Pp. 55–74. Cambridge: Cambridge University Press.

Heller, Robert. 1977. "Choosing an Exchange Rate System." *Finance and Development*, June: 23–27.

Ickes, Barry W., and Randi Ryterman. 1993. "Roadblock to Economic Reform: Inter-Enterprise Debt and the Transition to Markets." *Post-Soviet Affairs* 9(3): 231–52.

International Monetary Fund. 1993. *IMF Staff Papers on Financial Relations Among Countries of the Former Soviet Union.* Washington, D.C., September.

Kenen, Peter. 1969. "The Theory of Optimum Currency Areas: An Eclectic View," in Robert Mundell and Alexander Swoboda, eds., *Monetary Problems of the International Economy.* Pp. 41–60. Chicago: University of Chicago Press.

Krugman, Paul. 1992. "Policy Problems of a Monetary Union," in *Currencies and Crisis.* Pp. 185–203. Cambridge: MIT Press.

Masson, Paul, and Mark Taylor. 1993a. "Currency Unions: A Survey of the Issues," in Paul Masson and Mark Taylor, eds., *Policy Issues in the Operation of Currency Unions.* Pp. 3–51. Cambridge: Cambridge University Press.

———. 1993b. "Fiscal Policy within Common Currency Areas." *Journal of Common Market Studies* 31(1): 29–44.

McKinnon, Ronald I. 1993. *The Order of Economic Liberalization.* Baltimore and London: Johns Hopkins University Press.

Melvin, Michael. 1985. "The Choice of an Exchange Rate System and Macroeconomic Stability." *Journal of Money, Credit and Banking* 17 (November): 467–78.

Michalopoulos, Constantine, and David Tarr. 1993. "Energizing Trade of the States of the Former Soviet Union." *Finance and Development* 30(1): 22–25.

Sachs, Jeffrey D. 1996. "Economic Transition and the Exchange Rate Regime." *American Economic Association Papers and Proceedings*, May: 147–52.

Sachs, Jeffrey D, and Xavier Sala-i-Martin. 1989. "Federal Fiscal Policy and Optimum Currency Areas." Working Paper, Harvard University.

Tarr, David. 1992. "The Terms-of-Trade Effects on Countries of the Former Soviet Union of Moving to World Prices." Working Paper, The World Bank, October.

Tavlas, George. 1993. "The New Theory of Optimum Currency Areas." *The World Economy* 16(6): 663–85.

———. 1992. "Trade Policy and Exchange Rate Issues in the Former Soviet Union." Policy Research Working Papers WPS 915. Washington, D.C.: The World Bank, May.

Ukrainian Economic Trends. 1996. Kyiv, Ukraine: European Center for the Ukrainian Economy, January.

Vavilov, Andrey, and Oleg Viugin. 1993. "Trade Patterns after Integration into the World Economy," in John Williamson, ed., *Economic Consequences of Soviet Disintegration.* Pp. 99–174. Washington, D.C.: Institute for International Economics.

Wihlborg, Clas, and Thomas D. Willett. 1991. "Optimum Currency Areas Revisited. On the Transition Path to a Currency Union," in Clas Wihlborg, Michale

Fratianni and Thomas D. Willett, eds., *Financial Regulation and Monetary Arrangements after 1992*. Pp. 279–97. Amsterdam: North-Holland.

Willett, Thomas D., and Fahim Al-Mahrubi. 1994. "Currency Policies for Inflation Control in the Formerly Centrally Planned Economies." *The World Economy*, 17(6): 795–815.

Williamson, John, ed. 1993. *Economic Consequences of Soviet Disintegration*. Washington, D.C.: Institute for International Economics.

Winckler, Georg. 1993. "Comment," in John Williamson, ed., *Economic Consequences of Soviet Disintegration*. Pp. 307–9. Washington, D.C.: Institute for International Economics.